A FEW OF 'THE FEW'

A FEW OF

'THE FEW'

AUSTRALIANS AND
THE BATTLE OF BRITAIN

DENNIS NEWTON

AUSTRALIAN WAR MEMORIAL

First published in 1990 by the
Australian War Memorial, Canberra, ACT 2601

© Dennis Newton
Produced by the Historical
Research and
Editorial and Publications
Sections, Australian War
Memorial

National Library of Australia
Cataloguing-in-Publication entry

Newton, Dennis.
A few of the few.

Bibliography.
Includes index.
ISBN 0 642 14991 7.

1. Britain, Battle of, 1940. 2, World War,
1939–1945 — Australia. I. Australian
War Memorial. II. Title.

940.541294

Designed by Falkenmire Cullen
Graphic Design, Candelo, NSW
Typeset by Abb-typesetting, Melbourne,
Printed by Macarthur Press, Parramatta
AGPS Indexing Service

CONTENTS

FOREWORD

Fifty years ago in the skies over south-eastern England, the North Sea and the English Channel, a battle was fought the likes of which the world had not previously experienced, a battle between aerial armadas. Although better described as a campaign than a battle, the battle of Britain has passed into history as the first major military conflict which was resolved by operations between military aircraft.

Important, too, was the fact that this conflict was not a minor skirmish occurring at the strategic margin. This was a battle for survival; certainly for the British and possibly for the free world. An evil madman was ascendant in Europe. Adolf Hitler had convinced a great nation to act in barbarous, uncivilized and inhumane ways. He had to be stopped. Having over-run Europe, he and the forces he controlled were poised to destroy Britain and his vanguard was his air arm, the *Luftwaffe*.

Such is the pace of modern technological development that a weapons platform that had first been used in combat less than 30 years before was now to be the instrument used to destroy a nation's will and capacity to fight.

Fortunately that offensive aerial instrument was opposed by a defensive aerial instrument, Fighter Command, which, though grossly underprepared through neglect, inaction and lack of wisdom and foresight, was to prove itself equal to its essential task. At the operational heart of the command were its pilots, only 1495 of them. Those few, who were the combat soldiers of Fighter Command, have been immortalized by their deeds and through the words of Winston Churchill. They will never be forgotten.

Dennis Newton has focused on those few of the few who were Australians. He has done so through the device of a diary. This gives to his work an immediacy which takes you into the battle and captures the atmosphere of Britain, the Royal Air Force and Fighter Command — its operations and its people — in those tumultuous and fascinating days.

His prodigious research has illuminated for us the part which Australian pilots played in the battle of Britain. He tells of Ron Lees, the Australian-born commanding officer of 72 Squadron, who spent a full and rewarding career in the RAF and who as Sir Ronald Lees KCB CBE DFC is now retired and living again in the land of his birth. He tells of young Richard Hillary, the author of that wonderful book, *The last enemy*, who tragically died in 1943, and of Ian Bayles who enlisted with Richard Hillary from the Oxford University Air Squadron and who has been the driving force behind the Australian veterans' return to England to celebrate the 50th anniversary of the battle. Also there is my old commandant from Queensland Squadron Air Training Corps, Gordon Olive, whose relatively recent death denied him the opportunity to make a pilgrimage he would have greatly valued, and Gordon's coursemate from Point Cook, Pat Hughes, the highest scoring Australian ace in the battle, the inspiration of 234 Squadron, whose death during the battle was a severe blow.

This is a rich and illuminating history. It offers us an account of an important event of modern times in a way that describes the major events while highlighting for us the efforts of our own countrymen. As Chief of the Air Staff I warmly welcome this excellent contribution to Australian military history.

Air Marshal R.G. Funnell AC
June 1990

ACKNOWLEDGEMENTS

A work such as this cannot reach fruition without the help and co-operation of many people and organizations. Over six years of researching and writing there have been many, and I am pleased now to acknowledge their help. Individuals who have given support and assistance include:

Ian Bayles, John Cock, Desmond Fopp, Harry Hardman, John Hewson, Ron Lees, Gordon Olive, Doug Peterkin, Dick Power, Desmond Sheen, Alan Butement, Alan Cooper, R.C. de Bruin, Rowena Bayles, Len Bennett, Helen Andrews, Simon Parry, Kenneth Wynn, Joan Bowden, Pat Caban, Royce Stewart, Geoff Pittman, Michael Fopp, Robert Clyde, Robert Burridge, John Hamilton, Bill Fogarty, Philip Markham, John Lindsay, Lovat Dickson, Christine Hillary, S. G. Beaumont, Bill Hughes, George Bailey, David Moor, H. A. Hughes, Henry McDonough, Margaret McGaw, Peter Townsend, John Wallen, Colin Burgess, Lydia Crawford, Margaret Hopton, Marjorie Horn, Jim Beedle, Brenda Walch, James Coward, Christopher Deansley, Maera Galloway, E. Latham Withall, Alison Pilkington, P.A. Williams, Harry Daish, David Innes, Annette Donger, Andy Saunders, Winston Ramsey, A.J. Dwyer, F.S. van Zetten, G.W. Haysom, I.D. Blackwood, Tom Gleave, N.P.W. Hancock, Charles Palliser, Michael Piggott, Alec Mathieson, Derek Wood, Frank Kruta, Jim Thorn, Mrs. Q.M. Green (Penny Penrice), John Holloway, G.J.S. Gardiner, M.H.C. Parks, E.A. Munday, Margaret Browne, Ron Gilchrist, Bronwyn Self, Jenny Bell, Lynne Losik, Shirley Purchase, Mary Carse, Mary Hutchison, Neil Mulligan, Clive Huggan, H.J. Kissoon, D.N. Callighan, Peter Fox, R.L. Molony, Dennis Taylor, J. Grendowicz, P.B. Laddie Lucas, Frank F. Robins, Bryan Philpott, Anneliese Todd and W.R.J. Pullen.

I am particularly grateful for the work of Peter Stanley and Merrilyn Lincoln, of the Australian War Memorial and Brett Cullen of Falkenmire Cullen Graphic Design, who have spent long hours editing and designing this book, and without whose skills it would have been much the poorer.

Organizations which have assisted me include: In Britain — Ministry of Defence, Public Record Office, Commonwealth War Graves Commission, the Imperial War Museum, Battle of Britain Museum, FAF Museum, *Kent Messenger*, Battle of Britain Fighter Association of Great Britain, The Caterpillar Club, The Goldfish Club, *Air Mail Aviation News*; in Australia — the Australian War Memorial, Australian Archives, the National Library of Australia, the Department of Defence, the *Sun* (Sydney), the *Sun* (Newcastle), the Battle of Britain

Fighter Association—Australian Branch, Broken Hill City Council Library, *Sun* (Melbourne), *Mufti*, *Australian Aviation*, *Wings*, NSW State Library, *Advertiser* (Adelaide); Overseas — Public Archives of Canada and the *Bundesarchiv-Militararchiv* of West Germany.

No serious study of the battle of Britain could be made without particular reference to three books because of their originality, wealth of detail and accuracy. I owe a special debt to Derek Wood & Derek Dempster (authors of *The narrow margin*), Francis Mason (*Battle over Britain*), Winston Ramsey (*The battle of Britain then and now*). I acknowledge in particular the help given to me by the editor and contributors of the latter.

Lastly, and by no means least, I include a special acknowledgement of the many hours put into the project by my wife, Helen. Without her support, and the help of my son, Scott, this work could not have been finished.

ABBREVIATIONS AND RANKS

AAF	Auxiliary Air Force (RAF)
AASF	Advanced Air Striking Force (RAF)
AFC	Air Force Cross, also Australian Flying Corps
AFLT	Acting Flight Lieutenant
AI	Aircraft Interception
AIF	Australian Imperial Force
ASF	Australian Striking Force (AIF)
AVM	Air Vice-Marshal
AWM	Australian War Memorial
BBC	British Broadcasting Corporation
BEF	British Expeditionary Force
CFS	Central Flying School
CSIR	Commonwealth Scientific and Industrial Research
DFC	Distinguished Flying Cross
DP	Death Presumed
DSO	Distinguished Service Order
EFTS	Elementary Flying Training School
FIU	Fighter Interception Unit
F/L	Flight Lieutenant
F/O	Flying Officer
JG	*Jagdgeschwader* = fighter wing
KG	*Kampfgeschwader* = bomber wing
KIA	Killed in Action
LAC	Leading Aircraftman
MID	Mentioned in Dispatches
MU	Medically Unfit
NCO	Non Commissioned Officer
OKW	*Oberkommando der Wehrmacht* = Armed Force Supreme Command (German)
ORB	Operations Record Book
OTU	Operational Training Unit
PC	Permanent Commission
P/O	Pilot Officer
PDU	Photographic Development Unit
POW	Prisoner of War
PRO	Public Record Office (London)
PRU	Photographic Reconnaissance Unit
RAAF	Royal Australian Air Force
RAF	Royal Air Force
RAFVR	Royal Air Force Volunteer Reserve
RAN	Royal Australian Navy

RFC	Royal Flying Corps
RN	Royal Navy
RNAS	Royal Naval Air Service
RNZAF	Royal New Zealand Air Force
SSC	Short Service Commission
St	*Staffel* = Squadron
S/Ldr	Squadron Leader
ZG	*Zerstörergeschwader* = destroyer wing

The following list of *Luftwaffe* and RAF rank equivalents is necessarily approximate in certain cases: various German ranks existed which have no exact British parallel.

Flieger	Aircraftman (2)
Gefreiter	Aircraftman (1)
Obergefreiter	Leading Aircraftman
Hauptgefreiter	Corporal
Unteroffizier, Unterfeldwebel	Sergeant
Feldwebel	Flight Sergeant
Oberfeldwebel, Stabsfeldwebel	Warrant Officer
Leutnant	Pilot Officer
Oberleutnant	Flying Officer
Hauptmann	Flight Lieutenant
Major	Squadron Leader
Oberstleutnant	Wing Commander
Oberst	Group Captain
Generalmajor	Air Commodore
Generalleutnant	Air Vice-Marshal
General	Air Marshal
Generaloberst,	Air Chief Marshal
Generalfeldmarschall	
Reichsmarschall	Marshal of the Air Force

INTRODUCTION

According to Air Ministry Orders to be eligible for the much prized Battle of Britain Clasp to the 1939–1945 Star an airman must have served with the Royal Air Force's Fighter Command and flown at least one operational sortie between 00.01 hours on 10 July and 23.59 hours on 31 October 1940.[*]

There were no Royal Australian Air Force fighter units in operation during the battle of Britain but Australian airmen were sprinkled through RAF Squadrons in all commands and the fact of their being so scattered has made an accurate assessment of their numbers somewhat difficult. However, most historical works written in the United Kingdom, with one notable exception, seem unanimous that only 21 Australians took part and that of these, 14 were killed. The notable exception is the Roll of Honour at Westminster Abbey which contains the names of 24 Australians who lost their lives during the battle of Britain (Appendix 3). The apparent anomaly is obvious — if there were only 21 Australian participants how could 24 have been killed? But, what at first seems to be a glaring error, is explained by the fact that Westminster's Roll of Honour contains not only the casualties of Fighter Command but also those of Bomber and Coastal Commands. Meanwhile, in Australia, the official history of Australia in the war of 1939–45, John Herington's *Air war against Germany and Italy 1939–43*, stated:

> . . . some thirty Australians who had survived the hurly-burly of May and June fought in Fighter Command during these vital months of constant readiness for action. Australian records which have been preserved are skeletal, patchy and unsatisfactory, but do give some glimpse of the tumult in the clouds, although the details of much that was worthily and nobly done have passed from human knowledge because the men did not live to tell the tale. Ten Australians were killed and one became a prisoner, and it is worth noting that the distinction subsequently earned by those who survived gives, no less than their deeds, the measure of the loss to the RAF of those who did not. This group, though a minute portion of 'The Few' extolled in the Prime Minister's stirring tribute, were scattered among many squadrons, but did achieve much.[1]

A partial reason for this discrepancy in numbers occurred because, at the time of writing the official history, the three Coastal Command squadrons which were temporarily attached to Fighter Command

*Refer Appendix 1

were not considered to be members of 'The Few'. Lists of the Australian personnel eligible for the Battle of Britain Clasp, which were prepared before 1960, showed 25 names. This was later modified in accordance with Air Ministry Orders No. 850 and added 4 more names to total 29 (Appendix 4). Obviously, 8 of the men included in the Australian lists had been declared 'British' by authorities in England.

How could there be such confusion? Why were so many declared to be 'British'? Several circumstances contributed to this. In those days Australians travelled using a British passport and Australia was proudly part of the British empire. There was a sense of closeness with England and some of these airmen were being educated in English universities or were working in business in Britain. Many had relatives living in England, so for most to be Australian was to be British anyway. Sometimes, because of the scarcity of accurate records or evidence to the contrary, 'British' nationality was assumed.

Obviously, for the purpose of this history, it was necessary to clearly define the term 'Australian' so that a valid decision could be made as to whom should be included in the book. The guidelines decided upon were:

1. 'Australian' by birth;
2. 'Australian' by immigration;
3. if an official organization, or organizations (e.g. RAF, RAAF, Battle of Britain Fighter Association, etc.), had declared a person as 'Australian';
4. born of Australian parents while overseas if Australian identity had been preserved;
5. if a person's closest living relative(s), or the person himself, expressed the wish for inclusion in this history under the nationality of 'Australian'; and
6. declared by a biographer to be 'Australian'.

A number of battle of Britain veterans took up residence in Australia after the war and became as 'Australian' as any of us but at the time of the battle they were otherwise. Some have been mentioned in this War Diary.

Although eligibility for the Battle of Britain Clasp is restricted to those who served with RAF Fighter Command between 10 July and 31 October 1940, both of these dates for the battle are not universally accepted by historians, particularly those who are non-British. German historians, in particular, insist that the campaign was much longer, even suggesting that it started as early as 28 May 1940, the day the *Luftwaffe* first met the RAF head on over Dunkirk, or 30 June, a week after the end of the French campaign when Goering issued his 'General Directions' for the operations of the *Luftwaffe* against England. Others have put forward 2 July when the *Luftwaffe* received its first specific operational instructions for the campaign against England or the following day when regular attacks on shipping began. As to the end of the campaign, the Germans insist that it lasted, albeit on a reduced scale, well into 1941 and finally tapered off completely with the need to concentrate on the assault into Russia.[2]

On the British side, it has been pointedly asked why forget the early

Four of the original aircraft captains of 10 Squadron, conferring at Pembroke Dock in December 1939 (AWM 128163).

days of July? In the first 9 days of that month RAF pilots shot down at least 56 German aircraft for the loss of 28 planes with 23 pilots either killed or wounded, men who were therefore declared ineligible to receive the Battle of Britain Clasp. Perhaps 1 July, when the Germans occupied the Channel Island of Guernsey, their first invasion of British sovereign territory, should be considered as an equally valid date for the commencement of the battle.[3] Likewise, when looking at the so-called end of the battle, fighting tapered off throughout November and December but there were sporadic and sometimes fierce clashes. These last two months of 1940 are often called the 'forgotten months' of the battle of Britain.[4]

In this history it has been decided to stay close to the requirements for the Battle of Britain Clasp, except for the beginning of July, and to fully chronicle the four months of July-October 1940 in the War Diary. This is because, at the beginning of July, aerial activity began to increase sharply over the English Channel as the *Luftwaffe* strove to close this shipping lane by bombing shipping and smashing the harbours from Dover to Southampton. This tactic brought the RAF fighters into action and, as the destruction of Fighter Command was essential to obtain air superiority before any invasion attempt could be staged, the suggestion of the beginning of July is as valid as any. However, Battle of Britain Day is celebrated on 15 September.

Australians were not only in Fighter Command; they were in other commands as well. There were 26 Australians on duty in Coastal Command and of these 8 were killed, while in Bomber Command there were 47 pilots of whom 5 were killed and 6 became prisoners of war.[5] Because the decision was made to include airmen from all commands on the Roll of Honour at Westminster Abbey, it is also valid to include these men in the War Diary and to mention a random selection of others.

Australians were to be found elsewhere throughout Britain too, all prepared to play their part in repelling the enemy. Operating under the direction of Coastal Command was 10 Squadron RAAF, and stationed on Salisbury Plain were 8 000 officers and men of the Australian Imperial Force, part of the 6th Division. Working in Woolmer Forest near Longmore was the Railway Construction and Maintenance Group, and cutting timber in Northumberland were 400 Australian foresters. Members of the Royal Australian Navy were scattered throughout ships of the Royal Navy and the cruiser HMAS *Australia* saw active service with the British Home Fleet. In science and technology men such as Alan Butement, Marcus Oliphant and Sidney Cotton had already made contributions towards the war effort and were willing to make more. Because of the need to assess the work of Australians within the whole framework of the battle of Britain, the War Diary makes mention of many of these as well.

The purpose of this book is therefore threefold. First, it is an effort to at last set the historical record straight. Second, it is to pay tribute to the efforts and achievements of Australians during the battle of Britain. Finally, it is to honour and remember those who lost their lives. In the pages which follow, the War Diary, written in the present tense, attempts to capture the day-to-day mood of the times through the eyes of Australians, concentrating on the men who were in, or attached to, RAF Fighter Command between July-October 1940, as they played their parts in the drama going on around them. Biographical outlines are presented and, finally, there is statistical information and documentation.

Although this book concentrates on Australians, it does not seek to imply that they 'did it all'. They were part of the whole, a representative group, fighting alongside their comrades-in-arms from Britain, Canada, New Zealand, South Africa and even the United States of America, together with those who had escaped from occupied Europe, from Poland, Czechoslovakia, Belgium and France. The Australians were . . .

a few of 'The Few'.

PRELUDE TO THE BATTLE

At the outbreak of war on 3 September 1939 there were about 450 Australians serving in the RAF in various parts of the world. Nearly all were operational pilots on short-service commissions. Aside from these, there was another distinct group who held long-service commissions, most having transferred from the Royal Flying Corps, the Royal Naval Air Service or the Australian Flying Corps during or after the first world war. Some older men had risen to responsible positions at command or group level and there was also a smattering of technical and medical specialists. Among these was Air Vice Marshal W.A. McClaughry who, in September 1939, was director of training at the Air Ministry.

Other Australians already living in England were joining up. At Oxford, student members of the University Air Squadron reported to the Volunteer Reserve Centre as soon as possible. These included Ian Norman Bayles and Richard Hope Hillary. Others living in England included Richard Carew Reynell, who was a leading test pilot at Hawker Aircraft Ltd, Kenneth Christopher (Dutchy) Holland, who had joined Airspeed Ltd in 1936, and Charles Alexander McGaw, who had been an aeronautical inspector for the Air Ministry and had joined the RAF in June at the same time as John Curchin. Meanwhile, Charles Arthur Pritchard had joined No. 600 (City of London) Squadron, Auxiliary Air Force, in 1936, Desmond Fopp had joined the Royal Air Force Volunteer Reserve in November 1938, and Harry Hardman was already a member of 111 Squadron, RAF.

However, most Australians in the RAF at this time were there under a special Short-Service Commission Scheme. It was at the Imperial Conference of 1923 that the United Kingdom first proposed offering 4-year short-service commissions in the RAF to RAAF officers who had just graduated from Point Cook Flying School, Victoria, Australia. By this method, it was reasoned, a reserve of trained pilots would be built up which could be used to reinforce RAF squadrons in an emergency and the RAAF would benefit when the men returned after 4 years operational training at British expense. The scheme began in 1927 when the first Point Cook graduates took up their commissions. It was officially suspended in Australia in July 1938, but RAF short-service commissions continued to be advertized in the Australian press and intakes continued until mid-1939. Those accepted at this later date did not have the benefit of initial flying training at Point Cook and some, such as John Dallas Crossman, a member of the last contingent, had no formal preliminary military training at all. (Refer to Appendix 5)

The Point Cook cadet class of 1936, many of whom served in the RAF and the RAAF. Four became eligible for the Battle of Britain Clasp to the 1939-45 Star (photo courtesy of Bill Hughes).

Typical was the Point Cook cadet class of 1936 from which, out of 34 cadets, 25 were accepted for RAF training and left for England in January 1937. Among those who would eventually end up in RAF Fighter Command were Paterson Clarence Hughes, Charles Gordon Chaloner Olive, Desmond Frederick Bert Sheen, and Richard Morris Power.

With the war only a few days old, the air was crisp with anticipation and tension. It was a time for making sure one's affairs were in order before anything happened — there might not be another chance. At Church Fenton, while he was waiting for instructions, Pat Hughes of 64 Squadron wrote to his brother in Australia on 6 September:[1]

Will,

I feel that I owe you a letter merely to let you know I'm still hale and hearty and not doing anything like hard work. I'm trying to get abreast of my correspondence now because in this first week we've got not much else to do except sit and wait till it breaks . . . Up till now nothing much has happened, except for a few sort of tentative prods from either side, but some of our coves did sling some good stuff into the Kiel Canal the other night. Rumours have just come through of the first raids on London, how true they are I don't know, but it's quite possible the fun has started in earnest at last.

There's no use muttering about things Will, and to my mind the chances of living through it are equal anyhow, and that's all one can ask after all . . . Until this has been going on for a while we won't be able to

Families all over Australia farewelled pilots leaving to join the RAF. Here, Pat Hughes's family farewell him on the RMS *Narkunda* in Sydney on 9 January 1937. The man in the light coat is 'Peter' Pettigrew who was also to join the RAF. Pettigrew was killed in a mid-air collision on 24 August 1944 (photo courtesy of Bill Hughes).

judge much about their men and machines or whether they fight well or indifferently, but one thing is certain both of these Air Forces are out to show just how bad the other one is, and how long it will take I'd hate to guess.

Well brother mine, after we've cleared these Huns from the blue skies of England I'll come home to that tankard of old ale and the beach and forget that I've spent five years in fog and rain in Yorkshire.

Will write as soon as I can.

Yrs

Pat.

[Paterson Clarence Hughes was born on 19 September 1917, son of Paterson Clarence Hughes, a teacher from Branxton, New South Wales, and Caroline, née Vennel. Pat was the youngest of 12 children and was educated at Cooma Public School and later at Fort Street High School,

Sydney. He was good at swimming and football and had a keen interest in making model planes. He was accepted by both the air force and navy and chose to join the air force.]

Besides those in the RAF, there was one other group of Australian airmen in England at this time. There were 21 members of a RAAF contingent which had been instructed to take delivery of the first three of 9 Short Sunderland Mk 1 flying boats for the RAAF and fly them back to Australia. The aircraft were not yet ready so the men were attached to RAF Station, Pembroke Dock, Wales, for training. Between 15-26 September, 4 pilots, Flight Lieutenants Charles Pearce and J.A. (Dick) Cohen, and Flying Officers Hugh Birch and Ivan Podger, were released to fly with 210 Squadron on convoy and anti-submarine patrols over the Atlantic and St Georges Channel to gain experience of operational conditions.

Just a few days after Britain's declaration of war some Australians were flying in France. Almost immediately Nos 1 and 73 Squadrons went to the continent with the Advanced Air Striking Force, together with air component squadrons Nos 85 and 87. All were equipped with Gloster Gladiator biplanes soon to be exchanged for Hawker Hurricane Mk Is. The Point Cook graduate in 1 Squadron was Leslie Redford Clisby. Robert Wilton Bungey, from Adelaide, was also in France but flying Fairey Battle light bombers in 226 Squadron. Bungey had his 25th birthday on 4 October and Clisby flew 300 miles (480 km) across France to celebrate the occasion. No. 87 Squadron had two Australians, neither of whom had joined the RAF in the usual way. Richard Lindsay Glyde had worked his passage to England to join the RAF direct. He had received his commission in 1937, the same year that his companion in 87 Squadron, John Reynolds Cock, had paid his way to England to join up.

While both sides were settling into a period which became known as the 'Phoney War', the Orient Line Steamship *Orama* reached England with the last group of Australian volunteers. Among them were John Douglas Peterkin, Jack Clarence Burraston, John Francis Pain and John Dallas Crossman. On 30 October they arrived at Ansty and next day John Crossman wrote the first entry in his *Royal Air Force — pilot's flying log book* recording a 35-minute flight in Tiger Moth N6579.[2]

On 10 April 1940, John Crossman received his appointment as an acting pilot officer in the Royal Air Force upon completion of his elementary training. His days on Tiger Moths were over and he reported with others from his intake to the RAF College, Cranwell, for advanced training.

Not all managed to complete the earlier pilot training. Doug Peterkin had passed out of the course back in December 1939 but had retrained as an air gunner. He was posted to 248 Squadron and joined Clarence Charles Bennett and Alexander Lewis Hamilton as the third Australian on strength.

A month after John Crossman received his commission, the peace of the 'Phoney War' ended abruptly when the Germans marched into neutral Belgian territory. Early on 10 May 1940, *Luftwaffe* bombers ranged over north-east France, Belgium and Holland, attacking 23 airfields and destroying most of its potential opposition on the ground.

EXODUS OF PILOTS
From Australia To England

Australian pilots leaving for Britain on the SS *Orama*, under the RAF short-service commission scheme, on 12 August 1939. Some of these men fought in the battle of Britain; at the top of the gangway is John Crossman, next to him is Jack Burraston and, in the light suit, sixth from the top, is John Pain (newspaper clipping, source unknown).

George R.I.

Temporary.

George VI *by the Grace of God*, OF GREAT BRITAIN, IRELAND AND THE BRITISH DOMINIONS BEYOND THE SEAS, KING, DEFENDER OF THE FAITH, EMPEROR OF INDIA, &c.

To Our Trusty and well beloved *John Dallas Crossman* Greeting:

WE *reposing especial Trust and Confidence in your Loyalty, Courage, and good Conduct, do by these Presents Constitute and Appoint you to be an Officer in Our Royal Air Force from the* Tenth *day of* April 1940. *You are therefore carefully and diligently to discharge your Duty as such in the Rank of* Acting Pilot Officer *or in such higher Rank as We may from time to time hereafter be pleased to promote or appoint you to, and you are at all times to exercise and well discipline in their Duties both the inferior Officers and Airmen serving under you and use your best endeavours to keep them in good Order and Discipline. And We do hereby Command them to Obey you as their superior Officer and you to observe and follow such Orders and Directions as from time to time you shall receive from Us, or any your superior Officer, according to the Rules and Discipline of War, in pursuance of the Trust hereby reposed in you.*

GIVEN at Our Court, at Saint James's the Tenth day of May 1940 in the Fourth Year of Our Reign

By His Majesty's Command

The battle for air superiority was over before it even started. Any resistance that the Allied air forces could now make was piecemeal and unco-ordinated, although at times desperately heroic. Stuka dive-bombers roamed the skies without fear of being seriously molested and they systematically destroyed and disrupted troop concentrations, communications, pockets of resistance or anything which stood in the path of the advancing *Panzers*.

Many Australians distinguished themselves. Just after 3.30 p.m. on that first day, a Tasmanian, F/O Walter Michael Blom of 150 Squadron led two Fairey Battles in a low-level bombing attack against a German motorized column advancing from Neufchateau to Bertrik in Luxembourg. After crossing the frontier at Bouillon, Blom's aircraft was hit in the main fuel tank by machine-gun fire from the ground. Petrol spurted into the cockpit drenching the Australian and seriously impairing his vision. In spite of this, he and his crew, who were also affected by strong fumes, continued to fly the remaining 20 miles (32 km) to the target area but once there could not locate the column. A low-level search revealed a second German column so the two bombers attacked this instead. They were again subjected to concen-

The gunners of 248 Squadron at Dyce in July 1940. Doug (J.D.) Peterkin is standing third from the left. He was declared missing in action on 5 July 1944. He escaped from captivity and worked for a time with the French resistance (photograph courtesy of Doug Peterkin).

trated machine-gun fire and Blom's plane was hit repeatedly but he placed his bombs in the midst of the new target. The bomber was now almost beyond control but he managed to fly the 90 miles (145 km) back to his base at Ecury-sur-Coole where he landed safely. His Battle, K9369, was the only one to return and it had been so badly shot up that it was beyond repair.

In England while John Crossman, Jack Burraston, John Pain and their classmates were learning techniques of low flying at Cranwell, the RAF was being decimated in France. As its Fairey Battles were cut down over the Albert Canal, and two RAF pilots were earning posthumous Victoria Crosses, Leslie Clisby of No. 1 Squadron was among the Hurricane pilots trying to hold off the *Luftwaffe* fighters. On that day he destroyed three German aircraft. Described as an aggressive and fiery pilot who rushed in regardless of the odds, Clisby is believed to have shot down at least 16 German planes before being killed on 15 May. So died Australia's first air ace of the war. That same day Desmond Sheen's Point Cook classmate, F/O H.N. (Bill) Fowler, was shot down and captured near Namur.

[He would later earn the distinction of being one of the few Allied airmen to escape from Colditz].

While escorting Blenheims to bomb the bridges, John Cock and Dick Glyde of 87 Squadron were attacked from behind by Messerschmitt Bf 109s.[3] They managed to evade but the third pilot in their section was shot down. Next morning Cock intercepted a Heinkel He 111 near Lille and caused it to crash-land near Armentières, France.

In a desperate move to bolster the situation the French government begged for reinforcements from Britain. Churchill pledged his support and in spite of objections from the Commander-in-Chief of RAF Fighter Command, AVM Sir Hugh Dowding, the British Cabinet sanctioned the despatch of 32 precious Hawker Hurricanes to the continent. However, in a blunt letter to Cabinet, Dowding stated the situation plainly:[4]

> I believe that, if an adequate fighter force is kept in the country, if the fleet remains in being, and if home forces are suitably organised to resist invasion, we should be able to carry on the war single handed for some time, if not indefinitely. But, if the Home Defence Force is drained away in desperate attempts to remedy the situation in France, defeat in France will involve the final, complete and irremediable defeat of this country.

Dowding's letter had the desired effect and no more Hurricanes were committed to France. Meanwhile, the newer Spitfires, now coming more and more into service, were kept in England. At Leconfield in Yorkshire, much to Pat Hughes' delight, 234 Squadron, to which he had been posted as a flight commander, was re-equipped with them. Another new arrival was P/O Vincent ('Bush') Parker.

Spitfire squadrons were committed to cover the evacuation of the British Expeditionary Force from Dunkirk. Operating with them was 72 Squadron. In the afternoon of 2 June, led by S/Ldr Ronald Beresford Lees, who had taken up his short-service commission early in 1931 and had been granted a permanent commission in the RAF in 1936, the squadron shot up a formation of Ju 87 Stukas, claiming three kills and 4 probables, Lees himself disposing of one. No. 266 Squadron also saw fighting over Dunkirk but one of the two Australians in this unit, P/O J.W.B. Stevenson, was killed during a violent clash with Messerschmitt Bf 109s. The one remaining was Francis Walter Cale who had come to England early in 1939 with Lewis Hamilton, Clarrie Bennett and Bryan Martin McDonough, all of whom were now flying Blenheims. Killed in action, too, was Ian Bedford Nesbitt Russell from Melbourne who, in air battles over France and the beaches, shot down 11 enemy aircraft and probably 6 others. He was shot down on 1 June while flying with 609 Squadron.

Gordon Olive of 65 Squadron had been listed as 'missing in action' a few days earlier on 28 May. He had, in fact, become separated from his squadron and while flying alone had been caught up in a *mêlée* with a *Staffel* of Bf 109s. After a frantic dogfight he managed to escape unscathed, hurtle at low level across the English Channel and force-land at Manston aerodrome very late and almost out of fuel. When he tried to return to his squadron at Hornchurch, he discovered that it had moved to Kirton-in-Lindsay and had to follow it. His return seems never to have been properly recorded and even now some documents still list him as 'missing in action'.[5]

Another Australian went missing on 7 June. P/O John Frederick ('Peter') Pettigrew, who was a close friend of Pat Hughes, simply disappeared. His unit, No. 151 Squadron, flew its Hurricanes to Manston, refuelled and, together with 56 Squadron (Hurricanes), carried out a patrol from Abbeville to Amiens. There was a brief clash with enemy

Air Chief Marshal Sir Hugh Dowding, who promised during the battle of France that 'not one fighter will be sent across the Channel however urgent and insistent the appeals for help might be . . .' (Imperial War Museum photograph D1417).

A Fairey Battle light bomber over the German frontier during the 'phoney war' (Imperial War Museum photograph C1001).

fighters identified as Heinkel He 113s[6] but it did not develop into a fight. All the Hurricanes, except Pettigrew's, returned to Manston and refuelled.

[An unconfirmed story has it that he was shot down and eventually smuggled back to England. He eventually attained the rank of temporary squadron leader and was posted to the Aeroplane and Armament Experimental Establishment at Boscombe Down. On 24 August 1944 while he was leading another aircraft in Hurricane HW 187 there was a mid-air collision. Pettigrew crashed and was killed.]

On 11 June the Inter-Allied Supreme War Council met in Briare. Present were the French prime minister, Paul Reynard, Winston Churchill and Anthony Eden. In spite of Reynard's desperate plea for more RAF involvement, Churchill refused because he now had to face the stark reality of a *Luftwaffe* offensive against Britain. Meanwhile, RAF units had been getting out of France as best they could. In 11 days of fighting 87 Squadron had lost 6 pilots killed, 1 seriously wounded, and 19 aircraft. Only 9 of its Hurricanes remained serviceable and these flew off to England escorting an Airspeed Ensign and 2 DH Dragon Rapides.

A pre-war photograph of
Spitfires of 65 Squadron.
Gordon Olive is flying FZ-A
(Imperial War Museum
photograph HU 1664).

It was only a matter of time before France collapsed but a few RAF
squadrons stayed on as long as possible. Even now, the obsolete Fairey
Battles were being risked in daylight and on 13 June a flight of 3 from
142 Squadron, led by John Minchin Hewson, set out to attack German
columns and troop concentrations around Rouen. After they had
dropped their bombs they were bounced by Messerschmitt Bf 109s
and Bf 110s. All of the bombers were shot up. Amid the frantic fight
Hewson's Battle burst into flames. His gunner was wounded but
claimed to have shot down two He 113s (sic) and one Bf 110. Realizing
that his gunner could not bail out, Hewson ordered his third crewman
to bail out and then, in spite of the fire, he brought the Battle down to a
successful forced landing, made his way back to his aerodrome at
Villiers-Faux and three days later, led what remained of 142 Squadron's aircraft out of France.

The RAF's need for rapid expansion was now vital. Potentially
serious, especially after losing many experienced men in France,
Norway and over Dunkirk, was the need for replacement pilots. No.
238 Squadron had been reformed at Tangmere on 16 May and
equipped with Spitfires but these were replaced by Hurricanes in June.
The unit had two Australian flight commanders, Stuart Crosby Walch
and John (Jack) Connolly Kennedy, both Point Cook graduates, who
had come to England in 1937. There was also an experienced Australian flight commander, Latham Carr Withall, in 152 Squadron at
Acklington and among the newcomers were Ian Bayles and 'Dutchy'
Holland. William Henry Millington was now a member of 79 Squadron at Biggin Hill. This unit was one of those which had been sent to
France when the Germans had marched into Belgium and Holland.

While all this was happening, the third troop convoy (carrying
about 8 000 officers and men) had left Australia. On 17 June they
disembarked at Gourock and went to Salisbury Plain where a base

camp was to be established. Major General H.D. Wynter commanded the Australian force in the United Kingdom.

Elsewhere, out to sea, Charles Pearce and his crew in Sunderland P9604, RB-J, surprised a German U-boat on the surface of the sea and made a fast attack before it could completely submerge. Six 250 lb (114 kg) bombs were dropped 20 feet (6 m) ahead of the submarine's track and a large dirty brown patch of oil and bubbles spread out on the water a moment later. The Sunderland circled for almost three hours but, as there were no further signs of damage, the submarine was judged to have sustained only superficial damage. So ended 10 Squadron's first attack on a positively identified hostile submarine. This RAAF unit had been formed from the original group of 21 airmen who had been meant to take delivery of the Sunderlands and fly them back to Australia. Two officers and 183 men had been sent from Australia to join them and to form the new squadron which was now to remain in England. It had been officially incorporated into 15 Group, RAF Coastal Command, on 3 January 1940.

In spite of the devastating losses suffered on the European continent, in England the almost normal routines of life went on. At Cranwell John Crossman's training continued. In east Yorkshire Pat Hughes had met a girl, Kathleen (Kay) Brodrick of Hull, and they were seeing each other regularly. He had also acquired a dog which he named 'Flying Officer Butch' and occasionally the dog went up flying. Gordon Olive was due to marry Helen Thomas in a few days time. On 18 June Winston Churchill stated:

> What General Weygand called the Battle of France is over. I expect that the Battle of Britain is about to begin. Upon this battle depends the survival of the Christian civilization. Upon it depends our own British life and the long continuity of our institutions and our Empire. The whole fury and might of the enemy must very soon be turned on us. Hitler knows that he will have to break us in this island or lose the war . . . Let us therefore brace ourselves to our duties, and so bear ourselves that, if the British Empire and its Commonwealth last for a thousand years, men will say
> 'This was their finest hour.'[7]

And what a conflict the battle was shaping up to be. RAF Fighter Command under Dowding was now in the process of building up and numerous new squadrons were being formed. Depleted units were being brought up to full strength in terms of pilots and aircraft.

For the purpose of defending Britain Fighter Command was divided into 4 main groups:

11 Group — covering south-eastern England against the *Luftwaffe's* attacks, commanded by the resourceful New Zealander, AVM Keith Park;

12 Group — commanded by AVM Trafford Leigh-Mallory, covering the Midlands behind 11 Group;

10 Group — commanded by AVM Sir Quinton Brand, covering the southern coast and Wales; and

13 Group — covering northern England and Scotland to meet the threat from Norway and Denmark and commanded by AVM Richard Saul.

'Flying Officer Butch', Pat Hughes's dog which occasionally flew with him (photograph courtesy of Bill Hughes).

On 1 July 1940 the command had on its strength 463 Hurricanes, 286 Spitfires, 37 Defiants and 114 Blenheims. Of these 347 Hurricanes, 160 Spitfires, 25 Defiants and 59 Blenheims were serviceable, giving a total of 591 machines at the ready.

On the other side the *Luftwaffe* was in the process of redeploying and strengthening its forces after the fall of France. It was divided into three major groups:

Luftflotte 2 had its new headquarters in Brussels and was under the command of the highly capable *Generalfeldmarschall* Albert Kesselring. It was preparing to operate from bases in north-eastern France, Belgium, Holland and Germany against the south-west of England;

Luftflotte 3 was commanded by *Generalfeldmarschall* Hugo Sperrle who was setting up his operational headquarters in Paris. His aircraft were to operate from northern and western France to threaten southern England; and

Luftflotte 5, under *Generaloberst* Hans-Jurgen Stumpff, was smaller in numbers than the other two and was to fly from bases in Norway and Denmark to threaten north-eastern England and Scotland in order to thin out the English defences. Its headquarters was now at Stavanger in Norway.

Supermarine Spitfire Mk I, K9959, (RN-J) of 72 Squadron, RAF, was built in the first production order of 310 aircraft. Powered by a Rolls Royce Merlin II engine driving a mahogany, two blade, fixed pitch propeller, it was delivered to 72 Squadron on 8 May 1939. Later, a three blade, constant speed de Havilland propeller was substituted. It was flown regularly by Desmond Sheen, hence the Boomerang symbol (brown on a white circle), until he left in April 1940 to join the PDU. K9959 went to No. 1 PRU next October but crashed when its engine failed during a forced landing on 22 January 1941.

Clearly, units under Kesselring and Sperrle were to spearhead the assault. By 20 July redeployment was almost complete and the processes required for making them combat ready were well under way. *Luftflotten* 2 and 3 had available 1 131 twin-engined bombers, Do 17s, He 111s and Ju 88s (of which 769 were serviceable); 316 Ju 87 Stuka dive-bombers (248 serviceable); 246 Bf 110 twin-engined fighters; and 809 Bf 109 single-engined fighters (656 serviceable). In addition, Stumpff's *Luftflotte 5* had 129 (95 serviceable) twin-engined bombers and 34 (32 serviceable) long range Bf 110s, plus 84 single-engined Bf 109s which did not have enough range to be of use until they were later moved south to support *Luftflotten* 1 and 2. Between them they also had over 200 long and short range reconnaissance aircraft. In other words, RAF Fighter Command (Coastal and Bomber Command figures not included) was outnumbered nearly four to one.

However, to offset this advantage the British defences held a trump card — radar or RDF (radio direction finding) as it was known then. Back in 1934 the British government had set up a committee, under the leadership of Henry Tizard, to determine the best scientific methods of defence against bombers. It sought the advice of Robert Watson-Watt, a scientist at the National Physical Laboratory. He advocated the use of radio waves to detect approaching aircraft, communication between a ground controller and interceptor pilot by means of a radio-telephone for directions, and the standard use of a coded radio signal (IFF) from friendly aircraft to distinguish them from others. With Tizard's backing and Dowding's full co-operation, scientists created a radar network, called the Chain Home (CH) range, along Britain's coastline which formed an electronic wall facing out to sea. In the 'Biggin Hill Experiment' of 1936, a series of practical tests was carried out. RAF officers and scientists headed by Tizard used ground controllers and plotting tables to create a reliable system of using radar for the interception of enemy aircraft by defending fighters. After this, and the successful air exercises of 1937, the Air Ministry sanctioned the building of a further 17 new Chain Home Low (CHL) radar stations to supplement the CH range. These were more precise and accurate installations designed to plot low-flying aircraft and were the work of a team of designers headed by the 'Australian' scientist, Alan Butement. (For details refer to entry 13 July in the War Diary.)

A weakness which remained in the system was that after an aircraft crossed the coast it could no longer be plotted by radar and visual tracking had to be carried out by the Observer Corps. The difficulties created by unsuitable weather and darkness were obvious.

The battle lines were being drawn . . . Time was running out!

On 30 June 1940 German troops landed unopposed on the Channel Island of Guernsey to occupy British sovereign territory for the first time . . .

WAR DIARY

JULY, 1940

MONDAY 1

Records indicate that the Australian personnel listed below are on strength in RAF Fighter Command squadrons at 9.00 a.m. on 1 July 1940:

SQUADRON	[AIRCRAFT]	AIRMAN	BASE	
17	[Hurricane]	Sgt D. Fopp	Debden	[11 Group]
65	[Hurricane]	AF/Lt C.G.C. Olive	Hornchurch	[11 Group]
72	[Spitfire]	S/Ldr R.B. Lees	Acklington	[13 Group]
73	[Hurricane]	P/O C.A. McGaw	Church Fenton	[13 Group]
79	[Hurricane]	P/O W. Millington	Biggin Hill	[11 Group]
87	[Hurricane]	P/O J.R. Cock	Church Fenton	[13 Group]
		F/O R.L. Glyde DFC		
141	[Defiant]	P/O A.N. Constantine	Turnhouse	[13 Group]
152	[Spitfire]	AF/Lt L.C. Withall	Acklington	[13 Group]
		P/O I.N. Bayles		
		Sgt K.C. Holland		
234	[Spitfire]	AF/Lt P.C. Hughes	St Eval	[10 Group]
		P/O V. Parker		
238	[Hurricane]	AF/Lt J.C. Kennedy	Middle Wallop	[11 Group]
		AF/Lt S.C. Walch		
257	[Hurricane]	S/L D.W. Bayne	Hendon	[11 Group]
264	[Defiant]	LAC V.W.J. Crook	Duxford	[12 Group]
266	[Spitfire]	P/O F.W. Cale	Wittering	[12 Group]
600	[Blenheim]	F/Lt C.A. Pritchard	Manston	[11 Group]
609	[Spitfire]	P/O J. Curchin	Northolt	[11 Group]
		P/O R.F.G. Miller		

In addition, in three Coastal Command squadrons which are or will be attached to Fighter Command or operate under its control, are:

SQUADRON	[AIRCRAFT]	AIRMAN	BASE	
235	[Blenheim]	AF/Lt F.W. Flood	Bircham Newton	(A Flight)
			Thorney Island	(B Flight)
236	[Blenheim]	F/Lt R.M. Power	Middle Wallop	
		P/O B.M. McDonough		
		F/O W.S. Moore		
248	[Blenheim]	P/O C.C. Bennett	Dyce	
		P/O A.L. Hamilton		
		P/O J.D. Peterkin		

Short Sunderland Mk I, N9048, RB-A of 10 Squadron RAAF. Four Pegasus XXII medium-supercharged engines gave the Sunderland a maximum speed of 210 m.p.h. (338 km/hr) and its defensive armament of a twin 0.303 in. (0.77 cm) Browning machine-gun turret in the nose, a four 0.303 in. (0.77 cm) Browning machine-gun turret in the tail and a single hand-held 0.303 in. (0.77 cm) machine-gun in two beam positions in the top of the hull aft of the wings, plus its ability to withstand punishment, resulted in its being dubbed 'the Porcupine' by the Germans. N9048 was the first Sunderland delivered to 10 Squadron on 11 September 1939. During an air raid on Plymouth on 27 November 1940 it was destroyed by fire in a hangar at Mount Batten.

In the darkness of the early hours Sunderland P9603 (RB-H) taxis out for take-off from Mount Batten. The crew, captained by F/Lt. W.N. 'Hoot' Gibson, has been instructed to carry out an anti-submarine patrol but while moving out a message is received that a merchant vessel, the SS *Zarian*, has been torpedoed during the night about 250 miles (400 km) west of Ushant. Their orders are changed to providing escort to the outward-bound convoy OA175 while destroyers and corvettes search for the guilty submarine.

Several hours later, just as dawn is breaking, the Australians sight the *Zarian* about 3 miles (5 km) off. Gibson circles overhead. The ship is down at the stern and a destroyer stands guard nearby. Before the Sunderland's arrival the destroyer HMS *Gladiolus* had dropped depth charges and it is believed that the U-boat has been damaged. Gibson searches for the possibly crippled German craft.

The enemy submarine is the U-26 and it has indeed been damaged. Water is penetrating its hull and the commander, Oblt Heinz Scheringer, gives orders to resurface at 5.20 a.m. when he believes his U-boat is clear of the attacking British ships. He hopes to escape at high speed before encountering other ships. As the submarine reaches the surface the Germans are shocked to find that an escort vessel is only a few hundred metres away, though, in the semi-darkness, Scheringer manages to slip away undetected.

As the light brightens, he notices a British flying boat circling over the position where he had torpedoed the merchantman and there is another escort vessel sailing not far off in the opposite direction. It is the corvette HMS *Rochester*. The U-26 is obliged to steer a course directly between the approaching destroyer and the orbiting Sunderland.

At 6.12 a.m. F/O Geoff Havyatt spots a disturbance in the water 2 miles (3 km) away on the Sunderland's starboard bow about 30 miles (50 km) from the wallowing *Zarian*. In almost the same instant lookouts on the *Rochester* also sight the U-boat. On the U-26, Scheringer watches the *Rochester* turn and give chase but he may be able to maintain the distance between them if the Sunderland does not interfere. His hopes are dashed when the aircraft suddenly turns towards him and he has to immediately order an emergency dive.

By the time the RAAF Sunderland arrives, Gibson can only see a round patch of disturbed water. Making a run over the spot the Australians drop four 250 lb (114 kg) anti-submarine bombs. The water convulses and erupts as Gibson circles to observe the spectacular results. The U-boat's bow suddenly projects up amid the foam at a very steep angle and then it heaves up fully onto the surface. Four more bombs are dropped and these explode about 40 yards (36 m) from its conning tower, buffeting the vessel violently, then a salvo of shells fired from the *Rochester* at a range of 1 100 yards (1 000 m) thunders down.

It is all over. Scheringer gives the order to abandon and scuttle the ship. The crew lines up on the after deck to indicate surrender.

Gibson reports to Mount Batten at 6.15 a.m., 'Have attacked enemy U/Boat. Estimate five hits. Surfaced — sunk — survivors'.

Rochester picks up the German seamen as the Sunderland continues to circle. It is 10 Squadron's first confirmed success against the U-boats and only the second so far achieved by Coastal Command.

*

Around the same time as Gibson is attacking the U-26 some 250 miles (400 km) west-south-west of the Scilly Isles, three Spitfires of Blue Section, 72 Squadron, based at Acklington, Northumberland, and commanded by S/Ldr Ron Lees, are ordered up to look for an aircraft seen near a convoy sailing east of Sunderland. They encounter an all-white Heinkel He 59 floatplane (D-ASAM), of *Seenotflugkommando 3*, displaying Red Cross markings. Because of its proximity to the convoy the Spitfires attack, causing the German biplane to land in the water. A Royal Navy cruiser picks up the crew as the plane sinks and the Germans complain that the British have violated the symbols of the Red Cross. They insist that they have been on a search and rescue mission. The British suggest that they have been shadowing the convoy to report its position.

*

Flight Lieutenant 'Hoot' Gibson attacked this U-boat south-west of the Scilly Isles on 1 July 1940. The U-boat (U26) was scuttled shortly after this second attack (AWM 128165).

At 6.10 p.m. F/Lt Harry Daish of 212 Squadron photographic development unit (PDU), takes off from Heston, Middlesex, in Spitfire P9385. His is no ordinary Spitfire but a modified Mk IA aircraft which has been stripped of its guns, highly polished, loaded with extra fuel, painted duck-egg green and fitted with special cameras for high altitude reconnaissance.

[Harry Christian Daish trained at Point Cook and took up a short-service commission in the RAF in July 1936. Daish was trained as a bomber pilot to fly Fairey Battles but in February 1940 he was posted to the PDU at Heston.

The PDU was the brainchild of another Australian, Sidney Cotton, a colourful character from Queensland. Cotton was a first world war veteran, having flown with the Royal Naval Air Service, and it was during this time that he invented the 'Sidcot' flying suit. He was an adventurous and determined aeronautical engineer and businessman who, between the wars, among other things, pioneered air mail and aerial survey work in Newfoundland and also carried out pioneering work in aerial photography. In 1938 he was approached by British Intelligence to carry out clandestine aerial photography of military installations in Germany, Italy and the middle east. He agreed and used hidden cameras installed in his own Lockheed 12A. In August 1939 Cotton's Lockheed was the last civil aircraft to leave Berlin. His cameras were rolling all the way and they obtained valuable photographs which revealed the disposition and preparedness of German naval units.

Cotton's successful work with aerial photography led to the Air Ministry authorizing him to form his own unit and commissioning him with the rank of honorary acting wing commander. What was to eventually become the PDU started in secrecy in a spare hangar at Heston aerodrome in September 1939, as No. 2 Camouflage Unit. With F/Lt M.V. Longbottom, who was assigned to him, the Australian evolved the concept of using high performance fighter aircraft specially modified for maximum speed and range and stripped of armament for fast, high-altitude reconnaissance. Cotton's individualism, single mindedness, impatience with service delays and methods and his success had already created friction within the RAF hierarchy but he was provided with one Spitfire. Operating from France, it flew missions over western Germany with such success that by January 1940, No. 2 Camouflage Unit had become the PDU with four Spitfires at Heston and six in France. It was unofficially known as 'Cotton's Club'.

Early in 1940 a mysterious appeal had been circulated throughout RAF squadrons asking for pilots with navigational experience to volunteer to fly 'something very fast'. Among other airmen, two Australians, Harry Daish and Desmond Sheen, had responded. By July, all reconnaissance was directed towards evaluating the enemy's preparations for invasion and, because of the need for co-ordinated effort, both Bomber Command and Coastal Command vied for control of the PDU instead of having it nominally under Air Ministry supervision. It was transferred to Coastal Command on 18 June and Cotton was dismissed; he was posted instead to the pool depot at Uxbridge.]

Climbing steadily, Harry Daish sets his course from Shorham to Le Havre. The weather over the continent is now fine and the Australian estimates that visibility is up to 60 miles (100 km). Just north of Le Havre at 31 700 feet (9 700 m), he starts the cameras and takes photographs from the harbour to Trouville, Honfleur, and back to Le Havre again. Well satisfied with the mission, he sets course for Heston.

*

The British Broadcasting Corporation announces that communications with the Channel Islands have been severed as they are now occupied by the Germans. This is the first German invasion of British sovereign territory and is considered by some historians as a valid date for the beginning of the battle of Britain.

[During the ensuing first 9 days of the month Hurricane and Spitfire pilots would shoot down at least 56 German aircraft for the loss of 28 planes. Twenty-three Fighter Command pilots would be either killed or wounded. Those who were killed and those who could not return to operations before 31 October, and flew at least one sortie, are considered ineligible to be recipients of the coveted Battle of Britain Clasp.]

TUESDAY, 2 JULY

Flying conditions over most of England are poor, cloudy and rainy, and there is only limited aerial activity. Fighter Command shoots down only one German aircraft, a Dornier Do 215 reconnaissance plane.

Adolf Hitler orders the Armed Force Supreme Command, *Oberkommando der Wehrmacht (OKW)*, to make provisional plans for an invasion of England. After two weeks Field Marshal von Brauchitsch, commander-in-chief of the German army, and General Halder, his chief of staff, will submit ambitious proposals for the operation. These will receive Hitler's approval and he will direct them to begin active preparations, but at the same time he will stress that the attainment of air superiority is the indispensable prelude to carrying out a landing.

The *OKW* also issues its first operational instructions to the *Luftwaffe* for the campaign against the United Kingdom. There are two basic tasks assigned:

1. The interdiction of the English Channel to merchant shipping to be carried out in conjunction with German naval force by means of attacks on convoys, the destruction of harbour facilities and the laying of mines in harbour areas and approaches.
2. The destruction of the Royal Air Force.[1]

*

No. 238 Hurricane Squadron is declared operational for the first time. This squadron had been reformed at Tangmere on 16 May but on 20 June it had moved to Middle Wallop. Within the core of experienced officers responsible for training the new pilots are two Australians, Jack Kennedy and Stuart Walch.

[*John Connolly Kennedy was the son of John and Frances Kennedy of Sydney, NSW, and was educated at St Charles College, Waverley. He trained at Point Cook in early 1937 and sailed from Australia in July. In December Kennedy was posted to 65 Squadron at Hornchurch which at the time was equipped with Gloster Gladiators. His promotion to flying officer was recorded in the* **London Gazette** *of 26 May 1939, and at this stage the squadron had just converted to Spitfires. On 16 May 1940 he was promoted to acting flight lieutenant and on the 31st took up a new appointment as a flight commander in the newly forming 238 Squadron at Tangmere where he found that the other flight commander was Stuart Walch from the days at Point Cook.*

Stuart Crosby Walch was born in Hobart, Tasmania, on 16 February 1917, son of Percival and Florence Walch, née Pidgeon. Stuart was educated at The Hutchins School, Hobart. On 15 July 1936 he joined the RAAF as an air cadet at Point Cook and in due course accepted a short-service commission for five years in the RAF. In January 1940 he was promoted to acting flight lieutenant and in May he was posted to the newly formed 238 Squadron at Tangmere.

The new squadron had been worked up on Spitfire Is but early in June the unit moved to Middle Wallop where Hurricanes were waiting. Kennedy and Walch were required to train and prepare the new pilots for the fighting which now loomed.]

A constructive rivalry has been generated between the two Australians as to whose flight will score the squadron's first kill.

*

During a conference at Amesbury Abbey, General Wynter's headquarters, the officers of the Australian force in the United Kingdom learn of the serious, and completely unsatisfactory position, which exists in regard to the supply of war equipment, transport and ammunition. If the Germans begin large scale attacks on Britain tomorrow the Australian force will not only be immobile owing to lack of transport; it will also be inadequately equipped with the means to protect itself.

WEDNESDAY, 3 JULY

[*With the commencement of operations according to instructions issued to the* **Luftwaffe** *by the* **OKW** *on 2 July, most German historians regard the preliminary phase of the battle of Britain as commencing on this day.]*

*

Weather conditions are fine over most of England and there are several raids against coastal targets. German reconnaissance planes are also active.

In stormy conditions around 5.00 p.m. Jack Kennedy of 238 Squadron clashes briefly, south of Middle Wallop, with a Junkers Ju 88A. Both planes are slightly damaged and both manage to return safely to their respective bases. It is 238 Squadron's first clash with the enemy.

THURSDAY, 4 JULY

For the first time the *Luftwaffe* conducts co-ordinated attacks against British shipping in the Channel, with good results. One bombed ship beaches itself on the coast near Deal but the Germans' biggest successes come from a raid on Portland Naval Base by 33 Junkers Ju 87 Stukas. A merchant tanker is set alight and the auxiliary anti-aircraft ship *Foyle Bank* is sunk. One Ju 87 is shot down.

Because the English Channel is becoming more dangerous, the Admiralty accelerates its plans to divert ocean traffic to west coast ports.

Eight Hurricanes of 79 Squadron, Bill Millington's unit, are scrambled from Hawkinge at 2.05 p.m. to intercept bombers over a beleaguered convoy off Dover but they are surprized by the escort of 30 Messerschmitt Bf 109s. One Hurricane is shot down.

*

Newly operational, No. 247 Squadron, commanded by S/Ldr David Bayne, moves from Hendon to Northolt. The transfer is almost completed by 2.00 p.m. Bayne has 8 of his pilots carry out air-to-ground firing practice to keep his training programme going.

Also on the move, 236 Squadron (Dick Power and Bryan McDonough) transfers from Middle Wallop to Thorney Island for long range fighter and reconnaissance duties.

[Records show that David Walter Bayne was born in Sydney, NSW.

On 15 December 1928 he was granted a permanent commission in the RAF and by 1 August 1938 had attained the rank of acting squadron leader. That year he was involved in a flying accident which resulted in the loss of one leg. Such was his courage and determination, however, that he recovered and, with the aid of a wooden leg, was able to eventually return to flying duties. In May 1940 Bayne was stationed at Kenley. On 17 May he was posted to Hendon to form and take command of 257 Squadron. Reporting for duty at the same time, Bayne found an adjutant, 10 officer pilots, 10 airmen pilots, one engineer officer and 141 airmen to form his command. He was informed that the unit would be equipped with Spitfires plus a Master and a Magister aircraft for training purposes. The Spitfires arrived and they began to work on them. They reached the stage of air firing exercises but in June these aircraft were withdrawn and replaced by Hurricanes, so that training had to start all over again.

Throughout June the squadron had worked to become a cohesive unit and the men displayed an obvious confidence in their commanding officer. He was '... just the sort of man we needed. Determined, conscientious and brave,' wrote P/O Geoff Myers, the squadron's intelligence officer.]

*

At night RAF Bomber Command sends 73 aircraft out to bomb northern Germany's ports and blockade them by dropping antishipping mines. In Kiel harbour, the *Scharnhorst* lies in dry dock and this is the target for Hampdens from 83 Squadron, including aircraft

L4124 flown by Henry Ross. Flak and searchlights make results difficult to observe but Ross and his crew believe that they have made a successful run at the target.

[*Ellis Henry Ross was born at Tamworth, NSW, and became a Point Cook cadet in 1936. He sailed for England in July 1937, under the RAF Short-Service Commission Scheme, and joined 83 Squadron. For his exploits he was awarded the Distinguished Flying Cross (DFC) for his successful bombing of Aalborg aerodrome under adverse weather conditions on 20 April 1940. His aircraft was the second to attack and, in spite of intense anti-aircraft fire, he carried out 5 runs over the target.*]

FRIDAY, 5 JULY

Weather conditions over England are poor with rain occurring in East Anglia and the north and air operations are restricted.

In London Kenneth Slessor lunches with Stuart Smith, private secretary to Stanley Bruce, former prime minister of Australia and now Australian high commissioner. Slessor then visits the Australian Troops' Centre at the Strand Theatre, London. Outside is a huge sign, 'Aussie, Your London Home'. Each Australian soldier on 48-hour leave must report here in order to receive his payment of £2. The centre contains a continuous canteen organized by the Australian Women's Voluntary Service Association, members of which are drawn from Australian women living in Britain. Slessor is impressed by their thorough organization.

Kenneth Slessor, official Australian war correspondent (AWM 1830).

[One of Australia's most famous poets, Slessor was official Commonwealth government war correspondent between 1939–44. He was born at Orange, NSW, in 1901 and educated at Sydney Church of England Grammar School. He later worked for the Sydney **Sun**, and for Melbourne **Punch** and the **Herald**.]

*

At 5.55 p.m. Lockheed Hudson T9270 of 233 Squadron takes off from Leuchars, Fifeshire, in Scotland, to carry out a patrol over the North Sea. On board as second pilot is P/O James Horan.

Lockheed Hudsons of 233 Squadron. Australians James Horan, Bill Weaber and John McIntosh flew with this unit; they were all killed between July and October 1940 (Imperial War Museum photograph CH 989).

[James Henry Horan received a short-service commission for four years in the RAF, effective from October 1938. After training he was posted to Coastal Command and 233 Squadron, which used Ansons for general reconnaissance work. The squadron moved to Scotland in August 1939, and re-equipped with Hudsons with which it flew anti-shipping sweeps after the Germans invaded Norway in April 1940. It continued with this type of work during the period of the battle of Britain.]

SATURDAY, 6 JULY

In the north there is a spell of fine weather but in the south rain and low cloud persist throughout the day.

As more fighter squadrons become operational through the influx of new pilots and equipment, Air Chief Marshal Sir Hugh Dowding, Commander-in-Chief of RAF Fighter Command, with his Group commanders, Air Vice Marshal Keith Park (11 Group) and Air Vice Marshal Trafford Leigh-Mallory (12 Group), initiates the redeployment of several squadrons to meet the threat of the German bomber units being established in the Cherbourg and Brest peninsulas.

Among the changes 87 Squadron, containing John Cock and Dick Glyde, completes its move from Church Fenton to Exeter; from there it will cover the western approaches to Bristol and Plymouth.

No. 236 Squadron, equipped with Blenheims, shifts from Middle Wallop to Thorney Island to patrol at night over the Solent, Southampton and Portsmouth. For this duty the crews have to rely solely on directions from ground control and then visual contact. Britain is poorly prepared for German night attacks. Richard Power and Bryan McDonough are in this squadron.

No. 609 Squadron, containing John Curchin and Rogers 'Mick' Miller, both of them new arrivals to replace losses suffered over Dunkirk, comes from Northolt to Middle Wallop on Salisbury Plain.

Meanwhile, Harry Hardman rejoins 111 Squadron at Croydon and Richard Hillary joins 603 Squadron at Turnhouse. Upon his arrival Hillary learns that 603 Squadron is operating from two other airfields; 'A' Flight is at Dyce and 'B' Flight is at Montrose. Hillary goes to the latter.

[Richard Hope Hillary was born in Sydney on 20 April 1919, son of Michael Hillary and Edwyna, née Hope. Richard was educated at Shrewsbury School, England, and in 1937 went to Trinity College, Oxford. His flying career began when he became a member of the University Air Squadron. He was still at Oxford when war broke out in 1939 and he joined the RAF.]

There is a tragedy at RAF College, Cranwell. Jack Burraston is the passenger in a Hawker Hind which is being flown by another cadet when it stalls while performing low-level aerobatics over the airfield and crashes. When observers on the ground reach the wrecked plane they find that Burraston is dead.

Jack Burraston, who was killed in an air crash during training (photograph courtesy of Doug Peterkin).

SUNDAY, 7 JULY

In spite of another day of low cloud and rain patches, the *Luftwaffe* launches attacks on a convoy proceeding through the Channel. By evening it is off Dover and being subjected to a heavy attack by 45 Dornier Do 17s. One ship is sunk and three are damaged. Meanwhile 6 Spitfires of 65 Squadron, Gordon Olive's unit, which are scrambled from Hornchurch to intercept, are bounced from above by escorting Messerschmitt Bf 109s. Three Spitfires are shot down and the pilots killed.

*

No. 73 Squadron, Charles McGaw's unit, is declared operational once more; it had been one of the last units to leave France on 17 June. Now, it has been built up to strength again at Church Fenton and detached to Sherburn-in-Elmet for night-fighter training. However, it will be another month before it will be ready for this other duty.

[Charles Alexander McGaw, the son of William and Agnes McGaw, was born on 3 November 1915 in Peebleshire, Scotland. The family migrated to Australia in 1920 and settled at Stanthorpe, Queensland. Charles was educated at Scots College, Warwick, and began an engineering apprenticeship in Glasgow. He completed his trade in 1936 and for advancement went to another Glasgow firm as a draftsman. Afterwards he became an aeronautical inspector with the Air Ministry. With the situation in Europe becoming more serious, McGaw enlisted in the RAF on 13 June 1939 and on 5 August was granted a short-service commission for 6 years. After he had received his wings in 1939 he and Margaret Duncan of Paisley had married. On 12 June 1940 his appointment as a pilot officer was confirmed and he was posted to 73 Squadron.]

*

At night RAF Bomber Command sends over 50 aircraft to attack targets on the continent and to carry out minelaying operations. For Richard Taylor of 50 Squadron the target is the railway marshalling yards at Soest. He and his crew leave Lindholme in Hampden L4075 at 10.09 p.m. and have a quiet trip to the target. By the time they arrive several fires are already burning and the German defences have been stung into action. The area is alive with searchlights and anti-aircraft fire. Taylor makes his bomb run from south to north and drops six 250 lb (114 kg) bombs and a load of incendiaries.

[F/Lt George Richard Taylor remained a bomber pilot in 50 Squadron during the period of the battle of Britain. From Hawthorn, Victoria, he was a Point Cook cadet in 1937 and went to England in January 1938. His five-year short-service commission was granted in February. At 22 he received a DFC:

He has many times found his target in spite of adverse weather and severe enemy opposition. His devotion to duty and determination in pressing home his attacks are most praiseworthy . . .

RAF sources list him as 'Death Presumed', 13 August 1941.]

Charles McGaw, who flew with 73 and 66 Squadrons (photograph courtesy of Margaret McGaw).

MONDAY, 8 JULY

Weather conditions during daylight are clear but with plenty of cloud, ideal for the *Luftwaffe* to stage convoy attacks, and Fighter Command is kept busy flying cover.

Operating from Exeter John Cock of 87 Squadron flies an early patrol over Weymouth in Hurricane P3596, LK-N. The fruitless sortie lasts for one hour and 10 minutes. Later in the day, while on patrol between Salcombe and Dartmouth, the Hurricanes encounter a twin-engined German aircraft making good use of the available cloud cover. It is identified as a Dornier Do 215. John Cock is again flying P3596. He manages to fire 4 short bursts at the elusive Dornier before it escapes into the clouds with its starboard engine apparently damaged.

At 3.40 p.m. 79 Squadron, Bill Millington's unit, finds trouble. The squadron's 9 Hurricanes are scrambled from Hawkinge to cover a large convoy which had put out from the Thames Estuary. It is attacked off Dover by Messerschmitt Bf 109s. Two Hurricanes and two pilots are lost in a short, sharp encounter. The squadron has seen continuous action since May and has suffered casualties — the strain is showing . . .

At 6.15 p.m. Blue Section of 234 Squadron, led by Pat Hughes, is on convoy patrol at 21 000 feet (6 400 m), 25 miles (40 km) south-east of Lands End. The three Spitfires encounter a lone Junkers Ju 88 above the cloud layer. After Blue 2 makes a firing pass and breaks away, Hughes closes in from astern. The Ju 88 climbs steeply into a cloud but Hughes follows, firing bursts at 30–50 yards (25–45 m) range until they merge. Throughout the engagement the German rear gunner keeps up defensive fire but it is inaccurate and the Spitfire receives only one bullet hole in the leading edge of its starboard wing. As the Junkers goes into a shallow dive Hughes fires twice more and then breaks off to port, making way for the next attack.

The Operations Record Book of 234 Squadron notes this Ju 88 as the squadron's first confirmed kill.

*

Meanwhile other squadrons are still training. In the north Lewis Hamilton of 248 Squadron flies Blenheim L9392 as a target for the Spitfires of 603 Squadron as they practise interceptions and attacks with the new pilots. Replacement Spitfire pilot, Richard Hillary, will not be declared operational until he has completed a week of such training.

*

Thomas Frederick Umphelby Lang came to England from Melbourne, Victoria, and in December 1931, was granted a five-year short-service commission in the RAF, which was changed to a permanent commission in February 1936. Today the *London Gazette* records his promotion to acting wing commander. With his promotion comes greater responsibility as senior controller at No. 11 Group, Fighter Command Headquarters, Uxbridge.

Since the fall of France it has become obvious that 11 Group, covering an area from Portland to Felixstowe and commanded by the resourceful New Zealander AVM Keith Park, will bear the brunt of the German air attack. To meet the threat a careful routine based on the results of extensive manoeuvres carried out by the RAF in August 1938 has been established. During these tests the new radar (RDF) system and the Observers' Corps organization have been tried and found successful.

Lang has to fit in to an entirely new routine. At Group Headquarters itself, when a hostile raid is plotted, the floor supervisor blows a whistle and the entire Group Operations table is immediately fully manned. At the same time the staff officer rings an electric bell which summons the duty controller from his office above ground. The whole process only takes a matter of minutes.

In the coming months Lang and the whole system will be put severely to the test . . .

TUESDAY, 9 JULY

Rain and low clouds cover most of England in the morning, inhibiting operations. Conditions improve later in the day and three major raids take place, one of them on Portland naval base.

At 3.30 p.m. Bill Millington of 79 Squadron is flying as Red 2 of 'A' Flight carrying out an interception at 15 000 feet (4 500 m) over mid-Channel, south-east of Dover.

[William Henry Millington was born in England, son of William Henry and Elizabeth Millington. While he was a young child the family migrated to Australia, settling at Edwardstown, South Australia. Bill Millington arrived back in England on 14 June 1939 and in September was granted a short-service commission in the RAF. He was posted to 79 Squadron stationed at Biggin Hill and flying to cover Channel convoys. The squadron moved to Hawkinge to facilitate these operations.]

Enemy aircraft are sighted some 7 000–8 000 feet (2 100–2 400 m) overhead, heading for Dover and making full use of moderate cloud cover. As they climb after the Germans, Millington and his leader lose contact with the other four Hurricanes. They level out at 20 000 feet (6 100 m) and orbit, searching the sky, until they spot a dogfight developing between the other Hurricanes and Messerschmitt Bf 109s. They rush to join in and during the battle Millington notices two Bf 109s emerge from thick cloud. He climbs up behind them and carries out a stern attack on the rear machine. At 300 yards (275 m) range, he presses the button for three seconds. Belching thick black smoke, the 109 dives steeply and crashes a few miles from the French coast.

Meanwhile, the other Bf 109 has gone down in a diving turn with a second Hurricane hard on its tail. Millington joins the pursuit but the other Hurricane, Yellow 1, is well in front. The 109 crosses the French coast trailing black smoke but the Australian can follow no longer because he is due to switch to his reserve fuel tank.

During the afternoon, at about 5.30, another Heinkel He 59 air-sea rescue floatplane of *Seenotflugkommando 1* is brought down intact by 54 Squadron and its crew taken prisoner. This action, and that of 72 Squadron on 1 July, causes the Air Ministry to discuss whether or not the *Luftwaffe's* Red Cross aircraft, operating close to important British convoys, should have immunity under the provisions of the Geneva convention.

The overnight target for 83 Squadron at Scampton is the heavily protected *Tirpitz* at Wilhelmshaven. The Hampdens begin taking off at 10.15 p.m. and among them 'Mull' Mulligan and 'Rossy' Ross are flying L4051 and L4057 respectively. Flak, as usual, is heavy and accurate but all of the bombers manage to make an accurate run over the German port and drop their loads. It proves impossible, however, to observe the results of their bombing.

[Allan Roy Mulligan was born at Bingara, NSW, on 23 February 1915 and trained as an air cadet at Point Cook before sailing to England in July 1937 to take up a RAF short-service commission.]

WEDNESDAY, 10 JULY

[This day is generally accepted by British historians as marking the beginning of the battle of Britain.]

Weather conditions over south-east England and the Channel are showery. A large convoy, code named 'Bread', sets out early from the Thames Estuary and by 1.30 p.m. German forces are building up over Pas de Calais for a major attack. Radar plots the raid and several fighter squadrons, including 111 Squadron from Croydon, with 9 Hurricanes, are scrambled to intercept.

About 24 escorted Dornier Do 17s are sighted and 111 meets them head on. It is believed that this type of standard attack is unique to 111 Squadron at this time. While undeniably effective, the risks are obvious. The Hurricanes, in line abreast, charge in, firing as they close. Unnerved, the bombers break formation and one is shot down but there is a collision and a Hurricane loses its wing as it slams into a bomber. The British pilot is killed but the Dornier, also minus its wing, crashes.

Meanwhile, the remaining Hurricanes come through the German formations unscathed and occupy themselves attacking the rearmost bombers from behind. In the *mêlée* one of the Messerschmitt Bf 109 escorts is shot down into the sea and two Hurricanes are damaged.

Harry Hardman will later recall this type of action as 'thirsty work'.

[Harry Gordon Hardman was born on 4 May 1915 at Arncliffe, NSW, son of a leather goods manufacturer. Harry received his later education at Cottingham Commercial College, Bexleyheath, England, and between 18–21 years of age spent much of his time at Brooklands Flying Club learning to fly. In February 1938 he was granted a short-service

Harry Hardman of 111
Squadron (photograph
courtesy of Harry Hardman).

commission for four years in the RAF and on 17 September 1938 was
posted to 111 Squadron at Northolt. Hardman stayed with the squadron
until March 1939, when he was posted away on the 9th. His promotion to
flying officer was gazetted in December. On 6 July 1940 he returned to
111 Squadron just in time for the battle of Britain.]

Later in the day, another Hurricane from 111 Squadron is damaged
when it is mistakenly attacked by a Spitfire over Kent.

*

There is movement at Biggin Hill as 141 Squadron, equipped with
Boulton Paul Defiants, arrives from Turnhouse. Noel Constantine
and the others fly down between 8.30–9.40 a.m. The Australian is at
the controls of aircraft L6994 with P/O Webber in the turret position.

[Alexander Noel Constantine was born at Moama, NSW, on 13 December 1914. He apparently joined the RAF direct and received his four-year
short-service commission in July 1938. In July 1940 he joined 141 Squadron which just beforehand had become operational.]

While 141 Squadron's headquarters is to be established at Biggin Hill,
the Defiants are to operate from the satellite airfield at West Malling.
Hawkinge is also to be used as an advanced airfield.
     The Boulton Paul Defiant is a slim, Rolls Royce Merlin powered
monoplane requiring a crew of two, a pilot and a gunner. Unlike the
Hurricane or Spitfire, it has no forward-firing armament (a serious
fault), but carries instead a power-operated, four-gun turret positioned
in mid-fuselage. Designed to destroy slow-moving bombers which stay
in formation, it is the result of a concept which is completely out of
date for day fighting. In terms of performance, it does not compare
favourably with the Hurricane and Spitfire and therefore will be at a
disadvantage when it meets Willi Messerschmitt's Bf 109. An alarming
feature from the gunner's point of view is that, because of the narrow
confines of the turret, it is difficult for him to make a quick exit in an
emergency.
     No. 141 Squadron has not yet met the enemy in the air and many of
its aircraft are not yet fully modified for combat. In order to improve
performance, a programme of fitting constant speed propellers is
inaugurated. The complete change will take about a week, during
which time much-needed flying practice will be lost.

THURSDAY, 11 JULY

Over southern England the weather is clear but overcast in the morning with some rainy patches later in the day. Conditions are worse in
the north. German reconnaissance planes pick up the movement of
another convoy off the south coast. Just after 7.00 a.m. aircraft set off
from the Cherbourg peninsula to make the first attacks.
     At Warmwell, 'B' Flight of 609 Squadron is scrambled. Five Spit-
fires instead of the usual 6 are airborne in two sections, Blue Section

with three planes, followed by Green with two. John Curchin is Green 2. They reach the convoy just as a string of ten Ju 87s goes down to attack it. Blue Leader orders Green Section to remain aloft to cover Blue Section from any escorting Messerschmitt Bf 109s while it goes after the dive bombers. What 'B' Flight does not know is that a second formation of enemy planes has been picked up on radar. Control issues a warning but the radio message is not received. It is John Curchin's first combat and he suddenly finds himself fighting for his life when 20 Bf 109s sweep down on the Spitfires from out of the sun. Blue 1 and Blue 2 are shot down and killed.

[John Curchin was born at Hawthorn, Melbourne, Victoria, on 20 January 1918, son of Henry Wallace Curchin and his wife Suzanna. The family moved to Enfield, Middlesex, England, while John was young and he was educated at Merchant Taylor's School. He joined the RAF in August 1939 and in June 1940 was posted to 609 Squadron at Northolt. This unit's early war work consisted mainly of convoy patrols. On 5 July 1940 it was transferred across to Middle Wallop in 12 Group where it would remain for the duration of the battle of Britain.]

*

Around 11.00 a.m. another force from *Luftflotte 3* consisting of 15 Junkers Ju 87s with an escort of 30–40 Messerschmitt Bf 110s builds up over the Cherbourg peninsula and sets course for Portland. It is intercepted during its attack by 6 Hurricanes of 601 Squadron from Tangmere, whose pilots believed they would find a lone German aircraft! When the size of the enemy formation is revealed other RAF units, including 87 and 238 Squadrons, are vectored into the attack and a running battle ensues.

Dick Glyde is Blue 2 in a section of Hurricanes from 87 Squadron. At midday, when Blue Section pounces on the escort, he closes with the nearest Bf 110 and, after firing off two deflection shots, manoeuvres onto his opponent's tail. He fires again and thickening white vapour flows from the German's engines. Glyde fires again as the 110 looms in front before he has to swing away sharply. Throwing the Hurricane into a tight turn, he comes around onto his target's tail again but now comes under attack from behind by another Bf 110. Before he can roll out of the way a large hole is shot through the rear panel of his hood and three others are punched through his starboard wing tip. Once clear, he searches for his original adversary but cannot sight him. However, Glyde is convinced that the 110 has been badly damaged.

The Australian then locates a Hurricane engaging a Bf 110 lower down at 6 000 feet (1 800 m), and because he cannot see any disengaged enemy aircraft he joins in. Both Hurricanes carry out a series of deflection attacks without any apparent effect except for driving the German plane lower. Suddenly, at 3 000 feet (900 m), the enemy pilot tries to escape by pushing his heavier fighter into a dive. It is a mistake because Glyde, who is higher, dives after him and is able to overtake. He fires and white vapour issues from both of the 110's engines. The rear gunner puts up a good fight, firing repeatedly at Dick Glyde's machine. One bullet tears a long hole in the central panel of the Hurricane's hood and strikes the armour plating close to his head — a near thing. Undeterred, he pursues the 110 until it levels out at 100 feet (30 m) above the water and he fires again as the range closes. It is enough. The Bf 110 lands in the water near Portland Bill and sinks within 30 seconds.

[*Richard Lindsay Glyde was the only child of Frank Cave Glyde and Phillis Napier Birke, and was born in Perth, Western Australia, on 29 January 1914. He trained at Point Cook in 1935 and was the fastest air cadet put through the flying course, achieving his solo in a total of only 5 hours tuition. Unfortunately it was discovered that he had a slightly crooked spine, which was considered enough to prevent his being granted wings. Determined to be an aviator, Glyde sought medical treatment, boarded a freighter bound for England and joined the RAF direct. He was commissioned in 1937 and on 27 November 1939 he transferred into 87 Squadron, then serving in France. During the fighting in France Glyde accounted for at least 4 enemy aircraft and for his exploits he was awarded a DFC.*

Back in the United Kingdom, 87 Squadron operated from Church Fenton and on 5 July moved to Exeter. Now, after their first combat over England, the pilots are elated over their success. They claim 4 destroyed and one probable without loss, Dick Glyde's share being one destroyed and the one probable.]

Meanwhile Oblt Kadow and Gefr Scholz are in difficulties. Their Messerschmitt Bf 110 has been subjected to numerous attacks by British aircraft and just before 12.10 p.m. they run into three Hurricanes from 238 Squadron led by Stuart Walch. Kadow is wounded but in spite of his injury, he manages to force-land his aircraft at Grange Heath. Both he and Scholz are captured. Stuart Walch has scored 238 Squadron's first confirmed victory.

*

While this running battle is taking place, further to the west, a clash occurs between an Avro Anson of 217 Squadron, a general reconnaissance squadron based at St Eval, and an air-sea rescue Heinkel He 59 of *Seenotflugkommando 1*. The German aircraft sustains damage and has to land in the Channel. A second He 59 notices the rescue plane come down and although the English coast is in sight, it lands close by to help. An alert Cornish coastguard reports the incident and two RN destroyers from Plymouth are despatched in the hope of capturing the German seaplanes. The destroyers are covered by three British Blenheims of 236 Squadron, one of which is piloted by Bryan McDonough.

At 12.30 p.m., as the British force arrives, a Ju 88A attacks the ships but the Blenheims quickly counter-attack, shooting it down into the sea.

Shortly afterwards a Heinkel He 111H arrives on the scene and McDonough goes after it alone. He chases it down to sea level, firing all the way with his belly pack of 4 .303 inch (7.7 mm) machine-guns but it manages to escape, although heavily damaged.

[*Bryan Martin McDonough was born at Ulverstone, Tasmania, on 15 August 1916, son of John and Ellen McDonough. When the family moved to Victoria he finished his education at St Kevins College, Heyington, Melbourne, and joined the RAF on a short-service commission early in 1939. His commission was granted on 13 May and he was sent to 236 Squadron at Stradishall. This unit had only been established a week earlier.]*

FRIDAY, 12 JULY

The weather is mainly cloudy with early morning fog which hampers German air activity until approximately 8.50 a.m. when sorties are mounted towards Convoy 'Agent' near North Foreland and Convoy 'Booty' north-west of Orfordness.

No. 17 Squadron's 'A' Flight is ordered forward to Martlesham from Debden for the day's patrols.

At 8.45 a.m. two Hurricanes of Red Section (Desmond Fopp is Red 2) are ordered to patrol over Convoy 'Booty' east of Aldeburgh. Five minutes later they receive information that enemy aircraft are approaching the ships from the south. Nine Heinkel He 111s are observed flying in three vic formations. Fopp and his companion, P/O Geoff Pittman, dart in and out of the cloud cover making co-ordinated attacks on the Germans, and then concentrate on a third machine which lags behind in the last formation. A quarter attack silences the rear gunner and another puts the starboard engine out of action. Shortly afterwards, the Heinkel crashes into the sea.

[Desmond Fopp was born in Adelaide on 13 March 1920 and was educated at St Peter's College, Adelaide. In 1936 his father died and he and his mother returned to her family in England. Desmond joined the RAFVR as a volunteer pilot in 1938. When war broke out in September 1939 he was almost fully trained and he joined 17 Squadron early in 1940. By the end of June the unit was operational and based at Debden in 11 Group. It operated from there and Martlesham Heath until mid-August when it moved to Tangmere for two weeks.]

*

Red Section of 609 Squadron encounters a Heinkel He 111 over Portland Bill at 10.04 a.m. The three Spitfires are patrolling at 10 000 feet (3 000 m) when Red 3, John Curchin, spots the enemy machine to starboard. In 'line astern' the British fighters intercept before the Heinkel can escape into cloud cover. Curchin delivers a quarter attack in thick haze. There is no return fire. He follows the bomber in a slow climb and makes a beam attack. The other Spitfires continue their assault and seconds later Curchin again finds the bomber and delivers another quarter attack. He sees pieces falling off the starboard engine and wing but then the Heinkel dives steeply and disappears into cloud. It has obviously been heavily damaged.

Although Red Section claims a kill, the Heinkel manages to force-land at Cherbourg.

*

F/O Desmond Sheen DFC arrives back in England.

Desmond Fopp of 17 Squadron (photograph courtesy of Desmond Fopp).

[Desmond Frederick Bert Sheen was born in Sydney on 2 October 1917 but was living in Canberra when he decided to join the RAAF. He was accepted for a cadetship at Point Cook in 1936 and went to England for a RAF short-service commission in 1937. Late that year he joined 72 Squadron at Church Fenton which at this stage was equipped with Gloster Gladiators. Sheen was on squadron strength when, in December 1938, it received an Australian commanding officer, S/Ldr Ron Lees. No. 72 was one of the later units to receive Spitfires and the first of these arrived in April 1939. When war broke out Sheen had been a flying officer for a year and the squadron became operational immediately. It became engaged on coastal patrols, fighter protection of the Humber and Midlands areas, convoy escort duties and the protection of Edinburgh.

Desmond Sheen experienced his first clash with the enemy on 21 October 1939 when he and F/O Elsdon in Spitfires K9959 and K9950 encountered 14 Heinkel He 115s over the North Sea and shot down 2 of them. For this Sheen was awarded the DFC. In October 72 Squadron moved to Drem. In April 1940 Sheen transferred to No. 212 Squadron, Photographic Development Unit, which had been formed by Sidney Cotton, and he moved to France with a detachment for the AASF.]

After the PDU's aircraft had been destroyed by bombing Sheen and the others had to make their way back to England via Gibraltar.

SATURDAY, 13 JULY

Early fog over southern England clears by mid-morning for a day of sporadic attacks on convoys moving off the south coast.

Bill Crook flies his first operation as a gunner in Defiant L6967. His pilot is P/O Desmond Hughes who is to become one of the RAF's most successful night fighter aces. Operating from Duxford, 264 Squadron has been flying mainly night and dawn patrols since 7 June after its daylight loss rate over Dunkirk had become too high.

[Valton William James Crook was born at Orange, NSW, on 11 May 1913. His family moved to Sydney and he was educated at Newtown Technical School. In 1939, while in New Zealand, he joined the RNZAF. He went to the Ground Training School, Werweoa, in January 1940, after which he was sent to the Air Observers' School at Ohakea for gunnery training. In June Crook was posted to 264 Squadron, RAF, at Duxford. On 26 July he went to Aston Down for gunnery training and more flying experience and was awarded his air gunner's badge and promoted to sergeant.]

*

Around noon the three Spitfires of Red Section, 152 Squadron, led by Carr Withall, are ordered to patrol Portland Bill to intercept an enemy aircraft approaching from the south-east. Withall positions himself so that he can attack from out of the sun. After three minutes he closes in to a range of 350 yards (320 m). His target is a Junkers Ju 88 but, having fired two bursts into its centre section, he loses contact when the cloud layer becomes too solid.

Back at Warmwell Withall finds oil streaks covering most of the upper surface of his Spitfire's port wing, probably from the enemy's port engine.

[The victim of Carr Withall's attack may have been a Ju 88A-4 which landed at Rouen with 20% damage.]

[Latham Carr Withall lived in Canberra before he went to England to join the RAF. He was the son of Latham and Mabel Withall. He was granted a short-service commission for 4 years in the RAF in December 1936. One of the pilots who knew him as a flying officer in 19 Squadron was James Coward (Air Cdr J. Coward AFC, RAF (Retired)) who at the time of writing lived in Canberra:

> . . . Withall, affectionately known as 'Granny' because of his great age and wisdom, was a very keen gliding pilot with the London Gliding Club. He was an excellent pilot with a lot of Spitfire experience, as 19 Squadron was the first to be equipped with Spitfires in September 1938.[2]

James Coward had a deft hand with a pencil and he drew caricatures of the characters in his squadron as he sat in the Ante-room at Duxford.

Withall's promotion to acting flight lieutenant was gazetted in May 1939 and in October he was posted to Acklington to help with the formation of a new unit, No. 152 Squadron. This Squadron was initially equipped with Gladiators but in January 1940, began converting to Spitfires. After a period of defensive patrols in the north-east the unit moved to Warmwell, Dorset, on 12 July and remained there throughout the battle of Britain for the defence of this sector which included Portland naval base.

There were two other Australians in the squadron, P/O Ian Bayles and Sgt Ken Holland. Like the other members of the unit they had nicknames. Withall's new one was 'Elsie' because of his initials. The slow-moving Ian Bayles (whose background is outlined on 26 August of the War Diary) was called 'Dimmy' and Ken Holland of course retained 'Dutchy'.

Kenneth Christopher Holland was the son of Harold George and Ina Gladys Christopher Holland of Sydney, NSW. He was born c.1920 but details of his early life are not clear. By 1936–37 he was in England at Airspeed Aeronautical College. He was called up into the RAFVR in September 1939, did his training on Tiger Moths at Perth, Scotland, and eventually joined 152 Squadron at Warmwell.]

*

Just before 3.00 p.m. 12 Hurricanes of 238 Squadron and a section of Spitfires from 609 Squadron are ordered up from Warmwell to cover Convoy 'Bread' which is approaching Portland. However, the ships have been delayed. When the British fighters arrive at the anticipated position they find no ships but there are over 20 enemy aircraft.

The Hurricanes are at 11 000 feet (3 400 m) while the German planes are 4 000 feet (1 200 m) above. Mick Miller, who is flying as Yellow 3 in the section from 609 Squadron, is the first to point out the

This caricature by James Coward shows Latham Withall, who was a keen glider pilot with the London Gliding Club at Dunstable (AWM 28487/4).

Before the war both Jack Kennedy and Gordon Olive flew in 65 Squadron. Jack Kennedy is standing third from the right, and Gordon Olive is on the far left. Kennedy was killed in action on 13 July 1940 (photograph courtesy of John Wallen).

Germans to the other Spitfires. All the British fighters start climbing but as he does so Jack Kennedy, who is leading 238 Squadron's Red Section, spots a Dornier Do 17 crossing his bow 1 000 feet (300 m) below. He orders his section into line astern and sets off in pursuit. The Dornier dives away, heading out to sea as Kennedy closes in and launches two attacks which damage the German machine and silence the rear gunner. Suddenly, the Australian's Hurricane breaks off and dives sharply to disappear, hurtling towards the coast. Red 2 and Red 3 continue after the Dornier, attacking in turns until it crashes into the sea.

People along the shore have been watching the dogfight. They see a Hurricane shoot down an enemy aircraft but it is then attacked by three enemy fighters. It manages to escape but it has been damaged and the pilot tries to force-land along the shore. Tragically, the plane stalls and crashes during its low-level approach when it swerves suddenly to avoid high tension cables. The Hurricane's number is P2950, Jack Kennedy's machine. F/Lt John Connolly Kennedy is the first Australian fighter pilot to be killed in the battle of Britain.

Meanwhile Stuart Walch and the remaining Hurricanes of 238 Squadron with the Spitfires of 609 Squadron, launch attacks on about 20 Messerschmitt Bf 110s holding on a defensive circle 6 miles (10 km) south of Portland. The German pilots label this manoeuvre the 'death circle': all aircraft enter into a continuous circle over a fixed point whenever the threat of being overwhelmed by more nimble British fighters presents itself. In this way each plane covers the tail of the one ahead with the rear gunners affording added protection. The Hurricanes are unable to bring down any of the big, heavy, German fighters although two are severely damaged — one of them by Stuart Walch and his section.

In the same fight Mick Miller and his section leader claim one Bf 110 shot down and one Do 17 probable. Miller fires off all his ammunition at the Dornier and when he breaks contact it is losing height with one of its engines on fire.

*

Around the same time, west of Ushant Island, a stray Messerschmitt Bf 110 encounters Sunderland N9050, RB-D, flown by 'Hoot' Gibson and his crew. The 110 positions itself 500 feet (150 m) above and to starboard of the flying boat and then dives to attack. It closes to about 300 yards (275 m), exchanging fire with the Australian gunners, before breaking away and quickly turning in behind for a second assault. Again there is an exchange before it breaks away, flying towards France with smoke trailing from its starboard engine. Twenty-five bullets have struck the Sunderland, piercing both the port inner and outer fuel tanks but there is no fire and nobody is hurt.

For this action, and his attack on U-26 on 1 July, Gibson will receive the DFC.

In another action on the same afternoon, a Sunderland flown by F/Lt Dick Cohen and his crew chases a Heinkel He 111 away from a convoy under its protection.

From this day on, the *Luftwaffe* will mount an increasing number of air attacks on convoys on the approaches to England.

*

Alan Butement is principal scientific officer and assistant director of science research at the United Kingdom's Ministry of Supply headquarters in London. Before the war he had devised a radio location (radar) system which was effective in both accurately locating the position of a ship at sea and detecting low-flying aircraft. Under his supervision the CHL radar wall had been constructed along the east and south-east coastline of England to complement the main CH radar units in service which had a longer range but could not pick up low-flying planes.

[Although William Alan Stewart Butement CBE (1959), OBE (1945), Doctor of Science (Adelaide), has been one of Australia's leading scientific figures for many years he was actually born at Masterton, New Zealand, on 18 August 1904, son of Dr William Butement, physician and surgeon, and Amy Louise, née Stewart. In 1914 William Butement brought his family to Sydney so that he could join the Australian army. Alan attended Scots College, Sydney, until his father was detached overseas whereupon the family moved to England. He continued his education at Hampstead University College School, London, and from there he attended London University for a Bachelor of Science degree. After post-graduate research he commenced work as a scientific officer at the Signals Experimental Establishment, War Office Outstation, Woolwich, a position he held for ten years. In 1933 he married Ursula Florence Parish of Devon.

By 1938 Butement was the senior scientific officer of the War Office's Bawdsey Research Station and the threat of war loomed over Europe. Now, at last, there was a War Office requirement to provide a more accurate measurement of a target's bearing than could be obtained optically. Butement evolved what became known as the split beam method of target location, i.e., a radar beam switched rapidly to the left and right of the object gave much greater accuracy in bearing measurement than had hitherto been possible and also provided a means of determining in which direction to follow the target, to left or to right. The older methods did not give this information. He also developed a mechanical switch for the purpose and directed work on an electronic version. Finally, he applied to this radar equipment a spiral time base for accurate range measurement.

Butement's work had further important implications. Having devised a radar system which was effective not only in accurately gauging the position of a ship and which could do so at a much greater range than before, he had also provided equipment capable of detecting a low-flying aircraft. After initial testing in May 1939 his experimental installation was inspected on 29 June by Winston Churchill who was suitably impressed when a flying boat used as a demonstration target was easily detected low down at a range of some 25 miles (40 km). In August the Air Ministry ordered a number of sets which became known as CHL (Chain Home Low — for low-flying aircraft) and under Butement's supervision these were installed around the country to complement the CH radar chain. The first CHL unit became operational in November and it was situated in the Thames Estuary where low-flying German planes were already laying mines. By the spring of 1940 the CHL chain extended along the east and south-east coastline, in time to play an important role in the battle of Britain.

Early in the war it was found necessary to have an improved method of directing a defending fighter to intercept its target, particularly at night.

The tall transmitter masts of a chain home station. British radar was seriously underestimated by the Germans during the war (Imperial War Museum photograph CH15173).

What was required was a radar station on the ground which could detect not only the enemy bomber as it approached but also the defending fighter. Alan Butement adapted the CHL unit to perform this task.

It became obvious to Butement that a method of gunfire control could be devised if the splashes caused by shells from coastal batteries fired at a target ship could also be detected by radar. The success of his experiments was demonstrated when an enemy convoy passing through the narrows off Calais on a dark night was decimated by Dover's guns. This method of fire control remains standard even now in most of the world's navies.

Six adapted CHL radar sets were erected in the Shetland Islands and it was found that they could detect a fully surfaced submarine up to 25 miles (40 km) off, and low-flying aircraft up to 70 miles (113 km) away. Because of these capabilities, they proved extremely useful in warning of surprise low-level raids approaching to attack Scapa Flow, the home of the British Fleet.

When the war started the Ministry of Supply took over the business of the War Office in conjunction with radar and a new establishment was set up at Christchurch on the south-east coast of England, a mile or so inland. On the very edge of the coast, a small establishment was built to conduct experiments over the sea. Alan Butement was placed in charge.

A few months later the available methods of putting a searchlight onto an enemy aircraft at night were proving totally inadequate. Butement and his team assessed the possibility of adapting pieces of existing radar equipment and using them for searchlight location. During trials an enemy bomber was swiftly located by the searchlight beam as soon as the light was uncovered. The plane tried desperate evasive action without success and production of the device was soon under way.

By the time of the battle of Britain in late 1940 Alan Butement was principal scientific officer and assistant director of science research, Ministry of Supply headquarters, London. He was also secretary of the RDF (Radio Direction Finding) Applications Committee under Professor Edward Appleton charged with the invention and development of a radio proximity fuse for anti-aircraft shells. The idea was that the fuse, actually a tiny radio transmitter, receiver and aerial all in one, was enclosed in the nose of the shell itself so that when it passed within a certain distance of an aircraft the shell would be detonated.

After preliminary discussions Butement and another scientist independently proposed the use of a 'Doppler operated' fuse. The principle of the fuse was proved sound but the Americans took over work on it in mid-August 1940 so that, although he had invented it, Butement ceased to be involved in its development.]

Butement is also secretary of the RDF Applications Committee under Professor Edward Appleton. Another member is Professor Marcus Oliphant, head of research at the University of Birmingham.

[Sir Marcus Laurence Elwin Oliphant KBE, FRS, MA, PhD, DSc was born in Adelaide on 8 October 1901. He was educated at Unley and Adelaide High Schools, the University of Adelaide and afterwards at Cambridge. He was professor of physics at the University of Birmingham in 1937–50 and headed the design team which studied transmitters for the development of airborne radar during 1939–40. Later during the war

*years, he was a member of the Atomic Energy Technical Committee and
carried out much of the research work in this field.]*

On this day Butement submits a report on his preliminary work
indicating highly encouraging results.[3]

*

There is much to suggest that German plans to invade England can
be described as hasty and ill-conceived. Just two weeks have passed
since Adolf Hitler ordered the *OKW*, to make provisional plans for
an invasion of England. Now Field Marshal von Brauchitsch,
commander-in-chief of the German army, and General Halder, his
chief of staff, submit ambitious proposals for the operation. Misunder-
standing a naval staff statement that the best place to cross is the
eastern half of the English Channel, army strategists have assumed that
troops can be put ashore at such widely-spaced points as Ramsgate in
the east and Lyme Bay in the west. Thus, the stage is set for numerous
disagreements between the two services.

The naval point of view, as expressed on the 11th, by Admiral Erich
Raeder, commander-in-chief of the German navy, is that an invasion
of Britain should be a last resort. He advocates a blockade, supported
by air attacks on Liverpool and other centres of distribution. Should
this not succeed and an invasion is necessary, a vital prerequisite would
be the need for air supremacy over southern England.

It is on this last point that both the army and navy are in accord —
without air superiority over the Channel and southern England there
can be no landing at all. In accordance with this, the *OKW* had issued
its first operational instructions to the *Luftwaffe* for the campaign
against the United Kingdom back on 2 July. Two basic tasks had been
assigned. Firstly, the closing of the English Channel to British merchant shipping was to be carried out in conjunction with German
naval attacks on convoys, the destruction of harbour facilities and the
laying of mines in harbour areas and approaches. Secondly, the destruction of the Royal Air Force.

Hitler orders von Brauchitsch and Halder to begin active operations. The operation will be called *Seelöwe* (Sea Lion).

SUNDAY, 14 JULY

Nine small coastal convoys use the cover of poor weather and successfully evade detection by the *Luftwaffe*. Only one, Convoy 'Bread',
is attacked.

After considering interception and shooting down of German air-
sea rescue planes on 1 and 9 July, the Air Ministry decides that the
enemy should not be granted immunity through their use of the Red
Cross. Fighter Command is therefore directed to order all pilots to
shoot down such aircraft encountered.

*

At RAF College, Cranwell, John Pain and John Crossman are graded as pilot officers on probation.

[John Dallas Crossman was born on 20 March 1919 at Mossman, Queensland, son of George Edward Crossman and Gladys Allyne Dallas. He was educated at Cook's Hill Primary School and later at Newcastle Boys' High School, NSW. In response to an advertisement calling for volunteers to apply for short-service commissions in the RAF, John travelled to Sydney for an interview and medical examinations. His first attempt was not successful on the grounds that his chest expansion was not good enough. Not deterred, he spent the next six months in training for the next intake. This time his efforts were rewarded and in August 1939, he sailed for England.

John Crossman's words in letters to his family back in Australia, together with those of his English aunts living in Buckinghamshire, capture the image of a cheerful young man going off to a career of adventure and excitement only to be engulfed by the irresistible vortex of war. After 15 hours tuition he flew solo for the first time on 20 November 1939. On 10 April 1940 he reported to RAF College, Cranwell, and was posted to No. 32 Squadron at Biggin Hill on 15 July, though up to this stage he had only flown Tiger Moths, Harts and Hinds.]

*

One unit flying aircraft carrying new experimental airborne radar sets to test Air Interception (AI) under operational conditions is 600 Squadron at Manston. Four Blenheims, BQ-B, BQ-G, BQ-H and BQ-X, have it and Charles Pritchard takes off in BQ-X at 8.45 p.m. for a test run. At this stage of its development the 'magic box' (or 'magic mirrors') is suffering from numerous teething problems. These, coupled with the need for specialist training for the operators, are causing delays in the widespread introduction of this equipment for the night fighter defences. Pritchard's aircraft lands again at 9.30 p.m.

[Charles Arthur Pritchard's place of birth was Manildra, NSW. He apparently went to England at an early age, was educated at Highgate School and for a time served in the Scottish Regiment. In 1936 he enrolled in the Auxiliary Air Force with No. 600 Squadron. From 10 May 1940 he was in action over Holland and Belgium, flying fighter Blenheims.

Another Australian who flew Blenheim night fighters was Richard Maurice Power from Melbourne. He attended Point Cook as a cadet in 1936 and in January 1937 sailed for England. Granted a five-year short-service commission in the RAF, a month later he was doing advanced flying training at Wittering. In November 1939 Dick Power was promoted to acting flight lieutenant and posted to a newly reforming squadron, No. 236 at Stradishall. Among the other newcomers, most of them young and inexperienced, was Bryan McDonough. There was a third member of the squadron who came from Melbourne. William Storey Moore received his short-service commission in the RAF in August 1937. In December 1939 he was promoted to flying officer and twelve months later to flight lieutenant. On 1 March 1942 he became a squadron leader and served with 143 Squadron, flying Beaufighters. He was 27 when he was killed on 24 December 1943.

Although 236 Squadron was to be a fighter unit it was equipped with Bristol Blenheim Mk Is and was stationed at Middle Wallop in 11 Group; this was responsible for the air defence of southern England at night. The authorities then decided to use the unit in a daylight offensive role and it began attacking, in squadron strength, aerodromes at Cherbourg and Le Havre and reconnoitring Brest and other French ports for German activities. Losses were heavy and it was apparent that the Blenheim was inadequate in speed, manoeuvrability and armament to cope with German fighters, so again its role was changed to patrol of the seas, escort of aircraft, and shipping. This meant transfer to Coastal Command and a move to St Eval in Cornwall.[4]

The first radar-equipped night fighters had been requested in a secret minute from the Air Staff dated 17 July 1939. This called for the fitting of radar to 21 Bristol Blenheim IF long-range fighters as soon as possible. Deliveries of these began on 31 July 1939, to 25 Squadron. By 3 September, when war was declared, 15 had been delivered and the order was completed by the end of the month.

Three of these Blenheims were sent in November to a 'special flight' of 600 Squadron at Manston of which Charles Pritchard was a member.

*Meanwhile other AI-equipped Blenheims were issued in ones and twos to existing Blenheim squadrons. Here, once the operators became familiar with their new 'magic mirrors' (as they were called) was an answer to the **Luftwaffe's** night attacks but in July 1940 many difficulties had yet to be solved.]*

MONDAY, 15 JULY

The day is overcast with a solid cloud base of 200 feet (60 m) in most areas and some local storms later.

Air activity is inhibited on both sides and German reconnaissance planes have difficulty finding gaps in the cloud to locate convoys. Only Convoy 'Pilot' is attacked by 15 Dornier Do 17s but their bomb run is disrupted by Hurricanes from 56 Squadron. Altogether, from the few minor clashes throughout the day, Fighter Command loses 1 aircraft and the *Luftwaffe* loses 3.

*

At 1.42 p.m. at Mount Batten, home of the Sunderlands of 10 Squadron, RAAF, a lone Junkers Ju 88 is spotted approaching from the south-east. Two Spitfires are on patrol at a lower altitude nearby but the German ignores them and they do not spot him as he makes a run over the base. He then returns and drops four bombs before escaping out to sea. Damage is minor and one fails to explode. It is afterwards defused by Sgt Eric ('Lucky') Long of Ryde, NSW.

Meanwhile Hugh Birch and his crew in Sunderland P9603 are on patrol south of Bishop's Rock on the Scilly Isles when they sight a merchant ship under attack by five Heinkel He 111s. Using the cloud cover, Birch surprises a Heinkel which is just climbing away after its bomb run. The Australian front gunner opens fire at maximum range and then as the startled German machine turns to port he shoots into its belly — it is last seen losing height and trailing smoke. There is little time to watch because a second Heinkel dives onto the Sunderland's tail. A third Heinkel comes in from below making a determined attack but, at 200 yards (180 m), the tail gunner opens up and this Heinkel too breaks away. The last two German planes hover behind the flying boat for ten minutes but do not attempt to launch an assault.

The Germans are beginning to have a healthy respect for the Sunderland flying boat which they nickname 'flying Porcupine'.

TUESDAY, 16 JULY

Luftwaffe operations are hampered by poor weather with fog covering south-east England and northern France. Likewise, there are few RAF sorties.

*

From his headquarters, Hitler issues his Directive No. 16 on preparations for a landing operation against England. It states (in part):[5]

> Since England in spite of her hopeless military situation, shows no signs of being ready to come to an understanding, I have decided to prepare a landing operation against England, and if necessary, to carry it out.
>
> The aim of this operation will be to eliminate the English homeland as a base for the prosecution of the war against Germany and, if necessary, to occupy it completely.
>
> I therefore order as follows:
>
> 1. The *landing* will be in the form of a surprise crossing on a wide front from about Ramsgate to the area west of the Isle of Wight. Units of the Air Force will act as artillery, and units of the Navy as engineers . . . Preparations for the entire operation must be completed by the middle of *August.*
> 2. These preparations must also create such conditions as will make a landing in England possible, viz.:
>   (a) The English Air Force must be so reduced morally and physically that it is unable to deliver any significant attack against the German crossing . . .
>   (b) It is desirable that the English Navy be tied down shortly before the crossing, both in the North Sea and in the Mediterranean (by the Italians). For this purpose we must attempt even now to damage English home-based naval forces by air torpedo attack as far as possible . . .
>
> The invasion will bear the cover name *Seelöwe* (Sea Lion) . . .
> *The task of the Air Force will be:*
>   To prevent interference by the enemy Air Force.
>   To destroy coastal fortresses which might operate against our disembarkation points, to break the first resistance of enemy land forces, and to disperse reserves on their way to the front. In carrying out this

task the closest liaison is necessary between individual Air Force units and the Army invasion forces.

Also, to destroy important transport highways by which enemy reserves might be brought up, and to attack approaching enemy naval forces as far as possible from our disembarkation points ...

WEDNESDAY, 17 JULY

Again the weather is dull with widespread drizzle and occasional rain. *Luftwaffe* activities are restricted to reconnaissance by individual aircraft and some light raids.

*

In Germany the *OKW* allocates forces for *Seelöwe* and General von Brauchitsch orders 13 picked army divisions to embarkation points on the Channel coast to be the first wave of the invasion.

*

Harry Hardman of 111 Squadron is posted to Kenley for a course of instruction.

*

The headquarters of the Australian Railway Construction and Maintenance Group, under Lieut-Colonel K.A. Fraser, arrives at Liverpool. It consists of a company and a half of men who will go into camp in Woolmer Forest where they will build a large number of storage sidings before transferring to the middle east in January 1941.

Also, the Australian Railway and Forestry units, a total of 728 men, are now camping at Alton.

Men of an Australian forestry unit roll logs on to a tramway for a sawmill (AWM 4526).

THURSDAY, 18 JULY

Overnight radar plots show that German aircraft are active over the Bristol Channel, apparently mining the approaches to the port. RAF night fighters have to rely upon directions from control to place them in the near vicinity. Interceptions are a matter of good luck and it is being discovered that Blenheim Ifs, while able to keep pace with lumbering Heinkel He 111s, have little chance of catching the faster Junkers Ju 88s or Dornier Do 17s. Day fighters such as the Hurricane and Spitfire are speedier but unsuitable for night fighting as flaring from the engine exhausts impairs the pilot's night vision.

Operating from St Eval, 234 Squadron keeps two or three pilots at 'Readiness'. Between 1.00 a.m. and 6.55 a.m. Pat Hughes flies three fruitless patrols.

Daylight brings cloudy, cool weather with occasional rain over the south of England. These conditions will limit the *Luftwaffe* to sporadic attacks against shipping and the Channel ports plus isolated reconnaissance sorties.

*

Off the Isle of Wight at 10.30 a.m., Spitfires from 152 Squadron clash with a Dornier Do 17 and are counter-attacked by escorting Messerschmitt Bf 109s. The British are on patrol at about 8 000 feet (2 400 m), when suddenly the Dornier drops through cloud almost in front of them. It is the first enemy aircraft that Ian Bayles and his companions have seen. After recovering from their shock they give chase. The German pilot has also had quite a surprise and he zooms up for cover. As it disappears into the cloud layer, three Messerschmitt Bf 109s, apparently answering the Dornier's call for help, plunge down behind the British fighters. In this, his first combat, Bayles can see a Messerschmitt close on his tail and cannon fire coming from its nose. The two planes become locked into a circle which steadily decreases in diameter as they whirl around. Gradually the Spitfire gains on the Messerschmitt, until Bayles is almost into a position where he can open fire ... but, before he can do so, the 109 melts into the covering cloud.

*

A RAF reconnaissance over Boulogne discovers preparations for invasion for the first time. Bomber Command sends a force of 18 Blenheims escorted by 2 squadrons of Hurricanes. Nine Blenheims are from 40 Squadron and Brian Best is at the controls of aircraft L8796. Hits are made on jetties, a warehouse and several vessels. A stray Henschel Hs 126 encountered near the target is so badly damaged by the Hurricanes of 111 Squadron that it crashes afterwards.

[S/Ldr Charles Brian Best, DFC, *received his short-service commission in December 1938 and his promotion to flying officer was recorded in the* **London Gazette** *of 3 September 1940. The same publication noted the award of his DFC on 12 November 1940 for:*

carrying out 26 Operational Flights. During night operations late in 1940 against the German invasion bases, Best showed great ingenuity and

A dreaded sight in a pilot's rear vision mirror; a Messerschmitt Bf 109E (author's photograph).

foresight in planning his missions. His courage and initiative were of the highest order and the results achieved were highly successful.

He attained the rank of temporary squadron leader late in June 1944 but he is listed as 'Missing (flying battle), presumed dead', later that year.]

*

Sections of 141 Squadron fly a few uneventful patrols throughout the day. Modifications to the Defiants are mostly complete but valuable flying time for practice manoeuvring and drill at squadron strength has been lost. Noel Constantine flies two patrols in Defiants L7011 and L7015. On both occasions his gunner is P/O W.F.P. Webber. They are both fortunate not to be rostered for next morning . . .

*

The RAF inspector-general visits Mount Batten and while discussing policy with S/Ldr Charles Pearce, commanding officer of 10 Squadron, RAAF, he requests that Sergeant Eric Long be congratulated for his excellent work defusing an unexploded bomb on the 15th.

Meanwhile an unofficial tradition is beginning. As time goes by it will become common practice for personnel returning to camp after a few beers at the local hotel, to urinate in the holes left by bombs as a gesture of contempt for Hitler and the Germans who had dropped them.

*

Overnight RAF Bomber Command keeps pressure on Boulogne and five other targets. In action as well as the usual Hampdens and Wellingtons, are Fairey Battles from 142 Squadron at Eastchurch. John Hewson takes off at 8.30 p.m. in aircraft L5569. Over the French port bombs are dropped on the harbour. The squadron suffers no casualties.

FRIDAY, 19 JULY

At 8.00 a.m. two PRU Spitfires take off from Heston and head off in different directions. One is to photograph areas of Germany around Hamburg and Bremen. Harry Daish is the pilot of the other, Spitfire N3116, and his objective is to fly a reconnaissance over Boulogne, Dieppe and Le Havre.

*

Over southern England the weather is showery but with increasing bright intervals and, because of this noticeable improvement, Fighter Command Group commanders move strong forces to the forward satellite airfields in anticipation of increased *Luftwaffe* activity. There are 9 separate convoys off various parts of the coast.

Shortly before 1.00 p.m., Hannes Trautloft of 9/KG 51 peers out of the cockpit of his Messerschmitt Bf 109 Emil at 9 RAF fighters climbing rapidly just after leaving the coast. They turn towards the middle of the English Channel, apparently unaware of the 16 German fighters lurking in the sun. The distance between them narrows to 800 metres before Trautloft notices that each English plane has a gun turret behind its cockpit. They are Defiants maintaining a tight formation as if on parade. Then, unexpectedly, they turn back towards England. After searching the sky for signs of other RAF fighters, Trautloft gives the order to attack — 141 Squadron is about to receive its baptism of fire.

The 109s have been spotted and as they dive the Tommies open fire. Trautloft feels hits on his plane but he bores in, selects the starboard Defiant at the rear of the formation and fires. He misses with the first burst but is successful with his second. Smoke appears below his victim's fuselage and an instant later it explodes. Using speed gained from his dive, Trautloft curves in for another attack and at the same time he notices a second Defiant going down behind and to the left.

Suddenly his engine starts vibrating and begins to run roughly. Turning back across the Channel, he is joined almost immediately by another Bf 109 trailing smoke flown by Oblt Kath, a member of his own *schwarm*. Over their earphones both German pilots can hear their comrades shouting on the radio. More English fighters have obviously joined the fight but there is nothing they can do about it. Both Germans make successful emergency landings after crossing the French coast.

The German pilots claim to have shot down 12 Defiants.

Twelve Defiants had in fact come forward from West Malling to Hawkinge that morning. At 12.23 p.m. they had been ordered to take off to patrol 20 miles (32 km) south of Folkestone but three had aborted because of engine trouble. At 1.00 p.m. transmissions over the radio transmitter (R/T) had left no doubt that a violent battle was taking place. At Hawkinge anxious groundcrew, gunners and pilots, including Noel Constantine, who had not been scheduled to fly, scan the skies for the returning planes. At long last, 4 Defiants, two of them in obvious trouble, come into sight. Three make it to the airfield but the engine of the fourth cuts out and it crashes on the outskirts of

MAP 1   RAF Fighter
Command sector and group
boundaries, 1940

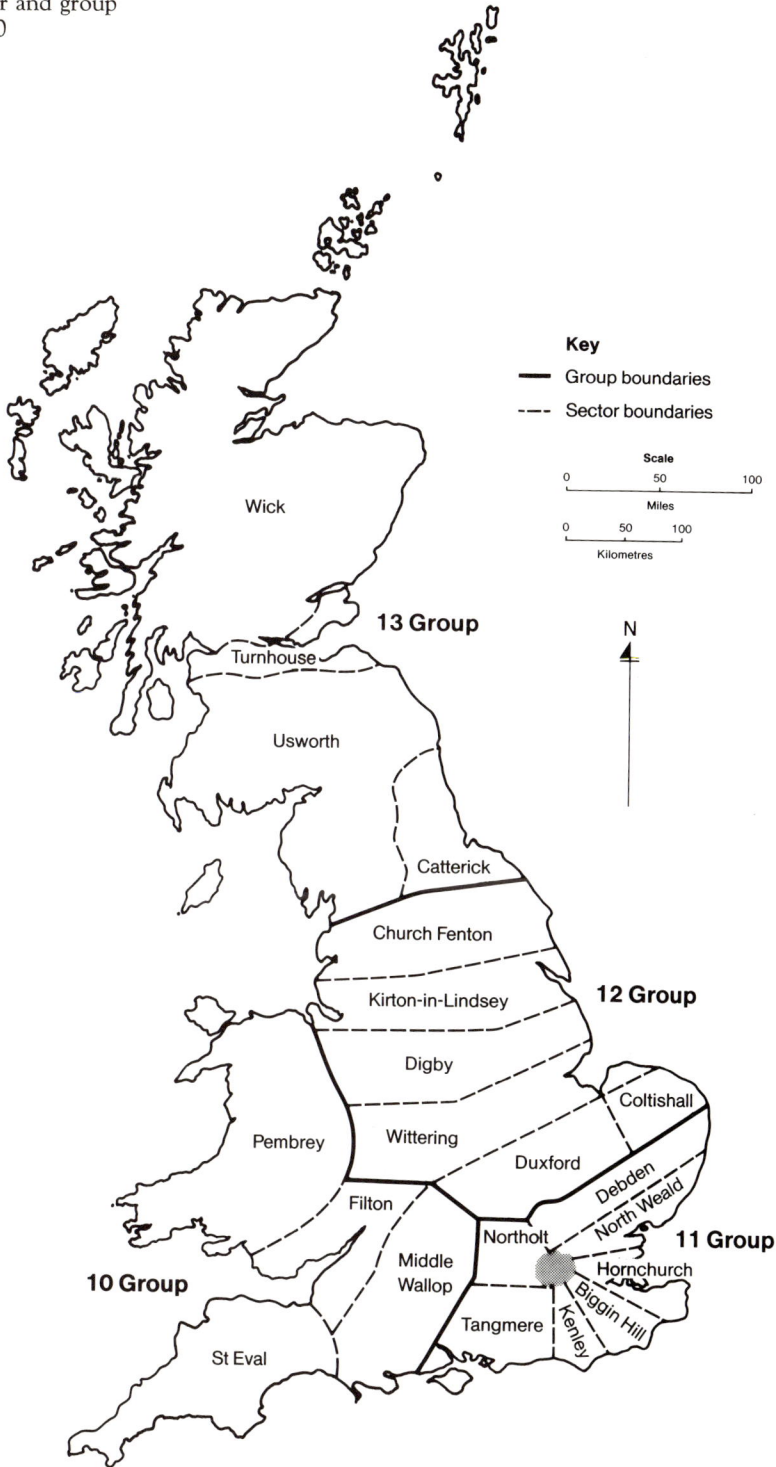

Key

— Group boundaries

--- Sector boundaries

Scale

0   50   100

Miles

0   50   100

Kilometres

N

Wick

13 Group

Turnhouse

Usworth

Catterick

Church Fenton

12 Group

Kirton-in-Lindsey

Digby

Coltishall

Pembrey

Wittering

Duxford

Debden

North Weald

Filton

Northolt

11 Group

10 Group

Middle
Wallop

Hornchurch

Biggin Hill

Kenley

Tangmere

St Eval

Hawkinge village. One Defiant which has managed to land is so badly damaged that it is written off as scrap. This is all that remains of the 9 aircraft which had set out.

In terms of human casualties, 4 pilots have been killed and two wounded, and 6 gunners have been killed. One pilot and one gunner are rescued from the sea.

There is no doubt that the Defiants would have been wiped out except for the timely arrival of No. 111 Squadron, which had been scrambled and vectored to the scene to cover 141's retreat. This is the heaviest defeat suffered by any Fighter Command squadron to date and it soon becomes known as 'the Slaughter of the Innocents'.

The survivors of 141 Squadron are released from operations. Because of the disastrous losses the squadron has lost all cohesion as a fighting unit. What is left of it is moved to Prestwick in Ayrshire, Scotland, for rebuilding.

*

Adolf Hitler delivers his 'last appeal to reason' speech in the *Reichstag*:

> If the struggle continues it will end in annihilation for one of us. Mr Churchill thinks it will be Germany. I know it will be Britain. I am not the vanquished begging for mercy. I speak as a victor. I can see no reason why this war must go on. We should like to avert the sacrifices which must claim millions. It is possible that Mr Churchill will once again brush aside this statement of mine by saying that it is merely born of fear and doubt of victory. In that case I shall have relieved my conscience of the things to come.[6]

Leaflets containing the translated text of this speech will be showered all over the British Isles during the next few weeks. Hitler also takes the opportunity to announce that Hermann Goering has been promoted to the rank of *Reichsmarschall*.

Less than an hour after the German leader's speech the BBC, without any official authorization, rejects Hitler's offer.

*

During the night, RAF Bomber Command sends nearly 90 aircraft to 5 targets in Germany. For Henry Ross of 83 Squadron the target is the battleship *Admiral Scheer* at Wilhelmshaven. He takes off at 10.35 p.m. in Hampden L4124 and drops his stick of bombs over the target area.

SATURDAY, 20 JULY

Overnight German bombers carry out minelaying activities from the Isle of Wight to Land's End, the Bristol Channel and east-coast waters. Even the huge four-engined Focke-Wulf FW 200 Condors of 2/KG40 are used. Just after midnight a Condor is caught by searchlights over Sunderland and shot down by flak. About 3.00 a.m. another Condor is lost off the coast of Northern Ireland.

Daylight brings occasional thunderstorms with clouds clearing to bright intervals over the Straits of Dover, part of which is nicknamed 'Hellfire Corner' because of so much bombing and aerial activity.

*

No. 238 Squadron is ordered to maintain standing patrols over Convoy 'Bosom' in Lyme Bay. Blue Section, led by Stuart Walch, arrives over the convoy at 12.20 p.m. By 1.00 p.m., after having lost contact with Blue 2 and Blue 3 and having twice investigated aircraft which turned out to be other Hurricanes, Walch switches to his reserve fuel tank to return to base.

He flies towards Swanage, gaining altitude to 8 000 feet (2 400 m). Around 5 miles (8 km) from Swanage, he sights 15 aircraft above, flying north in formation towards the convoy. He is too far away to identify them but judging from the direction in which they are flying they could be hostile. He turns back towards the convoy and gains altitude to get into the sun. Five miles (8 km) off he sees bombs exploding around an escort destroyer and pulling the boost, he goes after the enemy aircraft which have turned southwards. As he comes round to the south-east of the convoy he spots 3 Messerschmitt Bf 109s flying in a wide vic 3 000 feet (900 m) below. He immediately attacks the fighter on the port side, closing in behind it to 50 yards (45 m). He fires two two-second bursts. Black smoke pours from under the Messerschmitt's engine as it twists to the right and falls into a vertical dive but Walch cannot follow because the other 109s are turning onto his tail. He evades them in a steep stall turn and heads for home with fuel critically low.

Back at Middle Wallop he claims one unconfirmed victory. No. 238 Squadron will account for at least 3 German aircraft through the day, another Bf 109 and an air-sea rescue Heinkel He 59 spotted near the convoy.

A second He 59 is encountered by Hurricanes from 601 Squadron, which attempt to force the floatplane to fly inland. Rather than be captured, the German crew of 4 bails out but at an altitude too low for their parachutes to open. They are all killed.

*

About 6.15 p.m. No. 65 Squadron leaves Manston to engage enemy aircraft attacking the convoy which is now off Dover. The Spitfires are forced to take off in sections and at intervals and the effect of this is that they arrive too late. The Germans have already dropped their bombs, damaging a destroyer.

Meanwhile, Yellow Section, the last to leave the airfield, is led by Gordon Olive. He leads his section south of Folkestone on the lookout for enemy aircraft. He notices a Bf 109 coming up behind a lone unsuspecting Hurricane. Yellow Section is too far away to intervene. The Hurricane's tail is shot off and its fuselage plummets down in a vertical dive. Fortunately, the pilot bails out and lands safely near Dover. Olive's blood is up and he is determined to catch the 109. He chases it across the Channel and manages to overtake it near the French coast. At a range of 150 yards (140 m), he presses the firing button until all of his ammunition is used up. Towards the end of the burst the 109 catches fire and crashes into Cap Gris Nez.

Olive has scored the squadron's only victory for the day.[7]

[Charles Gordon Chaloner Olive was born at Bardon, Queensland, on 3 July 1916, son of H.C. Olive. Educated at Brisbane Grammar School and Queensland University, he became an engineering cadet with the RAAF and commenced training in January 1936. He was awarded his pilot's flying badge in December and in January 1937 took up a short-service commission with the RAF. By May he was with 65 Squadron, which was then equipped with Gloster Gauntlet IIs but in June it converted to Gloster Gladiators. He was promoted to flying officer in August 1938 and in July 1939 was made acting flight lieutenant. By then 65 Squadron had converted to Spitfires.

The squadron achieved its first kill in May 1940 and that month began flying offensive patrols over France and the Low Countries to cover the evacuation of the British Expeditionary Force from Dunkirk. On 26 May Gordon Olive claimed a Messerschmitt Bf 109 probably destroyed when the squadron became mixed up with about 30 German fighters near Calais. Next day, east of Dunkirk, he probably shot down a Dornier Do 17, silencing the rear gunner and setting the plane's port engine on fire. On 28 May he was listed missing 'as a result of air operations'. (Refer to Prelude).

After action over Dunkirk 65 Squadron moved to Lincolnshire to refit but a week later it was back at Hornchurch ready to play its part in the battle of Britain.]

*

No. 248 Blenheim Squadron is transferred out of Fighter Command back to Coastal Command and commences a move which will take it from Dyce to Sumburgh in the Shetland Islands.

*

To make room for the arrival of 248 Squadron's Blenheims, the Gloster Gladiators of the Sumburgh Fighter Flight, which had been formed to defend the Shetland Islands, move to Exeter to provide air cover for Plymouth.

[There were three Australians in 248 Squadron. Clarence Charles Bennett was born on 28 November 1916 at Mallala, South Australia, son of Septimus Bennett and Catherine, née Hobbs. He attended high school at Kapunda after which he joined the railways as a junior clerk. Two of his major interests were motor bikes and flying. At 19 he built his own glider and joined the Adelaide Gliding Club in 1936. Next year he took flying instruction at Mount Gambier.

'Clarrie' Bennett was a person of untiring energy with a happy-go-lucky manner, ready to lend a hand to all and sundry. This quickly made him popular amongst his workmates who nicknamed him 'Rattler'. In December 1938 he was accepted for a short-service commission in the RAF and left for England on 2 February 1939. With him were other Australians, among whom were Lewis Hamilton, Bryan McDonough and Frank Cale, destined like him to take part in the battle of Britain. Bennett was graded as pilot officer on probation on 6 November 1939 and posted to 248 Squadron.

Alexander Lewis Hamilton was born on 17 December 1914 in Adelaide, South Australia, son of John Alexander Hamilton, a mining engineer, and his wife Alice, née Lewis. He was educated at Sturt Primary and Technical High School to Leaving Certificate standard and was afterwards employed by the Adelaide Electric Company. He was also attending part-time commerce courses at Adelaide University. In August 1938 he applied for a short-service commission in the RAF and was posted to 248 Squadron. The unit was being equipped with Bristol Blenheim Ifs for night defence duties. However, because of the lack of airborne radar, the squadron's initial night flying was ineffective. At the end of February 1940 it was transferred from Hendon to Coastal Command and commenced re-equipping with Blenheim IVfs. A number of quick shifts from station to station followed in a matter of weeks. In April at Gosport it obtained its full complement of long-nose Blenheims. Around this time the third Australian, Doug Peterkin, joined the unit as an air gunner.

John Douglas Peterkin was born on 8 April 1915 at Cottesloe, Perth, Western Australia, son of John William Peterkin, railway officer, and his wife Ruby, née Jennings. He received his education at Kalgoorlie and Perth state schools and St Patrick's Christian Brothers College, East Perth. Afterwards he attended night school at Perth Technical College, matriculating in science in 1938. From 1935 he had been a member of the Western Australian Gliding Club. He left Fremantle in August 1939 for a short-service commission in the RAF and by the time he reached England in mid-October the second world war had already begun. Unfortunately, Doug Peterkin was not selected for further flying training. He retrained as an air gunner at the Gunnery School in south Wales, and was then posted to 248 Squadron as a commissioned air gunner/fire controller at RAF Station North Coates where he reported for duty on 5 March 1940. He soon established himself as something of a character, picking up the nicknames of 'Wild Man' Peterkin and 'The Big Bushman'.

On 22 May No. 248 Squadron was again attached to Fighter Command and it moved to Dyce, with a detachment sent to Montrose to extend the range of its patrols over the coastal waters of eastern Scotland. Three weeks later, Lewis Hamilton flew his first interception patrol.

Meanwhile, romance entered Clarrie Bennett's life when he began courting Dorothy Handle, an Australian girl working in England. They became engaged.

By now too Bennett and Hamilton, who had become close friends, had made a mutual pact 'to take care of things' in the event of one failing to return from a mission. The survivor was to take on the task of writing to his friend's relatives and putting his affairs in order. Before the battle of Britain will reach its conclusion the pledge will have to be honoured.

From 20 July the squadron began to shift northwards to Sumburgh in the Shetland Islands. The move was completed by the 31st and it reassumed the Coastal Command duties of anti-invasion patrols, reconnaissance flights over the Norwegian coast, attacks on enemy shipping and long-range air covers for convoys.]

*

At Marham a message is received by 38 Squadron from Headquarters, No. 3 Group, Bomber Command. Twelve aircraft are required to bomb targets at Hamm and Göttingen, Germany.

Between 9.35 and 10.10 p.m., the heavily-laden Wellingtons take off one by one. P/O Phillip Allen Leach is the tail gunner of Wellington P9287 with Sgt Swales in the pilot's seat. The Australian is actually the ranking officer as all the other members of the crew are sergeants.

Leach had arrived to join the squadron the day before and because he was both an air gunner and an officer he had been appointed squadron gunnery leader.

Up until now the main opposition faced by British night bombers over occupied France and Germany has been anti-aircraft fire but tonight a new and sinister element will be added. Situated between the two targets is the airfield at Gutersloh and stationed here are the Messerschmitt Bf 110s of NJG 1, Germany's first night fighter unit. The Germans have no airborne radar and have to rely on directions from the ground and visual contact. For weeks they have been trying to intercept the elusive British bombers but without success. Towards midnight Oblt Werner Streib and his radio operator Hgefr Lingen commence patrolling their allotted area, waiting directly in front of the incoming RAF bombers . . .

SUNDAY, 21 JULY

It is a clear moonlit night and, seated in the narrow cockpit of his Hampden bomber, Angus Robson of 144 Squadron nears the enemy coast. With others of his unit he has been detailed to attack warships in the harbour at Wilhelmshaven. Other RAF bombers are on their way to Hamburg where the *Tirpitz* is being completed and Kiel where the *Scharnhorst* and *Gneisenau* are based. At Wilhelmshaven the huge and powerful *Bismarck* is being fitted out. Bomber Command, whenever the weather is suitable, seizes every opportunity to attack these battleships because of the serious threat they pose to British shipping if they put to sea.

Robson can pick out the harbour and several ships as he nears the target. Narrow searchlight beams roam blindly in an effort to locate the bombers. It is to be a low-level raid so after lining up the largest ship he can find he dives to the attack. The Hampden lurches and jumps in the turbulent air as tracer bullets from shore batteries and moored ships float lazily towards him at first then accelerate and flash by. In spite of the barrage he continues on course until the ship looms in front and his bomb aimer releases the stick of bombs. The rear gunner, between bursts from his twin machine-guns, reports explosions. Then, to their great relief, the Hampden is back into the safety of darkness.

Robson sets course for home, RAF Station Hemswell across the North Sea.

*

For Oblt Werner Streib and Hgefr Lingen, on patrol in their Messerschmitt Bf 110 somewhere near Gutersloh, two frustrating hours drag by. They know the British are in the area but have been unable to sight them. At 2.00 a.m. German time (1.00 a.m. Greenwich) Streib notices what he believes to be an English plane. He creeps closer but it is not until he is flying alongside that the moonlight on a gun turret and a large RAF roundel on the fuselage betray it to be an Armstrong Whitworth Whitley.

Without taking his eyes off the bomber, Streib turns away in a tight circle to come around onto its tail. As he closes in, the British rear gunner opens fire but Streib replies with two short bursts of cannon and machine-gun fire and then swings to the side to observe results. The Whitley's starboard engine is on fire and seconds later two figures bail out. However, the British pilot is still at the controls and he tries to corkscrew away from danger. Streib attacks again and this time the Whitley's wing bursts into flames and the aircraft hurtles down to explode on the ground. Werner Streib has achieved the *Luftwaffe's* first night victory.

Twenty minutes later Wellington P9287 is droning its way over Gronau when it is suddenly jarred violently as a salvo of cannon and machine-gun fire from a German night fighter strikes its rear fuselage. Tail gunner Phillip Leach is badly wounded. The British pilot, Sgt Swales, through violent evasive action, manages to escape his attacker. Once clear, a check reveals that the Wellington has been severely damaged but Swales is able to nurse it home.

Leach is carried gently from the plane but he later dies in hospital. He is one of the first of many who will fall victim to German night fighters before the war is over.

P/O Phillip Allen Leach is listed on the Battle of Britain Roll of Honour in Westminster Abbey.

*

In contrast to the past two days, apart from an attack on a west-bound convoy in the Channel and scattered coastal reconnaissance over southern England, German air activity is relatively low. Fighter Command, determined to give Convoy 'Peewit' adequate fighter cover, maintains an escort of at least one squadron. The ships are at last raided

Wellington bombers were the backbone of RAF Bomber Command during 1940. Two Australians, Nugent Bull and Phillip Leach, were killed in Wellingtons between July and October 1940 (Imperial War Museum photograph CH 467).

about 10 miles (16 km) south of the Needles at 2.30 p.m. by Dornier Do 17s escorted by 50 Messerschmitt Bf 109s. Hurricanes from 43 Squadron manage to break up the bomber formation and shoot down one Bf 109 for the loss of one of their own. Shortly afterwards, 43 Squadron is relieved by Hurricanes from 238 Squadron. Stuart Walch is the leader of Blue Section in 'B' Flight. They patrol at 12 000 feet (3 600 m).

At 3.40 p.m. No. 238 is vectored towards enemy aircraft. As Blue Section approaches the Needles Walch sees the convoy being attacked by 15 Messerschmitt Bf 110s. He instructs Blue 2 and Blue 3 to select a target each and attack independently. He then dives after the last Bf 110 in the enemy formation. The range closes to within 500 yards (450 m) before the Hurricanes are seen. The Messerschmitts swing around to the right into a 'death circle' but the plane Walch is following mistakenly swings too wide and finds itself on the outside of the circle. The Tasmanian pounces and fires. At the same time he notices Blue 2 attacking the enemy aircraft to his right. Walch's target tightens its turn and dives towards the sea with its starboard engine emitting smoke but he has to break off and loses sight of it. Seconds later he spots a Bf 110 flying at sea level. It keeps a straight course for about a mile (1.6 km) and then plunges into the sea. Walch is unsure if this is his own victim or the one belonging to Blue 2 but he has no time to give the matter thought because there are three Messerschmitt Bf 109s coming towards him. They do not attack, turning away in a south-easterly direction. All hostile aircraft have now disappeared.

*

Thirty-four-year-old P/O Geoff Myers is 257 Squadron's intelligence officer and with the adjutant he is summoned to S/Ldr David Bayne's office. They find the commanding officer in a sombre mood. He has been promoted to wing commander and is leaving the squadron. His place will be taken by S/Ldr T. Harkness. The news is a shock to the two men because to them, and indeed to all of the men, 257 is Bayne's squadron. He had formed it and had built it up to become operational. Everyone had confidence in his leadership. Obviously the flying accident which had cost him his leg two years earlier had caused 'the powers that be' to decide that it was impractical to have an operational commander with a wooden leg. The only outward sign of the injury is Bayne's slight limp and the walking stick he uses. In spite of it, he has led the men in the air and on the ground but now that is to end. He is to go to a fighter control room.

*

In Germany on this day Adolf Hitler, apparently considering England's position to be hopeless, instructs his General Staff to commence preliminary feasibility studies for an attack on the Soviet Union.

*

Bomber Command makes its largest night effort since the fall of France. Over 80 aircraft are sent to attack 7 targets in Germany while others bomb airfields in France, strike barges in the Dutch ports and carry out minelaying operations.

Hampden P4389 of 50 Squadron, flown by Richard Taylor and his crew, is one of 4 aircraft of that unit detailed to bomb the Dornier aircraft works at Wismar. He arrives over the area just on midnight and drops his four 250 lb (114 kg) bombs from a height of 12 000 feet (3 700 m). Large fires are seen to break out but because of cloud Taylor and his crew are not certain that they are coming from the factory.

MONDAY, 22 JULY

Weather conditions over the English Channel are mostly fine but cloudy and *Luftwaffe* daylight activity is markedly reduced.

During a patrol over Portland Hurricanes from 87 Squadron intercept a German reconnaissance aircraft which is making good use of the cloud cover. John Cock is flying Hurricane P3596. He gives chase but the German proves too elusive.

Three Blenheims from 236 Squadron at Thorney Island escort a reconnaissance aircraft to Cherbourg at 11.30 a.m. Blenheim L1119 (ND-C) is flown by Bryan McDonough with Sgt F.A.P. Head as his gunner. Six aircraft are observed crossing northwards from south-west of Cherbourg but they are too far away to identify.

*

Ron Lees, commanding officer of 72 Squadron, is promoted to acting wing commander and posted to Headquarters 13 Group (Air Staff Operations Training Duties). He has been the Squadron's C.O. since December 1938, but now he hands over to S/Ldr A.R. Collins.

[Ronald Beresford Lees was born at Broken Hill, NSW, on 27 April 1910, son of John Thomas Lees. He was educated at Prince Alfred's College and St Peter's College, Adelaide, and later attended Adelaide University. In January 1930 he joined the RAAF as a cadet at Point Cook and in January 1931, took up a short-service commission in the RAF. He was graded as a pilot officer in March 1931. In August he married Rhoda Lillie Pank.

*Lees had his short-service commission extended and by October 1935 had risen to flight lieutenant. Next June he was granted a permanent commission in the RAF. In October 1938, his promotion to squadron leader was gazetted and he was given command of 72 Squadron two months later. The unit was stationed at Church Fenton. In October 1939 it moved to Leconfield and its first clash with enemy aircraft took place on the 21st when Desmond Sheen and F/O T.A.F. Elsdon encountered 14 Heinkel He 115s over the North Sea and shot down 2. Later that month the unit transferred to Drem in Scotland to counter long-range **Luftwaffe** flights taking place over the Firth of Forth.*

From Gravesend, early in June 1940, Ron Lees and 72 Squadron flew numerous patrols to cover the evacuation of Dunkirk. On 2 June their Spitfires intercepted a formation of Junkers Ju 87 Stukas and Lees dived through an anti-aircraft barrage and shot down a Stuka. After Dunkirk the squadron had returned to Acklington.]

*

At night almost 70 aircraft from Bomber Command, including Fairey Battles, attack targets in Germany, barges in Holland, and airfields in

France, and carry out minelaying. Three Battles from 150 Squadron are detailed to bomb the aerodrome at Schipol near Amsterdam. Walter Blom takes part in the operation in aircraft L5447. This is only the second night that Fairey Battles have operated under Bomber Command control since their return from the disastrous French campaign.

[F/Lt Walter Michael Blom, DFC, was born in Hobart, Tasmania, on 6 March 1917. He was an air cadet in the RAAF at Point Cook and took up a short-service commission in the RAF in August 1937. He was promoted to flying officer in May 1939. His squadron went to France with the AASF and he was heavily engaged in combat when the Germans invaded Belgium and France in May 1940.

He was awarded a DFC for his courageous action on 10 May 1940. (Refer to Prelude)].

TUESDAY, 23 JULY

During the night the *Luftwaffe* carries out minelaying operations from Dover to the Tyne and Forth Estuary. The radar station at Poling picks up an enemy aircraft on its screen and a radar-equipped Bristol Blenheim If of the Fighter Interception Unit (FIU) is vectored to intercept. Its all-British crew shoot down a Dornier Do 17 from 2/KG 3. This is the first victory using airborne radar in night fighting.

*

Daylight brings slightly hazy conditions in the Straits of Dover and German air activity throughout the day is minimal.

*

Six Blenheims of 236 Squadron leave Thorney Island and fly to Detling where they refuel and act as escorts for RN minesweepers operating in the North Sea. Bryan McDonough is the pilot of aircraft L6797 (ND-A). They return to Thorney at 3.30 p.m.

Fred Flood of 235 Squadron in his Blenheim 'Buskarlet's Brig' leads several aircraft on a similar escort mission between 7.30 and 10.00 p.m.

[Frederick William Flood was born at Roma, Queensland, on 18 March 1915, son of E. Flood. When he joined the RAAF he was living in Mosman, NSW. His training at Point Cook finished in 1935 and he sailed for England in January 1936 for a RAF short-service commission. When war broke out in September 1939 he was an acting flight lieutenant but was soon promoted to flight lieutenant and posted to Manston as a flight commander in 235 Squadron. In February 1940 the unit's new aircraft, Bristol Blenheims, began to arrive and it was transferred from Fighter to Coastal Command for long-range fighter reconnaissance duties.

When the German invasion of the Low Countries began in May 1940 the squadron flew sorties over Holland and was involved in numerous defensive patrols to cover the evacuation of Dunkirk. On 1 June, off

Blenheim IF of 248 Squadron. By July 1940 the unit's 'short-nose' versions had been superseded by 'long-nose' Blenheim IVFs. Both types were used as long range fighters. Blenheims were also used as interim night fighters but their lack of speed and teething troubles with airborne radar impeded their effectiveness (Imperial War Museum photograph MH 165).

Dunkirk, Flood sighted a Heinkel He 111. Flood attacked. The bomber managed to escape into cloud but not before the Australian's bullets silenced two of the bomber's gunners. When the evacuation was over, 235 Squadron reverted to convoy protection and long-range offensive patrols around Cherbourg. On 19 June Flood flew a reconnaissance mission over St Malo in aircraft N3531, (QY-F). This machine became his usual aircraft and he christened it 'Buskarlet's Brig'.[8]

On 24 June the squadron moved to Bircham Newton, though detachments were operated at Detling, Thorney Island, St Eval and Aldergrove. Flood normally operated from Thorney Island.]

*

Correspondents Kenneth Slessor and Ronald Monson travel from Amesbury Abbey to Alton where the men of the Australian Railway and Forestry units are camped and begin interviewing the men. Most, they discover, have been billeted out in the homes of villagers and are enthusiastic about the hospitality they have received.

WEDNESDAY, 24 JULY

There is rain in most districts with heavy cloud over the English Channel and Straits of Dover. In the west there is fog. During the morning, the *Luftwaffe* sends out isolated reconnaissance sorties and light nuisance raids.

At Acklington, Red and Yellow Sections of 72 Squadron fly
uneventful patrols early in the morning.

*

After 10 days with 32 Squadron at Biggin Hill John Crossman has
flown as many flights in the unit's Magister as the weather has per-
mitted but he has yet to fly a Hurricane!

THURSDAY, 25 JULY

The day is fine with haze over the Straits of Dover and German
reconnaissance planes locate a heavily protected convoy of colliers and
coasters heading west approaching the Straits. These unfortunate
ships of Convoy C.W.8 will be the main targets for the *Luftwaffe*
throughout the day.

The Germans send out large fighter formations to engage the RAF
covering aircraft so that while these are being refuelled and rearmed,
bombers can be sent in before fresh Hurricanes and Spitfires can
arrive.

Realizing the German tactics, the RAF 11 Group controller sends
only light forces to cover the convoy until a major bomber attack is
sighted, then reinforcements are quickly scrambled into the area.

At 2.30 p.m. 8 Spitfires of 64 Squadron on patrol over the ships spot
an incoming raid of 30 Junkers Ju 88s escorted by about 50 Messerschmitt Bf 109s. As they intercept, three more of 64 Squadron's
Spitfires are scrambled from Kenley and 12 Hurricanes of 111 Squadron scramble from Hawkinge. The Hurricanes again adopt their terri-
fying line abreast head-on charge and cause the Ju 88s to break off. On
seeing the bombers retreat the Bf 109s follow. In the confused fighting
several 111 Squadron pilots claim to have been fired on by Spitfires.

As the convoy leaves Dover behind it is briefly without fighter cover
as the patrols change shifts, and the inevitable happens. Passing Folkestone, 60 Junkers Ju 87 Stuka dive-bombers strike. Many ships are hit,
5 being sunk, and three others suffer damage including the two
destroyers. Nine Hurricanes of 56 Squadron arrive in the middle of the
raid and attack in spite of the odds.

Meanwhile 9 German E-boats close in on the convoy causing many
of the ships to scatter and damaging three before the destroyers can
drive them off. Before the convoy is out of danger, of 21 ships, 11 are
sunk or badly damaged and only two will reach their destination
unscathed. The men in the coastal ships will call it 'Black Thursday'.

*

At Biggin Hill, after flying half an hour of demonstration take-offs and
landings in Magister N7570 John Crossman climbs into Hurricane
L2062 and carries out a similar series of exercises for the next hour. It is
his first experience at flying a modern fighter.

*

After dark RAF Bomber Command sends almost 170 aircraft to attack
7 major targets in the Ruhr industrial area and airfields in Holland.

Because of haze and heavy cloud, coupled with searchlights and heavy flak, many of the bomber crews, including those of Richard Taylor and Bob Reed of 50 Squadron, are unable to locate their targets. Rather than bring their bombs home, they search for targets of opportunity.

At midnight Reed in Hampden P1327 bombs a self-illuminating target on the south bank of the canal north-east of Essen. Twenty minutes later Taylor in Hampden P4389 drops his bombs on the railway line at Dortmund.

Seven bombers fail to return.

FRIDAY, 26 JULY

Weather conditions are poor with low cloud, heavy rain and bad visibility over much of England, causing a low level of aerial activity.

At noon 238 Hurricane Squadron patrols over Swanage. The leader of 'B' Flight is Stuart Walch. The squadron is informed of bandits south-west of Portland. Walch sees three Bf 109s in a loose formation at 14 000 feet (4 200 m) and, ordering his section into line astern, he climbs up after them. The Hurricanes come up in the enemy's blind spot. Walch lines up the 109 on the right and fires a one-second burst and the German fighter plunges into the sea. The other two 109s have disappeared.

*

Major General H.D. Wynter, General Officer Commanding Australforce, calls a conference at his headquarters in Amesbury Abbey and explains that the force's role has now been clarified. The 18th Brigade, with artillery, the machine-gun battalion and other attached troops will become the 'Southern Command Striking Force', if a mobile striking force is needed. At this stage Wynter regards the 25th Brigade as suitable only for a local protective role in the Salisbury Plain area. Australforce's responsibility for the protection of Middle Wallop and Andover aerodromes and for the provision of a mobile striking column will therefore end from 27 July.

*

With darkness, the *Luftwaffe* commences minelaying in the Thames Estuary, off the Norfolk coast and the Bristol Channel. Several RAF squadrons, including day fighters, are alerted for night patrols.

At St Eval, Pat Hughes of 234 Squadron is one of three pilots alternating on this duty.

No. 87 Squadron at Exeter is also on alert. At 11.30 p.m. John Cock in Hurricane P3394, LK-M is on patrol from Hullavington when he sees an enemy aircraft caught overhead in the searchlights. He climbs up after it, identifying it as a Heinkel He 111 and opens fire from 250 yards (230 m). The bomber turns left and spirals away. Because his night vision has been ruined by the lights the Australian is unable to follow. Shortly afterwards a Heinkel crashes at Longfield and all except one of its crew are killed.

[John Reynolds Cock was born on 3 March 1918 at Renmark, South Australia, son of Vivian Ernest Cock and Katherine, née Farley.

John was educated at Renmark High School, Prince Alfred College, Adelaide, and Roseworthy Agricultural College. He first began flying at the age of 16 and by 1938, when he left Australia to join the RAF, he had almost 50 hours in his log book. In May 1938 he was granted a short-service commission and was posted to 87 Squadron at Debden which was then equipped with new Hawker Hurricane Mk Is. Another member of the squadron was Western Australian, Dick Glyde.

With the outbreak of war in September 1939 No. 87 Squadron went to France. On 14 April 1940 Cock shot down a Heinkel and on 10 May he destroyed a Junkers Ju 88. On the 12th he accounted for a Heinkel He 111 and on the 13th he shot down a Bf 109. On 17 May he shot down a Junkers Ju 87 Stuka.

Late in May, 87 Squadron flew its remaining Hurricanes out of France to Debden, England. It did not become operational again until 21 June and on 5 July it moved to Exeter.]

SATURDAY, 27 JULY

The weather all morning is fair and cloudy with some rain over the Midlands and North Sea.

*

Two Spitfires of 152 Squadron are scrambled from Warmwell early in the morning to intercept a German weather reconnaissance aircraft. One is flown by Ian Bayles. They find a Junkers Ju 88 making good use of the cloud cover but before they can attack it heads for France at full throttle. The Spitfires pursue. Bayles and his wingman use up all of their ammunition during an unsuccessful chase over the Bristol Channel.

*

Later that morning three Spitfires of Green Section, 609 Squadron, are on patrol over Convoy 'Bacon' when the section leader simply disappears. The other two machines, one flown by P/O D.M. Crook and the other by John Curchin, have been covering his tail but as both pilots simultaneously turn their heads to search behind he vanishes. Crook and Curchin conduct a wide search. However Green 1, P/O J.R. Buchanan, will never be found.

*

At 2.45 p.m. Blue Section of 234 Squadron, led by Pat Hughes, is ordered up to patrol Land's End. By 3.00 p.m. it is in position and upon receiving new instructions Hughes leads the three Spitfires up to 23 000 feet (7 000 m) where they find a Ju 88. The German apparently sees the oncoming fighters and dives vertically. Hughes fastens onto his tail and his Spitfire is buffeted by the Junker's slipstream. They level out at 50 feet (15 m) and hurtle across the water at 300 m.p.h. (500 km/h). Hughes fires until his ammunition runs out. Tracer, which had been snaking back from the German rear gunner, stops

This photograph, showing 87 Squadron scrambling for their planes in France during the 'phoney war', was staged for the photographer. Australian John Cock flew aircraft LK-N, third from the camera (Imperial War Museum photograph C465).

abruptly. Shattered perspex flies off the cockpit canopy and both engines are visibly damaged. Hughes breaks away. The Ju 88 is claimed as 'damaged'.

Hughes has flown 6 sorties in less than 24 hours.

*

RAF Fighter Command is fully aware of the problems of fatigue faced by its airmen. On this day Dowding rules that henceforth pilots must have a minimum of 8 hours in every 24 hours off duty and a continuous 24 hours off each week.

*

Around 4.00 p.m., at Newton airfield in Nottinghamshire, Fairey Battle L5528 is being prepared for operations under the supervision of Walter Blom. Four bombs are already loaded but as a flare is being attached it falls to the ground and bursts into flames. After 7 minutes the first bomb detonates followed shortly afterwards by a second explosion and then a third. Everyone in the immediate vicinity is cut down by flying shrapnel and pieces of wreckage. Ambulances and rescue parties go immediately to the aid of the injured men but the carnage is horrific. Five are already dead, among them the Tasmanian,

Blom. Another dies in the ambulance on the way to hospital and a seventh will die in the morning.

In spite of the tragedy, 150 Squadron's 'A' Flight is put on 'Stand By' for operations at 9.30 p.m.

*

It is a bad day for the Royal Navy too. Heinkel He 111s sink the destroyer HMS *Wren* off Aldeburgh.

There are also two attacks on Dover. Five high explosive bombs fall on the barracks and the destroyer flotilla leader, HMS *Codrington*, is sunk.

SUNDAY, 28 JULY

The weather is fine and clear over much of England, clouding over in the evening.

A breathless silence has settled down over the area of British coastline most likely to be invaded. The beaches are hedged with scaffolding, barbed wire, mines and concrete blocks and behind these the coast is sealed off by checkpoints on the roads. There is a tangible feeling of tension . . . of waiting for something to happen.

Blue Flight of 234 Squadron, led by Pat Hughes, is up early for convoy patrol. Orders have been received to investigate enemy aircraft over Plymouth. As the three Spitfires arrive over the port they spot a Junkers Ju 88 diving steeply towards an inland target. There is no chance to intercept so Hughes positions his flight and cuts the enemy off when he pulls up. He closes in to 50 yards (45 m) and holds this position while firing off short bursts. The German rear gunner replies. About 30 miles (50 km) south-east of Plymouth, grey-yellow smoke pours from the Junker's starboard engine and a red-hot object falls off. Hughes breaks off so Blue 3 and Blue 2 can attack it in turn. The crippled bomber bursts into flames and sinks within seconds.

*

Early in the morning, Sunderland P9601 (RB-F), of 10 Squadron, RAAF, flown by F/Lt Hugh Birch and his crew, is on an anti-submarine patrol when it encounters six Junkers Ju 88s but neither side takes action.

At 9.50 a.m. the Sunderland locates four life-boats in an area strewn with floating wreckage from the *Auckland Star* which had been torpedoed 80 miles off Valencia, Ireland. He radios their position.

After completing his patrol Birch returns to the scene and, deciding that the sea is calm enough, he lands next to the life-boats to take off any survivors requiring urgent medical attention. This is the first time that a RAAF flying boat has taken part in the rescue of survivors of a U-boat attack and it is also the first successful open-ocean landing.

*

After a heavy afternoon raid German air-sea rescue He 59s patrol looking for ditched airmen. Two Heinkels encounter Hurricanes from 111 Squadron and are shot down.

All remaining destroyers of Dover Command are withdrawn to Portsmouth. The Admiralty's decision to make this move has taken into consideration the mounting shipping losses during daylight, the sinking of two destroyers, and the potential menace of new heavy German guns on the French coast near Calais. Dover is no longer safe as a base. This means that the *Luftwaffe's* so-called 'Flying Artillery' has cleared the way across the Channel for an invasion but has yet to secure a safe air umbrella to cover it.

MONDAY, 29 JULY

This is a day of cloudless skies and fine weather.

At 7.20 a.m. Kent Sector Operations Rooms are informed of a large raid building up behind Calais. As the raid moves towards the British coastline it becomes obvious that Dover itself is about to be hit. Fifty Junkers Ju 87 Stukas and 80 Messerschmitt Bf 109s are intercepted over the port and a huge dogfight develops. The Hurricanes and the Spitfires prevent the Stukas from making accurate dive-bombing attacks.

*

After weeks of deliberation the Air Ministry releases an official communique concerning the problems posed by German air-sea rescue planes with Red Cross markings:

> His Majesty's Government desire to accord to ambulance aircraft reasonable facilities for the transportation of the sick and wounded, in accordance with the Red Cross Convention, and aircraft engaged in the direct evacuation of the sick and wounded will be respected, provided that they comply with the relevant provisions of the Convention.
>
> His Majesty's Government are unable, however, to grant immunity to such aircraft flying over areas in which operations are in progress on land or sea, or approaching British or Allied territory, in British occupation, or British or Allied ships.
>
> Ambulance aircraft which do not comply with the above requirements will do so at their own risk and peril.[9]

Fighter Command's instruction of the 14th has at last received official sanction.

*

A sudden low-level attack against a small group of ships off Portland catches the air defences off guard. HMS *Delight*, a destroyer, is sunk.

The Admiralty orders half of the English Channel closed to British destroyers during daylight hours.

*

Desmond Sheen who has been with the PRU Squadron at Heston since arriving back in England on the 12th, transfers back to his old unit, 72 Squadron, at Acklington. Harry Daish will continue flying in the PRU until he is posted away in December.

*

At Biggin Hill John Crossman is delighted to find the familiar face of John Pain who has joined 32 Squadron.

[RAF records indicate that John Francis Pain was born in Scotland but he was living in Brisbane in 1939. Gordon Olive, also from Brisbane, remembered him well when interviewed in 1985:

> John Pain was quite a character. He was the stepson of Sir Alan Mansfield who was Governor of Queensland for some time. His mother was Lady Mansfield who had previously been married to a gentleman named Pain but the marriage had broken up and as far as I know John was the only child of the marriage. He was a fairly wild young boy, known as 'Tiger' Pain, at school and also in the Air Force, and he had a somewhat . . . cat-like look about him . . . at least, I thought he had.[10]]

TUESDAY, 30 JULY

The weather is unsettled with low cloud over England. Air activity is limited.

*

Commencing at 4.30 a.m. Australforce conducts its first real brigade exercise, designed to test the force's ability in turning out, moving at short notice and giving the commanders practice in the rapid occupation of a defence position.

Meanwhile the newly formed 2/3rd Australian General Hospital, under Lieut-Colonel D.B. Loudon, is opened in Godalming and is under the complete control of the Australian military administration.

*

During the morning Dick Power of 236 Squadron flies with two passengers in Blenheim R2777 from Thorney Island to Carew Cheriton.

In the afternoon, while attempting to take off on the return flight, the plane collides with a Department of Works vehicle on the airfield. Neither Power nor his passengers are injured but the Blenheim is damaged beyond repair.

*

The *London Gazette* announces the award of the DFC to S/Ldr C.W. Pearce of 10 Squadron, RAAF:

> This officer has consistently displayed gallantry and devotion to duty whilst engaged on convoy and anti-submarine patrols. In June, 1940, Squadron Leader Pearce attacked an enemy submarine off the coast of Portugal, one bomb being observed to burst near the bow. This Officer has displayed courage and resource in anti-submarine work and, by his

personal energy and skill, has formed his Squadron into a highly efficient operational unit.

It is the squadron's first decoration and the first DFC to be awarded to a member of the RAAF since its formation in 1921.

WEDNESDAY, 31 JULY

Because of hazy visibility which persists all day, neither the *Luftwaffe* nor RAF Fighter Command score any significant successes.

*

At 8.50 a.m. James Horan of 233 Squadron takes off in Hudson N7224 from Leuchars and flies out over the North Sea on a patrol. Neither he nor the aircraft will ever be seen again . . .

[James Henry Horan received a short-service commission in the RAF in October 1938 and was posted to 233 Squadron, Coastal Command, which at that time used Avro Ansons for general reconnaissance work. The squadron moved to Scotland in August 1939, and re-equipped with Hudsons with which it flew anti-ship sweeps after the Germans invaded Norway in April 1940.]

P/O James Henry Horan is among those Australians whose names are listed on the Battle of Britain Roll of Honour at Westminster Abbey.

*

A RAAF Sunderland P9601 (RB-F), flown by Bill Garing and his crew, is detailed to escort the armed merchant cruiser *Mooltan* which has put to sea after a refit at Plymouth. The ship is being subjected to air attacks. After three and a half hours on patrol the Sunderland sights a Junkers Ju 88 and intercepts it, causing it to break off. The time is 8.55 a.m.

At 12.50 p.m. two more Ju 88s turn up and prepare to dive-bomb the ship. Garing attacks the rearmost machine and forces it to pull away so that its bombs fall well astern of the ship. A few minutes later the Sunderland's front and rear gunners engage the other Ju 88 as it dives out of a cloud towards the ship. Both German planes leave the scene.

A third attack comes at 1.20 p.m. when another Ju 88 is intercepted and its attack is again disrupted by the flying boat. Like the others, the dive-bomber does not stay.

Because of the persistent air attacks the *Mooltan* is diverted to Liverpool. Its captain highly commends the Sunderland's crew for their effective air cover and Garing will later receive the DFC.

By the end of the day Mount Batten, the home of 10 Squadron, has suffered a total of 41 air raid alerts since 1 July.

*

*[Throughout the first month of the battle of Britain the **Luftwaffe** has probed for weaknesses in the British fighter defences without obvious*

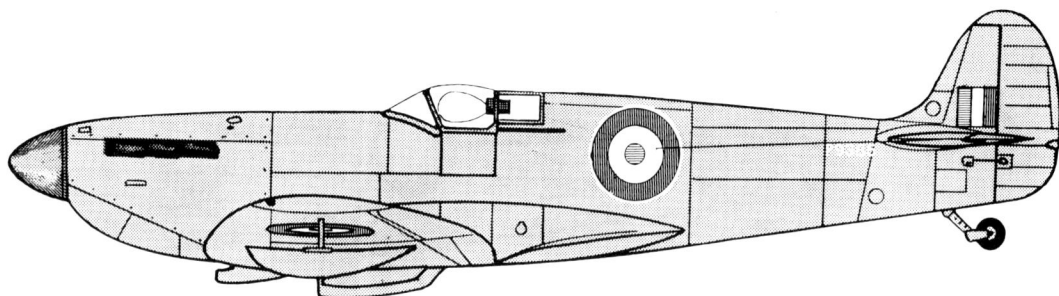

Supermarine Spitfire P9385 was a Mk I powered by a Rolls Royce Merlin III engine. It was delivered to Sidney Cotton's Heston Aircraft Ltd and converted into a PRIII Type C for the Photographic Development Unit (PDU) in April 1940. The port underwing blister contained 30 gals (136 l) of fuel and the starboard blister held two cameras. Desmond Sheen flew reconnaissance sorties over Italy in this aircraft during May/June 1940, operating from Le Luc in the south of France and Ajaccio in Sardinia. P9385 was later converted into a PRIV Type F.

success. While some weaknesses, such as the Defiant's inability to defend itself, have been exposed, Fighter Command's organization has been equal to the task of covering or reinforcing them. It has weathered the storm reasonably well so far but has not yet been subjected to full-scale assault and the threat of this now looms close.

Dowding receives encouraging news from the aircraft industry which has been making a maximum effort in the production of fighters. Hurricanes and Spitfires are rolling off the assembly lines at a rate well above official estimates. More than 1 200 have been delivered since the beginning of May.

On the other hand the pilot situation is a potential problem. While at the moment, in terms of numbers, battle losses are being made good, in terms of losing experienced pilots, there could be real difficulties ahead. Even before the battle had commenced, Fighter Command had lost more than 80 regular squadron leaders and flight commanders and their places were now being filled by pilots with considerably less experience in controlling large formations of aircraft or deployment of them in combat. The situation will become critical if the pilot loss rate begins to exceed the replacement rate and new pilots arriving on operational squadrons with only a minimum number of flying hours on Hurricanes and Spitfires prove to be more of a liability than an asset.

Only one Australian fighter pilot has been killed during July, F/Lt John Kennedy of 238 Squadron on the 13th. Bomber Command has lost two Australians, P/O Phillip Leach of 38 Squadron on the 21st, and F/Lt Walter Blom DFC of 150 Squadron on the 27th. And on this day, P/O James Horan of 233 Squadron, Coastal Command, has been posted missing.]

*

The operations continue . . .

Luftwaffe raiders during the night are mainly on minelaying operations.

RAF Bomber Command despatches 42 aircraft to attack a variety of targets and lay mines. Twelve Hampdens of 50 Squadron at Lindholme are detailed to carry out 'gardening' (minelaying) operations and plant 'radishes' (mines).

AUGUST, 1940

THURSDAY 1

Records indicate that the Australian personnel listed below are on strength in RAF Fighter Command squadrons at 9.00 a.m. on 1 August 1940:

SQUADRON	[AIRCRAFT]	AIRMAN	BASE	
17	[Hurricane]	Sgt D. Fopp	Debden	[11 Group]
32	[Hurricane]	P/O J.D. Crossman	Biggin Hill	[11 Group]
		P/O J.F. Pain		
65	[Spitfire]	AF/Lt C.G.C. Olive	Hornchurch	[11 Group]
72	[Spitfire]	F/O D.F.B. Sheen	Acklington	[13 Group]
73	[Hurricane]	P/O C.A. McGaw	Church Fenton	[13 Group]
79	[Hurricane]	P/O W. Millington	Acklington	[13 Group]
87	[Hurricane]	F/O R.L. Glyde	Exeter	[10 Group]
		P/O J.R. Cock		
111	[Hurricane]	F/O H.G. Hardman	Croydon	[11 Group]
		(Returns today after completing a course at Kenley.)		
141	[Defiant]	P/O A.N. Constantine	Prestwick	[13 Group]
152	[Spitfire]	F/Lt L.C. Withall	Warmwell	[10 Group]
		P/O I.N. Bayles		
		Sgt K.C. Holland		
234	[Spitfire]	F/Lt P.C. Hughes	St Eval	[10 Group]
		(On temporary attachment to 247 Squadron.)		
		P/O V. Parker		
238	[Hurricane]	F/Lt S.C. Walch	Middle Wallop	[10 Group]
264	[Defiant]	LAC V.W.J. Crook	Kirton-in-Lindsey	[12 Group]
		(Attending course at No. 5 OTU, Aston Down.)		
266	[Spitfire]	P/O F.W. Cale	Wittering	[12 Group]
600	[Blenheim]	F/Lt C.A. Pritchard	Manston	[11 Group]
603	[Spitfire]	P/O R.H. Hillary	Turnhouse	[13 Group]
609	[Spitfire]	P/O J. Curchin	Middle Wallop	[10 Group]
		P/O R.F.G. Miller		

In addition, in three Coastal Command squadrons which had been attached to Fighter Command or under its control, are:

SQUADRON	[AIRCRAFT]	AIRMAN	BASE	
235	[Blenheim]	F/Lt F.W. Flood	Bircham Newton	[A Flight]
			Thorney Island	[B Flight]
236	[Blenheim]	F/Lt R.M. Power	Thorney Island	
		P/O B.M. McDonough		
		F/O W.S. Moore		
248	[Blenheim]	P/O C.C. Bennett	Sumburgh	
		P/O A.L. Hamilton		
		P/O J.D. Peterkin		

German minelaying aircraft are active again during the night but their efforts are restricted by heavy mist. Using the mist, 4 British coastal convoys avoid harassment until evening, too late for the *Luftwaffe* to mount large-scale attacks.

Fighter Command flies numerous sorties to cover the ships but, while the Hurricanes are thus engaged, 30 Heinkel He 111s from KG 4 slip through the defences and bomb the Boulton Paul factory at Norwich.

*

After its move on 21 July Fighter Flight, Sumburgh, is now installed at Roborough to form the nucleus of No. 247 Squadron. It is passed for day operations immediately but needs a fortnight to settle down and become conversant with its new sector, patrol lines and operational duties. Pilots and personnel are billeted out. The new squadron comes under Mount Batten, Coastal Command, home of 10 Squadron RAAF, as its parent station.

For operational flying 247 Squadron is now in 10 Group controlled by Headquarters, Fighter Sector, St Eval. As all radio communications will come from St Eval and night operations are to be made from there as well, Pat Hughes, the unit's Australian flight commander, is appointed temporarily from 234 Squadron, to assist with organization.

Hughes has a busy day. He and Kathleen Agnes Brodrick are married at the Registry Office in Bodmin, with strangers as witnesses.

[*The airstrip at Roborough was suitable for 247 Squadron's Gloster Gladiators. During this period of the battle of Britain one Gladiator, No. N5585, was emblazoned with a map of Australia with a standing kangaroo superimposed upon it. Printed alongside were the words 'Anzac Answer'. Below these, there was a victory emblem in the shape of a miniature swastika (refer to sketch). The plane's usual pilot was P/O N.I.C. Francis whose nationality is listed as 'British'.*

The Australian motif has remained an enigma because there was no Australian known to have served as a pilot in the Fighter Flight or 247 Squadron at this time. Whilst at Sumburgh, the Flight had claimed two probable victories so it has been supposed that the swastika referred to one of these. Who was responsible for the 'Anzac Answer' has remained a mystery.

Research has produced two possible answers. The only Australian connection which can be established with certainty was the temporary attachment to 247 Squadron of Pat Hughes of 234 Squadron on 1 August 1940. Such was this man's imposing and outgoing character — we will see the great influence he had on 234 Squadron — that it does not stretch credibility to see him as being responsible for such an emblem. His combat record up to 1 August consisted of three attacks with his section on lone Ju 88s. The first was on 8 July and it was recorded in 234 Squadron as a victory for the whole section; the second, on 27 July, was unconfirmed; but in the third, the next day, Hughes played the major role and the Ju 88 crashed into the sea. The swastika on the 'Anzac Answer' could refer to this spectacular kill of 28 July.

There is another, less likely, possibility. No. 247's task was to provide air cover for the naval base at Plymouth and this was also the home of 10 Squadron, RAAF, at Mount Batten. Roborough became, in fact, a sat-

The 'Anzac Answer' emblem. The kangaroo, swastika and printing were black on white backgrounds.

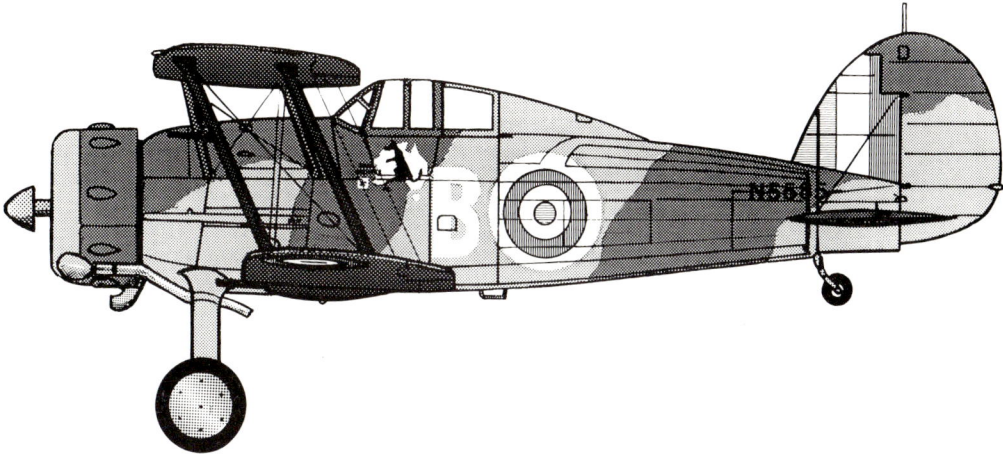

Gloster Gladiator II, N5585, of 247 Squadron RAF. The S.S.37 prototype Gladiator first flew in September 1934 and the type ended the era of single seat fighter biplanes for the RAF. 247 Squadron, previously known as the Sumburgh Fighter Flight, was established at Roborough on 1 August for the local defence of the Royal Naval Dockyards at Plymouth and was the only home-based RAF squadron so equipped during the battle of Britain. Although there was no Australian pilot known to be in the unit, N5585 has been depicted as having the 'Anzac Answer' emblem on its fuselage during this period. (804 Squadron FAA also used Gladiators during the battle of Britain.)

ellite airfield for Mount Batten and was often used by landplanes attached to the flying boat base. Australian personnel frequently used the field and Australian ground crew may have been 'borrowed' to set things up in the early stages. Certainly, 10 Squadron's successful part in sinking the U-26 on 1 July, was a matter of pride for the squadron — pride which could have manifested itself in the painting of a symbol of defiance on the side of one of 247 Squadron's Gladiators. Perhaps the 'Anzac Answer's' swastika referred to a submarine kill, not an aircraft kill.]

*

PRU aircraft report a large concentration of German planes at Cherbourg and in order to strike first the RAF orders a raid. At Thorney Island, 59 Squadron prepares 13 Blenheim IV bombers while an escort of 10 Blenheim long-range fighters is readied by the ground crew of 236 Squadron.

The escort is divided into three parts. First off at 3.00 p.m. is Dick Power in Blenheim N2799 (ND-Q) leading a section of three. Five minutes later two more Blenheims take off, the first flown by the squadron's commanding officer, S/Ldr P.E. Drew, and the second, N2774 (ND-N), with Bryan McDonough at the controls. There are supposed to be three planes in this section but Sgt Smith is late taking off. These sections led by Power and Drew are to follow 59 Squadron in and shoot up the aerodrome after the bombs have been dropped. The last section of 4 Blenheims, led by Bill Moore, is to wait 1–2 miles (2–3 km) off Cherbourg to cover the withdrawal of the others and it is with this group that Smith takes off. One of Moore's Blenheims suffers engine trouble and turns back.

Weather reports just before the mission predicted that conditions over Cherbourg peninsula would be fine and clear but this is not the case. Low cloud blankets the French coast causing Dick Power and his section to miss Cherbourg completely. The three Blenheims fly on searching for a landmark, not realizing that they are moving away from the target area.

Shortly afterwards, as 59 Squadron and Drew's section arrives, a break appears in the cloud cover and the bombers find the enemy aerodrome. As soon as the bombs are dropped, Drew leads McDonough and Smith down for a low-level strafing attack at 50–70 feet (15–20 m). Explosions erupt on the aerodrome and a fire breaks out, testifying to the accuracy of the bombing. The Blenheims separate to strafe machine-gun and coastal battery positions and German gun crews scatter. Smith's Blenheim is hit several times, damaging its tail and he loses contact with the other two but manages to finish his strafing run and fly out to sea. Bill Moore's section, waiting off Cherbourg, drives off a German aircraft and returns home.

The raid is an expensive one for three Blenheims do not return and others are damaged. The commanding officer of 59 Squadron, W/Cdr Weld-Smith, is missing with his crew and 236 Squadron has lost Peter Drew and Bryan McDonough and their crews.

It is recorded in 236 Squadron's Operations Record Book (ORB):

> Squadron Leader Drew commanded the squadron from the time it was reformed on 31st October 1939 and the loss of such a much loved leader is a bitter blow to the entire squadron. P/O McDonough who is an Australian was also another original member of the squadron, a pilot of great dependability and the utmost determination . . .[1]

Dick Power assumes temporary command of the squadron.

Bryan McDonough is the second of the Australians deemed eligible for the Battle of Britain Clasp to be killed in action.

*

From his headquarters Hitler issues Directive No. 17 for the conduct of air and sea warfare against England:

> In order to establish the necessary conditions for the final conquest of England I intend to intensify air and sea warfare against the English homeland. I therefore order as follows:
>
> 1. The German Air Force is to overpower the English Air Force with all the forces at its command, in the shortest time possible. The attacks are to be directed primarily against flying units, their ground installations, and their supply organizations, but also against the aircraft industry, including that manufacturing anti-aircraft equipment.
> 2. After achieving temporary or local air superiority the air war is to be continued against ports, in particular against stores of food, and also against stores of provisions in the interior of the country. Attacks on the south coast ports will be made on the smallest possible scale, in view of our own forthcoming operations.
> 3. On the other hand, air attacks on enemy warships and merchant ships may be reduced except where some particularly favourable target happens to present itself, where such attacks would lend additional effectiveness to those mentioned in Paragraph 2, or where such attacks are necessary for the training of air crews for further operations.
> 4. The intensified air warfare will be carried out in such a way that the Air Force can at any time be called upon to give adequate support to naval operations against suitable targets. It must also be ready to take part in full force in Operation *Seelöwe*.

Bryan McDonough of 236 Squadron, who did not return from a mission on 1 August 1940 and is presumed to have died on that date (photograph courtesy of Henry McDonough).

5. I reserve to myself the right to decide on terror attacks as measures of reprisal.

6. The intensification of the air war may begin on or after 5 August. The exact time is to be decided by the Air Force after completion of preparations and in the light of the weather. The Navy is authorized to begin the proposed intensified naval war at the same time.

Hitler also stipulates that all armed services should be ready to launch Operation *Seelöwe*, the actual invasion, on 15 September.[2]

In accordance with Hitler's Directive, tomorrow *Reichsmarschall* Goering will issue his final orders for the *Luftwaffe* to commence its major attack.

First priority will be to destroy the RAF with assaults on British fighters in the air and on the ground. These are to be carried out together with attacks on coastal radar stations and the entire ground organization in southern England. Attacks on objectives in the north and in the Midlands will be made from Norway. On the second day, operations are to be extended to airfields around outer London and maintained at full strength again on the third. It is hoped that a few telling blows will be sufficient to obtain air superiority within four days and cause the collapse of the RAF within four weeks. Six days will be allowed for preparation and build-up, operational details, final decisions and the fixing of the date.

The first day is to be called *Adler Tag*, the 'Day of the Eagle'.

FRIDAY, 2 AUGUST

The weather is mainly fine over the north of England but it is cloudy in the east and over the English Channel.

In the morning German aircraft carry out several reconnaissance sorties. Then they attack a small convoy off Harwich and sink a trawler.

To the north another small convoy off the east coast of Scotland is bombed by 10 Heinkel He 111s.

Bomber Command despatches 36 Blenheims to attack German airfields in France, Belgium and Holland. Brian Best of 40 Squadron carries out a low-level hit-and-run raid on the hangars and runway of Haamstedt aerodrome. One of the squadron's other targets is Flushing aerodrome.

John Crossman leaves 32 Squadron to report to Sutton Bridge, Lincolnshire, for intensive training to fly Hurricanes.

At Thorney Island 236 Squadron does not fly any sorties. Dick Power, now the acting commanding officer, receives orders to transfer to St Eval.

*

F/O Clive Mayers joins 601 Squadron at Tangmere.

[*Howard Clive Mayers was born in Sydney, NSW, on 9 January 1910, son of George and Penelope Mayers. He received his tertiary education at*

Cambridge University, where he became a member of the University Air Squadron, and was commissioned in the RAFVR in 1930. In March 1940 he was again granted a commission as a pilot officer in the RAFVR for the duration of hostilities. His promotion to acting flying officer was gazetted in April and he was posted to 601 Squadron at Tangmere.]

Mayers arrives to a squadron routine in which each pilot flies two days on and one day off. He also finds that in theory there are four stages of preparedness before a 'scramble':

'Released' — off duty;
'Available' — 15 minutes to become airborne;
'Readiness' — 5 minutes and
'Standby' — 2 minutes, and at this stage each pilot should be sitting strapped into the cockpit of his aircraft.

*

At Hornchurch Gordon Olive is becoming exhausted by the large number of sorties he has been flying lately. He is rostered to fly a night patrol but H.C. Sawyer, his squadron leader, decides to take his place. Reluctantly Olive complies.

It is 11.35 p.m. when the 25-year-old squadron leader sends Spitfire R6799 hurtling across the grass airfield. Just after becoming airborne the plane stalls and crashes. Sawyer is killed.

SATURDAY, 3 AUGUST

The weather is mainly dull with a few light patches and the *Luftwaffe* is relatively inactive.

In the evening German minelaying aircraft are busy.

*

Lockheed Hudson T9282 (VX-E) of 206 Squadron, takes off from Bircham Newton at 8.40 p.m. on a convoy patrol duty. On board are two Australians, John Gilbert in the pilot's seat, and Ben Gannon who is taking the place of one of Gilbert's regular crewmen.

[John Allan Gilbert received a short-service commission in the RAF effective from October 1938 and after training was posted to 206 Squadron. At the beginning of the war this unit flew anti-submarine patrols with its antiquated Avro Ansons and it was not until March 1940 that it received Lockheed Hudsons. Benjamin Peter Gannon was a relative newcomer to 206 Squadron.]

Weather for the patrol is described as fair to good but there is cloud and mist in some areas. When Gilbert heads the aircraft out over the North Sea it is for the last time ... Hudson T9282 does not return.

P/O John Allan Gilbert and Sgt Benjamin Peter Gannon are two of the Australians whose names are listed on the Battle of Britain Roll of Honour in Westminster Abbey.

SUNDAY, 4 AUGUST

A Lockheed Hudson of 206 Squadron is sent out to search for John Gilbert's aircraft but the task proves hopeless and is abandoned.

*

The *Luftwaffe* flies a few reconnaissance sorties over the Channel and as far across as the west of England but cloud and fog over much of Britain reduces its missions. Also preparations are under way for *Adler Tag*.

A flight of patrolling Hurricanes from 32 Squadron, one with John Pain at the controls, has a fleeting glimpse of an enemy aircraft but no combat ensues. It is the Australian's second operational sortie with the squadron.

MONDAY, 5 AUGUST

Expecting heavy German attacks because of the fine weather, Fighter Command flies numerous patrols during the morning but the *Luftwaffe*, organizing for *Adler Tag*, only makes minor appearances.

A small convoy sails free from attack until it comes through the Straits of Dover in the early afternoon. It encounters a small raid of Junkers Ju 88s escorted by Messerschmitt Bf 109s. Patrolling Hurricanes shoot down one of the escorts and damage one bomber. The ships escape harm.

More effective for the *Luftwaffe* than its direct air attacks at this stage, are its minelaying activities. Over a 24-hour period 4 naval trawlers are sunk by mines.

*

From today the Australian Imperial Force (AIF) contingent in England, previously named the Southern Striking Force, is to be known as the Australian Striking Force.

*

After dark RAF Bomber Command sends 85 Hampdens, Wellingtons and Whitleys to bomb targets in Hamburg, Kiel, Wilhelmshaven and Wismar. Airfields in Holland are also attacked and minelaying is carried out. Wilhelmshaven is the base for the *Bismarck* and this is the target that Henry Ross and the pilots of 83 Squadron are ordered to attack. Ross takes off from Lossiemouth in Hampden L4412 just after 9.30 p.m. Such targets are always heavily defended and tonight is no exception. Ross manages to drop his bombs but because of the darkness, searchlights and intense anti-aircraft fire, it is impossible to observe the results.

TUESDAY, 6 AUGUST

Over Hamburg 50 Squadron is attacking the *Tirpitz*. At 12.22 a.m. Dereck French in Hampden L4149 arrives over the area but he and his crew are unable to locate their primary target because of the darkness and haze. The Australian decides instead to bomb the neighbouring docks. The haze hides his results.

Bob Reed is over the target shortly after French leaves and he drops his bombs. Two explosions are observed in the area where the battleship is docked but again results are obscured by haze.

No RAF aircraft are lost overnight.

*

The day is cloudy with moderate to strong winds. Two deep sea convoys approaching the Cornish coast are given strong fighter cover by 10 Group. Few German planes venture near the coast of England. While on patrol from Start Point to Plymouth, John Cock and a flight of Hurricanes from 87 Squadron sight 10 or more Messerschmitt Bf 110s above them in the glare of the sun. The Hurricanes alter course and gain height but are unable to reach the Germans before they turn for home.

*

At Karinhall, Hermann Goering's mansion in Prussia, the *Reichsmarschall* holds a conference with his three *Luftflotte* commanders, Albert Kesselring, Hugo Sperrle and Hans-Jurgen Stumpff. Also present is Erhard Milch, inspector general of the *Luftwaffe*.

Goering has a precise plan of attack for *Adler Tag*. The three air fleets are to be ready by 10 August. The main attacking forces will be Kesselring's *Luftflotte 2* operating from north-eastern France, Belgium, Holland and Germany, and Sperrle's *Luftflotte 3* operating from northern and western France. Both are to conduct daylight missions over southern England up to and including the Midlands, and to operate wider afield at night. The third force, Stumpff's *Luftflotte 5*, which is smaller than the other two, will fly from its bases in Norway and Denmark to threaten north-eastern England and Scotland. On or after 10 August all that will be required for the order to launch the assault will be a forecast of three or four days of suitable weather.

*

The *London Gazette* announces the award of a DFC to F/Lt J.M. Hewson of 142 Squadron for his action of 13 June.[3] (Refer to Prelude).

[In considering who should be classified as 'Australian' for this history, John Minchin Hewson's background posed problems. His English father migrated to Australia, his mother was Australian-born, his brother and sister were born in Australia but John was born and raised in England. He learnt to fly at Brooklands and joined the RAF on a short-service commission in 1936.

After training he was posted to 142 Squadron at Andover on 22 May 1937. It was one of the squadrons in the Advanced Air Striking Force which went to France in September 1939. He stayed with that squadron until August 1940.]

P/O Angus Robson of 144 Squadron also had his DFC recorded in the *London Gazette*:

> This officer was detailed to attack Warships in the harbour at Wilhelmshaven from a very low level on the night of 20th July. He carried out the attack at a height of twenty feet above the houses in the face of a terrific barrage of enemy gunfire. In spite of this opposition he crossed the harbour and pressed home his attack on an enemy warship.
>
> This officer has consistently displayed great daring and devotion to duty when attacking the enemy on many other occasions.[4]

WEDNESDAY, 7 AUGUST

Dawn brings mainly fair weather with cloud over the south-east but *Luftwaffe* operations are mainly restricted to reconnaissance sorties.

*

It is often said that cats and fighter pilots need nine lives . . .

At 1.00 p.m. Gordon Olive, in Spitfire R6617, is leading 65 Squadron up from Hornchurch aerodrome when he runs into trouble. The squadron has been ordered to Manston and after take-off Olive is adjusting his oxygen regulator when suddenly it flares into a fire. The cockpit fills with smoke and to clear it he thrusts back the canopy. Realizing that an explosion is only seconds away, Olive must get out quickly but he finds that he is trapped. He cannot roll the plane over and fall out because he does not have enough height for his parachute to open. Also, with 11 Spitfires in formation behind and below he could be struck by someone's churning propeller. He must do something . . . and quickly. Heat is searing his face.

Olive's only chance is to try a stall turn to gain some height quickly and clear the others. Waving his wingmen away, he pulls back into a vertical climb, undoing his harness at the same time. While zooming upwards he pulls off his flying helmet and oxygen mask and then pushes open the entry hatch. He has gained between 500–1 000 feet (150–300 m), still not a great margin for error but there are no choices left. Standing the Spitfire on one wing, he kicks himself out of the cockpit and pulls his ripcord . . . but nothing happens. The parachute has not opened. Looking down, he sees that the small pilot chute has caught in his flying boots. While hurtling through the air he manages to untangle it and push it away so it can drag out the main canopy. A shoulder-wrenching jolt almost knocks him unconscious as the parachute opens and jerks him upright.

It takes a few seconds for Olive to recover his senses and realize that he is now floating gently down. He then notices something which terrifies him . . . He is drifting down towards high tension cables.

He must try to side-slip out of their way but, as he reaches up to manipulate the cords of his parachute, he gets another shock . . . The canopy is splitting in two! Any attempt to side-slip might collapse the chute completely . . .

As if these problems were not enough, the quiet is suddenly shattered by two loud reports. Someone is firing at him! Looking down again, he spots two home guardsmen who are shooting upwards with shotguns, but fortunately they are still out of range.

Everything seems to accelerate. He is dropping quickly now but at least he is going to miss the cables. More shots go wide. He thuds down into a potato field and the softness of its soil breaks his fall. He is uninjured and safe . . . or is he?

The two home guardsmen now rush up and demand to take him into custody. Olive tells them that he 'is not going to bloody well go', and finally two apologetic guardsmen retreat from the scene.

Seconds later, they are all surprised by the arrival of a fire engine and an ambulance. The whole incident had been witnessed and they have charged across country to the rescue. Olive agrees to ride back in the ambulance and waits while the driver turns around . . . but, unfortunately, it strikes a ditch and topples over. Luckily, the driver scrambles out uninjured.

The Australian now decides to return on the fire engine which will take him to Hornchurch. However it arrives at an unexpected hairpin bend and fails to negotiate the turn. It crashes through a rail and down into water. Olive manages to jump clear and he last sees the engine as it disappears in foam and spray. Luckily, except for wounded pride, nobody is hurt.

After climbing back to the road, Olive tucks his parachute under his arm and begins to walk home. There cannot be too many of his nine lives left!

An old bull-nosed Morris utility pulls up beside him and the driver calls out:

'Hey, can I give you a lift?'

'Not bloody likely', Olive replies, 'I'm going to walk'![5]

At Hornchurch the doctor tells him that the burns on his face will not take long to heal and suggests that he should take 48 hours leave in London to recover his composure.

*

Around dusk 25 coastal merchant ships, most of them colliers, leave the Thames Estuary to force their way through the Straits of Dover. The Admiralty is out to prove that the English Channel is not in German hands. Off Sheerness 9 RN escort vessels join them. Convoy 'Peewit' steams for the Isle of Wight.

The men on the ships are unaware that the Germans have set up a *Freya* radar site on the cliffs at Wissant, opposite Folkestone. It has picked up, and given ample warning of, the convoy and German E-boats creep across the Channel on an interception course. They select a position, cut engines and wait in ambush.

THURSDAY, 8 AUGUST

At 3.00 a.m. all hell breaks loose in Convoy 'Peewit'. The roar of powerful engines is mixed with gunfire as the lurking E-boats spring their trap. A ship is hit by a torpedo and others swing around desperately in wild evasive manoeuvres. There are explosions. Two ships are sent to the bottom with gaping holes in their hulls, the results of torpedo strikes. Another vessel is hit but remains afloat. Yet another sinks soon afterwards. The other ship, although badly damaged, continues on. Hundreds of tons of coke from a sunken collier float on the surface of the water.

Finally the fighting dies down but by dawn the surviving ships are hopelessly scattered over 10 miles (16 km) of sea . . .

Hugo Sperrle, commander of *Luftflotte 3*, orders an all-out assault on the scattered ships. Just after 8.30 a.m. Junkers Ju 87 Stukas escorted by Messerschmitt Bf 109s assemble over the Cherbourg peninsula and set out to hunt them down.

Fighter Command is alerted and 6 squadrons of fighters, 5 from 11 Group and one from 10 Group, intercept this force and drive it off. A battle takes place above the clouds. Down below, sailors can hear but not see the fight and cannot tell what is happening. Several bombs fall aimlessly to explode in the water and a Stuka crashes into the sea. Then all is quiet. The Germans have gone, this time without sinking a ship.

At 7.55 a.m. Spitfires from 234 Squadron set out from St Eval on patrol. Because of Sperrle's build-up over Cherbourg, they are kept up as long as possible and on their way home encounter thick fog. They have been up for almost two hours and fuel is running low. Separated from the others and believing he will be unable to make it back, Vincent Parker diverts and lands elsewhere. A second Spitfire with its fuel tanks empty crashes while making a forced landing.

The RAF maintains fighter patrols over the scattered ships. There are a few minor attacks but all is quiet until midday when the Germans send out 57 Junkers Ju 87s escorted by 20 Messerschmitt Bf 110s and a top cover of about 30 Bf 109s. The radar station at Ventnor on the Isle of Wight picks up the approaching raid. Eighteen Hurricanes from three squadrons, Nos 145, 238 and 601, are in the area to meet the attack and the Spitfires of 609 Squadron are scrambled from Warmwell. A huge dogfight develops and lasts for 20 minutes . . .

No. 601 Squadron is patrolling the coast between Worthing and the Needles when 'B' Flight sights the enemy and attacks. Red Section, in which Clive Mayers is No. 3, goes into line astern and sets out after the Bf 109s. The leader attacks one German fighter which turns left, cutting across Mayers' sights. The Australian turns onto the 109's tail and fires off a five-second burst, closing in until he is only 50 yards (45 m) behind. The 109 trails black smoke and dives into the sea.

The Spitfires of 609 Squadron tangle with the close escort. Blue 3, John Curchin, attacks a Bf 110 and silences the rear gunner before breaking away. Sweeping around in a steep turn, he spots another Bf 110 and attacks it on his starboard beam. A white puff of smoke comes out of the 110's fuselage. It dived vertically, too low for it to possibly pull out. Curchin breaks away knowing that he has made his first kill.

In the afternoon the remnants of 'Peewit' assemble south of St Catherine's Point and continue. At 4.00 p.m. the *Luftwaffe* launches another attack which is again met by RAF fighters. However, several of the raiders manage to break through and cause damage.

At 4.30 p.m. flying from his new base at St Eval, Dick Power leads 5 Blenheims to assist remnants of the convoy under attack off Swanage.

MAP 2 Britain's radar
defences 1940

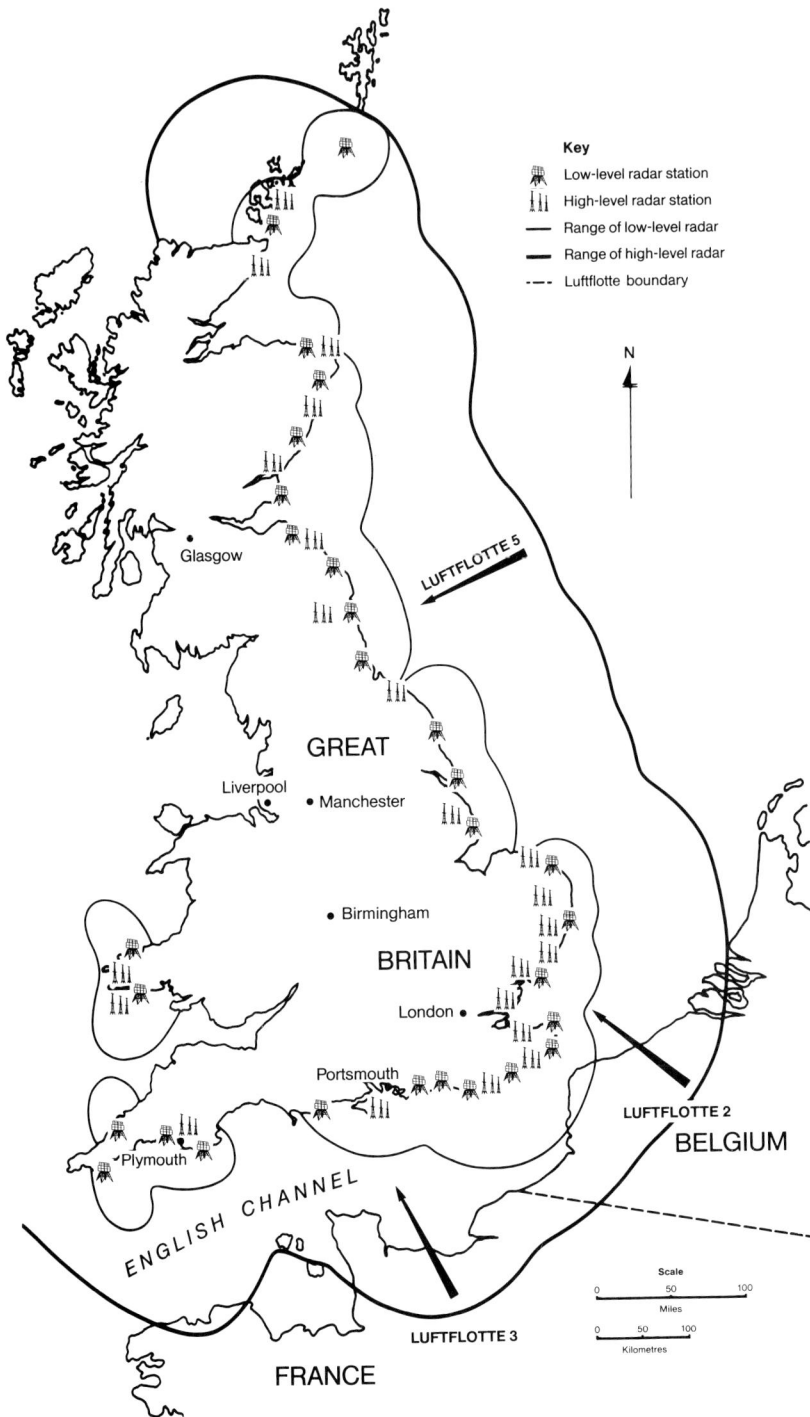

Key

Low-level radar station

High-level radar station

Range of low-level radar

Range of high-level radar

Luftflotte boundary

N

LUFTFLOTTE 5

Glasgow

GREAT

Liverpool   Manchester

Birmingham

BRITAIN

London

LUFTFLOTTE 2

BELGIUM

Portsmouth

Plymouth

ENGLISH CHANNEL

LUFTFLOTTE 3

Scale

0   50   100

Miles

0   50   100

Kilometres

FRANCE

They arrive after the Germans have gone but find ample evidence of where they have been. Two ships are on fire and heading for Poole while 5 others are well spread out heading for Portsmouth. Further out 5 more vessels can be seen, apparently on their way to Portsmouth at maximum speed. The Blenheims zigzag over the area to give cover.

Of the 23 ships which had set sail the previous night, only 4 reach their destinations unscathed. Besides the three sunk by E-boats, 4 other merchant vessels have gone down and 6 more are badly damaged.

[Because of the intensity of the air fighting some historians regard 8 August as marking the beginning of the second stage of the battle of Britain or the beginning of the battle itself. Strategically, however, it still belongs to the battle for air supremacy over the English Channel, the first part of the struggle. Perhaps it should be remembered simply as the battle of Convoy C.W.9. and a victory for the Germans.]

*

Overnight RAF Bomber Command despatches 46 Hampdens and Wellingtons to attack 7 different targets in Germany. From Lossiemouth, Henry Ross and his crew of 83 Squadron in Hampden P4402 are out between 9.05 p.m. and 3.45 a.m. They bomb their target but are unable to observe the results. Out of its 46 sorties Bomber Command loses one Hampden.

FRIDAY, 9 AUGUST

Most of England is cloudy with showers. After the hectic activity of the day before it remains relatively quiet although there are incidents involving small numbers of aircraft.

Between 8.05 a.m. and 12.25 p.m. Blenheim WR-S of 248 Squadron, flown by Charles Bennett and his crew, is on an anti-invasion patrol. In the squadron's ORB the adjutant notes the return of Douglas Peterkin from Warmwell on completion of a course.[6] He is now the squadron's senior gunner.

*

No. 266 Squadron (Frank Cale) moves from Wittering down to Tangmere in 11 Group.

[Francis Walter Cale was in the second last group of Australians to take up short-service commissions in the RAF. He attended Guildford Grammar School, Perth, Western Australia, where Dick Glyde had also been a student. He was described as an 'exuberant type' and was popularly known as 'Willie'.[7] He left Australia for England in March 1939 and after training was posted to 266 Squadron at Sutton Bridge. This unit had been reformed and was intended to be a Blenheim squadron but the Blenheims never came. In January 1940 Spitfires began to arrive. In March the squadron moved to Martlesham Heath but by 14 May the whole unit was established at Wittering.

Two other Australians in 266 Squadron were P/O J.W.B. Stevenson from Sydney and P/O J.L. Wilkie who was born in New Zealand but was living in Perth when he joined up. Wilkie was posted to 263 Squadron which took part in the ill-fated campaign in Norway. No. 266 Squadron saw its first action on 2 June over Dunkirk where Stevenson was killed in action.]

*

At a meeting of the War Cabinet, Sir Cyril Newall informs the ministers that the fighting of the previous day has been the biggest air action so far. Losses to the RAF are 19 for the destruction of 66 German aircraft, of which 52 are confirmed. The Cabinet drafts a telegram congratulating the chief-of-air staff on this fine achievement.

RAF Fighter Command under Dowding has been steadily building up its strength since June. Several new squadrons have been formed and most units have been brought up to full strength in terms of pilots and aircraft. In the north, No. 14 Group is being formed, and at Preston, Lancashire, Fighter Command's No. 9 Group exists in nucleus form.

In spite of the build-up, losses suffered during the previous day's fighting have Dowding worried. The RAF and its airfields in the south have not yet suffered a full-scale assault — one which everyone knows must soon eventuate.

The worst is yet to come . . .

Bristol Blenheim MK IF, L8679, BQ-D of 600 Squadron, Royal Auxiliary Air Force. Two Bristol Mercury VIII radial engines gave the Blenheim Mk IF long range and interim night fighter a maximum speed of 279 m.p.h. (449 km/hr at 15 000 feet (4 570 m) and its armament consisted of a 0.303 in. (0.77 cm) Browning machine-gun in the port wing; one/two 0.303 in. (0.77 cm) Vickers or Browning machine-gun(s) in the dorsal turret and a ventral pack of four 0.303 in. (0.77 cm) Browning machine-guns. L8679 was one of a batch of 50 built by Roots Securities Ltd. It was flown by Charles Pritchard during July 1940 but around 11.00 p.m. on 9 August 1940 it was damaged by British AA fire and the crew bailed out. L8679 crashed near Westgate.

SATURDAY, 10 AUGUST

Because of unfavourable weather forecasts by German meteorologists, *Reichsmarschall* Goering postpones *Adler Tag*. Air activity on both sides is minimal.

Overnight RAF Bomber Command sends nearly 60 aircraft to 9 separate targets in Germany, one of which is the synthetic oil plant at Homberg, south-west of Hamburg. Nine Hampdens of 50 Squadron are allocated this target and aircraft P4395 flown by Dereck French is over the area first at 11.30 a.m. He drops 4 bombs but is unable to see his results because of haze and cloud.

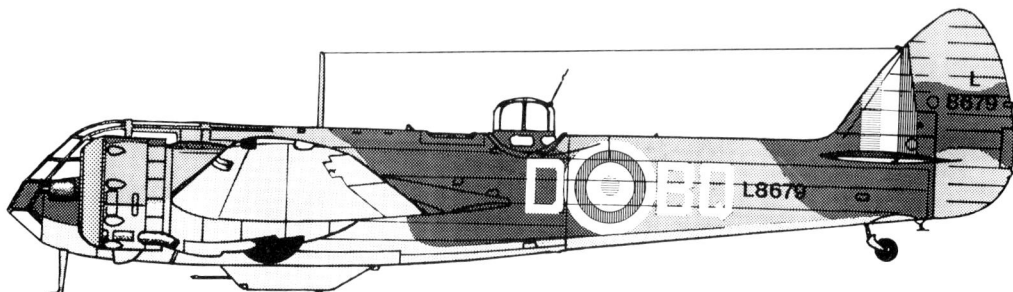

Bob Reed in Hampden L4097 arrives over Homberg at 12.25 a.m. to find ten-tenths cloud between 3 000–6 000 feet (900–1 800 m). He glides down below these and soon locates the refinery. After he drops 6 bombs and incendiaries from 2 500 feet (750 m) several large explosions occur and the sky is lit by a big fire.

The fire must have been quickly controlled because when Angus Robson of 144 Squadron in Hampden P4360 arrives around 1.30 a.m., he is unable to see the target owing to low clouds and darkness.

SUNDAY, 11 AUGUST

Dawn brings fine conditions but cloud gradually builds up throughout the day.

Aerial activity begins early with a series of marauding attacks by Messerschmitt Bf 109s near Dover. Shortly afterwards Bf 110s drop about 60 light bombs over Dover Harbour. The defences are caught by surprise and the Germans escape unscathed. Little damage is caused. The *Luftwaffe's* plan is to attract as many RAF fighters as possible into the Dover area and then mount a main strike at the Portland naval base. This is the Royal Navy's principal base close to the proposed invasion area and a target which must be neutralized.

Ventnor CH radar reports a heavy raid building up near Cherbourg peninsula. Both AVM Keith Park and AVM Sir Quinton Brand agree that this will be the main threat. Eight squadrons of Hurricanes and Spitfires are ordered up to patrol allotted areas and await instructions to intercept. No. 609 Squadron is the first to make contact with the enemy when it breaks into a group of circling Bf 110s south of Swanage.

*

At 10.08 a.m. John Cock is airborne with the rest of 'B' Flight of 87 Squadron to intercept the Germans coming to attack Portland. Dick Glyde leads the other section.

After 609 Squadron makes contact with the Bf 110s, the Hurricanes of 601 Squadron and 145 Squadron join in, while Bf 109s reinforce the German side and a huge dogfight develops. This successfully draws the British fighters away from the bombers, allowing the Junkers Ju 88s to approach Portland Bill unmolested. Eight Hurricanes from 213 Squadron are the only RAF planes to engage the bombers before they drop their bombs. Damage is extensive. Two oil storage tanks catch fire, causing a huge pall of smoke to billow out over the target. A fire breaks out in the hospital and several huts, buildings and nearby houses are destroyed.

Just after the bombing 1 and 152 Squadrons attack the remaining German fighters while 238 Squadron, followed later by 87 Squadron, makes a bid to reach the Ju 88s.

John Cock in Hurricane V7233 attacks a Bf 109. He fires several bursts and sees pieces of the German fighter break off. It is obviously badly damaged and Cock judges that it has little chance of making it back across the Channel. Meanwhile, one of the Australian's .303 inch

RAF identity card carried by John Cock when he was shot down on 11 August 1940 (photograph courtesy of Simon Parry)

(7.7 mm) machine-guns jams. Next he attacks a Ju 88 and fires off all the ammunition from his remaining seven guns. One wing of the bomber bursts into flames but Cock does not have a chance to see it crash because bullets strike the left side of his Hurricane and crash through into his cockpit. The instrument panel disintegrates and his engine begins to run roughly. One bullet nicks his left arm which is also struck by shrapnel. Looking up he glimpses the 109 which has hit him as it dives away.

The Hurricane is mortally hit and Cock has no choice but to bail out. He pulls back the hood and rolls the plane over onto its back but something catches and prevents him from falling out. Kicking at the control column, he is suddenly shot out into mid-air and instantly he pulls the ripcord. Other aircraft are whirling around and, when some of his parachute cords are cut, Cock realizes that a Bf 109 is shooting at him. A Hurricane is after the 109 and it is with satisfaction that the Australian sees the German fighter shot down without the pilot bailing out.

Cock lands in the sea and as the parachute billows on the surface of the water it acts like a sail and begins to drag him towards Portland. He wriggles out of the chute and, kicking off his boots, starts swimming towards the beach. His arm begins to throb and the left side of his Mae West, which is punctured by bullets, causes him to float crookedly in the water. He decides that it would be easier to swim if he removed his trousers.

Eventually Cock reaches Chesil Beach and as he staggers ashore he is greeted by several home guardsmen armed with shotguns. He is a sad sight, having lost his plane and his trousers and a £10 note, a recently repaid debt.

Cock will have a short stay in hospital and a month will pass before he will fly on operations again.

[On 1 June 1983 the remains of Cock's Hurricane were recovered from Portland Harbour. John, who was on hand, was interviewed by a television reporter. When asked for his thoughts he said quietly, 'I'm just glad I'm not coming up with it.']

*

The two flights from 238 Squadron separate and engage the enemy in two different areas. Leading 'B' Flight is Blue Section consisting of Stuart Walch, F/O Steborowski, an experienced Polish flier, and Sgt Gledhill. It is Gledhill's first engagement with the enemy — and his last.

Blue Section runs into a huge formation of Bf 109s and is wiped out — the Hurricanes are shot out of the sky. Walch's fighter is last seen tumbling down into Lyme Bay.

Stuart Walch is the third of those Australians who qualify for the Battle of Britain Clasp to be killed in action.

*

Just before noon Dornier Do 17s escorted by 20 Bf 110s and with an umbrella of Bf 109s attack Convoy 'Booty' off the Norfolk coast. Two ships are seriously damaged. Spitfires and Hurricanes from 74 Squadron and 17 Squadron account for 4 Bf 109s.

In the early afternoon a small convoy in the Thames Estuary becomes the target for 45 Do 17s and a *Staffel* of Ju 87 Stukas, escorted by Bf 109s. The attack is successfully driven off although 111 Squadron is hard hit by the Bf 109s and 5 Hurricanes are shot down.

*

At night the *Luftwaffe* carries out harassing raids aimed at Merseyside and continues minelaying in the Bristol Channel.

Stuart Walch, who was killed in action on 11 August 1940 (photograph courtesy of Brenda Walch).

MONDAY, 12 AUGUST

German meteorologists agree that there is likely to be fine weather and clear skies over the British Isles during the next few days so Goering's headquarters (*OKL*), orders *Luftflotten 2* and *3* to be ready for the beginning of *Adler Tag* at 7.00 a.m. on Tuesday the 13th.

The 12th dawns fine and clear except for patches of mist. Because of the weather prediction, the *OKL* decides to try and put out of action all known radar stations between the Thames Estuary and Portsmouth

Latham Carr Withall of 152 Squadron. Older than many of the other pilots, he was often called 'Granny' or 'Elsie', from his initials L.C. He is presumed to have died on 12 August 1940 after failing to return from a mission (photograph courtesy of James Coward).

and to conduct raids on the forward British airfields in preparation for the 13th. For the first time the battle will move inland from the Channel.

*

At Biggin Hill it is 610 Squadron's turn for dawn readiness while the pilots of 32 Squadron, including John Pain, relax. At 6.30 a.m. they are scrambled to patrol between Dungeness and Dover where they encounter Messerschmitt Bf 109s on a free chase, the first of the *Luftwaffe's* feints for the day. As the Spitfires take off, 32 Squadron comes to 'Readiness'.

*

Around 9.00 a.m. the Germans attack 5 radar stations. Those at Dover, Pevensey and Rye are temporarily put out of action but all are operational within 6 hours.

The next raid comes just after 10.00 a.m. Junkers Ju 87 Stukas attack two small convoys, 'Arena' and 'Agent', in the Thames Estuary.

Warned late because of the damaged radar chain, 65 Squadron, which is at Manston for the day, is not scrambled until 11.00 a.m. Leading 'A' Flight is Gordon Olive. The Spitfires are too late to prevent the bombing and they clash with the escort. Olive spots twenty Bf 109s ahead and above. He leads his section into a climb and wings it around onto the rearmost aircraft. Selecting a target, he fires a five-second burst at one Messerschmitt which breaks away with pieces falling off it. After attacking two other Messerschmitts, he pursues a third across the Channel but because he cannot close the distance he has to turn back. On the way home he sights yet another 109 and he tries to intercept but, because of the German fighter's built-up speed, he is easily outdistanced.

*

At Biggin Hill 32 Squadron is still at 'Readiness' as news of the morning's events filters through. It is not good. Not only has the *Luftwaffe* put out of action several radar stations and dive-bombed two convoys in the Thames Estuary, it has also made a successful raid on Portsmouth. Pain and the other pilots realize that the situation could become serious if the Germans continue this pressure throughout the afternoon.

*

The raid on Portsmouth is carried out by about 100 Junkers Ju 88s escorted by 120 Bf 110s and a high escort of 25 Bf 109s. The Ju 88s split into two groups, the largest consisting of over 70 bombers, and stage the attack on Portsmouth while the smaller force of about 20 aircraft makes for the Isle of Wight, its target being the Ventnor radar station. Arriving over the Isle, they break formation and one by one carry out steep dive-bombing attacks. They succeed in hitting the radar site with 15 bombs, demolishing practically every building in the compound.

British fighters do not succeed in engaging the Ju 88s until they are escaping over the Isle's south coast. On patrol over St Catherine's Point are the Spitfires of 152 Squadron and these dive to the attack while 609 Squadron engages the escorting Bf 109s and becomes involved in a vigorous dogfight over the Needles. Four Ju 88s are shot down into the sea while two others are damaged.

Pilots of 234 Squadron with one of their Spitfires at St Eval in August 1940. Pat Hughes is seated at front left and Vincent Parker is third from the right on the aircraft's starboard (right) wing. Parker was shot down over the English Channel shortly after this photograph was taken. Pat Hughes was killed in action on 7 September 1940 (photograph courtesy of Bill Hughes).

When 152 Squadron arrives home the pilots are jubilant over their successes but the joy is dampened by the fact that two of their planes have not returned. One of these is Spitfire P9456, the machine flown by Carr Withall. This quietly spoken Australian flight commander will be sorely missed.

F/Lt Latham Carr Withall is the fourth Australian deemed eligible for the Battle of Britain Clasp to be killed in action.

*

A serious situation is building up at Manston airfield. Located at the mouth of the Thames Estuary, it is in the front line and everyone knows that it will be one of the very first airfields to be hit when the *Luftwaffe's* assaults begin in earnest. Besides being a forward satellite airfield for the Biggin Hill Sector, it is also frequented by fighter squadrons based at North Weald, Hornchurch, Kenley and Northolt because of its key strategic position. It is also the home airfield for 600 (City of London) Squadron, a Bristol Blenheim night fighter unit, one of whose flight commanders is Charles Pritchard.

Manston has been busy since the days of Dunkirk. At that time, it had been used for refuelling, rearming and feeding squadrons which flew in from various other stations. They would operate from Manston during the day or night and afterwards return to their own bases. Since those days, the pace has not really slackened and at the beginning of June the first German bombs had fallen on the airfield. To meet the inevitable onslaught, Manston's defences had been strengthened. July had been a month of increasing pressure on the ground crews because of the air battles over the Channel convoys. Visiting pilots, fatigued by combat and tension had sometimes had bitter clashes with the equally tense and overworked ground personnel. Such things have eroded morale and inevitably the *Luftwaffe* must soon come . . .

The Spitfires of 65 Squadron are refuelled and rearmed. F/Lt Sammy Saunders, who is in temporary command, asks permission to move the aircraft to Manston's south-east corner after a wind shift and is refused by the controller. He discusses the situation with Gordon Olive, the 'A' Flight commander, and both men are agree that they are in a hopeless down-wind take-off position.

Suddenly the phone inside the dispersal hut rings and its message makes all pilots race to their machines. As they taxi forward, the radio crackles a warning of an air raid approaching the airfield. Seconds later, Messerschmitt Bf 110s sweep in over the field, bombing and strafing. At the same time, 18 Dornier Do 17s of KG 2 appear overhead and make a bomb run. Olive can see clouds of smoke and chalk dust bursting into the air as the bombs explode and the Spitfires taxi into a position to turn into the wind. Opening the throttle and pulling the emergency boost, Olive and the others hurtle across the field for the fastest take-off of their careers. One hangar erupts, shattering debris in a cloud of flame and smoke. Bombs explode one by one in a line which seems about to overtake the speeding Spitfires. Then, almost unexpectedly, they are airborne. Looking back as he climbs away, Olive sees the last Spitfire emerge from the huge billowing cloud of smoke and dust. Almost everyone is off safely.

The raid lasts 5 minutes but Manston has disappeared under a great mushroom cloud of smoke. The German crews believe that the airfield has been totally destroyed but as the smoke clears a different story is revealed. Two hangars have been damaged, workshops destroyed and the aerodrome has been pitted and scarred by bomb craters. It is declared unserviceable until next day but, even so, 65 and 54 Squadrons can still operate.

More damaging is the blow to morale. Many of the ground personnel refuse to leave the bomb shelters. They have had enough, their nerves have cracked and they refuse to come out for days, in spite of threats, orders and pleading by their officers.

*

Shortly afterwards, 32 Squadron is ordered to Hawkinge, another forward airfield. Perhaps their turn is coming.

The *Luftwaffe* keeps the pressure on in the afternoon with a series of three smaller raids. At 2.30 p.m. No. 32 Squadron is scrambled to patrol over Dover-Hawkinge but no enemy aircraft are sighted.

At 4.50 p.m. the 12 Hurricanes are ordered up again to patrol the same area. Five minutes before the patrol is due to end Do 17s, escorted by Bf 109s, are sighted heading for Dover. As the British fighters close in to intercept, a similar enemy force is spotted closer at hand so they have to alter their plan of attack. In the ensuing battle, 32 Squadron claims 11 enemy aircraft destroyed for the loss of one Hurricane.

Returning for fuel and ammunition, 5 Hurricanes go back to Hawkinge while the remainder return to Biggin Hill. At Hawkinge the pilots are dismayed to see the smoking remains of two hangars and numerous bomb craters. Nobody has enough fuel to go back to Biggin Hill, and Manston is out of the question. There is no other choice; they must land. Threading their way between the craters, they manage to come down safely.

As they climb out of their machines, approaching aero engines are heard — more Dorniers! When the pilots look around again the ground crew who were servicing their planes have gone. They have run for cover, leaving the pilots standing, but as the first bombs fall they too flee for the trenches.

Five minutes later it is all over. The men emerge and an inspection of their aircraft reveals that no Hurricanes have been hit.

*

It has been a good day for the *Luftwaffe* and German radio announces that heavy damage has been caused on the British mainland and claims the destruction of 71 RAF aircraft, including all of 65 Squadron at Manston. Actually 65 Squadron is alive and well back at Hornchurch.

*

Owing to the attacks on convoys 'Arena' and 'Agent' in the Thames Estuary that morning, 266 Squadron (Frank Cale) is moved from Tangmere to Eastchurch. Its role there is to thwart future anti-shipping attacks.

Frank Cale's squadron is not the only unit moving into Eastchurch. The Fairey Battles of 142 Squadron (John Hewson) have been bombing German barge concentrations in the Channel Ports from their base at Binbrook, Lincolnshire, but today they shift forward to shorten the range.

[The day's aerial battles are obviously a foretaste of what is to come and most historians consider this to be the end of the preliminary stage of the battle of Britain.

German claims for the day are somewhat optimistic. Of the fighter airfields attacked, all are operational again in a matter of hours with the exception of Manston which will be out of action for 24 hours. RAF Fighter Command has suffered 22 casualties. The attacks on the 6 radar stations have put one, Ventnor, out of action and it will remain so for several days.

Goering has promised Hitler that he will begin the full air assault on the RAF as soon as he has a forecast of three consecutive days of fine weather. During the evening he confirms that the all-out attack on RAF Fighter Command is to begin the next day.]

*

With darkness, the *Luftwaffe* continues light raids and minelaying sorties.

Bomber Command reciprocates by sending nearly 80 aircraft to attack 5 targets in Germany, bomb German-held airfields in France and carry out minelaying.

On this night the RAF launches one of its most dramatic raids of the early part of the war.

Earlier in August, 24 Handley Page Hampdens from 49 Squadron had made a successful attack on a bridge over the Ems Canal and it was then decided that another raid should be risked on the aqueduct carrying the vital Dortmund Canal over the River Ems.

A high precision low-level night attack is necessary and so 10 of the most experienced crews in Bomber Command are selected from the best squadrons in 5 Group. They have come from Nos 49 and 83 Squadrons and are specially trained for the attack. For a week they have practised by moonlight on the canals in the east Midlands of England, dropping practice bombs on mock-ups of the target, and studying table-top models of the Dortmund-Ems area. Each crew has known that a final assault force of only 5 aircraft would be chosen.

A reconnaissance over the Dortmund-Ems area on the night of 11–12 August by F/Lt R.A.B. Learoyd has revealed that the German defences have been strengthened by searchlights and light flak units and that more gun emplacements are being prepared. The attack has to be launched as soon as possible — tonight!

After 8.00 p.m. the 5 selected crews take off. The Hampdens are piloted by S/Ldr James Pitcairn-Hill DFC, F/O Ellis Henry Ross DFC, F/Lt Allen Mulligan, F/Lt Matthews and F/Lt 'Babe' Learoyd. Ross and Mulligan are the Australians in the group.

It is a good night for flying, cloudy with a half moon, and the journey to the target is uneventful. Cloud continues right up to the target area and then the Hampdens emerge into a clear moonlit sky. It is 11.00 p.m. The attack is scheduled to begin in 10 minutes. The Hampdens are to make their bomb-runs one by one at two-minute intervals so that the raid will be over by 11.18 p.m. Each bomb has been fitted with a ten-minute delay-action fuse which means that the first explosion should occur at 11.20 p.m. — if the last plane (Learoyd's) starts late, it risks being caught up in the first explosion.

Pitcairn-Hill attacks first, drops his bombs on target and climbs away although his aircraft is badly peppered by flak.

Ross is next but as he brings Hampden P4410 in low it meets heavy anti-aircraft fire and bursts into flames. He and his crew have no chance as the stricken bomber crashes into the ground.

It is now 'Mull' Mulligan's turn and like Ross he comes in low. Again the bomber is caught by concentrated ack-ack fire and its port engine is set on fire. Pulling back on the controls, Mulligan sends his Hampden into a steep climb up to a 1 000 feet (300 m) and holds it level while his crew bails out. Then he too jumps. His aircraft, Hampden P4340, crashes in flames.

The fourth Hampden makes its run and like the others it is heavily hit. Matthews has to feather one engine but he manages to release his load before escaping into the darkness.

Lastly comes Learoyd and, in spite of what has happened to his comrades, he presses home his attack. His machine, too, is badly shot up but he succeeds in bombing accurately and coaxing his damaged plane out over the North Sea. The first explosion occurs on schedule as the three remaining bombers limp home.

The raid is a major success and the aqueduct is breached. Water flows out of the canal and it will be 14 days before the damage can be

Four Australians — Raymond Earl, Robert Reed, Angus Robson, and Ellis Ross — were killed flying Handley Page Hampden bombers between July and October 1940 (Imperial War Museum photograph CH 3478).

repaired. River traffic will be seriously disrupted and raw materials for the Rhineland's heavy industry will be unable to get through. Also blocked is barge traffic going through to the invasion ports. The raid on the Dortmund-Ems Canal is the forerunner of future special attacks, such as the famous dambusters' raid, which will come later in the war.

[F/Lt Roderick Learoyd will receive the Victoria Cross for his determined action and S/Ldr J. Pitcairn-Hill DFC, who will soon be killed in action, will be awarded the DSO. When it is discovered that Allen Mulligan is alive and safe in a POW camp he will be awarded the DFC].

F/O Ellis Henry Ross DFC, known as 'Rossy' by his comrades in 83 Squadron, is one of the Australians listed on the Battle of Britain Roll of Honour at Westminster Abbey.

TUESDAY, 13 AUGUST

ADLER TAG

On this fateful morning the weather is mainly fair but with widespread early mist and drizzle.

German bombers begin taking off ready for their first major assault on British air bases. They are in the air forming up when there is a last-minute signal from Goering's Headquarters postponing the attack until the afternoon in the hope that the weather will clear. Frantic radio messages recalling all airborne formations are not received by all and 74 Dornier Do 17s from KG 2 set off without their escort.

At 6.30 a.m. the Hurricanes of 601 Squadron are scrambled from Tangmere. Clive Mayers is flying as Red 3 in 'A' Flight. They head east and then swing north. After 10 minutes about 24 Ju 88s, escorted by Bf 110s and 109s, are sighted. The German fighters are stepped up in tiers, seemingly all the way up into the sun. The Hurricanes fly alongside the bombers and when they are slightly ahead the squadron leader gives the order to attack.

Mayers starts to make his own run but he is wary as a formation of Bf 110s begins to dive. Waiting for the right instant he executes a climbing right turn into them. From almost head-on he presses his firing button and sees part of the roof and fuselage of one Messerschmitt break off. Swinging around in a tight turn he finds a Ju 88 below and dives after it. He fires a five-second burst and the bomber bursts into flames. Mayers is now alone and he searches the sky to locate his section. He spots 5 Ju 88s making for France and climbs up to intercept. He makes a beam attack, sweeping the whole formation from front to rear. One bomber falls behind and seeks safety in cloud cover. Mayers follows, manages to relocate his prey and fires off his remaining ammunition. With one engine burning, the German plane loses height.

Harried by three squadrons of British fighters, the Ju 88s miss their targets, disperse into small groups and make a disorderly retreat back to France.

'B' Flight of 87 Squadron arrives from Exeter too late to join the main battle but the Hurricanes find a stray Ju 88 and shoot it down. While reforming, the pilots notice white smoke coming from the engine of Dick Glyde's fighter. Return fire from the Junkers has hit his glycol tank. When they look around again his Hurricane is gone.

*

The unescorted Do 17s of KG 2 are intercepted by only two sections of Hurricanes from 111 Squadron and successfully bomb their targets, the naval base at Sheerness and the Coastal Command air base at Eastchurch.

Eastchurch in particular is heavily hit, receiving over a 100 high-explosive bombs and incendiaries. A direct hit destroys the operations block, injuring 48 personnel. Sixteen are killed in the airmen's quarters. All Frank Cale and the pilots of the newly-arrived 266 Squadron can do is run for cover; they have not even been ordered up. The men of 142 Squadron (John Hewson) do likewise. Every hangar is hit and the one allocated to 266 is set on fire. Firefighters manage to remove three Spitfires and two Magister trainers but one Spitfire is totally destroyed as is most of the squadron's ammunition and equipment. German bomber crews will claim the destruction of 10 Spitfires but it is 35 Squadron, Coastal Command, which is hardest hit when 5 of its Blenheims are reduced to wreckage. The airfield will be inoperable for most of the day. Four of the attacking Dorniers are shot down and several others damaged. Harry Hardman manages to score hits on one bomber before it escapes.

*

Confusion continues among *Luftwaffe* units. At 11.40 a.m. British radar picks up more than 20 aircraft apparently on course for Portland. They are, in fact, 28 Messerschmitt Bf 110s from I/ZG 2 which were to have escorted Junkers Ju 88s from KG 54 on a raid to bomb Portland Harbour. KG 54 had received the cancellation message but I/ZG 2 had not. Instead of finding friendly German bombers they meet two squadrons of hostile British fighters.

Clive Mayers of 601 Squadron is up again, still flying as Red 3, and he spots the enemy south of Portland. The Messerschmitts are already hotly engaged by other Hurricanes from 238 Squadron and have formed a defensive circle. 'A' Flight goes into line astern and the leader gives the order to attack.

Mayers selects a target and delivers a burst of machine-gun fire from almost head-on but it seems to have no effect. He comes round for a second attack, singles out one Messerschmitt and fires from dead astern for 8 seconds, stopping at 50 yards (45 m) when it seems that they must collide. One of the 110's rudders breaks off and it dives away out of control. Suddenly Mayers' Hurricane is hit and there is pain in his right leg. His first reaction is to pull back on his control column to get out of the line of fire but there is no response. Then he blacks out . . .

Next thing he is falling through the air, tearing off his flying helmet. His flying boots and socks have already gone. Giddy from lack of oxygen, he pulls the ripcord and his parachute cracks open level at 7 000 feet (2 100 m). As he floats down between cloud layers a Bf 110 fires a snap burst at him but misses. Shortly afterwards he lands in the water offshore from Portland.

*

After a lull *Adler Tag's* planned attacks take place between 3.45 and 5.00 p.m. with raids on Portland, Southampton, Kent and the Thames Estuary. The Germans make a simultaneous three-pronged assault. At 3.30 p.m. radar picks up several larger raids approaching on a 40-mile (65 km) front from the direction of Cherbourg peninsula and the Channel Islands. These formations consist of about 120 Junkers Ju 88s and 30 Messerschmitt Bf 110s. Further west there are 27 Junkers Ju 87 Stukas of II/*Staffel* G2. Believing British defences to be fully alert because of the earlier raids, these two forces are spearheaded by 30 Messerschmitt Bf 109s whose job is to lure RAF fighters away from the incoming bombers.

The *Luftwaffe* is right; Fighter Command is ready. Splitting up into sections, 152 Squadron engages the Bf 109s near Abbotsbury but the

German fighters are already short of fuel and do not stay to fight. Instead of drawing off the British fighters they have only stirred up a hornet's nest for the approaching Ju 88s.

Harried all the way to their target of Southampton, the main force of Ju 88s bombs successfully at 4.05 p.m. causing serious damage to dock facilities and numerous casualties in the residential area. However, Southampton's Spitfire factory is hardly damaged.

Meanwhile 40 Ju 88s have turned north looking for Middle Wallop aerodrome but have difficulty in finding their target. Although some bombs fall on Middle Wallop village, most of them land on Andover airfield by mistake. A German plane almost crashes on top of an AIF detention camp at Bulford. Guards and prisoners alike scatter through the wire. Australian engineers camped at Hedge End are asked to help search for German airmen who have bailed out nearby.

Ian Bayles is leading White Section of 152 Squadron and, coming through cloud south of Portland, he sights 20 to 30 Bf 110s in a defensive circle. After climbing to a favourable position he leads a dive through the orbiting formation and fires at a 110 from directly above but does not observe any strikes. Pulling into a climb he zooms up and positions himself for an attack on the last machine in the circle. He closes in firing bursts from 300 yards (275 m). Crossfire from the German planes is heavy but inaccurate. The 110 he is attacking trails smoke from its port engine but suddenly his Spitfire lurches as if struck by a bullet and Bayles breaks away.

At the same time 609 Squadron, west of Dorchester, discovers 20 Ju 87 Stukas without any covering fighters. P/O Mick Miller is flying as Yellow 2 in 'A' Flight. He follows Yellow 1 down onto the nearest group and closes in on a vic of three. He opens fire at 300 yards (275 m) and one Stuka hurtles down with black smoke billowing from its engine. In another stern attack he singles out three planes which are flying in an extremely tight vic and opens up on the leader at a range of 300 yards (275 m). All the German rear gunners return fire. Miller yaws the Spitfire slightly from side to side, spraying all three with bullets.

The Stuka formation has been cut to pieces.

*

Away to the east the third prong of the German assault strikes at 11 Group in two waves of heavily escorted Stukas from Kesselring's *Luftflotte 2*. They come in around 5.00 p.m. with two targets, Detling and Rochester airfields. The assault is spearheaded by Messerschmitt Bf 109s of JG 26 flying well ahead on a free chase to draw off the British fighters. These attract 65 Squadron which is still operating at Manston.

Gordon Olive and his Spitfires are at 19 000 feet (5 800 m) when they spot 20 Bf 109s flying at the same level. Leading off with his section, Olive engages one group in a twisting dogfight during which he notices 4 more 109s above to the east. Not wanting to leave them unmolested he climbs up and comes in behind the rear machine without being noticed. He touches the firing button. Almost instantly there is an explosion and the German fighter falls in flames. The remaining three 109s swiftly dive away towards France.

While returning to Manston Olive finds 4 more Messerschmitts at

26 000 feet (8 000 m). Again he climbs after them, approaching from a down-sun position. He selects a victim and within seconds another German fighter explodes. The other 109s have disappeared. Olive starts to descend but sights another large formation of 109s on the same level. They are turning to attack. Ramming the throttle open and using his built-up speed Olive zooms up into the sun, rolls out and attacks the nearest of his pursuers, forcing him to turn away. Because of his advantage of speed and height the Germans cannot catch him so they give up the chase.

There are too many enemy planes about so Olive dives for cloud but on the way he comes across a stray Bf 109 flying back towards France. With his air speed indicator registering 430 Olive sweeps in after his victim, firing off a four-second burst. The Messerschmitt sheds debris but remains in the air and heads for safety in the clouds. It has taken brutal punishment.

Because of the fighter engagement 40 Ju 87s reach Detling. At 5.16 p.m. they scream down on the airfield in well-aimed dive-bomb attacks. The results are devastating. The messes and cookhouses are all destroyed and all the hangars set on fire. Twenty-two aircraft (none of them fighters) are destroyed and 67 people are killed. The *Luftwaffe* has actually made a tragic mistake because Detling is not a Fighter Command airfield so the defence capability of 11 Group is not impaired.

Because of cloud the Stukas heading for Rochester cannot find their target and while turning back they draw the attention of Hurricanes from 56 Squadron. The Germans scatter into small groups, seeking individual targets of opportunity as they fly back across Kent.

[*The last German aircraft disappears off British radar screens around 6.00 p.m. The* **Luftwaffe** *will claim 84 RAF fighters destroyed while the British will claim that they have shot down 64 German aircraft. In fact the Germans have lost 46 planes while Fighter Command has lost 13. On the ground the RAF has had a further 47 aircraft destroyed but only one is a fighter.*]

*

After three fruitless interception scrambles throughout the day 234 Squadron (Pat Hughes and Vincent Parker) flies its Spitfires from St Eval to Middle Wallop to replace 238 Squadron which is to swap back to St Eval. Before leaving S/Ldr R.E. Barnett relinquishes command of 234 Squadron. Under his leadership morale in the squadron has been steadily declining and Hughes finds the men turning to him for leadership.

*

Two Australian pilots, Clive Mayers and Dick Glyde, have not returned to their bases. Mayers is on his way home to 601 Squadron. After being rescued from the sea, he was taken to Portland Naval Hospital where his shrapnel wounds were dressed. As they are superficial he returns to Tangmere.

At Exeter there is no news of Dick Glyde in spite of an air search. He is never seen again. He is the fifth Australian deemed eligible for the Battle of Britain Clasp to be killed in action.

*

Thirty-five Whitley bombers are despatched by RAF Bomber Command to attack Milan and Turin in the first raid on Italy since the French collapse in June. At the same time over 60 other aircraft are sent to targets in Germany.

At Lindholme Dereck French is one of three pilots detailed to bomb the Junkers factory at Bernberg. He and his crew take off at 9.01 p.m. but their radio transmitter refuses to function so French aborts the mission.

As Dereck French is taxying in, Angus Robson is taking off from Hemswell in Hampden P4360 bound for the same target. When he arrives bad weather makes location of the factory difficult. Only one bomb is dropped before Robson decides to turn for home. Twenty-five minutes later he is over Brunswick and he and his crew bomb searchlights and anti-aircraft guns.

WEDNESDAY, 14 AUGUST

The three Spitfires of Red Section in 234 Squadron's 'A' Flight, led by Vincent Parker, are the first to go on patrol from their new base at Middle Wallop. After an uneventful flight they return to base.

In the north at Sumburgh both Clarrie Bennett and Lewis Hamilton of 248 Squadron (Blenheims) log their first anti-invasion patrols. These are carried out day and night and form a link in the long interlocking chain of security patrols which are continually being flown all along the eastern and southern shores of Britain. Now they have been stepped up because of the *Luftwaffe's* increased air activity on the 12th and 13th. In the south-west the Sunderlands of 10 Squadron, RAAF, operating from Mount Batten, make up a link at the opposite end of the chain as they patrol to cover possible enemy excursions from Brest peninsula. These patrols are insurance against surprise attack and will remain an essential commitment for Coastal Command units until the danger passes.

*

During the morning the Defence Committee meets to discuss 'Pilot Wastage' and ministers are told the situation in cold, statistical terms:

> . . . the postulated wastage, which was taken as a basis for planning the production of pilots from training establishments, was at present fixed at 746 per month . . . this figure was reduced to 650 net by excluding those pilots who returned subsequently to duty. On the other hand, the actual figures for loss of pilots, in action and accidents, for June/July were as follows:
>
> June — 318 killed, 43 wounded, total 361;
> July — 208 killed, 70 wounded, total 278.[8]

It is obvious to those present that if, as the air fighting intensifies, actual wastage begins to exceed the Air Ministry's postulated wastage

Richard Glyde of 87 Squadron. Dick Glyde did not return from a mission on 13 August 1940 and is presumed to have died on that date (photograph courtesy of Robert Glyde).

and therefore the training output, the end result would be the decline of Fighter Command's strength and then . . . disaster.

At today's meeting of the War Cabinet the ministers are informed that the air raids of the day before have been the heaviest yet experienced.

*

Sir Henry Tizard, scientific adviser to the chief of air staff, leaves for the USA. He is taking to Washington top secret data on the latest developments in British technology which must not be allowed to fall into German hands should England be invaded. Amongst the confidential information being carried are details of Alan Butement's work on GCI radar and radar proximity fuses for anti-aircraft shells, plus the results of research into microwave radar transmitters, essential for airborne radar, the work of Marcus Oliphant's team of scientists at Birmingham University.

*

A new commanding officer takes over 65 Squadron. He is S/Ldr A.L. Holland who had been working at the Air Ministry. Gordon Olive and Sammy Saunders can hardly conceal their disappointment when they learn that he has never flown a Spitfire.

In spite of the previous day's fighting the morning passes quietly and it is almost midday before radar detects a build-up over Boulogne and Calais.

No. 65 Squadron is again operating from Manston where the situation is far from good. The ground personnel are still in a state of siege, remaining below ground in shelters where they have been since the bombing of 12 August. Because of this the men of No. 600 Blenheim night fighter Squadron, among them Charles Pritchard, help to refuel and rearm the visiting day fighters. They have also designed some of their own defences. The so-called 'Armadillo' is a truck converted to a primitive armoured car through the addition of concrete sides and a machine-gun fixed in the centre; and the 'Sheep dipper' consists of a set of Browning machine-guns mounted on a pole. These will soon come in handy.

At 11.50 a.m. 4 squadrons of Hurricanes and Spitfires are ordered to intercept 80 Junkers Ju 87 Stukas from Kesselring's *Luftflotte 2* with a heavy escort of Messerschmitt Bf 109s. At the same time, two *Staffeln* of *Hauptmann* Walter Rubensdorffer's Erpr. G1. 210 (Test Group 210) Messerschmitt Bf 110 fighter-bombers are on their way with one specific target: Manston.

So numerous are the German fighters that one *Staffel* takes its time attacking barrage balloons over Dover. The burning balloons are seen by 65 Squadron which proceeds to investigate. As they approach Gordon Olive sights 10 or 12 Bf 109s approximately 2 000 feet (600 m) above. Staying as much as possible in their blind spot, the Australian leads his flight up to engage them. Selecting a target on the edge of the formation, he closes in and fires off a five-second burst. The stricken Messerschmitt rocks violently and pieces break off. In the *mêlée*, Olive notices two Bf 109s above him and the leader seems intent on lining up a Spitfire. Pulling back on the control column he fires just as it is about to attack. Startled, the 109 breaks away and seeks cloud cover.

Olive is now alone and below he sees another 12 Bf 109s. Apparently he has not been seen and is well positioned for an attack. Diving swiftly he sends off a four-second burst, spraying as many enemy planes as he can and, before they react, he hurtles down into the safety of nearby clouds.

Meanwhile Rubensdorffer's fighter-bombers arrive over Manston and attack. They are met by a withering anti-aircraft barrage. On the edge of the airfield the Royal Artillery, manning a Bofors 40 mm gun, swings into action. So too do the machine-guns manned by 600 Squadron's personnel.

At 600 feet (180 m) a 40 mm shell smashes into *Uffz*. Hans Steding's Messerschmitt Bf 110, tearing off the whole tailplane. With its engines screaming the 110 slithers and bounces across the airfield to finally cartwheel and crash. Steding is killed but his gunner had managed to bail out.

The bombing continues and 4 hangars burst into flames. Three of 600 Squadron's Blenheims are destroyed and the dispersals are reduced to shambles. A second Messerschmitt Bf 110 is shot down by the improvized anti-aircraft guns.

When they return the Spitfires of 65 Squadron have to thread their way through a multitude of new bomb craters as they land.

*

Late in the afternoon Sperrle's *Luftflotte 3* attacks. The assault takes the form of 9 scattered and relatively small raids designed to spread 10 Group's defences. Advancing on the south coast over a 100-mile (160 km) front, the tactic is successful and AVM Brand's squadrons are obliged to scatter to meet the oncoming German bombers. Inevitably, some groups avoid the British fighters and reach their targets, one of which is Middle Wallop airfield.

No. 234 Squadron shares the airfield with 609 Squadron and 604 Blenheim night fighter Squadron but it is 234's turn to be on 'Readiness'. At 5.45 p.m. Vincent Parker's section is scrambled, followed 5 minutes later by Pat Hughes and 'B' Flight. One section from 609 is also up.

Ten minutes later three Heinkel He 111s appear over the airfield and unload their bombs. A single Junkers Ju 88 conducts a dive-bombing attack. In the same instant three airmen, realizing that the doors of 609 Squadron's hangar are open, run to close them to protect the Spitfires inside. They are cranking them shut when the hangar is struck by a bomb which blasts the doors down, killing them instantly. Inside the hangar, three Blenheims and several Spitfires are destroyed.

While the bombs are falling two 609 Squadron Spitfires manage to take off. They overtake the Heinkels and shoot down the leading bomber. Another 609 pilot, already airborne, tackles the Ju 88 which crashes and explodes near Romsey.

*

Nightfall brings the usual small scattered raids over southern England but British defences are keyed up for a possible heavy attack on Liverpool following the interception of German radio signals. RAF counter-measures include patrols by Blenheim night fighters, some of them carrying airborne radar, and several single-seat day fighters.

From Middle Wallop Pat Hughes flies an uneventful night patrol at 10.00 p.m. The expected raid does not eventuate.

At the same time RAF Bomber Command is not inactive. Among others 8 Hampdens from 50 Squadron carry out attacks on the oil refinery at Paullac near Bordeaux. Bob Reed, at the controls of Hampden P2124, takes off from Lindholme at 9.17 p.m. Three minutes later Dereck French follows in Hampden P4417 . . .

THURSDAY, 15 AUGUST

Dereck French is the first of the two Australians to arrive over the oil refinery at Paullac at 1.26 a.m. He makes his bomb-run at 5 500 feet (1 400 m) and drops 6 bombs on storage tanks. After vivid explosions fires spread swiftly.

Reed and his crew locate the target 14 minutes later and they bomb from 1 500 feet (450 m), their stick of 6 bombs falling on buildings and large tanks in the southern corner of the refinery. The whole area is heavily damaged.

*

Because German forecasters have predicted poor weather for the day Goering summons his senior air corps commanders to analyse the *Adler Tag* attacks.

With daylight the predictions seem to be correct and returning German bomber crews report extensive cloud over England. However, later in the morning, the skies clear and conditions also improve over northern France. Orders are issued for all *Luftflotten* to come to readiness in accordance with the plans outlined yesterday.

*

On the British side there is little indication of the huge air battles about to take place.

At 11.00 a.m. a two-pronged attack is picked up on radar. The first, consisting of 60 Junkers Ju 87s escorted by Messerschmitt Bf 110s, makes a heavy dive-bombing attack on the forward airfield at Lympne, putting it out of action for 48 hours.

The second raid of over 20 Stukas heads for Hawkinge with a strong escort of Messerschmitt Bf 109s of JG 26. Before the British can intercept, the Stukas are already diving on the airfield and they inflict heavy damage. The unintended severing of power cables, which puts the Dover radar system out of action, poses a most serious problem for the defences.

As the dive-bombers withdraw the British fighters pounce and 7 are claimed shot down. JG 26 responds by engaging the interceptors and the RAF loses two Spitfires and two Hurricanes.

*

Believing RAF Fighter Command to be almost exclusively concentrated in the south, the Germans launch a two-pronged daylight assault in the north. What they do not realize is that several experienced fighter squadrons are in the north 'resting'. Stationed at Ack-

Werner Restemeyer of 1/ZG 76 was probably shot down by Desmond Sheen over north-east England on 15 August 1940 (Bundesarchiv-Militararchiv photograph).

lington are 72 and 79 Squadrons while further south, at Church Fenton, is 73 Squadron.

At 10.00 a.m. 63 Heinkel He 111s from I and III/KG 26 take off from Stavanger/Sola in Norway. Their main targets are the northern British airfields of Dishforth and Asworth, with secondary targets listed as Newcastle, Sunderland and Middlebrough.

Shortly afterwards 21 Messerschmitt Bf 110s of I/ZG 76 stationed at Stavanger/Forus take off to escort the Heinkels. Leading the formation is the *Gruppe Kommandeur* Hptmn Werner Restemeyer. Specially installed in his aircraft is complex radio intercepting equipment with which he proposes to listen in on British transmissions and pass information onto his own formations for effective countermeasures. In effect he has created a flying command post. Underneath the fuselage of each Messerschmitt is attached a fat, bomb-like 1 000 litre drop tank nicknamed a *Dachshund* to enable the escorts to fly well beyond their normal range and accompany the bombers all the way across the North Sea.

Further south 50 unescorted Junkers Ju 88s of KG 30 are flying from Aalborg in Denmark, heading for RAF Station, Driffield.

Just after midday the northern-most raid is detected on radar. The controller contacts Acklington ordering 72 Squadron to 'Readiness'. Five minutes later it is scrambled. In the same instant the incoming raid swings southwards; the Germans have corrected a navigation error, bringing them head-on towards the orbiting Spitfires.

In temporary command of 72 Squadron is F/Lt Edward Graham. Des Sheen leads Green Flight consisting of two sections, each of two aircraft, which patrol as rearguard on either flank. Information from the controller keeps coming in, each time presenting a more dramatic picture. At first 10 bandits are reported. A few minutes later this jumps to 30 and then to 50, proving the inaccuracy of numerical estimates by radar at this stage of the war. The true picture is further confused by a diversionary mock raid by Heinkel He 115 seaplanes further north.

At last the enemy is sighted some 30 miles (50 km) east of the Farne Islands and the radio erupts into excited chatter. The British pilots identify the aircraft in the enormous broad-fronted formation as Heinkel He 111s followed by Junkers Ju 88s with Messerschmitt Bf 110s bringing up the rear. They have in fact encountered the force from Norway containing Heinkels and Messerschmitts but no Ju 88s — these are coming from Denmark to a target 100 miles further south. Leaving Sheen's Green Section to cover, Graham leads Blue and Red Sections down to attack on the starboard flank.

Apparently the Germans do not spot the Spitfires until the last minute and when they do, numerous objects, taken to be bombs, are seen to fall away from their planes into the sea. They are the long-range belly tanks carried by the Messerschmitts but Werner Restemeyer is unable to jettison his *Dachshund* which, although empty, is still full of highly explosive fumes.

The Bf 110s form defensive circles while the Heinkels split up into two major groups, one going towards the Clyde and the other towards Newcastle.

Sheen now orders Green Section into the fight. The Australian makes for a formation of 7 German aircraft, which he wrongly identifies as Junkers Ju 88s, and singles out one which carries what appears

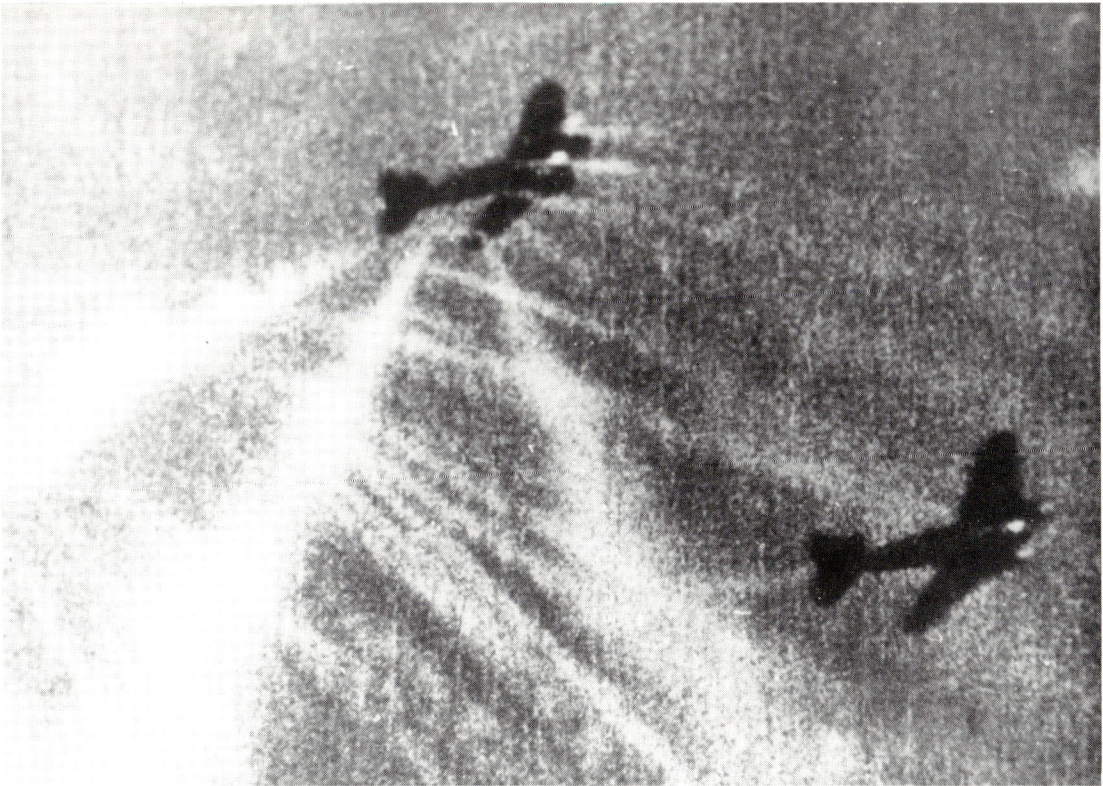

A firing pass on a formation of Heinkel He 111s. Bill Millington shot down at least three of these bombers on 15 August when he found himself alone against a large formation of them (Imperial War Museum photograph).

to be a very large bomb under its fuselage. He closes in from astern and presses the firing button. His bullets strike the 'bomb' and there is a huge explosion as the German plane blows up.

German pilots flying in Restemeyer's formation see the *Gruppe Kommandeur's* aircraft being riddled with bullets followed by a shattering explosion, apparently caused by a hit in the still attached fuel tank. It seems highly probable that he is Sheen's victim.

Sheen goes after another defensive circle of 6 Bf 110s. One turns to attack him but is discouraged by a quick deflection shot. A second 110 coming head-on suddenly looms in Sheen's sights and instinctively he fires. Immediately flames break out inside the Messerschmitt's port engine but the German plane keeps coming on. To avoid a collision Sheen breaks away violently and the Messerschmitt disappears leaving a trail of thickening smoke.

The sky is now suddenly empty of aircraft so Sheen returns to Acklington to refuel and rearm.

Meanwhile, knowing that a large raid is taking place, the controller puts more units into action.

No. 79 Squadron intercepts the raiders approaching Newcastle. Again aircraft recognition is faulty and Dornier Do 215s are identified. During the fight Bill Millington finds himself alone with a large formation of Heinkel He 111s but in spite of the odds, he launches a series of stinging attacks. Flak, which has been peppering the bombers, ceases as his Hurricane sweeps in. Firing on his first Heinkel he sees the big plane suddenly burst into flames.

Turning in to attack another bomber Millington fires off short bursts until it too begins to burn. It lurches and turns sharply in a steep dive. Still not satisfied he attacks a third Heinkel and shoots it down.

By 2.45 p.m. all of 79 Squadron is back at Acklington. One Hurricane has been heavily damaged. Bill Millington asks for confirmation of two destroyed and one damaged but investigations reveal later that he has shot down all three Heinkels.

One hundred miles (160 km) to the south the Junkers Ju 88s of KG 30 from Denmark sweep over the Yorkshire coast shortly after 1.00 p.m. and are engaged by 12 Spitfires of 616 Squadron and 6 Hurricanes of 'B' Flight, 73 Squadron. Flying at full throttle these bombers, the fastest in the *Luftwaffe* arsenal, speed relentlessly on and then suddenly swing south over Bomber Command airfield at Driffield. The Hurricanes and Spitfires have difficulty keeping pace. Over Driffield the Germans are greeted by accurate anti-aircraft fire but the airfield is heavily hit with serious damage to hangars and the destruction of several Whitley bombers.

A formation of Ju 88s has split from the main force and bombed Bridlington where an ammunition dump is blown up.

Lightened after dropping their loads the Junkers speed back over the North Sea. Seven of them have been destroyed and another three are so badly damaged that they have to crash-land.

Out of the 134 aircraft despatched from Norway and Denmark, *Luftflotte 5* has lost 16 bombers and 7 fighters and numerous others have been damaged. The losses are so severe that *Luftflotte 5* will never again make a major daylight attack.

The RAF has lost one Hurricane.

*

The battle switches back to the south. At midday 12 Messerschmitt Bf 110s suddenly swoop down on Manston airfield in a hit-and-run attack, raking it with cannon and machine-gun fire. Two Spitfires are destroyed and there are 16 casualties.

At 2.15 p.m. radar stations in Kent and Essex report concentrations of enemy forces over Pas de Calais and Belgium. The 11 Group controller cannot predict which way the Germans will go. Complicating things is the power blackout caused by the raid on Hawkinge which has put out of action the CH radar stations at Dover, Rye and Foreness.

Passing within 20 miles (30 km) of Foreness 16 Messerschmitt Bf 110 fighter-bombers escorted by 9 Messerschmitt Bf 109s bomb Martlesham Heath in a hit-and-run attack. The Hurricanes of 17 Squadron have been moved forward from Debden to Martlesham to fly convoy patrols. The Bf 110s come in low and drop over 30 bombs. Desmond Fopp is one of the pilots stranded on the ground. The damage is such that the airfield will not be operational for 48 hours. By the time a squadron of Spitfires arrives on the scene the raiders are heading for France.

*

Eighty-eight Dornier Do 17s of KG 3, escorted by over 130 Bf 109s, approach Deal at 3.30 p.m. At the same time over 60 Messerschmitt 109s of JG 26 fly in over Dover. The Biggin Hill controller is only able to direct three airborne squadrons to meet them. The British fighters find it almost impossible to engage the bombers because of the size of the fighter escort.

Over Faversham the Dorniers split into two groups. One continues westward to Rochester and the smaller force heads north-west to bomb Eastchurch again. The raid on Rochester is highly successful. Over 300 bombs rain down on the airfield and on the Short Bros factory where production is under way on the RAF's newest heavy bomber, the huge four-engined Stirling. Six completed planes and the spare parts store are destroyed. Serious though this is, the *Luftwaffe* has not hit Fighter Command and therefore has not contributed to winning the battle of Britain.

*

Around 5.00 p.m. two more raids materialize, this time in the south-west. One force of 40 Ju 87 Stukas, escorted by 60 Messerschmitt Bf 109s and 20 Messerschmitt Bf 110s, is detected on the way to Portland. The two Hurricane Squadrons at Exeter, Nos 87 and 213, are scrambled, while at Middle Wallop 234 Squadron is ordered up. Thirteen Spitfires take off. Vincent Parker is flying as Red 2 and 'A' Flight is led by Pat Hughes in the extra Spitfire. They patrol Swanage and await instructions.

Shortly afterwards 609 Squadron is brought to 'Readiness'. The second raid of over 60 Junkers Ju 88s of LG 1, escorted by 40 Messerschmitt Bf 110s, is heading for Middle Wallop. Minutes later the Ju 88s split up, half diverting for an attack on Worthy Down while the rest continue. At 5.50 p.m. 609 Squadron is scrambled and the crews are hardly airborne when the bombers appear overhead. Two stranded pilots run to parked planes which have been earmarked for maintenance and take off just before the bombs begin to rain down.

In sharp contrast to the previous day's raid very little damage is done to the airfield. Likewise at Worthy Down and Oldham damage is negligible. On the other hand, 609 Squadron pilots claim one Ju 88 and 4 Bf 109s destroyed plus three Ju 88s probables.

Over Portland the Spitfires of 234 Squadron engage the escorting fighters of the first raid while the two Hurricane squadrons from Exeter go after the Stukas. A vicious dogfight develops. In the *mêlée*, Pat Hughes shoots down a Bf 110 and shares in the destruction of a second.

Red Section is overwhelmed by enemy fighters. P/O Richard Hardy, Red 1, is wounded by machine-gun fire. Short of fuel and far out to sea, he heads for France where he manages to land safely and is taken prisoner. Red 2, Vincent Parker, comes under heavy attack by Bf 110s. His engine is hit and his shoulder injured. Low over the Channel he has to bail out near the Isle of Wight.

Over Bournemouth P/O Hight of Yellow Section is shot down and killed.

Against these losses 234 Squadron claims 5 Messerschmitt Bf 110s destroyed and one Bf 109 damaged.

*

The day's fighting is not over. A large force of Dornier Do 17s in several small formations aims for Biggin Hill. It flies in over the Kent coast at 6.20 p.m. with covering Messerschmitt Bf 109s following.

To defend Biggin Hill 610 Squadron has 8 Spitfires serviceable and 32 Squadron has 9 Hurricanes. The controller orders No. 610 off first and 10 miles south-east of Biggin Hill they meet the Dorniers and shoot several down. Those that continue attack West Malling by mistake. At the same time 32 Squadron is ordered up to orbit the airfield. From this position the Hurricane pilots can see a pall of smoke and dust to the west. Croydon is under heavy attack and they rush there as fast as possible.

Fifteen Messerschmitt Bf 110s are again active in a hit-and-run attack on Croydon, the home of 111 Squadron (Harry Hardman). They are escorted by 8 Bf 109s. The bombing is highly effective and numerous buildings are damaged. Sixty-eight people are killed and almost 200 injured.

Luckily the 9 Hurricanes of 111 Squadron had taken off moments before the bombing. They claw for height and counter-attack the German fighter bombers which immediately form a defensive circle.

At the same time 32 Squadron takes on the Bf 109s. John Pain sees 6 Messerschmitts diving from 1 500 feet (450 m) above. He avoids them by breaking his Hurricane into a tight turn just as they open fire. Completing his circle he lines up the last machine and presses the button. The 109 begins to trail smoke. Closing right in to 50 yards (45 m) he fires two more bursts. In the same instant he realizes that he is alone with 6 enemy fighters so he turns away to rejoin his squadron.

Down below the Bf 110s decide to make a run for it and break out of their circle into small groups to head for cloud cover. It is the chance that 111 Squadron has been waiting for and they dive to attack. Seven Bf 110s are shot down.

Meanwhile 266 Squadron is ordered up from Hornchurch. After surviving the bombing of Eastchurch on the 13th, it has transferred to the assumed relative safety of Hornchurch. Instructions have come through to intercept enemy aircraft off Dover but on the way the squadron falls victim to Bf 109s over Maidstone. Frank Cale's Spitfire N3168 is hit and he bails out. His parachute is seen to open.

Cale's is the only aircraft missing when the unit returns to Hornchurch although a second plane has been severely damaged.

*

At last it is time to take stock. Assessments of aircraft destroyed are exaggerated by both sides. The RAF claims to have shot down 182 German aircraft while the *Luftwaffe* claims 82 Hurricanes and Spitfires, 5 Curtiss Hawks and 14 others. Clearly aircraft recognition is a problem for both sides. While in some areas the RAF claims Ju 88s and Dornier 215s where none are flying, the Curtiss Hawks claimed by the *Luftwaffe* do not exist. (Post-war figures will put *Luftwaffe* losses at 75 and Fighter Command losses at 34, with 17 pilots killed and 16 wounded).

German airmen will remember this day as 'Black Thursday'.

*

Frank Cale of 266 Squadron. He was killed in action on 15 August 1940 (photograph courtesy of Henry McDonough).

Hermann Goering and his commanders remain in conference for most of the day. He demands better bomber protection from his fighters especially for the Stukas and also suggests that there is not much value in continuing attacks on radar sites because apparently none of them have been put out of action. This decision will prove a costly error.

*

Two Australian pilots are missing. Vincent Parker of 234 Squadron floats in the cold waters of the English Channel for almost 4 hours before a speed boat finds him. Unfortunately it is German. He is taken to Cherbourg.

Burnt-out wreckage from Spitfire N3168 is found at Teston in Kent. Later in the evening the Maidstone police report finding a parachute with burnt straps but there is no trace of the pilot. It is not known where Frank Cale is but police suspect that he may have fallen into the River Medway.

FRIDAY, 16 AUGUST

German air activity overnight is limited but incendiary bombs are dropped near the camp of the 18th Infantry Brigade, Australian Striking Force, close to Middle Wallop aerodrome. There is no damage.

*

The morning weather is fine and sunny but the *Luftwaffe* delays launching attacks until 11.00 a.m., taking time to build back to strength some of its units which have suffered casualties. Several light raids are despatched against airfields in Norfolk, Kent and the greater London area. Of these only an attack on West Malling airfield achieves any success.

After spending the night at Cherbourg Vincent Parker is flown to *Dulag Luft* at Operursel. Here the Germans interrogate him and hand him false Red Cross forms to fill in. The Australian gives only his number, rank and name. He is then taken to the cells.

*

At Mount Batten W/Cdr E.G. Knox-Knight, who has arrived from Australia, assumes command of 10 Squadron, RAAF, from Charles Pearce.

*

Around 12.25 p.m. three heavy attacks build up. The first, a raid of 50 aircraft consisting of 24 Dornier Do 17s plus escorting Messerschmitt Bf 109s heads for the Thames Estuary. The second, comprising 150 aircraft, appears off Dover while a third, estimated at 100, builds up over Cherbourg and sets course for the Portsmouth-Southampton area.

The first raid, apparently making for Hornchurch, is intercepted by Spitfires from 54 Squadron and is turned back.

The second raid crosses the coast near Dover and splits up into several formations. To meet this widespread threat three squadrons of RAF fighters are ordered up. British tactics are for Hurricanes to engage the bombers while the Spitfires keep the escorts busy. The two Hurricane squadrons find several groups of Dorniers and charge in, using highly dangerous head-on attacks. For 111 Squadron it is a standard tactic. The Hurricanes spread out in line abreast and fire wildly. Several bombers are hit but there is a wrenching collision as a Hurricane and a Dornier meet at a closing speed well over 500 mph (800 km/h). Both planes, their occupants dead, crash in flames.

266 Squadron, Frank Cale's unit, is trapped by Messerschmitt Bf 109s. Outnumbered two to one, 5 Spitfires are shot down and a sixth crash-lands near Faversham.

Bombing by the Dorniers is scattered and inaccurate.

The third raid consists of over 100 Junkers Ju 87 Stukas and escorting Messerschmitt Bf 109s followed by 12 Junkers Ju 88s and a *Staffel* of 18 Messerschmitt Bf 110s. Over the Isle of Wight the Stukas split into 4 groups, the largest continuing on to Tangmere airfield while the others head for Ventnor, Lees-on-Solent and Gosport.

The Stukas approach Tangmere from the east and peel off for a textbook attack but 601 Squadron is airborne and intercepts.

The Hurricanes dive in at well over 400 mph (650 km/h) and Clive Mayers, his controls stiffened by the pace, cannot line up a target and pulls up without firing. He finds a victim and attacks one of the dive-bombers until it falls. He immediately goes after a second Stuka. Coming in from dead astern he again fires briefly before overshooting and then sweeps in for another run. The Stuka crashes into the ground.

The Stukas inflict serious damage on Tangmere. Two hangars are destroyed and the other three are damaged. The station's workshops receive direct hits. Six Blenheims of the Fighter Interception Unit are destroyed on the ground and 7 Hurricanes and one Miles Magister are damaged. Bristol Beaufighter R2055 of the FIU is damaged. It is the first night fighter of this type to be delivered to the RAF. Forty motor vehicles are either destroyed or damaged and 20 people are killed.

At the height of the attack a burning 601 Squadron Hurricane crash-lands on the aerodrome. Before the pilot can scramble out the plane becomes an inferno. Courageous ground crewmen carry him to safety though he will die next day.

As the Ju 87s try to escape they are made to pay dearly. Many are shot down by the defending fighters. Over Selsey Bill Clive Mayers shoots down another Stuka which glides down into the sea. The CH radar station at Ventnor is practically flattened. Barely recovered from the attack on the 12th, it will be out of action for 7 more days.

The naval station at Lee-on-Solent has several Fleet Air Arm planes and three hangars destroyed.

*

The last raid of Ju 88s and Bf 110s heads for another naval airfield at Gosport. The force is met by three Hurricanes of 249 Squadron. The British fighters are overwhelmed by the escorting Messerschmitts.

*

In the late afternoon Kesselring's *Luftflotte 2* and Sperrle's *Luftflotte 3* launch three major bombing raids combined with 'free chases' by Messerschmitt Bf 109s.

It is 65 Squadron's turn to operate from Manston and Gordon Olive leads 'A' Flight. Near Deal they sight 60 Junkers Ju 88s in close lines of 6 abreast 2 000 feet (600 m) higher up. Around these are an estimated 200 German fighters.

Deciding that it is impossible to attack the bombers, 65 Squadron climbs to a favourable position to engage the fighters. Olive leads his flight onto 12 Bf 109s. The Germans break formation and dive for France but Olive chases one fleeing Bf 109 and fires 4 bursts. The German plane breaks downwards into a vertical dive.

A twisting dogfight develops but suddenly the radio warns that enemy aircraft are now over Chatham so, with his wingman, Olive sets off in that direction. As he arrives he spots the same large formation of enemy bombers still pressing relentlessly on but now the escorting fighters are more scattered and fewer in number.

The two Spitfires make a quick hit-and-run attack on 12 Bf 109s but in the same instant Olive notices a lone Ju 88 trailing below behind the main bomber formation. Seizing his chance he dives after it, closes in quickly and smoke pours from both of its engines.

Eight Bf 109s pay Manston yet another visit. They hurtle across the airfield, raking buildings and parked aircraft with cannon and machine-gun fire. One Spitfire and a 600 Squadron Blenheim night fighter are destroyed and a second Blenheim is damaged.

The Hurricanes of 32 Squadron are airborne for their fourth patrol and at 5.30 p.m., over Biggin Hill, they encounter over 30 Ju 88s escorted by Bf 110s, all flying in the opposite direction. John Pain is in Red Section as it circles around after the bombers. He selects a Ju 88 at the rear and discharges two bursts at it. Pieces fly off the German's port engine and tail assembly and it drops away out of sight. Pain turns his attention to the other aircraft, spraying as many bombers as he can with bullets until his ammunition is used up.

After their 4 patrols 32 Squadron is able to claim 9 enemy aircraft destroyed.

*

The 12 Spitfires of 234 Squadron are scrambled again at 5.25 p.m. Pat Hughes is Cressy leader.

At 6.15 p.m. they are patrolling south of the Isle of Wight when Hughes spots about 50 Bf 109s circling above. Ordering his sections into line astern, he leads them up to attack. The 109s form a circle. Hughes fires a deflection shot at the nearest which immediately blows up.

Hughes' plane is suddenly jolted and, reacting quickly, he throws it into a sharp turn to find himself chasing the Messerschmitt which has just attacked him from behind. It tries to climb away but only succeeds in presenting the Australian with an easy target. The German fighter bursts into flames.

Immediately afterwards Hughes finds 4 Ju 87s heading south and sets off in pursuit. As he attacks his Spitfire shudders as its tailplane is heavily damaged by cannon fire. He evades his attacker.

Hughes is credited with two Bf 109s and his plane, Spitfire R6896, can be repaired. The squadron claims 6 destroyed for the loss of two, with both pilots safe.

*

Nightfall brings a rest for both sides. After 'Stand Down' at Biggin Hill the pilots, learning that two captured German aviators are being held prisoner in the guard room, decide to entertain them. John Pain and the 32 Squadron pilots take charge of the taller man, leaving 610 Squadron with the other. They bring him into the mess for a drink. At first the German remains aloof and somewhat angry because he, an officer, has been imprisoned under the command of a sergeant of the RAF police. After a few ales he begins to relax.

*

The airmen of 266 Squadron at Hornchurch are not in the mood for celebration. They have lost 5 Spitfires and a sixth has been badly damaged. The commanding officer and two others have been killed and two more injured.

Added to this comes the news that police have recovered Frank Cale's body from the River Medway.

P/O Frank Cale is the sixth Australian deemed eligible for the Battle of Britain Clasp to be killed in action.

*

The *Luftwaffe* too is licking its wounds. Replacement aircraft and personnel are urgently needed. After the strenuous combat and maximum effort of the last few days, air crew need rest. Because of this German night raids are greatly reduced.

*

In contrast RAF Bomber Command is very active overnight and 150 bombers are sent to targets in Germany and Holland.

No. 50 Squadron at Lindholme details 11 aircraft to attack the synthetic oil plant at Merseburg. They begin taking off at 8.40 p.m.

At Hemswell 144 Squadron's target is the oil plant at Leuna.

SATURDAY, 17 AUGUST

At midnight Angus Robson of 144 Squadron in Hampden P4360 arrives over the oil refinery at Leuna. There are already fires below them and a thick column of smoke is mushrooming up. After circling for over half an hour Robson makes his bomb-run.

Dereck French encounters intense flak as he makes his bomb-run across the synthetic oil plant at Merseburg. It is 12.50 a.m. when he drops his 4 bombs but his Hampden runs into trouble. The starboard engine starts spluttering so he does not stay around to watch the results of his bombing. He reaches Lindholme after a tense three-and-a-half hours.

Richard Taylor makes a low-level attack 10 minutes after French. The hydrogeneration plant is already in flames. Their first run is a failure because the bombs fail to release so Taylor has to bring the

A message of sympathy from Buckingham Palace. At least 26 Australian families received these letters after men were killed during the battle of Britain (photograph courtesy of Joan Bowden).

BUCKINGHAM PALACE

The Queen and I offer you
our heartfelt sympathy in your
great sorrow.
    We pray that your country's
gratitude for a life so nobly
given in its service may bring
you some measure of consolation.

George R.I.

Hampden around again. This time they score a direct hit. Nearby incendiaries burst and start another fire.

Bomber Command loses 7 aircraft overnight.

*

Although the weather is fine the day presents a lull in the fighting. German air activity is limited to reconnaissance. Both sides are preparing for the next round.

Over the past 28 days Fighter Command has lost 78 pilots killed and 27 severely wounded, most of them experienced airmen. Their places are being taken by newly-trained pilots from Operational Training Units but Dowding realizes that there are not enough of them; the OTUs are having difficulty keeping up with this rate of attrition. On this day the Air Staff at last agrees to allow 5 volunteers from each of the 4 Fairey Battle squadrons and three volunteers from each of the 4 Lysander Army Co-operation squadrons in 22 Group to transfer across to Fighter Command. These men are to be given a brief conversion course to have them ready to join fighter squadrons by the end of the month.

As an additional drastic measure the Air Ministry decides to cut operational training to a minimum, just enough to give new pilots some basic knowledge of the aircraft they will be flying into combat. The dangers of this are obvious, with half-trained novices at the controls of high-speed fighters to be pitted against a numerically superior, highly skilled and dangerous enemy, but the risk has to be taken.

Meanwhile, to fill the gap in the radar defences caused by the bombing of Ventnor the previous day, a mobile installation is set up at nearby Bembridge.

SUNDAY, 18 AUGUST

The Air Ministry's notice calling for volunteers to join Fighter Command is circulated throughout units of 22 Group. Among those who come forward are two Australians, F/O Robert Bungey of 226 Squadron and F/Lt John Hewson DFC of 142 Squadron. Both are veterans of the fighting in France flying Fairey Battles. Bungey is posted to 79 Squadron at Acklington while Hewson goes to 616 Squadron at Leconfield.

*

Weather conditions are fine early but become cloudy.

Just after midday Dover radar reports a huge build-up of enemy aircraft and 11 Group brings every serviceable fighter to 'Readiness'. The German targets are airfields to the south and south-east of London including Kenley, Croydon, West Malling and Biggin Hill. The *Luftwaffe* intends to use a one-two punch in several attacks whereby two groups of bombers, one flying at medium height and a smaller formation coming in fast and low, hit the airfield almost simultaneously to try and catch the defences by surprize.

All fighters still on the ground at Kenley are ordered up in a 'survival scramble'. Aircraft able to fly but not fight are directed to fly northwest to safety. The 12 Hurricanes of 111 Squadron up from Croydon are ordered to assemble over Kenley.

At Kenley two raids of escorted Dornier Do 17s come in at 1.30 p.m. but the first group of about 50 aircraft at medium altitude is late. The German plan has mis-cued. At the same time 111 Squadron intercepts the low fliers and gives chase at full throttle. All hurtle into light flak and machine-gun fire from Kenley's defences. One Hurricane is hit either by return fire from the Dornier gunners or by flak. It breaks away and crashes. The others break off hurriedly to clear the ground fire and speed to the northern side of the airfield to catch the bombers as they emerge. One Dornier attracts concentrated anti-aircraft fire and crashes. A second bomber is brought down and most others suffer damage.

When the Dorniers are clear of flak 111 Squadron sweeps in again and a frantic low-level chase begins. Harry Hardman's section pursues a Dornier which is flying so low that when he opens fire they can see bullets kicking up dust from the ground. Hardman pulls his Hurricane away so the others can come in and attack in their turn.

More bombers are shot down until one by one the British fighters run out of ammunition and are obliged to turn back. Three Hurricanes are lost.

As the Dorniers are attacking Kenley 60 Heinkel He 111's supported by 40 Bf 109s are making a bomb-run on Biggin Hill untroubled by either fighters or flak. Shortly beforehand 32 Squadron and 610 Squadron were scrambled so the British fighters are well clear and racing for height. One bomb falls squarely on the motor transport sheds and another explodes close to a Bofors gun, killing one man and wounding others.

John Pain and the other pilots can hear the sound of bombs exploding over the radio as they meet the German bombers head-on. After hurtling through the Heinkels they pull up steeply to turn back and give chase. The pursuit is on in earnest with 32 Squadron determined to make the Germans pay but the Bf 109 escort fighters are equally determined to cover the bombers' retreat. Pain's Hurricane P3147 bursts into flames and Pain is wounded but he manages to bail out safely. As he floats down he loses consciousness because of loss of blood.

Pain awakens to find that he has landed in someone's garden near Penshurst. He is taken to the Kent and Sussex Hospital, Tunbridge Wells.

As the Germans retreat to France they must run the gauntlet of angry Hurricanes and Spitfires ordered to cut them off but the weather favours them. Thickening haze makes it difficult for a concentrated RAF counter-attack.

At Biggin Hill, with the raid over, personnel are organized to fill in the many bomb craters which pockmark the field. Unexploded bombs are marked by red flags. This effort is only interrupted briefly as the returning fighters come in to land carefully between the craters and red flags. Later a bomb disposal squad arrives.

The damage to Biggin Hill is superficial. Kenley is the airfield which has suffered most. Reported casualties are 9 dead and 10 injured.

A few bombs have also been dropped on West Malling and Croydon.

*

Just after 2.00 p.m. 4 separate formations of enemy aircraft are reported approaching the Isle of Wight. Three of the raids consist of about 30 Ju 87 Stukas while the fourth is made up of 25 Ju 88s. With memories of the heavy attack on Tangmere on the 16th, the controllers scramble their fighters up to patrol over their airfields and await instructions.

No. 601 Squadron orbits over Tangmere with a strength of 12 Hurricanes. As Clive Mayers gains altitude he realizes that his oxygen line is blocked so he leaves the formation and lands. He switches to a reserve aircraft and takes off again, climbing at full throttle to rejoin his squadron.

Five other squadrons of Hurricanes and Spitfires are also airborne and climbing but, in spite of the early scrambling, most of the Germans reach their targets before meeting opposition.

The naval airfield at Gosport is hit again by the Ju 88s and suffers further heavy damage. Fortunately there is no loss of life.

Almost at the same time one Stuka raid peels off over the Coastal Command airfield at Thorney Island. There are two Blenheim units stationed here, No. 59 Squadron with bombers and the detached flight of Blenheim If fighters from 235 Squadron commanded by Fred Flood. Just prior to the Stuka attacks the Blenheim fighters have been scrambled to assist in the airfield's defence. Three aircraft are destroyed while a visiting Wellington bomber is damaged.

The Fleet Air Arm Station at Ford, where there are only 6 post-mounted Lewis-guns for defence, suffers heavy damage. The *Luftwaffe's* attack is devastating and accurate. A huge column of black smoke whirls upwards after the fuel storage compound is set ablaze.

Poling radar station is so badly damaged that it will not be restored to full activity for over a week.

[A mobile radar unit is brought in to ensure that the enemy will not realize that the radar chain has been breached.]

As the Stukas try to regroup over the Isle of Wight they draw the concentrated attention of the British fighters. There is a running chase out to sea. To evade the attacking fighters the Stukas throttle back and make steep turns to the right or left so that the faster Spitfires will overshoot. This ruse is often successful but there are so many targets that the Spitfires simply close in on the next victim. German casualties mount. Hurricanes from 601 Squadron and Spitfires from 602 Squadron join 152 Squadron in the hunt.

Led by its new commanding officer, S/Ldr J.S. O'Brien DFC, 234 Squadron comes over the Isle of Wight and notices 20 Messerschmitt Bf 109s high above in the sun. The Spitfires climb, coming up in the enemy's blind spot. Taken by surprize, the German fighters scatter and a sprawling dogfight ensues which keeps the Stukas' fighter cover busy. Pat Hughes fires an ineffective burst at one Bf 109 but then realizes that two others are about to attack him from behind. One opens fire at extreme range but Hughes turns steeply after his attacker and an accurate short burst sets it on fire. The Australian is immediately attacked by the second 109. After successful evasive action he watches for a chance to counter-attack. The 109 climbs briefly and then begins to dive. Hughes follows and closes in to 30 yards (27 m) for another burst. The German plane is heavily damaged and its pilot bails out.

Clive Mayers, who is still endeavouring to catch up with his squadron, comes in on the end of the dogfight and, finding a stray Bf 109, turns onto its tail. As he rapidly closes in he fires a four-second burst. Pieces fall off the fuselage and it hurtles down in a steep dive.

Before they can escape the unprotected Stukas are severely mauled Altogether 17 Stukas have been shot down and 7 others have suffered damage.

Around 5.00 p.m. a final assault develops. Radar detects 5 separate formations converging on Kent but they are successfully engaged by Hurricanes from North Weald and Spitfires from Hornchurch so that bombing is inaccurate and scattered over Kent and Surrey.

*

To keep the pressure on overnight the *Luftwaffe* sends approximately 50 bombers over England to carry out widespread nuisance raids. They also lay mines in the Thames Estuary and Bristol Channel.

MONDAY, 19 AUGUST

The weather is mainly cloudy with showers. Air activity is light after the vicious battles of the last week.

[Many historians consider that the previous day's fighting marks the end of the second phase of the battle of Britain.]

It is time to assess the results. On the German side Goering is worried about his bomber losses and the lack of obvious weaknesses in RAF defences. For the third time in 4 days the *Luftwaffe* has lost over 50 aircraft. Now, for the second time in a week, Goering summons his *Luftflotte* commanders. He re-emphasizes the importance of smashing Fighter Command and gives priority to attacking inland airfields and sector stations. He is highly critical of his fighter pilots for their lack of aggressiveness and failure to protect the bombers, in spite of the fact that, in terms of fighter-vs-fighter combat, the Bf 109 pilots are shooting down more than they are losing. He orders them to give the bombers closer escort but by doing this he makes a tactical error because, as close escorts, his fighters will consume more fuel while tied to the slower bombers and also pass the initiative to the British interceptors.

Goering further instructs that the Bf 109s are to provide cover for the Messerschmitt Bf 110s, creating the ludicrous situation of fighters escorting fighters. Although he does not admit it, this means that the heavy twin-engined Bf 110 escort fighter has failed in its role. To do this he needs more Bf 109s. *Luftflotte 5* is to be stripped of its long-range fighters and from now it will concentrate on night attacks. These Bf 110s will go to *Luftflotte 3* in France to free its Bf 109 *Staffeln* so that they, in turn, can be transferred to *Luftflotte 2* to boost the number of short-range fighters available on the Channel Coast. This will ensure that *Luftflotte 2's* bombers can be sent over south-east England in daylight with the heaviest possible protection.

Finally, because the Junkers Ju 87 Stuka dive-bombers have suffered disastrous losses over the last few days, they are to be withdrawn from operations.

*

It is a chance for reassessment of tactics in RAF Fighter Command as well. Senior Controller, S/Ldr George Edward Sampson, studies a copy of Instruction No. 4, newly drafted by AVM Park, for the guidance of his sector controllers.

[Sampson was from Brisbane and joined the RAAF as a cadet, entering Point Cook in 1928. He came to England in 1929 to take up a short-service commission in the RAF. This was extended to a permanent commission in 1936 and from April 1938 he commanded the famous No. 74 'Tiger' Squadron. In March 1940 he was posted to this new position.]

Park's instructions emphasize the critical need to limit losses as much as possible. He orders his controllers to despatch the fighters to engage large enemy formations over land or within gliding distance of the coast to avoid losing pilots through forced landings in the sea. They are to avoid sending fighters out over the sea to chase reconnaissance aircraft or small formations of enemy fighters. Against incoming mass attacks they are ordered to despatch a minimum number of squadrons to engage the German escorts. The main object is to engage the bombers.

To deal with single reconnaissance aircraft he instructs that a pair of fighters is to be despatched to intercept those that come inland.

In the event that all the squadrons around London are engaged in action Park orders his controllers to ask No. 12 Group or the Command controller to provide squadrons to patrol Debden, North Weald and Hornchurch aerodromes.

[This instruction presumes the co-operation of 12 Group which will soon prove to be sadly lacking. It will cause a serious rift between Park and AVM Leigh-Mallory, the commander of 12 Group, and seriously threaten to split Fighter Command at the worst moment.]

To Park, the protection of his airfields is vital. He also directs that if heavy attacks have crossed the coast and are proceeding towards aerodromes a squadron, or even a sector training flight, is to patrol over each sector aerodrome. Furthermore, although it is still under training and there is a language problem, No. 303 (Polish) Squadron is to provide two sections for patrol of inland aerodromes, especially while other units are on the ground refuelling.[9]

The two Australian volunteer pilots from Bomber Command proceed to their new squadrons but, upon arriving at Acklington to join 79 Squadron, Bob Bungey immediately receives a new posting to 145 Squadron at Drem. When he reaches his unit Bungey will undergo conversion onto Hurricanes.

[Robert Wilton Bungey was born at Fullarton, South Australia, on 4 October 1914. He attended Glenelg Primary School and Adelaide High School and in civil life was an insurance clerk. In 1936 he entered Point Cook as a cadet, then took up a short-service commission in July 1937.

When war broke out Bungey was in 226 Squadron equipped with Fairey Battle light bombers. The squadron was moved to France immediately with the AASF.

No. 226 Squadron was evacuated from Brest in June and reassembled in Ireland at Sydenham.]

John Hewson reports to Leconfield but discovers that his unit, 616 Squadron, has just moved to Kenley. He makes his way south to join it.

Hewson's squadron is not the only one on the move. No. 111 Squadron (Harry Hardman) transfers from Croydon to Debden where it is joined by 601 Squadron (Clive Mayers) from Tangmere.

*

At *Dulag Luft*, Oberursel, Vincent Parker is transferred from the cells into the main prison camp. For 'Bush' Parker this marks the beginning of a captivity during which he will attempt to escape so many times and prove to be so elusive that the Germans will eventually place him in Colditz Castle in April 1942.

['Bush' Parker was an incredible character. He was born in Durham, England, on 11 February 1919. His mother died when he was only a few months old. In 1920, he was adopted by his aunt and uncle, Edith and Jack Parker.

In 1928 the Parkers migrated to Australia and Jack Parker obtained work with Queensland Railways.

Vincent was educated at Bohleville State School. He then moved to Townsville and his flair for magic and acrobatics enabled him to train to be a professional magician with 'The Great Levante', a visiting magician from New Zealand. When Levante returned home, Vincent went with him but soon came back to Australia. After his second trip to England he went to Durham, the home of his original family, where he stayed in 1938–39. During this time he decided to join the RAF and in July 1939 was granted a short-service commission.

Eventually he was posted to 234 Squadron in which Pat Hughes was a flight commander. He moved with it to Middle Wallop in August and two days later, as already related, he was shot down and captured.

Colditz was for the hard cases, those considered too elusive for ordinary POW camps. It was thought to be escape-proof.

When he was not making escape attempts himself 'Bush' helped his fellow POWs in their bids for freedom. In an interview after the war he recalled:

> *I was a member of the Escape Committee at OFLAG IV C (COLDITZ) from the beginning of 43 until liberation in Apr 45. I helped all intending escapers as it was impossible to get out of the castle without picking some locks, and I was the authority on this. In connection with this, I advised on places from which to escape and on sites for starting tunnels.[10]*

Of 'Bush' Parker, Patrick Reid wrote in **The latter days at Colditz:**

> *. . . he might equally well have been called 'Fingers' Parker, for his wits and hands were as quick as lightning. He learned to handle locks with consummate skill. Bush was a colourful character . . . Colditz would not have been quite what it was if Bush had not been there . . .[11]*

On 15 April 1945 American soldiers captured Colditz Castle. Four days later F/Lt Vincent Parker set foot on British soil again after a forced absence of nearly 5 years.

After a few weeks' leave he was posted to Milfield and began training on Hawker Tempests. On 29 January 1946 'Bush' Parker took off in an aircraft for the last time. Just 5 miles (8 km) north of the airfield at Duddo, his Tempest crashed and he was killed.]

TUESDAY, 20 AUGUST

Low clouds, strong winds and intermittent rain restrict German operations to a few small raids and reconnaissance sorties.

Spitfire R6598 of the Photographic Reconnaissance Unit takes off from Heston at 11.00 a.m. with Harry Daish at the controls. From high altitude he successfully takes photos of Le Havre, Dieppe, Boulogne, Gris Nez, St Omer and Calais.

[Harry Daish had completed his training at Point Cook and took up a short-service commission in the RAF in 1936. Daish was trained as a

bomber pilot to fly Fairey Battles but in February 1940 he was posted to the PDU at Heston to fly reconnaissance Spitfires. He flew with this unit until December 1940. In August 1942 he took command of No. 27 (Beaufighter) Squadron in India. Awarded an OBE in January 1943, he stayed in the RAF after the war and retired as a group captain in 1958.]

In his classic speech to the House of Commons, Prime Minister Winston Churchill states:

> The gratitude of every home in our Island, in our Empire, and indeed throughout the world, except those in the abodes of the guilty goes out to the British airmen who, undaunted by odds, unwearied in their constant challenge and mortal danger, are turning the tide of the world war by their prowess and by their devotion. *Never in the field of human conflict was so much owed by so many to so few . . .*[12]

The last sentence will be one of the most quoted statements in the history of the second world war. He continues:

> All hearts go out to the fighter pilots, whose brilliant actions we see with our own eyes day after day; but we must never forget that . . . all the time, night after night, month after month . . . our bomber squadrons travel far into Germany, find their targets in the darkness by the highest navigational skill, aim their attacks, often under the heaviest fire, often with serious loss, with careful discrimination, and inflicting shattering blows upon the whole of the technical and war-making structure of the Nazi power. On no part of the Royal Air Force does the weight of the war fall more heavily than on our daylight bombers who will play an invaluable part in the case of invasion and whose unflinching zeal it has been necessary in the meanwhile on numerous occasions to restrain . . .

WEDNESDAY, 21 AUGUST

Poor weather conditions continue throughout the day but the *Luftwaffe* carries out several hit-and-run attacks using small formations and single aircraft.

Goering pays his first visit to *Luftflotte 2's* headquarters. On the Channel coast at Cap Gris Nez, using high-powered binoculars, he peers across the water to the cliffs of Dover where tall radar masts are clearly visible. Adjacent to Cap Gris Nez the Germans have set up a battery of heavy guns pointing towards the English coastline.

*

Three Blenheims of 235 Squadron from Thorney Island escort a reconnaissance plane on its mission over Le Havre. The leading plane is 'Buskarlet's Brig' piloted by Fred Flood. Just off the port the Australian sights a Henschel Hs 126 army co-operation plane and in a diving attack shoots it down into the sea.

*

Pilots waiting near their aircraft for the order to scramble (Ministry of Defence, UK).

Kenneth Slessor is writing a despatch in his office in Amesbury Abbey when he receives a phone call informing him that the ship on which his wife is travelling to England is to dock at Liverpool tomorrow. Slessor drops everything and travels to meet her.

*

Luftwaffe activity overnight is minimal. RAF Bomber Command despatches 42 Hampden bombers to targets in Germany. Despite the inclement weather Dereck French of 50 Squadron takes off at 8.37 p.m. in Hampden P4408 as one of 10 aircraft detailed to bomb the synthetic oil plant at Magdeburg. Bob Reed follows in Hampden L4097 two minutes later. Angus Robson takes off in Hampden P4366 from Hemswell at 10.00 p.m. as part of a force of 4 from 144 Squadron.

THURSDAY, 22 AUGUST

Dereck French encounters bad weather on the way to Magdeburg and over the target. Anti-aircraft fire is intense. Nevertheless, his attack is pressed home and explosions are seen in the target area.

At midnight Bob Reed makes a low-level attack on the plant. He flies in at 2 000 feet (600 m) and drops 4 bombs.

Of the 42 Hampdens despatched only 29 manage to find and bomb their targets. One aircraft from 144 Squadron at Hemswell fails to return. P/O Angus Robson DFC and his crew will never be seen again. He is one of the Australians listed on the Battle of Britain Roll of Honour at Westminster Abbey.

*

With daylight inclement weather continues over Britain but RAF anti-invasion patrols are maintained. In the Straits of Dover a convoy of 18 ships, mostly colliers, creeps along close inshore bound for Scotland. They make an ideal target for new German heavy guns at Cap Gris Nez. The enemy barrage continues for over an hour but not one ship is hit and Convoy 'Totem' escapes.

*

Since being posted north to Scotland on 21 July No. 141 Squadron has received replacement pilots, gunners and aircraft. The Defiants are to be used as night fighters. After training 'B' Flight moves to Dyce while 'A' Flight, with Noel Constantine, is detached to Montrose.

*

The Blenheims of 600 Squadron (Charles Pritchard) have transferred from Manston to Hornchurch.

*

At Kenley the newly-arrived John Hewson familiarizes himself with his new aircraft. In France he had flown Fairey Battles but 616 Squadron, to which he has been posted, is a Spitfire unit.

At 6.45 p.m. he watches the squadron scramble. Fourteen Spitfires take off and an hour later they return minus one aircraft. Over Dover they were surprised by a dozen Messerschmitt Bf 109s and one Spitfire was shot down.

FRIDAY, 23 AUGUST

Low cloud and rain continue throughout the day, once again limiting the *Luftwaffe's* operations to hit-and-run attacks and reconnaissance.

In the north three Spitfires of 232 Squadron shoot down a German reconnaissance aircraft, a Heinkel He 111, 8 miles west of Fair Isle. Shortly afterwards, Blenheims of 248 Squadron set out to search the area for survivors.

Meanwhile the pilots and gunners of 264 Squadron settle in at Hornchurch in 11 Group. The unit's Australian member, Bill Crook, is still on a course at No. 5 OTU, Aston Down, for his air gunner's badge. This is fortunate because he is well away from the tragedies soon to come. For the men of the Defiants, history is about to repeat itself.

MAP 3   RAF Fighter
Command's groups and
stations mentioned in the text

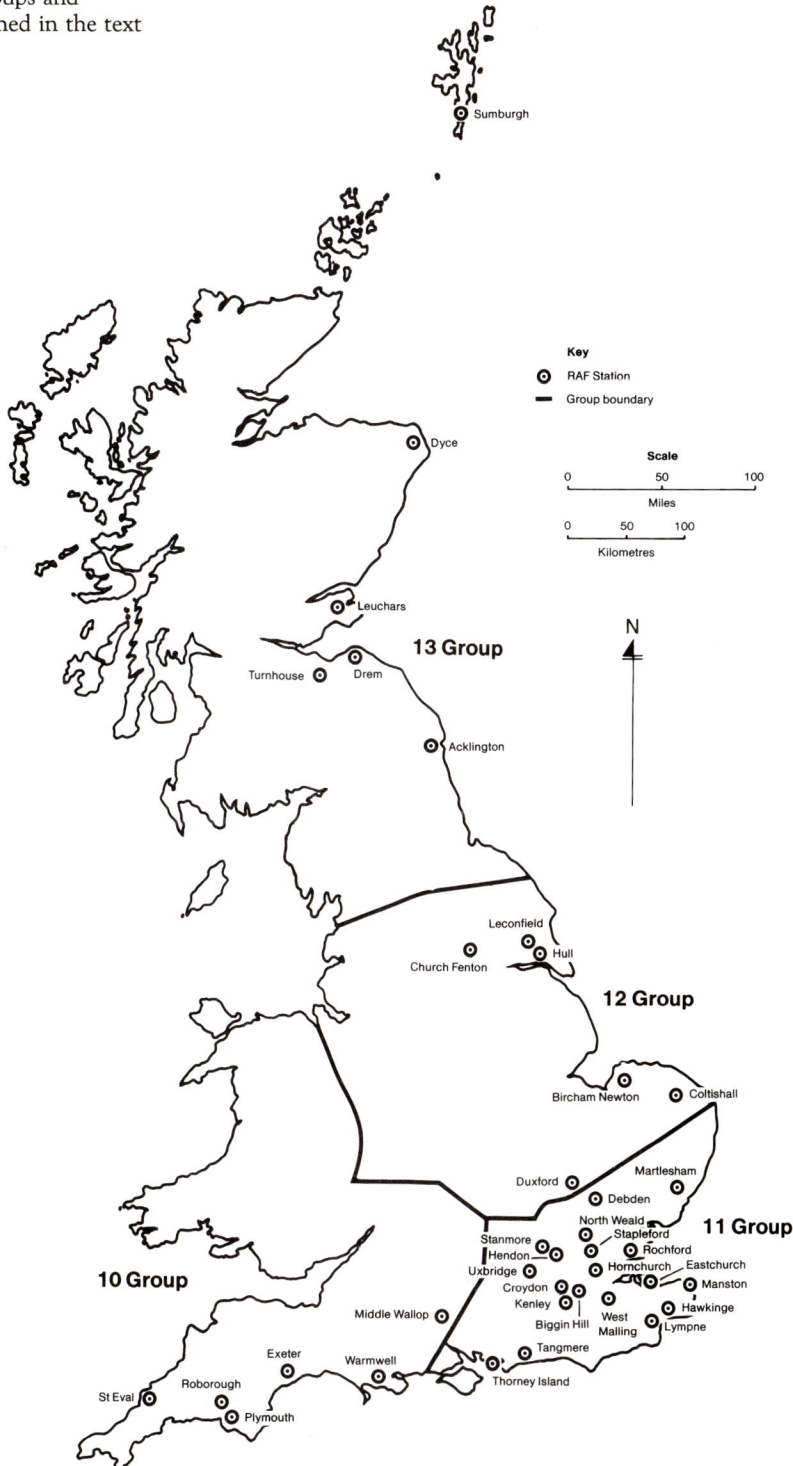

Key

⊙ RAF Station

▬ Group boundary

Scale

0 .... 50 100

Miles

0 ...... 50 100

Kilometres

Sumburgh

Dyce

Leuchars

13 Group

Turnhouse   Drem

Acklington

N

Leconfield

Hull

Church Fenton

12 Group

Bircham Newton   Coltishall

Duxford   Martlesham

Debden

North Weald

Stanmore   Stapleford   11 Group

Hendon   Rochford

Uxbridge   Hornchurch   Eastchurch

Croydon   Manston

Kenley   Hawkinge

10 Group   Biggin Hill   West   Lympne

Malling

Middle Wallop   Tangmere

Exeter   Warmwell

Roborough   Thorney Island

St Eval

Plymouth

SATURDAY, 24 AUGUST

*[With the arrival of fine weather both sides are ready for the main event. Most historians agree that this day marks the beginning of the most critical phase of the battle of Britain during which the **Luftwaffe** must devote its entire energy to the destruction of RAF Fighter Command if it is to succeed.]*

Early morning is fine and cloudless. At 11.00 a.m. a large build-up of aircraft is detected from Cap Gris Nez. The Germans are adopting a new tactic to keep the British guessing. About 20 miles (32 km) out to sea they maintain a constant stream of aircraft flying parallel to the Sussex coast. Occasionally these planes turn in towards England in feints to attract RAF fighters from their bases, only to quickly turn back to the coast and leave the British planes hopelessly out of position. Then, while the Hurricanes and Spitfires are returning to base to refuel, a real attack begins.

Out of this confusing mass, a raid by 40 bombers escorted by over 60 fighters materializes and drops bombs on Dover. The fighter escort is packed so tightly around the Dornier Do 17s and Junkers Ju 88s that intercepting British fighters have great difficulty breaking through and the Germans retire almost unscathed.

*

The British make a tactical blunder of their own. No. 264 Squadron has had difficulty settling into Hornchurch, a Spitfire base, because there are no personnel experienced in maintaining Defiants and there are no stores or spare parts for them. The decision itself to deploy the Defiants in 11 Group again is incomprehensible in view of the *débâcle* suffered by 141 Squadron. Over Dunkirk 246 Squadron had achieved outstanding results but there its Defiants had been mistaken for Hurricanes and been attacked from behind. It is hoped that, because the unit's pilots and gunners are veterans, they will be able to achieve similar results now.

Mistake follows mistake. The squadron is ordered forward to operate daily from, of all airfields, a patched-up Manston, where the least warning, a wild scramble and a zooming, full-throttle climb for height is the expected norm. The Defiants are slow-climbing two-seaters which require time for the crew to board and, once aloft, time to form up for a formation attack. They are hardly suitable for such a place.

Just after midday the Defiants are being refuelled when a warning is given of approaching enemy aircraft. Nine of the turreted fighters scramble, the last leaving the ground as the first bombs explode. Caught low, they are at the mercy of the Messerschmitt Bf 109 escort fighters. Three Defiants are lost. The survivors make their way back to Hornchurch. Fortunately for them, a Hurricane squadron operating in the area intervenes before more of the two-seaters can be shot down.

*

At 3.30 p.m. another large raid builds up over Le Havre and flies towards Manston. To the hard-working ground personnel who have been trying to effect repairs after the earlier attack, this new bombing is the last straw as the grounds are rendered virtually useless.

Before the bombing 65 Squadron, operating from its forward satellite, Rochford, had been ordered up to intercept raiders approaching Dover. Led by Gordon Olive, the 9 Spitfires encounter two formations of 30 and 40 bombers and 40 Messerschmitt Bf 110s. Higher up there are countless Messerschmitt Bf 109s. A desperate fight follows but all Spitfires return safely and lodge claims for two probable kills, a Bf 109 and a Bf 110. The 109 is Olive's.

Germans bombing Manston find so much smoke and dust created by the first bombing wave that they are unable to clearly define their target.

While the bombing is in progress, another large raid wings its way to targets north of the Thames Estuary where Hornchurch and North Weald come under attack. AVM Keith Park, the 11 Group commander, realizing that, because all his squadrons are engaged, his airfields are vulnerable, requests air cover from 12 Group. Apart from 6 cannon-armed Spitfires from 19 Squadron, no help arrives.

At Hornchurch the pilots and gunners of 264 Squadron have just finished lunch when they are ordered to scramble as they had been at Manston a few hours before. Again the last plane is just off as bombs begin to fall and again the squadron is unable to form up for its own defence. A large formation of Heinkel He 111s and Junkers Ju 88s is bombing from 12 000 feet (3 700 m) and the Defiants have no chance of reaching them.

Messerschmitt Bf 110. The Germans had great hopes for these long-range escort fighters but they were outmanoeuvred by the more nimble Hurricanes and Spitfires (Imperial War Museum photograph MH 4194).

While Hornchurch is under attack Do 17s and He 111s approach North Weald. Three British units including No. 111 Squadron intercept and succeed in turning back some of the bombers but about 20 arrive over North Weald and unload. Nine people are killed and 10 wounded.

[Park is bitterly angry over 12 Group's failure to arrive. AVM Leigh-Mallory had ordered his squadrons to assemble into a wing over Duxford, thus losing precious time and arriving too late to be of any assistance.]

*

At 3.40 p.m. Ventnor radar station, repaired with new equipment but experiencing teething problems, picks up enemy aircraft approaching the Isle of Wight. The British fighters are scrambled late, due in part to the *Luftwaffe's* confusing patrolling tactics. An error in judging the enemy's height causes controllers to order their interceptors to fly too low in anticipation of meeting Ju 87 Stuka dive-bombers again.

[They are unaware that these planes have been withdrawn from the fighting.]

Like others 609 Squadron finds itself over the Isle of Wight 5 000 feet (1 500 m) directly below the enemy aircraft. Fortunately the German escorts are not particularly aggressive and 609 manages to extricate itself from the situation with only two Spitfires damaged.

A flight of three Blenheims from 235 Squadron led by Fred Flood in 'Buskarlet's Brig' is put up to defend its base at Thorney Island but the German bombers, 50 Ju 88s of LG 1, continue to Portsmouth and drop over 200 bombs. Considerable damage is caused to naval installations and the city, with 104 civilians killed and 237 injured. There are 50 casualties among naval personnel.

Just after 5.00 p.m. Fred Flood's three Blenheims are patrolling over the Solent when they are suddenly attacked by fighters. They are shocked to realize that their opponents are Hurricanes. A patrol from No. 1 Squadron, RCAF, has mistaken the Blenheims for Ju 88s. One Blenheim is riddled by bullets and its crew killed — it plummets down into the sea. The second has its undercarriage shot up and has to crash-land. Through violent evasive manoeuvres Flood manages to escape the Hurricanes so that 'Buskarlet's Brig' suffers only slight damage.

*[The British defences have taken heavy punishment and results in the air for the **Luftwaffe** indicate that, while close escort of the bombers is unpopular with the fighter pilots, it has been successful in that the British have had difficulty in breaking through. Bomber losses have been less but fighter losses have been correspondingly higher. The **Luftwaffe** has lost 38 aircraft while RAF Fighter Command has lost 22.*

For the RAF the Defiant has again been shown to be useless as a front-line day fighter and there are now signs of a serious rift developing between the British commanders. AVM Park is highly critical of 12 Group's inability to back up his 11 Group.]

*

In the evening the *Luftwaffe* continues its pressure by sending over more than 150 bombers to various targets in Kent, Sussex and Surrey. Some are directed to bomb Rochester and the Thameshaven oil tanks. Because of a mistake in navigation, bombers instructed to hit the latter stray over London and drop their bombs on the city itself.

[Hitler had specifically ordered that London was not to be bombed and this, the first raid on the British capital since 1918, although an accident, will set in motion a chain of events which will completely change the course of the battle.]

SUNDAY, 25 AUGUST

Overnight RAF Bomber Command despatches 78 longer-range Wellingtons and Whitleys to targets in Germany and Italy while Blenheims attack targets in France. The Hampdens of 50 Squadron, including those of Dereck French and Bob Reed, carry out minelaying.

*

Fine weather covers southern and eastern England and *Luftflotte 2* continues the tactic of flying formations of planes along the coast with the occasional feint to keep the RAF on its toes but does not initiate any major raids. All squadrons in 11 Group are held at 'Available'.

In London Kenneth Slessor takes the opportunity to show his wife the sights but they soon find evidence of German bombing.

It is not until mid-afternoon that a change in the enemy's pattern of operations is detected when Ventnor radar picks up several groups of aircraft building up west of Cherbourg peninsula. It reports a raid of over 100 aircraft approaching Weymouth Bay. So that the previous day's mistakes will not be repeated (i.e. the defending fighters being caught too low) squadrons at Tangmere, Exeter, Warmwell and Middle Wallop are scrambled as early as possible.

There are actually over 300 German planes in the air. As they arrive over Weymouth, the Germans split into three major formations each consisting of about 30 Ju 88s and 40 Bf 110s. Their targets are Portland, Weymouth and Warmwell.

The Portland force is met by 12 Hurricanes from 87 Squadron and 12 Spitfires of 609 Squadron. The Hurricanes go after the bombers while the Spitfires take on the fighters. John Curchin is flying as Green 3 in 609 Squadron and he follows his companions into line astern as the Spitfires plummet into the centre of a Bf 110 formation. The Bf 110s split up and scatter with the British fighters giving chase but at the same instant Bf 109s join the fight. Curchin sends a Bf 109 down in flames.

The Spitfires of 152 Squadron from Warmwell find the Germans south-west of Portland at 5.35 p.m. Ian Bayles, perhaps because he is to go on leave the next day to get married, does not seem to be able to hit anything as he blazes away at any German plane which appears in front of him. The battle shifts out over the sea as the Ju 88s speed for home and one by one the Spitfires break off the action.

Only 7 bombers manage to reach Warmwell but these cause heavy damage, hitting two hangars and the sick quarters and severing almost all of the telephone lines — communications will not be restored until midday next day.

*[Again the presence of an overwhelming number of escort fighters effectively reduces bomber casualties. Of the 12 planes lost by **Luftflotte 3** only one is a bomber.]*

The pilots of 152 Squadron claim three confirmed victories and one probable but the men are far from happy because two of their number have been killed. Since coming to Warmwell the squadron has accounted for 40 confirmed and 15 unconfirmed but this success does not remove the depression when comrades fail to return. Because of the losses and the strong possibility of more German raids, Ian Bayles' leave to be married is cancelled.

*

After dark 103 planes from Bomber Command carry out raids on Germany and France. For half of these the nominated target is Berlin. The previous night's bombing of London has provoked Winston Churchill into ordering an immediate reprisal raid. It is a hasty and ill-conceived attack and Berlin is covered by thick cloud, making bombing highly inaccurate. Records indicate that only two people are slightly injured. On their return flights the British planes encounter strong headwinds which particularly affect the Hampdens because they are operating at the furthermost limit of their range. Six are lost, three of which ditch into the sea because they run out of fuel.

Five Hampdens of 50 Squadron are detailed to attack one of Berlin's electricity power stations. Richard Taylor takes off from Lindholme at 9.50 p.m. in aircraft L4062 and by 1.15 a.m. he is flying over the extensive cloud which covers the German capital. At 1.23 a.m. his bomb-aimer releases the Hampden's load of 8 bombs but no results can be seen because of the murk below. He lands back at Lindholme at 6.28 a.m. after an exhausting flight lasting 8 hours and 38 minutes.

Like the previous night's bombing of London, in spite of the raid's lack of military success, its political consequences will be far-reaching.

MONDAY, 26 AUGUST

The arrival of two replacement pilots for 152 Squadron at Warmwell is welcome news to Ian Bayles who takes leave to be married.

*

The weather is still good for flying and the *Luftwaffe* continues flying bogus sorties up and down the Channel to keep the RAF guessing. The first real raid, directed against Biggin Hill and Kenley, occurs at 11.00 a.m. when 40 Heinkel He 111s and 12 Dornier Do 17s, escorted by 80 Messerschmitt Bf 109s and 12 Bf 110s, cross the coast north of Dover. While the main group continues westward, a small force breaks away and bombs Folkestone. A few Bf 109s carry out low-level strafing attacks on targets of opportunity in East Kent and others shoot up the balloon barrage over Dover.

More than 70 British fighters are scrambled to intercept. Twelve pilots of 616 Squadron, among them John Hewson, are at 'Available' at Kenley. Hewson has had a few familiarization flights on Spitfires and is now scheduled for his first sortie. When the order comes to 'Scramble' there is confusion and only 7 Spitfires take off quickly. The remaining 5 are delayed. The first flight is directed to Dungeness but is too late to tackle the Heinkels and turns quickly north to find above and in front of it about 50 Bf 109s apparently unaware of its presence. For the next 15 minutes 616 Squadron manoeuvres to gain height and obtain a favourable position up-sun of the enemy which remains unaware of the stalking Spitfires. Hewson is flying on the outer port side. They are ready to attack but before the order is given they are suddenly bounced by 30 other Messerschmitts. The squadron is taken completely by surprise and its two weavers are shot down. Overwhelmed by the odds, the Spitfires are hit hard and over the next 15 minutes three more are lost. Hewson is one of the surviving pilots who land back at Kenley.

At about the same time the Defiants of 264 Squadron are taking on the formation of 12 Dorniers over Herne Bay but they are jumped by escorting Bf 109s. Two Defiants are shot down, a third crash-lands and a fourth is badly damaged but manages to land safely.

The Defiants of 264 Squadron and the Spitfires of 616 Squadron have not been sacrificed in vain because they have drawn off the German escort fighters. Hurricanes and Spitfires from other British squadrons are able to break into the main bomber force, inflicting casualties and turning it away from Biggin Hill. The Germans jettison their bombs as they retreat towards France.

*

At 12.30 p.m., in a meeting of the British War Cabinet, ministers hear for the first time of the retaliatory raid on Berlin from Sir Cyril Newall, the Chief of Air Staff.[13]

*

The Germans' second raid in the early afternoon has orders to attack the airfields at Hornchurch and Debden. Judging from the size and direction of the attack that the raid will be very heavy, AVM Park again requests 12 Group to cover his northern airfields and orders up every available squadron of his own.

No. 65 Squadron, led by Gordon Olive, has been airborne on patrol when it is ordered to intercept the incoming bandits approaching Ramsgate. Its strength is 11 Spitfires and they are in a good position to meet the enemy force which can be seen from a great distance. Olive can make out the escorting fighters in three or 4 formations about 30 to 40 strong.

As Olive leads his flight down onto a group of Bf 110s, they form a defensive 'death circle'. To counter this Olive changes direction and leads his flight into a circle of its own about 3 000 feet (900 m) above the Germans where they wait for a chance to attack. It is a stalemate. Olive realizes that by staying put in a threatening position, he is securing a tactical advantage because his pilots can keep the Germans circling indefinitely while the bombers they are supposed to be escorting continue with much of their protection gone.

This stand-off continues for about 20 minutes when, at last, some Bf 110s begin to break off and fly towards home. Olive immediately dives and attacks the rearmost machine which bursts into flames and dives into the ground. The others quickly swing back to the safety of the circle. The Australian returns to his position directly above. Every time the Bf 110s attempt to break off, a section of Spitfires dives . . . and so it goes on until the Spitfires run out of ammunition and are so low on fuel that they have to return to base. They claim two destroyed, two probably destroyed and one damaged, without casualties.

Meanwhile the bombers have split into two groups. One of 40 Do 17s and 40 Bf 110s heads for Debden while the rest turn towards Hornchurch. As each proceeds to its target, more British fighters and flak are encountered. The Bf 109s are now low on fuel and are obliged to turn back. The Hornchurch force is now virtually without cover and several Dorniers are shot down. Realizing they will be cut to pieces if they continue, the entire formation wheels around and retreats.

The other Dorniers heading north for Debden meet heavy flak and also run into a wall of defending Hurricanes and Spitfires. They too are obliged to turn back except for less than a dozen which reach the airfield.

From the German point of view this two-pronged attack is a complete failure but, on the British side, AVM Park is furious that AVM Leigh-Mallory's 12 Group has again failed to supply covering aircraft for his airfields. Spitfires from Duxford arrive over Debden long after the Dorniers have disappeared.

*

At 4.00 p.m. *Luftflotte 3* despatches 50 Heinkel He 111s against Portsmouth and the aerodrome at Warmwell. Escort is provided by over 100 Messerschmitt Bf 110s and Bf 109s. Park's 11 Group sends up 5 squadrons while AVM Brand scrambles another three from his 10 Group.

No. 234 Squadron takes off from Middle Wallop and once again Pat Hughes is Cressy leader. Thirty minutes later, south of the Isle of Wight, the Spitfires meet 8 red-nosed Bf 109s at 16 000 feet (4 900 m) plus another 30 higher up.

Hughes shoots down one of a pair of Messerschmitts but then finds that the other is now attacking from above. When he turns tightly to face it, the German plane immediately dives away but as it pulls out of its dive Hughes catches up and fires a long burst from dead astern. The Messerschmitt burns but continues to fly. Although out of ammunition, Hughes follows and a few minutes later sees the German pilot bail out. Hughes climbs towards Middle Wallop but spots more Messerschmitts ahead. As the gap between them closes, one Bf 109 fires a snap burst from maximum range but misses. Hughes cannot reply. They loom up and hurtle past, apparently intent on reaching France and probably low on fuel.

While this is happening three squadrons of Hurricanes and Spitfires intercept the German bombers and, after shooting down at least 4 Heinkels, succeed in turning them back.

One of the successful units is 43 Squadron from Tangmere but it loses three Hurricanes in the process and has three others damaged. Four of its pilots are wounded. Replacement pilots are usually short of flying experience but today one of the newcomers is Dick Reynell, a Hawker Aircraft Ltd test pilot on temporary attachment.

[Richard Carew Reynell was born on 9 January 1912, at Reynella, South Australia, son of Carew Reynell, vigneron and winemaker. After he had finished his schooling, he went to England in 1929 where he passed the Oxford University entrance examination. While there, his growing interest in flying led him to join the Oxford University Squadron.

In 1931 he joined the RAF and was posted to 43 Squadron where his flying skill enabled him to become a member of the unit's Hawker Fury Aerobatic Team.

After leaving 43 Squadron Dick Reynell went to the Met Flight at Duxford. He then returned to Australia for a short time and went back to England where his flying skills eventually led him to the position of test pilot at Hawker Aircraft Ltd in 1937.

When war broke out he was 'chafing at the bit' to rejoin the RAF but his work at Hawker had made him too valuable to let go. Then, in August 1940, the situation changed. The Air Ministry began allowing a selected few test pilots to fly for short periods with operational squadrons. Dick's posting came on 26 August when he rejoined 43 Squadron.]

*

Dick Reynell, celebrating after his aerobatic display at the Brussels Air Show in July 1939 (photograph courtesy of Marjorie Horn).

That night 99 Hampdens, Blenheims and Wellingtons set out to bomb targets in Germany and 11 Whitleys take off to attack Turin and Milan in Italy. For 50 Squadron the target is the Leipzig-Mockau aerodrome and the adjoining aircraft component parts factory. Six aircraft are involved.

Dereck French is over the target area just after 11.30 p.m. The weather is overcast but he is able to drop 6 bombs and incendiaries. Because of cloud he and his crew are unable to observe the results of their bombing.

By the time Bob Reed arrives over Leipzig-Mockau aerodrome the area is completely shrouded by cloud. He decides that there is no point in attacking so instead he bombs a heavy flak area north-west of Hannover.

The Luftwaffe makes scattered raids around Bournemouth and Coventry and approximately 50 bombers carry out a sustained attack on Plymouth. At St Eval in Cornwall a decoy aerodrome has been constructed and, by following a false flare path, several German bombers are attracted to the spot. They drop 62 bombs onto open heathland.

The German bombing of Plymouth lasts for 7 hours but RAF Station, Mount Batten, located on Plymouth Sound and home to 10 Squadron, RAAF, is not damaged. Many bombs fall into the Sound itself but the moored Sunderland flying boats are not hit.

TUESDAY, 27 AUGUST

No. 603 Squadron (Richard Hillary) moves south to Hornchurch.

Other moves are also taking place. From Hornchurch the Defiants of 264 Squadron shift to Rochford. Seven replacement Defiants have arrived but the men are disgusted to find that modifications to prepare the machines for combat have not been carried out. Among other things the Browning machine-guns have not been harmonized and some of the planes do not have self-sealing fuel tanks.

Also flying southwards are the Hurricanes of 79 Squadron (Bill Millington), on their way from Acklington to Biggin Hill to relieve 32 Squadron. The latter is overdue for a rest from combat. John Crossman had reported back to 32 Squadron the previous day after completing his training at Sutton Bridge.

The *Luftwaffe* does not appear except for several reconnaissance missions mainly in the Southampton-Portsmouth area.

At 7.00 p.m. Richard Hillary lands at Hornchurch. After Turnhouse he finds the atmosphere at his new base completely different. Instead of only one section of Spitfires at 'Readiness' there are 4 squadrons. One is Gordon Olive's 65 Squadron which is down to only 5 aircraft and 12 pilots and which is to move to Church Fenton to rest and rebuild.

*

[The German tactics of splitting their formations once they pass the British coastline, where the outward-facing radar cannot follow their progress, has consistently confused the defences which have to rely solely upon reports from the Observers' Corps. It becomes impossible to guide defending fighters onto the enemy formations as they become widely dispersed, so that quite often up to two-thirds of them do not manage to engage. AVM Park instructs his squadron leaders and flight commanders who make contact to pass a proper sighting report back to their controller before engaging the enemy.

Today AVM Park issues Instruction No. 7 to his controllers. In this, he begins by thanking 10 Group for its help in covering the Portsmouth area but then follows with an attack on 12 Group for its lack of co-operation. On two occasions when 12 Group had been requested to cover 11 Group's aerodromes, they had failed to do so and the airfields had been bombed. He directs that from now on 11 Group controllers are to put their requests for 12 Group assistance to the controller, Fighter Command.

The instruction brings into the open the friction between Park and Leigh-Mallory, who has fostered the idea of operating a large wing against large-scale raids instead of Park's tactic of sending squadrons up singly or in pairs. This argument, big wing versus squadron, will continue with increasing bitterness as the battle progresses.]

*

In the evening scattered enemy raids come in from Cherbourg. British defences reply with patrols by Blenheim night fighters, two-seater Defiants and single-seater fighters on 'cat's eyes' sorties. At Kenley John Hewson of 616 Squadron, because he has already logged numerous hours of night flying in bombers, is rostered for 'cat's eyes' patrols in his Spitfire.

WEDNESDAY, 28 AUGUST

The weather is cold and fair with cloud over the Straits of Dover — suitable for operations. Between 8.00 a.m. and 8.30 a.m. a heavy raid builds up over Pas de Calais and is soon estimated at over 100 planes. There are, in fact, two groups of bombers, 23 Dornier Do 17s of KG 3 and 27 Heinkel He 111s of KG 53, with the usual heavy escort of Messerschmitt Bf 109s and Bf 110s. No. 11 Group orders up three squadrons of Hurricanes including 79 Squadron from Biggin Hill and the 12 Defiants of 264 Squadron. As the raid crosses the coast of Kent it splits up, the Dorniers making for Eastchurch and the Heinkels for Rochford. No. 79 Squadron is first to find the Heinkels and it makes a sighting report as per AVM Park's instructions before launching an attack. The Hurricanes are quickly engaged by the escort fighters.

While the Bf 109s are busy with the Hurricanes, the 12 Defiants arrive on the scene to engage the bombers. The British crews do not notice another *Gruppe* of Bf 109s lurking in the sun. They manage to shoot down one Heinkel and damage another before they are bounced. Two Defiants crash in flames. The pilot of another manages to bail out but his gunner dies. Of the 8 Defiants which manage to return to base, two are severely damaged and only three are still serviceable.

[With only three airworthy aircraft, 264 Squadron has been decimated and it is now obvious, even to the most optimistic, that Defiants can never again be risked in daylight actions.]

*

Meanwhile the Hurricanes of 79 Squadron are fortunate and escape without loss in spite of the odds against them. The Heinkels continue to Rochford where they meet heavy flak while they are bombing. Only minor damage is caused to the airfield.

The story is similar at Eastchurch where two squadrons of defending Hurricanes are held at bay by the escorting Bf 109s. Just after 9.00 a.m. the Dorniers unload on Coastal Command's light bomber airfield. Two Fairey Battles are destroyed on the ground and the airfield is left with numerous craters but there are no casualties. The station remains in operation.

*

At Headquarters, Australian Striking Force, the commanding officers of all units are advised by the general officer commanding that the AIF in the UK is to transfer to the middle east but this move will not take place before 25 September.

*

At 12.30 p.m. Rochford aerodrome is attacked again, this time by 30 Dornier Do 17s. Again the defending fighters experience great difficulty in breaking through the escorts to the bomber formation but, as before, the target is not seriously hit and remains serviceable.

It now seems obvious that the *Luftwaffe* is following its usual tactic of dividing its main effort into three phases and the third attack, flying at 25 000 feet (7 600 m), sweeps over Kent and the Thames Estuary around 4.30 p.m. Seven RAF squadrons are ordered to intercept but they are shocked when they discover a huge group of Messerschmitt Bf 110s and Bf 109s — there are no bombers. The British become embroiled in a fighter versus fighter combat, the type of action which AVM Park has sought to avoid.

One of the units engaged is 603 Squadron from Hornchurch which loses two Spitfires and their pilots. A third Spitfire, its pilot wounded, manages to limp home. Although they have been caught at a height disadvantage, the pilots of 603 Squadron believe that they have done well.

*

With darkness the *Luftwaffe* steps up its night offensive and numerous sorties are directed against the industrial Midlands and the north. Liverpool receives the first of 4 consecutive night raids. It is the city's heaviest attack so far and widespread damage is caused to the dock area. There are more than 470 casualties. Scattered bombing occurs in other areas. The whole evening underlines the ineffectiveness of the British night defences. There are numerous 'cat's eyes' patrols by single-engined fighters and John Hewson of 616 Squadron is finding that a Spitfire is not good for night fighting. Flames from the aircraft's exhaust stacks render the pilot's night vision almost useless. Hewson also feels that it has an uncomfortably long landing run.

Of 5 Blenheim night fighter squadrons which fly more than 80 sorties, only one machine even sights an enemy raider. It is an aircraft of 600 Squadron flown by Charles Pritchard. The Australian is sent out to patrol over Hornchurch at 8.50 p.m. He is then ordered to patrol a line which enemy aircraft must cross on their way to the Midlands. Before long he sees the exhaust flames of an aircraft in front and above. Pritchard pushes the throttles wide and goes after it, climbing higher until the Blenheim's controls become sloppy. He manoeuvres the plane into position behind the German bomber and fires a long burst. The startled bomber immediately turns and dives. All Pritchard can do is watch because it is too fast for his poor old Blenheim to catch.

Resuming his patrol line a few minutes later he sights more exhaust flames below. He dives after them and the Blenheim rocks and bucks as it passes through the other plane's slipstream. There seems to be a good chance of a kill as he closes the gap but suddenly he is blinded by a searchlight. When he last sees it the German bomber, like the one before it, is diving away too fast for him to catch it.

Without ammunition and low on fuel Pritchard returns to Hornchurch. It has been an exhausting evening and he has difficulty landing.

If the British night defences are inefficient and ineffective, so too are those of the Germans. RAF Bomber Command sends nearly 80 bombers to 6 targets in Germany and several airfields in France. Berlin is attacked again and from now on it will be regularly included in routine raids. Out of the force sent out, only one Blenheim and one Hampden fail to return.

THURSDAY, 29 AUGUST

The night raids on Liverpool and other areas have an effect on British industry which is probably not anticipated by German planners. Almost 70% of the towns along the flight paths of the bombers are placed on a 'Red' warning (raid likely or imminent). The sirens send thousands of people to air-raid shelters while the lights of the factories, railway stations etc., are extinguished for lengthy periods. This disrupts industrial activity and production.

Daylight brings dull weather with showers in some areas. The *Luftwaffe* does not appear all morning.

The remaining few Defiants of 264 Squadron leave Hornchurch for Kirton-on-Lindsey. The effects of combat and stress are clearly evident. They are led out by a 20-year-old pilot officer, the only experienced man left.

*

Just after 3.00 p.m. radar detects enemy activity over Cap Gris Nez, Boulogne and the mouth of the Somme. No. 11 Group musters 13 squadrons of fighters to meet the threat. Each British pilot is aware of the recent warning issued by AVM Park not to engage in battle unless bombers comprise part of the enemy formation because the RAF cannot afford to lose fighters wastefully in fighter versus fighter combat. They encounter an obvious trap. There are two small formations of bombers, Dorniers and Heinkels, escorted by possibly 500 to 600 fighters. Most of the British squadrons shear off but a few become involved in desperate fighting. One of these is 603 Squadron which claims one Bf 109 destroyed and three probables for two Spitfires damaged.

*

German intelligence notices that the English fighters are avoiding combat and deduce that the RAF is weakening. In the evening *Luftflotte 2* despatches several *Staffeln* of Messerschmitt Bf 109s on free chases hoping to catch some unsuspecting victims.

At Hornchurch Richard Hillary of 609 Squadron climbs into the cockpit of his Spitfire with a feeling of suspense. A moment later his plane, along with 7 others, is airborne.

Over Manston the Spitfires encounter 20 yellow-nosed Messerschmitt Bf 109s. The British fighters are badly placed below the enemy. As the Messerschmitts begin to dive, flight leader Brian Carbury orders the Spitfires into line astern and he turns into the attack. Hillary sees Carbury fire at the leading 109 which goes into a half-roll to evade. Seizing his chance Hillary delivers a full deflection burst while it comes through his sights. The Messerschmitt bursts into flames and spins down out of sight.

Hillary does not have time to think about his first victory because for the next few minutes he is caught up in a wild *mêlée* as Spitfires and Messerschmitts twist and turn in all directions. Then suddenly and unexpectedly, the sky is clear.

The Spitfires are ordered back to base but Hillary finds a squadron of Hurricanes flying in sections of three with no rearguard. They are from 85 Squadron. Hillary decides to join them and act as their 'Arse-end-Charlie', the man who weaves back and forth above and behind the main formation to protect it from surprise attack. Unfortunately, it is Hillary who is taken by surprise as bullet holes start appearing in his port wing. He has been bounced from out of the sun and his Spitfire goes into a spin. Lower down Hillary recovers and checks his plane. Black smoke is pouring from his engine and the smell of glycol is very strong. There is no chance of reaching Hornchurch or Lympne so he chooses the closest corn field and makes a wheels-up belly-landing. A salvage crew from Lympne is swiftly on the scene and takes charge of Hillary's Spitfire which will be written off.

*

On this day in Gullane, Scotland, Ian Bayles and Rowena Dutton are married.

[Ian Norman Bayles was born in Melbourne on 13 August 1918, son of Norman Bayles, a noted solicitor and the representative of Toorak on the Legislative Assembly, and Roma Mary Hill Neill, née James. The family went to England in 1923 and Ian and his mother stayed. He attended Winchester College.

In 1937, before going to university, Ian Bayles returned to Australia with his father. It was decided that he would read for the law at Oxford University and take his Bar examination in England with the ultimate aim of practising in Melbourne. He enrolled at Oxford in 1938 and while there joined the Oxford University Air Squadron and therefore the RAF reserve. He was called up in October 1939, and from then until April 1940 was at the RAF Flying Training School, Cranwell.

P/O Ian Bayles was posted to 152 Squadron which was stationed at Acklington and had just converted to Spitfire Is. In May he went to No. 5 OTU at Aston Down for the very first OTU course on Spitfires. From there he was posted to 249 Squadron but by 11 June he was back in 152 Squadron.]

*

The *Luftwaffe* sends 200 bombers to attack Liverpool and Birkenhead for the second night running. The sky is cloudless making navigation easy so the Germans have no difficulty locating their target. Diversionary raiders bomb targets on the outskirts of London.

RAF Bomber Command sends 81 aircraft on scattered raids to airfields in France and Holland and to such centres as Bottrop, Essen, Mannheim and Soest. As on the previous night, one Blenheim and one Hampden are lost.

FRIDAY, 30 AUGUST

With weather conditions likely to remain fine for several days, *Luftwaffe* chiefs decide to increase operations against Britain. Just after dawn several light raids, designed as feints to test RAF reaction, are directed against a north-bound convoy in the Thames Estuary.

*

By now over 80% of the *Luftwaffe's* Messerschmitt Bf 109s are concentrated in the Pas de Calais area under Kesselring's command. Radar reports a major attack of over 100 planes building up over Cap Gris Nez at 10.30 a.m. It continues to gather strength until the first of three successive waves, setting off at half-hour intervals, advances on the coast. AVM Park, guessing that this will be a fighter sweep, does not react and his judgement is proved sound when three *Gruppen* of Messerschmitts Bf 109s cross the coast.

The second wave crosses at 11.00 a.m. and the Observers' Corps reports 40 Heinkel He 111s and 30 Dornier Do 17s escorted by up to 100 fighters — Messerschmitt Bf 109s and Bf 110s. This time Park acts, sending up 16 squadrons, two of which are assigned to guard the sector station airfields at Biggin Hill and Kenley. There are so many aircraft in the air that the fighting soon becomes confused and by 11.45 a.m. the air raid situation over Kent and Surrey is totally mixed up. The *Luftwaffe* is certainly after the vital Fighter Command sector stations.

At about 11.30 a.m. Green Section of 79 Squadron from Biggin Hill attacks an estimated 30 Heinkel He 111s, one of which is shot down. The 4 Hurricanes of Blue Section are led by F/O Ted Morris and Blue 2 is Bill Millington. Instructing Blue 3 and Blue 4 to keep the fighters off, Morris leads Millington down into a vertical dive through another bomber formation to split it up. Millington opens fire as a Heinkel looms up in front of him but at the edge of his vision he sees a collision — Morris has crashed into a Heinkel. There is no time to watch as he hurtles through, narrowly missing a collision himself. As he pulls out of his dive the Australian can see that the Heinkels have split up and over the radio Blue 4 calls that he has seen Morris bail out. To one side, a Heinkel goes down with both engines on fire.

As the dogfight is in progress a *Staffel* of Ju 88s, part of the third raid, arrives over Biggin Hill unsighted by the 12 Group squadron on patrol. Fortunately for the sector station, most bombs fall wide of the airfield but cause damage in the villages of Biggin Hill and Keston.

At 12.10 p.m. a lone Hurricane comes limping back to the airfield. It has been heavily damaged by Bf 109s but Millington manages to land safely. In the fight the Australian has destroyed one Heinkel, probably destroyed a second and damaged a Bf 110. The other 6 Hurricanes land 5 minutes later. Altogether 79 Squadron and its sister unit at Biggin Hill, 610 Squadron, claim 10 victories.

*

No. 43 Squadron from Tangmere is one of the units blocking Kesselring's third wave of bombers. The Hurricanes meet them crossing the coast. Over Brighton Dick Reynell becomes separated and realizes he is in danger of being attacked by 5 fighters which he identifies as Heinkel He 113s (*sic*). It is his first combat and he is trapped. The Germans have the advantage of speed and height but the Hurricane is more manoeuvrable and Reynell is no ordinary pilot. They adopt dive and climb attacks, coming down one at a time onto the Australian's tail while the remainder stay above to cut off any escape. Reynell quickly turns tightly as each German plane comes into range and completes his circle to come in behind. Needing to keep his eye open for the next incoming fighter, there is little chance for him to line up a target as the enemy dives away and zooms for height. It is a tense and frustrating situation and timing has to be perfect because one slow reaction could mean the end. The procedure is repeated for a full 10 minutes until the Germans, probably low on fuel, tire of it and leave.

*

Instead of waiting a couple of hours before launching the next attacks, Kesselring begins an assault just after 1.00 p.m., sending waves of bombers and fighters over the south coast of Kent at 20-minute intervals. The constantly mounting pressure is felt throughout Fighter Command and it seems that the Germans are building up toward their ultimate goal — invasion. The most critical period of the battle of Britain is obviously beginning.

At 4.00 p.m., again without pause, the third and perhaps heaviest group of raids is plotted building up. During the next two hours large and small formations of enemy aircraft flood in over Kent and the Thames Estuary. The Junkers Ju 88s which appear over Biggin Hill at 6.00 p.m. only number 9 but the havoc caused by their bombs is far worse than that of any previous attack. The airfield is taken completely by surprise. Six of 79 Squadron's Hurricanes manage to scramble before the bombs start falling but 610 Squadron, already up, is too far away to help defend its own base. There is wholesale destruction as workshops, cook houses, the sergeants' mess and WAAF quarters are wrecked and 90% of the station's transport is damaged or destroyed. All electricity, water and gas mains are cut and two parked aircraft are reduced to scrap. The airmen's shelter is pulverized by a direct hit and all those who had crammed in a few moments earlier are killed. Another bomb hits the airwomen's shelter and the concrete walls cave in, crushing and smothering those inside.

Everyone outside pitches in and digs furiously to free the trapped women. Ambulance and stretcher parties stand by. One-by-one the women are carried out: some are barely recognizable because of dirt and blood on their faces. Others are dazed and bruised but all, except one, are alive. Lena Button from Tasmania is the only casualty. Altogether, 39 personnel have been killed and 26 injured.

*

Today's fighting has been the heaviest so far experienced. Twenty-two Fighter Command squadrons have been in action, some of them 4 times and almost all twice. After dark there is no respite as bombers from *Luftflotte 3* make their way from France. At least 130 of them are aiming for Liverpool and numerous scattered raids are heading for other centres. RAF night fighters prove unequal to the task of stopping them although this is not through lack of effort. From Hornchurch the Blenheims of 600 Squadron have their busiest evening of the war so far. The pilots and their crews, including Charles Pritchard, each fly two sorties and one crew goes up three times.

*

The RAF is on the offensive as well. Throughout the night more than 80 Hampdens, Wellingtons, Whitleys and Blenheims fly to 5 targets in Germany and airfields in France, Holland and Belgium.

The target for 149 Squadron is Berlin. The crews are briefed to attack and destroy industrial targets and cause maximum disturbance.

A German Junkers Ju 88 bomber in British markings after capture (AWM SUK 15203).

The squadron leader's tail gunner is an Australian, Sergeant Nugent Joseph Bull.

At Lindholme 5 Hampdens of 50 Squadron are ordered to attack an oil refinery north-east of Gladbeck.

Close to midnight Bob Reed is flying over the Ruhr approaching Gladbeck when his aircraft is caught by dazzling searchlight beams and accurate anti-aircraft fire. The brightness renders map reading and target identification impossible. Reed has to break away and escape into the clouds. He drops his bombs east of Gelsenkirchen.

All except one of the 8 Wellingtons of 149 Squadron reach Berlin and release their bombs. From the night's operations Bomber Command loses 4 aircraft: two Whitleys, one Wellington and one Hampden.

SATURDAY, 31 AUGUST

Daylight at Biggin Hill brings the promise of a warm summer's day. The station is still operational despite the previous day's bomb damage and at the dispersals the fighters are being given their pre-flight checks.

Soon the remaining Spitfires of 610 Squadron will be flying north to Acklington for a rest. Its place will be taken by 72 Squadron (Desmond Sheen).

Just before 8.00 a.m. radar stations report 4 waves of enemy aircraft approaching, three flying up the Thames Estuary and the leading formation closing in over Dover. No. 11 Group despatches two squadrons to Dover but, when the Observers' Corps reports that the enemy force is composed of single-engined fighters, control tries to recall them. No. 1 Squadron RCAF does not turn away in time and is bounced by Messerschmitt Bf 109s. It loses three Hurricanes. Unable to tempt the RAF any further, the Messerschmitts shoot up the Dover barrage balloons.

The enemy force heading up the Thames estuary in three waves is estimated at 200. To counter this, 11 Group scrambles 13 squadrons from 7 airfields around London. One German formation proceeds to North Weald, a second group of Dornier Do 17s with escorting Messerschmitt Bf 110s heads towards the 12 Group sector station at Duxford and the third formation of Dorniers has Debden airfield as its target. The 12 Group controller at Duxford is caught by surprise and urgently requests cover for his airfield. AVM Park acts swiftly and diverts the 9 Hurricanes of 111 Squadron, already on patrol, to intercept. Luckily they are well positioned for a head-on attack, shooting down at least one Dornier and scattering the rest for the loss of one Hurricane.

The force heading for Debden arrives unchallenged over the base. Approximately 100 bombs fall on the airfield, damaging three barracks blocks and inflicting 18 casualties. Four Hurricanes are damaged on the ground but the base remains operational.

On their way back the Dorniers and their escorts are intercepted by 9 cannon-armed Spitfires of 19 Squadron from Fowlmere. The second section is led by F/O James Coward and the third by New Zealander F/O Francis Brinsden. Coward selects a Dornier but his cannons fail. Suddenly his own aircraft is hit and something strikes his leg, almost severing it below the knee. With extreme difficulty he manages to bail out and within half an hour is in an ambulance on his way to hospital where his leg will be amputated below the knee.

[Air Cdr James Baird Coward AFC retired from the RAF in September 1969, and eventually settled in Australia. At the time of writing he resided in the Australian Capital Territory.]

Meanwhile Frank Brinsden engages a Bf 109 head-on. His Spitfire is hit and immediately falls into a dive. He bails out successfully and lands unhurt.

[W/Cdr Francis Noel Brinsden retired from the RAF in 1966 and at the time of writing resided in Western Australia.]

*

At 9.00 a.m. two more groups of enemy aircraft are reported. The first, a heavily escorted formation of Dornier Do 17s, bombs Eastchurch airfield but damage is superficial. The second, another fighter sweep, strafes Detling where once again damage is light. For the rest of the morning there are numerous radar alerts and, while these strain the defences by requiring 11 Group squadrons to be brought to 'Readiness', RAF fighters are not committed once the Observers' Corps reports that the raids are all made up of Bf 109s. AVM Park cannot afford to lose aircraft or men needlessly.

*

Just after noon, 100 aircraft cross the coast near Dungeness and split up to fly up two clearly defined corridors. A formation of Dorniers heads towards Croydon and the other force of Heinkel He 111s appears to be aiming for Biggin Hill. Just near Maidstone this second group splits and one wave of Heinkels diverts towards Hornchurch. All of the bombers are heavily escorted.

At 12.30 p.m. all the Hurricanes of 79 Squadron are ordered to patrol over Biggin Hill.

Similarly 603 Squadron is scrambled from Hornchurch. The squadron is still using sections of three planes with Red Section leading and Blue and Green Sections to right and left. The last three machines form a rearguard section above and behind. Richard Hillary is Blue 2. By 12.40 p.m. the squadron is at 28 000 feet (8 500 m) and searching. Someone calls 'Tally ho' as 20 German fighters are spotted below. For once the Spitfires have a height advantage but they have obviously been seen because the Germans form a defensive circle. Hillary picks out one machine and sees his tracer bullets converging on the Messerschmitt's nose but then he has to pull back on the control column. When he looks again the German circle has broken up but he cannot see the plane he had attacked. Seconds later the sky is empty.

Hillary is of two minds. He realizes that to fly about alone in a hostile sky is to ask for trouble but he is still carrying ammunition which might be put to good use. Over Dungeness about 40 Hurricanes are on patrol and he climbs to join them. Suddenly he realizes that there are too many planes . . . Looking closely at the aircraft in front of him he discovers to his horror that there is a swastika on its tail. He is alone with 40 Messerschmitt Bf 109s! Luckily the Germans do not know that he is there and, seizing the chance, he closes in on the last 109 and fires. The stricken plane flicks over and spins down out of sight. Hillary heads as fast as he can for Hornchurch and supposed safety.

No. 79 Squadron has been vectored onto an incoming raid but is unable to break through to the bombers because of the protective Bf 109s. The Heinkels drone relentlessly on towards Biggin Hill. In the dogfight Bill Millington destroys a Bf 109 while two more are probably destroyed by the other pilots.

At Biggin Hill many bombs fall wide of the mark but the runways are so badly cratered that 79 Squadron, returning from the fight, is diverted to Croydon. Every available man and woman works to repair the airfield as quickly as possible so that 79 Squadron can come home.

While the bombs are falling on Biggin Hill 12 Hurricanes of 601 Squadron are taking off from Debden to intercept enemy aircraft over Colchester. Clive Mayers is Red 3 in 'A' Flight. They are climbing, approaching the Thames Estuary when the leader calls 'Tally ho' to indicate that 30 heavily escorted Dornier Do 17s have been sighted flying over the London dock area. Higher up there are at least 12 Messerschmitt Bf 109s which dive as 601 launches its attack. Red Section concentrates on the bombers and Mayers presses the firing button before diving below them. One enemy bomber crashes near

Tottenham. Mayers climbs back and attacks the formation from every quarter. Banking to follow them out to sea, he looks for an opportunity to make a final attack and notices two Dorniers flying to the coast of Kent. He overtakes them, notices that the port engine of the nearest machine is stopped and concentrates on it. The Dornier starts to dive but he follows, fires off his remaining ammunition and watches it crash into the sea.

Back at Hornchurch by 1.15 p.m. Richard Hillary hears over the loud-speaker that there is a large enemy formation approaching the airfield. He peers upwards but the bombers are not visible. Everything seems to happen at once. The Spitfires of 54 Squadron scramble to clear the aerodrome before the bombs rain down. Hillary watches as the last three begin rolling down the runway. The bombers are in sight now, about a dozen of them shining in the sunlight. With the scream of the first falling bomb, Hillary hunches his shoulders and ducks his head but watches the progress of the three Spitfires. The leading plane is piloted by the New Zealand ace, F/Lt Alan Deere. They have just become airborne when an explosion catapults them apart. Deere's Spitfire hurtles up 100 feet (30 m) losing its propeller and one wing and crashes down along the runway. The second machine digs a wing into the ground and spins around onto its airscrew while the third has both wings blasted off.[14] Hillary dashes into the air raid shelter which shakes and heaves from the concussion of each explosion. For three minutes the bombing lasts, then there is silence. The runways have gaping holes and piles of dirt are strewn everywhere but the damage is surprisingly light.

Miraculously the three crashed Spitfire pilots survive with only minor injuries.

Hillary inspects his own plane. There is a large bomb crater nearby and the Spitfire has been showered with dirt and rubble but it is intact.

The station commander orders all available personnel to assist in repairing the airfield's surface so that it will be ready for use as soon as possible.

*

The routine is the same at Biggin Hill where, by tea time, one runway is back in use allowing the Spitfires of 72 Squadron arriving down from Acklington to land at their new base. As he brings his plane in, Desmond Sheen is shocked by the condition of his new surroundings.

Around 4.30 p.m. the Hurricanes of 79 Squadron begin coming back from Croydon.

*

Throughout the afternoon small groups of bomb-carrying Messerschmitt Bf 110s, escorted by Bf 109s, mount low-level raids on radar stations in Kent and Sussex and the CHL installation at Foreness. What all the defence chiefs fear most, that the Germans will simultaneously knock out the sector stations and radar sites, seems to be happening. However all radar installations are back in operation again by evening.

Around 5.00 p.m. the *Luftwaffe* attacks Hornchurch and Biggin Hill again. At both airfields every available fighter is ordered into the air.

While the fighters are away the Germans arrive over Hornchurch again. Apart from further damaging the runway and dispersal pens the bombs destroy only two grounded Spitfires and one airman is killed.

At Biggin Hill the damage is far more serious. One bomb falls on the cables and telephone lines outside the operations block; now it is no longer possible to control or plot and everybody dives to the floor as the explosions draw nearer. The operations room is plunged into darkness as the lights fail and a portion of the roof caves in. Fragments of steel and glass from the walls and plotting screens shatter everywhere. Outside, two of the remaining hangars and the messes are destroyed but miraculously there are no deaths. Ambulances and fire engines racing to the scene from Bromley and Westerham find the roads reduced to craters and rubble and cannot make their way through.

The Hurricanes of 79 Squadron, although they are scattered, chase the retreating enemy. Bill Millington in Hurricane P3050 is closing in on a bomber when he is bounced by two Bf 109s. He manages to evade them and turn on them. He chases one down and causes it to crash and watches as the pilot struggles out of his burning machine.

Millington's preoccupation with what is happening below causes him to forget the second Messerschmitt. He realizes too late that it is behind him when he feels the concussion of cannon shells smashing through his plane's radiator and engine. Something strikes his left thigh and smoke seeps into the cockpit. His Hurricane is on fire and, choking and retching, half blinded by smoke, Millington forces the cockpit canopy back and prepares to bail out. The air clears his vision enough to see a small village below which he recognizes as Tenderden. His burning Hurricane is going down into the middle of it! Fighting the urge to jump, the Australian eases back into the cockpit, grasps the controls and manages to level out in spite of the increasing flames. There is no power but he is able to glide down and crash-land in an open field. Wounded in the thigh and suffering from burns, Millington climbs out of the cockpit just before the Hurricane's fuel tank explodes.

No. 603 Squadron encounters a large number of Messerschmitt Bf 109s over the Thames estuary and, in a large dogfight, loses two Spitfires. One pilot is killed. The second manages to bail out safely but his plane crashes into a house in Essex.

Flying back to Hornchurch after the fight Richard Hillary sights 12 Dornier Do 17s heading back to France approximately 5 000 feet (1 500 m) below him. He dives to attack and when he comes into range presses the button but nothing happens. He is out of ammunition! He has no time to turn away; all he can do is hurtle on and somehow he flies through the formation and emerges unscathed.

In spite of the craters 72 Squadron is able to land back at Biggin Hill. In its baptism of fire in 11 Group it has destroyed three enemy aircraft and damaged two others but at a cost — three Spitfires have not returned. Desmond Sheen is posted missing.

Sometime after the others have returned a lone Spitfire appears over Biggin Hill and makes its approach. It is recognized as belonging to 72 Squadron's Australian flight commander. Surveying the scene after he

Bill Millington, who flew with 79 and 249 Squadrons, with Pipsqueak. Millington found the dog and made him 249's mascot. Bill Millington did not return from a mission on 30 October 1940 and is presumed to have died on that date (photograph courtesy of Andy Saunders).

lands Des Sheen notes that nearly all of the station's hangars and workshops have been destroyed.

*

Peter Townsend of 85 Squadron has been shot down. Now he is transported to to Hawkhurst Cottage Hospital and then to Croydon General Hospital but on the way, as demanded by some newly-made tradition, his driver conducts him to the Royal Oak Tavern where the locals toast him as a hero and raise their tankards to the damnation of the enemy. Later a short, chubby Australian in his dark blue uniform, is brought in and, despite the obvious discomfort of burns and a wounded thigh, he introduces himself as 'Bill Millington' and immediately has a pint thrust into his outstretched hand. The airmen are warmed by the hospitality of the people.

*

Overnight more than 150 German bombers are active, most of them visiting Liverpool and Birkenhead for the fourth evening in a row. Widespread nuisance bombing also occurs. A single delay-action bomb falls on the airfield at Duxford.

*

RAF Bomber Command mounts attacks on Berlin and Cologne and on airfields in Holland and Belgium. No. 61 Squadron at Hemswell despatches 5 Hampdens charged with bombing the aero engine factory at Spandau near Berlin. Weather conditions make accurate bombing impossible. Hampden X2906, flown by Ray Earl, has to abort the mission because of radio failure.

*

Of those airmen deemed eligible for the Battle of Britain Clasp, 5 have been killed during August:

1 August	P/O Bryan McDonough	236 Squadron
11 August	F/Lt Stuart Walch	238 Squadron
12 August	F/Lt Carr Withall	152 Squadron
13 August	F/O Dick Glyde DFC	87 Squadron
15 August	P/O Frank Cale	266 Squadron

Of those deemed ineligible for the Battle of Britain Clasp but included as Australian on the Battle of Britain Roll of Honour at Westminster Abbey, four have been killed in August:

3 August	P/O John Gilbert and Sgt Ben Gannon	206 Squadron
12-13 August	F/O Ellis Ross DFC	83 Squadron
21-22 August	P/O Angus Robson DFC	44 Squadron

Three Australians are still recovering from injuries:

P/O John Cock of 87 Squadron, wounded 11 August
P/O John ('Tiger') Pain of 32 Squadron, wounded 18 August
P/O Bill Millington of 79 Squadron, wounded 31 August.

Dornier bombers over Biggin Hill in August 1940 (Ministry of Defence, UK, photo no. ZZZ 5620F).

Two Australians have been made POWs:

F/Lt Allen Mulligan of 83 Squadron, bailed out and captured 12/13 August
P/O Vincent ('Bush') Parker of 234 Squadron, bailed out and captured 15 August.

*

With 39 aircraft written off on this day Fighter Command has suffered its heaviest losses to date although aircraft loss is not the major cause for alarm because the output of Hurricanes and Spitfires for the month exceeds the projected estimates by 69%. Far more critical is the loss of aircrew. Of the 46 squadron commanders who began the battle of Britain early in July, 11 have been killed or wounded. Of the 97 flight commanders 27 have been killed, 12 seriously wounded and 7 promoted to take command of squadrons. The loss of these skilled airmen is Dowding's most serious problem. The training programme has been cut, volunteers have been obtained from other commands and Czech, Polish and Canadian squadrons, previously held in reserve, have been ordered into battle. Even so Dowding and Park are coming to the dreadful realization that they are not winning.

With pressure mounting day by day, the fight for survival is reaching its most dangerous period . . .

SEPTEMBER, 1940

SUNDAY 1

Records indicate that the Australian personnel listed below are on strength in RAF Fighter Command Squadrons at 9.00 a.m. on 1 September 1940:

SQUADRON	[AIRCRAFT]	AIRMAN	BASE	
17	[Hurricane]	Sgt D. Fopp	Tangmere	[11 Group]
32	[Hurricane]	P/O J.D. Crossman	Acklington	[13 Group]
		P/O J.F. Pain		
		(In hospital recovering from wounds received 18-8-40)		
43	[Hurricane]	F/Lt R.C. Reynell	Tangmere	[11 Group]
65	[Spitfire]	AF/Lt C.G.C. Olive	Church Fenton	[13 Group]
72	[Spitfire]	F/Lt D.F.B. Sheen DFC	Croydon	[11 Group]
73	[Hurricane]	P/O C.A. McGaw	Church Fenton	[13 Group]
79	[Hurricane]	P/O W. Millington	Biggin Hill	[11 Group]
		(In hospital recovering from wounds received 31-8-40)		
87	[Hurricane]	P/O J.R. Cock	Exeter	[10 Group]
		(Recovering from wounds received 11-8-40)		
111	[Hurricane]	P/O H.G. Hardman	Debden	[11 Group]
141	[Defiant]	P/O A.N. Constantine	Turnhouse	[13 Group]
145	[Hurricane]	F/O R.W. Bungey	Dyce	[13 Group]
152	[Spitfire]	P/O I.N. Bayles	Warmwell	[10 Group]
		Sgt K.C. Holland		
234	[Spitfire]	AF/Lt P.C. Hughes	Middle Wallop	[10 Group]
264	[Defiant]	LAC V.W.J. Crook	Kirton-in-Lindsey	[12 Group]
		(On course at 5 OTU, Aston Down)		
600	[Blenheim]	F/Lt C.A. Pritchard	Hornchurch	[11 Group]
601	[Hurricane]	P/O H.C. Mayers	Debden	[11 Group]
603	[Spitfire]	P/O R.H. Hillary	Hornchurch	[11 Group]
609	[Spitfire]	P/O J. Curchin	Middle Wallop	[10 Group]
		P/O R.F.G. Miller		
616	[Spitfire]	F/Lt J.M. Hewson DFC	Kenley	[11 Group]

In addition three Coastal Command squadrons have been attached to Fighter Command or have operated under its control:

SQUADRON	[AIRCRAFT]	AIRMAN	BASE	
235	[Blenheim]	AF/Lt F.W. Flood	Bircham Newton	(A Flight)
			Thorney Island	(B Flight)
236	[Blenheim]	F/Lt R.M. Power	Middle Wallop	
		F/O W.S. Moore		
248	[Blenheim]	P/O C.C. Bennett	Sumburgh	
		P/O A.L. Hamilton		
		P/O J.D. Peterkin		

For Desmond Sheen and the men of 72 Squadron it is the beginning of a busy day. Because of the damage inflicted on Biggin Hill the squadron is to move to Croydon. No. 79 Squadron remains at Biggin for air defence.

Other changes are taking place and No. 46 (Hurricane) Squadron, which is back to strength after being wiped out at the end of the Norwegian campaign, is moved from Digby to Stapleford Tawney, changing places with the battered No. 151 Squadron.

At Tangmere after losing two commanding officers within days, 43 Squadron is taken over by S/Ldr Caesar Hull, the popular South African.

*

Taking advantage of cloudless conditions the *Luftwaffe* begins building up its first raid around 10.20 a.m. After the usual diversionary feints 60 bombers, escorted by 60 fighters, advance on Dover where the force splits into two groups. The German plan is for each to split up again so that 4 targets can be hit: Biggin Hill, Detling, Eastchurch and London docks.

At Croydon 72 Squadron is directed onto a formation of Dorniers coming in south of the Thames. Over Beachy Head, Des Sheen lines up one bomber but, before he can fire, a glance behind reveals that 6 Messerschmitt Bf 109s are after him. The situation is the same for all of the 72 Squadron pilots and in the frantic dogfight which takes place three Spitfires are shot down. One pilot is killed and one wounded. Two other Spitfires have to force-land.

One of the aircraft shot down is Desmond Sheen's. In a twisting, turning encounter he manages to break free of the 6 Bf 109s but not before his engine is hit by a cannon shell and bursts into flames. The Australian bails out. As he floats down Sheen surveys a scene that will live in his memory forever. On his right he can see explosions from bursting bombs in the Dover area with answering anti-aircraft fire from the defences. On his left he can see bombs falling on London Docks. The air is pungent with the acrid smell of cordite and it throbs to the engines of the bombers punctuated by the whining, straining sounds of fighters as they dive, climb and turn somewhere above. Not far off a Bf 109 falls in flames. A parachute blossoms out but its harness must be faulty because the airman dangling beneath suddenly falls away to oblivion. Another 109 turns towards him but there is a Spitfire on its tail. It twists away and both planes merge into the panorama.

Sheen lands lightly in the middle of a field.

*

At Biggin Hill the funeral of those killed in the earlier raids is held in the small cemetery beyond the airfield. Over 50 coffins lie next to the newly-dug graves. There are not enough flags to cover them all. Representing the station is Group Captain Grice and his senior WAAF officer. There are many civilians present, friends and relatives of the deceased. Just as the padre begins the air raid siren wails and 79 Squadron's Hurricanes prepare for take-off. Grice insists that everyone takes cover and only when he is satisfied that they are as safe as possible does he allow the ceremony to continue. Anti-aircraft guns open fire and bombs whistle down as Biggin Hill suffers its fifth raid in

Headstone of Aircraftwoman Edna (Lena) Button, a Tasmanian serving in the WAAF, killed during an air raid at Biggin Hill in August 1940 (RAF official photograph 0065/87/10).

48 hours. As the noise fades the dead of Biggin Hill, including Lena Button, are laid to rest.

Biggin's runway is now so pitted by craters that 79 Squadron's returning Hurricanes are diverted to Croydon. The airfield is out of service until late afternoon.

*

After another heavy midday attack the *Luftwaffe's* last wave of operations begins around 5.30 p.m. when several formations sweep in over the coast of Kent. They are mostly fighters and, following AVM Park's instructions, the RAF fighters avoid contact. However, there are small groups of bombers and 50 aircraft bomb Hawkinge and Lympne while a small formation of Dorniers bombs Biggin Hill which suffers its third raid in one day. Within an hour effective communications are re-established and next day the airfield will be operational.

*

The cruiser HMAS *Australia*, which has been serving with the British Home Fleet on a patrol in the Arctic Sea north of Norway, returns to the Clyde. The ship's 850 men look forward to shore leave after action against the Vichy French and their Arctic patrol.

*

Up until midnight the *Luftwaffe* is relatively quiet but afterwards over 100 bombers carry out widespread single and small-scale attacks. The Germans' greatest success occurs between Swansea and Neath where 6 10 000 ton (10 160 tonne) oil storage tanks are set ablaze.

RAF Bomber Command also stages widespread attacks with 131 aircraft sent to 10 targets in Germany and to airfields in Holland and Italy.

For Raymond Earl of 61 Squadron the target is the aircraft components factory at Stuttgart. Over Stuttgart he has difficulty identifying his target because of thick haze but he does locate a marshalling yard nearby and attacks this instead. As a result of his bombing fires break out.

MONDAY, 2 SEPTEMBER

The weather continues to be fine with early fog. No. 17 Squadron (Desmond Fopp) moves forward to Debden, changing positions with 601 Squadron (Clive Mayers). Even while Fopp is landing at Debden the *Luftwaffe* is building up a heavy raid behind Calais. Radar indicates formations of 30 and 40 aircraft and shortly afterwards the Germans come in over Dover, with 40 Dornier Do 17s closely escorted by Messerschmitt Bf 110s and high-flying Messerschmitt Bf 109s. They break up for separate attacks on Eastchurch, North Weald, Rochford and Biggin Hill. This change of tactics (early morning sorties by the *Luftwaffe* have always been confined to single reconnaissance aircraft before this) catches many sector controllers by surprise because they only have standing patrols over their airfields.

No. 11 Group despatches 11 squadrons altogether and of these only

5 make contact. Consequently, as 9 Spitfires from 72 Squadron, which has moved forward to Hawkinge for the day, are heavily engaged over Maidstone, 9 Dorniers slip through and carry out a sharp, low-level thrust at Biggin Hill. Joining 72 Squadron for the day is its former C.O., Ron Lees, who is on 'leave'.

At Hornchurch 603 Squadron is scrambled and as soon as it is realized that the airfield is in no danger, the Spitfires are ordered over Kent in an effort to catch the retreating enemy. Richard Hillary is flying with P/O R. Berry when they chase three Bf 109s out over the sea towards France. They are half-way across the Channel when Berry catches his victim and Hillary's finally crashes off the French coast.

*

A second attack forms up over France about noon and a raid of 250-plus approaches Dover. Determined not to be caught unprepared again, the 11 Group controllers send their squadrons forward as soon as possible and they encounter the enemy as the German formations begin to split up for their separate attacks. The Spitfires of 72 Squadron are among the first to engage the enemy over Herne Bay. During the battle one Spitfire crashes and two others are damaged.

Five miles (8 km) east of Sheppey, Spitfires from 603 Squadron encounter an estimated 80 Bf 109s. There is the usual dogfight and as it breaks up into individual combats, Richard Hillary sights a single Messerschmitt heading for France. He tracks it for 10 minutes determined that it will not escape and he is over France before he can attack. The enemy plane turns to engage him head-on, firing wildly. The German's cockpit canopy breaks off and a second later they flash past each other.

Hillary is in a dangerous position alone over France and he discovers 12 Bf 109s turning in formation on the same level. He is well positioned to attack one of the fighters at the edge of the formation and sends it spinning down. He sees the Messerschmitt burst into flames before he scurries off at full throttle leaving 11 angry German fighters behind. Landing back at Hornchurch well after everyone else, he lodges claims for one destroyed and one damaged.

While Richard Hillary is chasing Messerschmitts over France, the Biggin Hill controller requests reinforcements from neighbouring sectors. Four more squadrons are sent in, one being 43 Squadron from Tangmere. Dick Reynell is flying as Red 3 in 'A' Flight. Over Ashford at 1.10 p.m. they encounter Bf 109s. Reynell singles out a victim and after a short burst, white vapour appears from the Messerschmitt's fuselage. It starts to climb away but the Australian gives chase and fires off two more bursts from dead astern which appear to have no effect. Still climbing, Reynell's Hurricane is losing ground but then unexpectedly the 109 turns back towards England and he is able to head it off. The German pilot seems to sense danger but, before he can slip away, Reynell fires another short burst which hits the Messerschmitt's engine. The fight has brought both planes close to the ground and the 109 crash-lands and breaks up.

*

Pressure from the *Luftwaffe* continues. By 3.15 p.m. another large raid is detected over Calais. Again 250 German aircraft come in over Dover and fan out over Kent to various targets. Biggin Hill is hit again and so are the airfields at Detling, Kenley, Eastchurch and Hornchurch.

One target of special concern to Dowding and Park is Brooklands airfield where the Hawker and Vickers factories are situated. The two commanders have been fearing a move to bomb aircraft factories. To meet this potential threat Park has a standing patrol of fighters from Tangmere along a line from Weybridge to the south coast over Guildford. At this time of the afternoon Spitfires from 234 Squadron (F/Lt Pat Hughes) are on patrol but they are ordered forward to tackle the enemy over Kent, unfortunately leaving enough of a hole in the defences for the enemy raiders to break through. The Germans have been briefed to attack the Hurricane factory but they bomb instead the Vickers works in which Wellington bombers are being assembled. Damage is moderate. The force sent to raid Hornchurch is so heavily engaged by British fighters that fewer than a dozen bombs fall within the airfield's boundaries.

Eastchurch suffers badly when its bomb dump is hit and the resulting explosion demolishes practically every building nearby, smashes water mains and sewers, destroys 5 aircraft and puts the communication system out of action.

Around 4.00 p.m. No. 72 Squadron runs into a swarm of Messerschmitt Bf 110s. South of Dungeness, Ron Lees' Spitfire is struck by enemy fire and he is wounded in the leg. He manages to bring his damaged machine back to Hawkinge.

*

Around 5.00 p.m. a fourth major attack appears over Dungeness. The Germans are after the airfields again and Eastchurch is struck a second time and a hangar is destroyed. Casualties for Eastchurch for the day are 4 killed and 12 wounded. Detling receives approximately 100 bombs, wrecking a hangar and rendering the airfield unusable for two hours.

Over Hornchurch 11 Spitfires from 603 Squadron are vectored onto a large force of 50 bombers escorted by 50 Messerschmitt Bf 109s. Richard Hillary shoots up a 109 but loses track of it so when he lands at Hornchurch he can only claim a probable. Nevertheless this has been his most successful day because in three combats he has claimed two destroyed, one probably destroyed and one damaged.

Soon afterwards 72 Squadron is up again, heavily involved in combat over the Thames Estuary. The 72 Squadron records that it has been 'a hell of a day' but it can claim 18 victories.

At Kenley 616 Squadron has lost one Spitfire during the day but its pilot has bailed out safely. John Hewson DFC who has been mainly flying 'cat's eyes' patrols, is to be posted to No. 7 ETS at Peterborough as an instructor. He decides to stay with the squadron as long as he can before reporting to Peterborough.

*

The last hours of the day are not kind to Dick Cohen and the crew of Sunderland P9602/G of 10 Squadron, RAAF. Their aircraft crashes into the shore and sinks while landing at Oban on the Firth of Lorne, Scotland, in the haze and darkness. The crew evacuates safely.

*

Darkness brings some rest and respite for the defences until 1.30 a.m. when individual raiders are plotted coming in over East Anglia. Seventy-five bombers from *Luftflotte 3* come over during the next few hours, approximately half of them carrying out minelaying operations while the rest conduct scattered raids on Liverpool, the Midlands and south Wales.

RAF Bomber Command despatches over 80 aircraft to a wide variety of targets including the U-boat base being established by the Germans at the French port of Lorient. A fire raid on the Black Forest is also launched. At Lindholme the Hampden of F/O Bob Reed is one of two 50 Squadron aircraft briefed to bomb the viaduct of the Dortmund-Ems Canal. As they arrive over the target they find that the Germans are employing a smoke screen so that only the eastern branch of the canal is visible. Reed makes his bomb run at 6 000 feet (1 800 m) travelling along the canal and drops a stick of eight 250 lb (114 kg) GP bombs.

TUESDAY, 3 SEPTEMBER

Weather conditions are dark and overcast but in the south the day turns out fine and warm.

At Hornchurch the Spitfires of 603 Squadron are brought out onto the tarmac at 8.00 a.m. Richard Hillary's machine, Spitfire X4277, has had a new hood fitted but it refuses to slide open. Hillary and the corporal fitter hastily work on it, taking turns filing and oiling but it proves stubborn and only slowly responds.

While they toil the first raid of the day, which will turn out to be the heaviest, commences building up behind Pas de Calais at 8.30 a.m. When it is reported that the leading formations are mostly fighters, the controllers instruct the defending Hurricanes and Spitfires to avoid combat by disengaging and flying north.

German bomber crews have been briefed to attack the airfields at Hornchurch, North Weald and Debden. At 9.45 a.m. over 50 Dornier Do 17s escorted by about 80 Messerschmitt Bf 110s fly up the Thames Estuary and turn for North Weald. The fighter controllers who have been delaying the decision to scramble to see which way the raid would turn, now scramble all available squadrons to take off.

At Hornchurch Hillary's cockpit canopy can now slide half-way but it refuses to budge any further. Suddenly the moment he has been dreading arrives as the loud-speaker orders 603 Squadron to take off. Squeezing into his cockpit Hillary presses the starter and the Rolls-Royce Merlin bursts into life. Altogether 8 Spitfires take off.

At Debden No. 17 Squadron's Hurricanes scramble into the air.

While the British fighters are climbing, the Dorniers have time to make a thorough attack on North Weald. They drop over 200 bombs, many of them delay-action, and the airfield is severely damaged. Four personnel are killed and the runways are heavily cratered but the airfield remains operational. As the Dorniers set course for France they come under attack from 6 squadrons of Hurricanes and one of

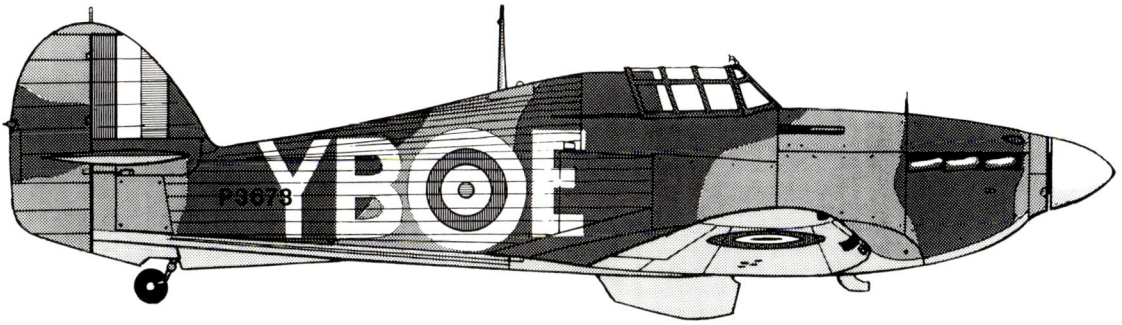

Hawker Hurricane Mk I, P3673, YB-E of 17 Squadron RAF. This was the aircraft flown by Desmond Fopp on 3 September 1940 when he was shot down and severely injured. It was not his usual machine, this being P3539, YB-I, which had earlier had the tips of its propeller damaged in a taxying accident (not by Fopp). The tips had been cut off by 3 inches (7.6 cm) with a hacksaw, throwing the prop hopelessly out of balance. P3673 crashed and burned near a dairy farm close to Ingrave, Essex. Aviation archaeologists from the London Air Museum have since recovered numerous minor parts.

Spitfires. The latter are the cannon-armed Spitfires of 19 Squadron but 6 out of the 8 have gun stoppages and are obliged to disengage immediately.

The Hurricanes of 17 Squadron are unable to reach sufficient height for a favourable attacking position. When they encounter the Dorniers they have to engage them head-on, hoping to break their enemy's formation. After hurtling through, they twist back for individual combat and as he does this Desmond Fopp loses contact with his section leader. He attacks a Dornier and after several bursts one of its engines begins to burn. Closing in he fires again but at the same time he notices three Messerschmitt Bf 110s behind him. In the same instant his guns stop firing — out of ammunition! Fopp, in a split second, decides that his best chance is to simulate an attack on the enemy fighters to catch them off guard. He turns into the Bf 110s and to his amazement they break away. Seizing his chance he dives for the ground.

Suddenly there is an explosion. A Messerschmitt has put a cannon shell into the radiator of his Hurricane and it blows up. The Australian is immediately surrounded by flames. In severe pain he tries to struggle out of the cockpit but his straps still clamp him in place. After releasing them, he succeeds in escaping from the blazing machine and falls several thousand feet before pulling his ripcord. The parachute cracks open with a jerk on his shoulders. As he floats down he realizes that his vision has been impaired by the flames but he can see that his uniform is smouldering. Suddenly he begins to crash through the leaves and branches of trees. He has descended into a wood in Essex.

Freeing himself from his parachute harness which is still smouldering, Fopp staggers blindly through the trees until he reaches a clearing. He is at once confronted by farm labourers armed with pitch forks. They are ready for anything and Fopp is in such a state that they are unable to tell whether he is British or German. The vigour of his language dispels their doubts but he is close to exhaustion and can now hardly see anything. Gentle hands cover his burns until an ambulance arrives.

Richard Hillary of 603
Squadron. Author of *The last
enemy* and a member of the
Guinea Pig Club, he was killed
in an aircraft accident on 8
January 1943 (Public Archives
of Canada photograph
139031).

Besides Fopp's Hurricane, No. 17 Squadron loses one other aircraft
and its pilot. On the credit side, it claims destruction of two Bf 110s
and two Do 17s plus two Bf 110 probables.

*

While Fopp is in combat with the Dorniers the controller warns 603
Squadron of 50 enemy aircraft directly above them. They are Bf 109s
from JG 26. Almost automatically the Spitfires go into line astern but
in the same instant the Messerschmitts dive. Seconds later both sides
meet and in the ensuing dogfight it is every man for himself.

Richard Hillary climbs steeply in a bid for height, the Spitfire
hanging on its air screw. Just below to his left he sees a lone 109
climbing as he is but slanting away. Hillary has the sun at his back and
attacks. The 109 takes punishment but it refuses to fall. He continues
firing from dead astern and sends off a four-second burst. The Messerschmitt suddenly bursts into flames and spins down towards the
sea.

As Hillary delivers his last burst his plane is rocked by an explosion.
Instantly the cockpit becomes a mass of flames. He reaches up to open
the canopy but it is jammed shut. In pain and panic he tears off his
straps and with a superhuman effort forces the hood to slide but then
drops back exhausted into his seat. He reaches for the control column
to turn the crippled plane onto its back but the heat is too intense. He
raises his hands to his eyes and faints. The burning Spitfire spins down
to about 10 000 feet (3 000 m) where Hillary's unconscious form falls
into space. As he hurtles down he recovers his senses and pulls the
ripcord. His plunge is arrested with an uncomfortable jerk and the
parachute brings him down into the sea off Margate.

Observers on shore have seen him come down but the Margate
lifeboat has difficulty finding him, searching in vain for three hours.
The crew is about to give up when one man spots the floating parachute. Hillary is drifting in and out of consciousness. At last he is lifted
to safety but he has suffered cruelly; once a handsome young man, he
has been grotesquely mutilated by fire.

*

In the afternoon another attack develops but it is not as big as the
morning raids and is successfully beaten off.

Low cloud at night hinders German operations but about 60 raiders
reach London and other scattered targets. The General Aircraft Co. at
Feltham in Middlesex is damaged.

WEDNESDAY, 4 SEPTEMBER

The weather is fine and warm over the south of England while in the
north there is occasional rain and strong winds.

Several 12 Group Squadrons move southwards closer to 11 Group
as reinforcements for the squadrons around London. Among them, 9
Hurricanes from 73 Squadron (Charles McGaw) transfer from
Church Fenton to Duxford.

Spitfire X4277, XT-M, the aircraft in which Richard Hillary was later shot down on 3 September 1940 (photograph courtesy of Bryan Philpott).

In accordance with *Luftwaffe* Operations Staff Orders issued on 1 September, targets for *Luftflotte 2* are divided between sector airfields and aircraft factories to halt the seemingly endless flow of fighters and equipment to British squadrons. The first major raid in the morning concentrates on the airfields with the Germans coming in via Dover and the Thames Estuary. Dover's barrage balloons receive their usual harsh treatment and Lympne airfield is strafed. At Eastchurch bombs make 6 large craters on the runway and destroy ration stores.

*

Large concentrations of German aircraft are detected by radar around noon. By 1.00 p.m. about 300 enemy planes cross the coast at Beachy Head, Hastings, Folkestone and Dover. Fourteen RAF fighter squadrons are scrambled and of these 9 make contact. The squadrons on the edge of the danger zone are ordered up to cover the sector stations. No. 73 Squadron patrols over North Weald, a target of the previous day's bombing.

Near Testerton, Spitfires from 72 Squadron encounter two formations of German escort fighters but almost immediately they form defensive circles. Desmond Sheen checks that there are no other enemy aircraft above before he attacks a Messerschmitt Bf 110 about to join one of the circles. As he fires smoke comes from the 110's port engine but Sheen is closing in too fast and has to break away. As he climbs again for height he looks around for other aircraft but there are none to be seen. One instant the sky had been a mass of planes, now . . . nothing.

153

Patrolling over Tangmere the 12 Spitfires of 234 Squadron led by Pat Hughes have spiralled up to 15 000 feet (4 600 m) by 1.20 p.m. Down below, on the airfield, the Hurricanes of 601 Squadron are taking off. At the controls of one is Clive Mayers.

Hughes spots two groups of German aircraft. About 50 Bf 110s are coming in over the coast while 15 others are already circling over Haslemere lower down. Detailing Red, Yellow and Green Sections to attack the larger formation, Hughes leads Blue section down after the others. As soon as the Spitfires are sighted the 110s form their usual defensive circle. Hughes attacks the leading Messerschmitt head-on. His aim is deadly. The 110 rears up and another short burst strikes its fuselage, causing it to erupt in flames.

Seconds later the Australian comes in directly behind another 110 and fires briefly twice. The heavy escort fighter crashes and blows up. Suddenly Hughes is surrounded by three Messerschmitts and he notices a fourth slipping in behind. Manoeuvring wildly he fires three snap bursts to break them up and causes one to dive away. He pounces after it and empties the remainder of his ammunition. The 110 sinks and turns slowly towards the coast. It cannot get far because both engines are burning.

While all this is happening 601 Squadron intercepts bandits near Worthing. Clive Mayers goes into line astern following Red 1 who attacks a defensive circle of Bf 110s. Mayers finds a Messerschmitt slightly below him and fires briefly from above and behind. He attacks again from dead astern and sees smoke coming from both engines. He dives underneath and, as he does so, notices Red 1 attacking. He leaves his section leader to deliver the *coup de grâce* and he last sees the Messerschmitt trailing smoke with Red 1 in dogged pursuit.

Looking around he sees another aircraft flying out to sea. It is a Dornier bomber. Gradually he overhauls it but as he draws abreast it suddenly turns towards him. Mayers reacts quickly and charges in head-on. He presses his firing button and the bomber's glasshouse nose shatters to pieces as he flashes past. As he hauls back on his Hurricane's controls, the crippled German plane rolls over onto its back and dives vertically into the sea.

The German escort fighters have suffered badly and 234 Squadron alone claims a record 14 Bf 110s and one Do 17 destroyed for only one damaged Spitfire.

However, while the RAF fighters are successful in the air, a formation of bomb-carrying Bf 110s reaches Brooklands and drops 6 bombs on the Vickers works, destroying the Wellington bomber assembly sheds and inflicting 700 casualties, among them 88 dead. It is an unintended success for the Germans because they had been after the Hawker factory nearby — which escapes unscathed. Another raid reaches Rochester where the Short Bros factory producing the new four-engined Stirling bombers is damaged.

*

News of the expected arrival of a 'very important visitor' has the men of the 25th Brigade, Australian Striking Force at Salisbury Plain, making preparations all day. The VIP turns out to be the British Prime Minister, Winston Churchill, accompanied by detectives and a military secretary. The party drives to Lipcombe Corner to the 12th and

9th Battalions where Churchill, standing on a wooden platform, addresses the men through loudspeakers:

> Speaking to you in the name of the British Parliament and the people I express to you our deep gratitude not only because we know you would fight to the death — for after all no one wants to live forever — but because of the encouragement it gives us here, now that we are all alone ... I used to see the Anzacs in the last war, and I am certain that this new expeditionary force from Australia will revive and equal — it cannot excel — the glories of the famous Anzac Corps ... we are certain that the divisions sent from Australia will preserve the same glorious reputation which made them renowned twenty-five years ago and which caused the Australian Corps to be recognized by friend and foe alike as unsurpassed in all the valorous manhood of Europe ...

After this the convoy goes to the '72nd' Battalion at Tidworth Park and the 3rd Field Battalion at Arena Road where Churchill joins in a sing-song around a piano.[1]

*

With the day's air fighting obviously over the support squadrons return to their bases. Charles McGaw and 73 Squadron leave Duxford and arrive back at Church Fenton by 8.00 p.m.

*

Churchill is not the only leader making speeches to boost morale. Hitler addresses an audience of nurses and social workers at the *Sportpalast* in Berlin. In his speech he accuses the RAF of indiscriminate bombing. His address is, of course, well covered by the German press.[2]

THURSDAY, 5 SEPTEMBER

The stress of the sustained fighting is beginning to show on airmen and machines on both sides of the Channel but today will bring no respite, for once again the weather is ideal for combat.

Beginning around 10.00 a.m. *Luftflotte 2* launches numerous raids over southern England. There are at least 22 separate formations despatched although two are larger than the others. Kesselring has targeted the airfields of Croydon, Biggin Hill, Eastchurch, North Weald and Lympne.

Biggin Hill is still only able to operate No. 79 squadron. No. 72 Squadron, Desmond Sheen's unit, which is down to 9 serviceable Spitfires, remains at Croydon. No. 79 Squadron is scrambled to cover Biggin Hill and breaks up a raid of 30 bombers and their escorts. Six Hurricanes meet the Dorniers at 15 000 feet (4 600 m) and split them up so effectively that bombing is well off target.

Also up are 12 Hurricanes of 43 Squadron from Tangmere. It is obviously going to be a very busy day and reinforcements are brought in including 73 Squadron which moves from Church Fenton to Castle Camps.

After the raid on Biggin Hill Group Captain Grice makes an aerial inspection of his airfield. One hangar, although it is only a burnt-out shell, appears undamaged. This, he reasons, is why the enemy persists with attacks. Arrangements are made to place explosive charges in the hangar so that when the next raid occurs they can be detonated and the building brought down.

*

Just after lunch radar tracks a large concentration sweeping in over the Thames Estuary at extremely high altitude. These Heinkel He 111s and Junkers Ju 88s bomb the oil storage facility at Thameshaven and cause serious fires.

British squadrons are scrambled from everywhere.

Clawing for height over Kent, the Spitfires of 72 Squadron climb in the old tight formation of vics of three with the rear section providing two 'weavers' while the leader flies in the box position at the rear. It is the duty of the weavers to guard the others against surprise by German fighters but this time the warning comes too late. Over Canterbury Desmond Sheen hears a shout in his earphones but, before he can react, he is bounced from behind. His Spitfire shudders from a heavy burst of cannon and machine-gun fire and flying metal strikes his leg, hand and face. He passes out . . . The stricken Spitfire, with large pieces missing from its port wing, heels over into a vertical dive. Lower down Sheen regains consciousness and tries the controls but they do not respond. He has no idea how close he is to the ground although he senses that it is not far away. Releasing the harness pin to rid himself of his straps, he is instantly sucked out of his seat but he does not fall free because his feet get caught at the top of the windscreen. Pinned against the top of the fuselage, he struggles with all his strength but in vain.

Suddenly his feet are released and instinctively the Australian pulls the ripcord without even waiting to ensure that he is clear of the aircraft's tail. With a bone-jarring snap the parachute opens at only 800 feet (250 m). Sheen has only a split second glimpse of trees beneath him before he is crashing through boughs and branches. Fortunately the crown of a tree catches the top of his parachute acting as a brake so that his fall is slowed and he lands lightly. Apart from his wounds in the leg, hand and face he has suffered only a few extra scratches and bruises.

He notices a policeman on a bicycle coming towards him. He reaches Sheen, swiftly produces a flask and asks 'Why didn't you bail out earlier?'.

[Sheen is taken to Queen Mary's Hospital, Sidcup.]

The Hurricanes of 73 Squadron engage the Ju 88s but they run into a swarm of Bf 109s. Three Hurricanes are shot down with one pilot killed and one wounded. A fourth Hurricane is obliged to force-land. Two others, although badly damaged, limp back to base.

No. 43 Squadron is luckier and, although it too becomes involved with the Bf 109 escorts, no Hurricanes are lost. A member of Dick Reynell's flight shoots down a 109.

By now 234 Squadron is heading towards Gravesend where they

have noticed anti-aircraft fire. Pat Hughes is Blue Leader. Without warning the Spitfires are attacked from out of the sun by three Bf 109s. As Hughes breaks to counter-attack he spots 12 more Messerschmitts coming up the Thames Estuary. He is joined by two Hurricanes and together they attack the advancing 109s. A dogfight breaks out and, seizing his chance, Hughes fires a full deflection shot at one German fighter which blows up. He then goes after a vic of three more 109s, selects a new victim and gives chase from dead astern. The 109 drops away and lands in a field. The German pilot climbs out of his cockpit and a few soldiers run up and surround him.

The Messerschmitt Bf 109E of Franz von Werra in a field in Kent. Von Werra later escaped from the British in Canada into neutral America and returned to Germany, the only German airman to escape from captivity. Evidence strongly suggests that he may have been shot down by Pat Hughes (photograph courtesy of Fox Photos).

[This man is believed by many to be the German ace, Oblt Franz von Werra.[3] The bravado von Werra displayed as a fighter ace among his comrades remained with him as a POW. He proved difficult to hold and made numerous escape attempts.

With other prisoners, he was transferred to Canada. In Nova Scotia the prisoners were transported by rail from Halifax to their new camp and en route von Werra forced open a window and jumped from the moving train. This time he was not recaptured and made good his escape by crossing the nearby border into the United States which was still neutral. He was the only German aviator to escape from British custody and return to fight for his country again.

Concerning the combat which resulted in von Werra's fall into British hands, there is confusion. That he crash-landed on 5 September at Winchet Hill is not disputed but other circumstances surrounding the incident are open to question.

After returning to Germany, von Werra eventually became commanding officer of 1/JG 53 on the Russian front. He shot down 13 Russian planes to bring his tally to 21 but on 25 October 1941 the engine of his Bf 109 failed and it plunged into the sea near Vlissingen. He was drowned.]

*

Waiting at Biggin Hill for the usual 6.00 p.m. raid Group Captain Grice is almost disappointed when the *Luftwaffe* does not turn up. The Royal Engineers have set their charges and he can wait no longer to give the signal to demolish the burnt-out hangar. With probably the loudest explosion ever experienced at Biggin Hill the hangar disintegrates and from the air, the destruction of the base now seems complete.

[As he predicts Biggin Hill does not have another major raid. Whether this is because of Grice's action or the change in German tactics is open to conjecture.]

*

With darkness the German Air Force steps up its activity and London begins what will be its longest night alert so far. The targets are spread all over England and, although Sperrle's bombers can be tracked by radar on precise courses from Cherbourg, RAF night fighters are again unequal to the task of interception.

Night raids extend well to the north and, operating from Turnhouse in Scotland, Noel Constantine of 141 Squadron takes off on a patrol. After its disastrous debut as a daylight interceptor unit the previous July, the squadron has trained to use its Defiants as night fighters. In the middle of his patrol Constantine spots an enemy aircraft caught up in searchlights over St Albs Head but the bomber disappears into the blackness.

*

Bomber Command despatches 82 planes to targets ranging from Turin to Stettin and Berlin is raided for two hours. Three Hampdens and one Wellington are lost.

Hampden P4408 flown by Dereck French and his crew of 50 Squadron is one of 4 aircraft allocated to bomb the oil refinery at Stettin. They set out on a course to the target which will go north of Heligoland and south of Kiel. Over Denmark they encounter troublesome searchlights and accurate anti-aircraft fire and, between Brunsbruttel and the target, numerous flares, presumably dropped by German night fighters, are seen floating in the air. Visibility remains good all the way and Stettin is found easily but the flak put up by the defences is intense.

At 12.27 a.m. French carries out a bomb-run at 10 000 feet (3 000 m) and unloads 4 bombs and incendiaries. Three direct hits are observed causing bright explosions with white flames.

*

A Defiant of 141 Squadron; their effectiveness as night fighters left much to be desired (Imperial War Museum photograph CH 2523).

[On this day the first Empire Air Training Scheme contingent of Australian airmen consisting of 40 pilots, 42 observers and 72 air gunners, leaves Sydney for Canada to complete their training.]

FRIDAY, 6 SEPTEMBER

In London the air raid alert lasts a record seven-and-a-half hours.

*

Daylight brings fine weather once again and the British commanders, particularly Dowding and Park, know that the *Luftwaffe* will not allow any respite. The first radar plots appear at 8.30 a.m.

Numerous early morning reconnaissance sorties by single *Luftwaffe* aircraft suggest to Park that, as well as airfields and sector stations, the vital factories at Weybridge may be in danger. He requests AVM Brand to divert fighters to cover them and the task falls to 609 Squadron but a small raid reaches Brooklands while 609 Squadron is back on the ground refuelling. The Hawker factory is hit several times but damage is superficial.

The burning oil tanks at Thameshaven still ablaze from the previous day's raid are revisited by a large formation of bombers. The British squadrons scramble to intercept. At 8.45 a.m. 6 Hurricanes from 73 Squadron take off from Debden. Charles McGaw is in Green Section but it is Blue Section which falls foul of the escorting Messerschmitt Bf 109s. In a swift encounter one Hurricane is shot down and its pilot bails out wounded. The remaining two claim one 109 destroyed and a probable. Flying further back Green Section is unable to help.

Twelve Hurricanes of 43 Squadron scramble from Tangmere at 9.00 a.m. to patrol Mayfield. The unit is led by Caesar Hull while Dick Reynell leads Yellow Section. Shortly afterwards about 20 bombers are sighted flying below some distance ahead while an escort of 30 fighters is stacked up behind them. The bombers are too far away to be taken by surprise so 43 Squadron engages the fighters.

From within the ensuing dogfight Dick Reynell notices a lone Junkers Ju 88 straggling behind the rest. It loses height and he sees another Hurricane also going after it. The Australian dives towards them and as he draws closer he realizes that Caesar Hull is flying the other fighter. Joining forces they make two quarter attacks after which the Ju 88's guns no longer reply and they are all rapidly losing height. Reynell makes one more assault to use up his remaining ammunition on the heavily-damaged German machine and is about to fire when his Hurricane shudders from the impact of a cannon shell. Waiting for the right instant he breaks away, takes skilful evasive action and makes his escape.

High over Dover the Spitfires of 234 Squadron position themselves above 25 Bf 109s. Ordering his section into line astern, Pat Hughes launches the attack and his victim is mortally hit.

Hughes hauls back on his controls to regain height and finds 5 Bf 109s escorting a damaged Messerschmitt Bf 110. He stalks them from behind. The 110 has one engine on fire and just past Dover the crew bail out. By now Hughes is positioned behind the rearmost 109 and commences firing but three more Messerschmitts are diving at him from the beam. Determined to finish his target off, he keeps the button down until the last possible second. The 109 is hit badly and apparently has a ruptured oil tank. Breaking off Hughes turns swiftly into the three 109s, fakes an attack because he is out of ammunition and gives himself a chance to escape in the opposite direction. He lands at North Weald to refuel on his way home.

*

Ian Bayles of 152 Squadron flies his first sortie after reporting back from his honeymoon. The flight out over the sea is a low-level patrol looking for a downed airman.

*

Throughout the day there are three main attacks. Just before 1.00 p.m. 43 Squadron and Dick Reynell are again on patrol over Kent when they encounter some elusive Messerschmitt Bf 109s. After a fast, indecisive clash one German fighter leaves the scene with smoke pouring out of its engine.

*

Kenneth Slessor and Ronald Monson, the London representative for Sydney's *Daily Telegraph*, are relaxing at the Avon Hotel, Amesbury, when they are startled by a huge pale grey bomber with twin engines which thunders very low overhead. The Nazi swastika is clearly displayed on its rudder and huge black crosses decorate its wings. It disappears in seconds flying in a south-westerly direction. Monson rushes to telephone the Australian Headquarters at the Abbey. No British fighters are to be seen anywhere. Slessor is impressed by the German pilot's nerve.

*

HMAS *Australia* sails from the Clyde to join the RN naval force on its way to Dakar. The expedition is a joint British-Free French amphibious landing to capture Dakar in French West Africa to block its possible use by Germany as a submarine base.

*

Pat Hughes, photographed the day before his death on 7 September 1940. Hughes was the highest-scoring Australian pilot in the battle of Britain (photograph courtesy of Bill Hughes).

[By the evening of the 6th it has become obvious to British commanders that their situation is becoming grim. Between 24 August and 6 September Fighter Command losses have amounted to 295 fighters destroyed and 171 badly damaged. During the same period 103 pilots have been killed and 128 wounded. The average pilot strength of each squadron has sunk from 26 to 16.

AVM Park reports that the German bombing attacks on his aerodromes and sector stations have caused extensive damage to 5 forward airfields and 6 out of 7 sector stations. Manston and Lympne are out of action temporarily and Biggin Hill has been so badly battered that only one squadron can use it at a time. Material damage has been widespread and so severe that in terms of communications and facilities, crisis point is at hand. No. 11 Group is being crushed . . .]

Many veteran pilots who have been continually in combat over the past couple of weeks are reaching the end of their endurance. In the evening at Middle Wallop 234 Squadron's intelligence officer, Gregory Kirkorian, has an unexpected visitor — Pat Hughes. He looks tired . . . very, very tired. The Australian is in a depressed and unsettled state. As they talk, Kirkorian studies the man who is regarded by them all as the real hero of 234 Squadron. It is Hughes who has welded it into a real fighting force. His leadership in the air has been tough and uncompromising and on the ground he has remained 'one of the boys', very much a man to inspire others and to be followed.

Kirkorian tries to reassure the Australian.[4]

*

Headquarters Home Forces issues its preliminary Alert No. 3:
    'Invasion probable within three days'.[5]

*

Throughout the night the *Luftwaffe* is not as active as usual. Only single raiders are despatched to strategic areas of England, keeping the air raid sirens screaming and the people confined to shelters. Most fighter controllers feel that the Germans are resting after their sustained effort and heavy losses over the past fortnight but some suspect a more sinister reason for the relative quiet. Aerial reconnaissance has revealed that more invasion barges have arrived in the captured French ports. Heavy concentrations of troops are already nearby. Perhaps the Germans are husbanding their forces for the final blow . . . invasion?

SATURDAY, 7 SEPTEMBER

Apart from a few reconnaissance sorties by isolated German aircraft the first half of the day passes quietly.

During the morning the latest reports of increased German barge concentrations in captured French ports, building of new airfields close to the coast, construction of new heavy gun emplacements, rumours of bomber group deployments and information from captives are passed on to the British Chiefs of Staff (COS) together with a forecast that moon and tide conditions will favour a landing on the British coastline between 8–10 September. A COS meeting headed by Lieut- General Alan Brooke is scheduled for 5.20 p.m. to discuss whether or not 'Alert No. 1' (invasion imminent and probable within 12 hours) should be issued.

Meanwhile AVM Park instructs his controllers and squadron commanders to follow orders from Group Operations 'exactly' and 'without modification'.

[This statement was made necessary because squadrons had too often been positioned too high to successfully intercept the German bombers and instead had become embroiled with the escorting fighters.

Two days earlier, Park had also instructed that wherever practical, two squadrons were to operate together, with the Spitfires, because of their better performance at high altitudes, engaging the escort fighters while the Hurricanes attacked the bombers. He emphasized that it was vital to harass and destroy as many bombers as possible.]

Bearing in mind the *Luftwaffe's* continuous pressure on his airfields and sector stations, Park gives orders for the deployment of his squadrons and leaves Uxbridge to attend a conference called by Dowding at Fighter Command Headquarters, Bentley Priory.

*

The oppressive lull continues and radar screens remain empty. Sector controllers relax their fighter states but for many the quiet is nerve-racking.

At Tangmere after the midday meal the pilots of 43 Squadron, including Dick Reynell, relax outside the officers' mess. Someone produces a camera and takes photographs of them. Within a few hours two of the 8 men in the pictures will be dead.

At Fighter Command Headquarters a marker is placed on the huge map table just before 4.00 p.m. Radar has detected a build-up of over 20 aircraft over Pas de Calais. The *Luftwaffe* is beginning to move . . .

*

The pilots of 43 Squadron relax at Tangmere on the morning of 7 September; only hours later two of them were dead (photograph courtesy of Marjorie Horn).

On the cliffs near Calais the *Luftwaffe's* commander-in-chief, Hermann Goering, stands poised and waiting for an incredible passing parade. With him are Kesselring and Bruno Loerzer, commander of *Fliegerkorps II*, an entourage of high-ranking officers and a following of war correspondents and reporters. Goering had arrived earlier in his special VIP train for the purpose of personally commanding the assault against London. He poses for the press, looking skywards through his binoculars as 348 bombers and 617 fighters, almost 1000 planes, the largest aerial armada so far assembled, thunder overhead on course for the British capital. The rationale for the attack is that it should draw the few remaining English fighters into the air to be destroyed by the escorting fighters. It will also carry out the promises which Hitler had shouted to his audience in Berlin's *Sportpalast* a few days before:

> . . . In England they're filled with curiosity and keep asking: 'Why doesn't he come?' . . . Be calm. Be calm. He's coming! . . . He's coming! . . .

*

Park finds that besides Dowding and an NCO shorthand-typist to record the minutes of the meeting, there are 4 others present. These are Sholto Douglas, assistant chief of the Air Staff, a group captain from the Air Ministry, AVM H. Nicholl of Fighter Command and Australian-born AVM D.C.S. Evill, senior air staff officer.

Dowding paints a grim picture. Up to now his policy has been to concentrate most of his squadrons in the south-east with supporting units just outside 11 Group to be brought into action upon Park's request when needed. As squadrons become fatigued they have so far been rotated out of the combat zone and replaced by fresh ones drawn from the surrounding groups but if the present scale of attack is maintained this procedure cannot continue. He is after decisions on the best measures to be adopted so that a rapid recovery can be made should the situation change.

Evill has figures to confirm the worsening situation. Disregarding accidents and illness, total pilot casualties for the 4 weeks ending 4 September amount to 348. During the same period the three OTUs have turned out only 280 fighter pilots, resulting in a decline in numerical strength of 68. Park adds that the casualty rate in 11 Group is nearly 100 per week.[6]

There is a big difference between a pilot fresh out of an OTU and a seasoned combat pilot. Park suggests that new pilots should go from the OTUs to squadrons in the north for extra training and his squadrons should only receive fully trained pilots from the north to replace losses. It is agreed that a few fresh squadrons must be kept ready to relieve Park's most tired units when necessary and that the importing of airmen will come into effect when a squadron's strength falls to only 15 pilots.

For this purpose the squadrons are re-classified:

Class A: All squadrons which are based in 11 Group and those in 10 and 12 Groups which might be called upon by AVM Park to provide first line reinforcements.

Class B: Squadrons of all groups (other than 11 Group) fully established in men and machines, which the southern Groups can call into action with consideration of fatigue or lack of combat experience.

Class C: All remaining squadrons which, although possessing combat experience, have suffered crippling losses in action and are obviously overdue for rest and the training of new pilots. Experienced airmen will be 'milked' from these squadrons after a short rest to provide replacements for those in Class A and Class B.[7]

These will not be popular measures, particularly with such veteran 'resting' units as 32, 65, 85, 145, 151 and 615 Squadrons whose members have achieved much and paid a heavy price. Strong bonds have grown up between the survivors.

*

As the meeting continues, British radar operators are chilled by what they detect. It is not just another raid ... At 4.17 p.m. Park's controllers scramble 11 squadrons and 15 minutes later all fighter squadrons within 70 miles (110 km) of London are airborne or preparing to scramble.

The COS meeting at Whitehall begins at 5.20 p.m. and as it proceeds the first bombs whistle down on London's dockyard areas of Woolwich and the Isle of Dogs. The attack is concentrated because the leading bombers have arrived unmolested. British defences have been wrong-footed, most of Park's squadrons having been deployed to meet the usual airfield attacks. They are hurriedly redirected, only to arrive one by one and be confronted by a mass of German planes.

Nine Hurricanes from 43 Squadron had been scrambled at 4.35 p.m. under the leadership of Caesar Hull with Dick Reynell and F/Lt John Kilmartin as section leaders. The controller had directed them all over the place but now they find, crossing the coast near Folkestone, 25 Dornier Do 17s escorted by a huge number of fighters. Coming into

A publicity photograph showing test pilot Dick Reynell and Lord Nuffield with a Hurricane manufactured by Hawker Aircraft Ltd. Lord Nuffield signed the photograph on 8 July 1940 for Marjorie and Dick Reynell. Reynell was killed in action on 7 September 1940 (photograph courtesy of Marjorie Horn).

view at the same time are two other similar sized groups of bombers and fighters.

Hull leads his Hurricanes towards the front formation, climbing until they are 1 500 feet (450 m) above it. Ordering Kilmartin's section to keep off the fighters, Hull and Reynell lead their sections down on the Dorniers. They sweep around in a co-ordinated attack from astern, firing for all they are worth and then break away to make individual attacks. Time and again they dart in until most are out of ammunition but at the same time the escorting Messerschmitt Bf 109s shoot down three of the Hurricanes. Killed in action are the squadron's popular South African commanding officer, Caesar Hull, and its Australian flight leader, Dick Reynell. The latter, his plane shot up by Bf 109s, manages to bail out before it bursts into flames but his parachute fails to open.

Over the Thames Estuary, 73 Squadron encounters 25 bombers escorted by 30 Messerschmitt Bf 110s. Blue Section has the job of attacking the fighters but it has little chance to gain enough height, so the three Hurricanes attack the bombers instead. Each plane fires a short burst from about 350 yards (320 m) without any obvious effect and then zooms up into the sun. As they climb, a *Staffel* of Bf 110s in a defensive circle looms up into view. In a series of diving attacks on this formation the Hurricane pilots claim two Messerschmitts destroyed and one damaged.

Coming all the way from Middle Wallop, the Spitfires of 609 Squadron catch a formation of enemy bombers as it turns southwest of London. John Curchin manoeuvres Green Section to engage a group of Dornier Do 17s from the beam but at the last instant the Germans turn so that a co-ordinated assault becomes impossible. Curchin instructs his men to break up and make individual attacks while he goes after the leading Dornier. He turns in, closing fast, and fires a four-second burst before diving underneath and swinging around for a second attack from the other side. Again he fires for 4 seconds. The leading Dornier seems undamaged but suddenly the second bomber in the formation breaks away and falls in a dive. As the Australian turns off, he spots a single Messerschmitt Bf 109 below and ahead. He follows it through the thick smoke billowing over the Thames and finally catches up with it over the Estuary. He fires for three seconds. The 109 is hit and Curchin closes to 50 yards (45 m) as he fires for the last time. Pieces of the German fighter are torn away before it crashes into the sea.

*

The scene below is devastating. A huge cylinder of black smoke from burning warehouses near the docks billows steadily up into the clouds. The streets are full of the noise of racing fire engines and the shouts of running men. The docks and warehouses are ablaze as London's East End is hammered. Twenty percent of the bomb loads carried by the He 111s and Ju 88s are incendiaries and 30% are delayed action bombs of 2–4 hour and 10–14 hour delay. The sinking sun glints on the wings of the German bombers as they turn followed by the flak. Smaller planes dart in and out of the enemy formation but the sound of fighting overhead is drowned out by the noise in the streets. The German planes are being scattered but there are so many that they seem impossible to stop.

*

No. 234 Squadron runs into 60 German aircraft consisting of Dornier Do 17s and escorting Messerschmitt Bf 109s south-east of Folkestone. Pat Hughes is leading Blue Section in Spitfire X4009 and, ordering them to follow suit, he dives down after the bombers. He is well ahead of the others as he closes in on a straggling Dornier. Blue 2 follows the Australian down and sees him make a quarter attack on the German bomber. Large pieces fly off the enemy machine, then a wing crumples and it goes down spinning. An instant later Blue 2 sees a Spitfire, which he assumes to be that of Pat Hughes, spinning down with about a third of its wing broken off . . . Has there been a collision?

The Australian's plane spins wildly and he has no chance to bail out. It crashes at Bessels Green at 6.30 p.m.

In the same dogfight, 234 Squadron's commanding officer, S/Ldr 'Spike' O'Brien, is shot down and killed.

[In the confusion of a dogfight it is difficult to be certain about anything and uncertainty exists with regard to the events of this day. The combat report of Pat Hughes' wingman infers rather than states that the Aus-

tralian collided with a Do 17. Other sources suggest that he flew into the firing line of another British fighter.[8]

About one thing there is no dispute or controversy — Pat Hughes was the inspiration and driving force of 234 Squadron. When morale was dangerously low, it was his leadership which welded it into an efficient fighting unit.[9] Between 13 August and 7 September the squadron shot down 63 enemy aircraft and fought to exhaustion. Four days after his death it returned to St Eval, a much quieter sector.]

The British fighters, ammunition exhausted and fuel tanks close to empty, land back at their airfields in ones and twos. Pilots climb wearily out of their cockpits in grim silence carrying in their minds an unforgettable picture of the seemingly impregnable bulk of the German formations and of the terrible firestorm in London.

Flames spread furiously along the waterfront, granaries and warehouses collapse, falling into the river or crashing down into the streets, and rows of houses are obliterated. Every fire-fighting appliance for miles around is sent into the area. A huge pall of smoke prematurely darkens the sky but as night falls, London's agony is not over because the first of 318 German bombers are approaching, guided in by the huge fires. It is the start of a series of violent attacks which will go on for 57 consecutive nights — the blitz has begun.

Against the incoming stream of German planes British night defences are almost powerless and have to rely solely upon the 264

The work of German bombers; huge fires blaze out of control, in London's dock area on 7 September 1940 (Imperial War Museum photograph HU 653).

anti-aircraft guns ringing the city. There are only two squadrons of Blenheim night fighters available and one of these, No. 600 Squadron (Charles Pritchard) at Hornchurch, is unable to take off through the thick smoke which swirls across the airfield. All night the Germans cruise over London, a target impossible to miss, dropping 330 tons of high explosive and 440 incendiary canisters to stoke the inferno below. By morning 306 civilians will be dead and 1 337 badly injured.

*

At 8.07 p.m. Lieut-General Alan Brooke issues the code word 'Cromwell', Alert No. 1, to his Eastern and Southern Commands. The signal is received in some places with panic. Numerous Home Guard and army units order the ringing of church bells, the universal signal that an invasion is already taking place.

The 'Cromwell' alert comes into Headquarters, Australian Striking Force, at Amesbury Abbey at 9.30 p.m. and all units are placed at one hours notice to move. The 18th Infantry Brigade is handicapped by its incidence of leave, with almost 50% of its personnel absent. Many of the men of the 10th Battalion who are due back are unable to leave London because of the bombing.

War correspondent Kenneth Slessor, who is stationed at the Abbey, is awakened at 11.00 p.m. with the news that the Germans have landed on the south coast and that everyone has been ordered to stand by for an immediate move. Although this is unconfirmed, everyone appears to accept it as correct. General Wynter who had been absent when the signal had come in, is now back in his office. The Abbey has become a hive of activity and all available troops parade in full battle dress. One guard mutters to Slessor, 'I'll be glad when the bastards come'.[10]

With the passing of time the bustle gradually diminishes as they tensely wait for orders. By midnight the men are allowed to return to their tents and sleep but are told to be ready to move at one hours notice. The signal will be two or three blasts of a whistle. Some listen to the midnight news on the radio and learn that London has been under heavy attack and that fires in the East End are still out of control.

*

In the space of two hours, two of the most experienced Australian pilots have been killed in action. The news of Pat's death is broken to Kay Hughes late in the evening. After only 5 weeks of marriage, she is a widow.

For Marjorie Reynell the pain is the same. She and Dick would have had their second wedding anniversary in less than three weeks.

Both F/Lt Paterson Clarence Hughes and F/Lt Richard Carew Reynell are among those Australians deemed eligible for the Battle of Britain Clasp.

*

Overnight RAF Bomber Command, for the first time, concentrates most of its effort against the invasion barges being assembled in the Channel coast ports. Brian Best of 40 Squadron carries out a high-level attack on Dunkirk. His is one of several aircraft from the squadron ordered to bomb Calais and Dunkirk. His bombs are observed bursting in the target area.

A Heinkel He 111 over London's dockland on 7 September 1940 (AWM 128166).

SUNDAY, 8 SEPTEMBER

The bombing of London stops at 4.30 in the morning. After 12 hours, the people emerge, shell-shocked and silent, from their shelters. The air is full of fumes and smoke as the fires along the dock areas burn freely. So many are dead and injured and so many homes have been reduced to rubble. The stark horror and reality of war has struck home. Air raid wardens, rescue workers and volunteers, including many Australian soldiers on leave, dig amongst the ruins searching for the injured. Three main railway stations, including London Bridge, Waterloo and Victoria, are out of action.

At Amesbury Abbey, orders cancelling leave are issued and uncon- firmed rumours about invasion are rife. In case of invasion the tasks allotted to the 18th Australian Brigade are:

(a) Action against paratroop landings in the Salisbury Plain area,
(b) Reserve to V Corps in the South of England.

But there is no invasion. Early morning reconnaissance planes reveal that no fleet of German barges has crossed the Channel or even set sail.

Nevertheless anti-invasion patrols are stepped up all along the coast as far north as the Shetland Islands where Lewis Hamilton of 248 Squadron sets off on one such patrol.

*

In Berlin the Sunday morning papers carry the headlines:

'BIG ATTACK ON LONDON AS REPRISAL'[11]

The weather is fair in the early morning and late evening but the *Luftwaffe* only makes a few minor raids on airfields.

*

During the morning AVM Park flies in his Hurricane over the smok- ing British capital. His immediate reaction is one of anger but at the back of his mind he sees a glimmer of hope. If the Germans continue to strike at London and leave his airfields unmolested there is a chance.

Dowding uses the quiet of the day to rotate some of his weary squadrons. For the battered 'Fighting Cocks' of 43 Squadron, it is now time to rest and refit for it has suffered heavy losses, particularly of key personnel including three squadron commanders. It leaves Tangmere for Unsworth and will be replaced by 607 Squadron.

Likewise Bill Millington's unit, 79 Squadron, moves to Pembrey from Biggin Hill. It will be replaced by 92 Squadron.

The hard-working 'Treble One' Squadron flies north from Croy- don to Drem with its remaining 7 battered Hurricanes. Harry Hard- man leaves the squadron for two months of instructing in Flying Training Command.

Pat Hughes's widow, Kay, with the posthumous DFC awarded to her husband of 5 weeks (clipping from *Evening News*, London, 23 June 1942, held in P. Hughes's personal file, AWM 65).

Pilots were not the only Australians serving in Britain. Australian nurses are shown here, outside Australia House in London, in September 1940 (AWM 2811).

[On 6 November Hardman again rejoined 111 Squadron. In December his promotion to flight lieutenant was recorded in the **London Gazette**. Hardman stayed with the squadron until January 1941 when he was posted to Training Command.]

*

Communications are slow and by 7.00 p.m. at Amesbury Abbey reports of enemy landings have still not been confirmed but the status of the 18th Brigade is lowered to three hours notice to move. All day, personnel of the 10th Battalion have been returning in small groups and by 8.00 p.m. the unit is almost back to full strength.

*

At 7.30 p.m. the air raid sirens wail in London again as Sperrle's *Luftflotte 3* sends over a procession of Heinkel He 111s, Junkers Ju 88s and Dornier 17s loaded with high explosive bombs and incendiaries. The huge fires which have blazed out of control all day are re-stoked. During the night 412 more people will die and a further 747 will be injured. Damage to private homes, factories and docks is extensive.

For the second night in a row, RAF Bomber Command concentrates its efforts on enemy ports and barges, despatching 130 aircraft to Hamburg, Boulogne, Ostend, Bremen and Emden. The heaviest raid is to be by 49 Hampdens on the Blohm and Voss shipyard in Hamburg. Eight of these come from 61 Squadron and they take off at 8.30 p.m. for their long flight. At 8.38 p.m. Hampden X2911 with Ray Earl at its controls, leaves the ground.

One hour later, 6 Hampdens from 50 Squadron (Bob Reed) take off for the same target.

MONDAY, 9 SEPTEMBER

Just after midnight Wellington P9245 of 149 Squadron takes off from Mildenhall. It is one of 8 aircraft sent to attack enemy shipping and barges at Neuerbinnenhaven and Boulogne. Sgt Joe Bull is one of the gunners.

Of the 8 aircraft despatched from 61 Squadron to attack the dock-yards at Hamburg, 7 locate and bomb the target. Ray Earl and the others encounter intense anti-aircraft fire, not only over the target but all along the Elbe and from flagships moored at the mouth of the river.

Over Hamburg at 12.40 a.m. Bob Reed meets the same heavy con-centrations of searchlights and anti-aircraft fire. Reed's aircraft is caught in a beam but he carries out evasive action and successfully shakes it off. After this, he drops his bombs from 10 000 feet (3 000 m). Three of his 4 bombs land in the target area and explosions are seen.

Of the 49 Hampdens involved in the Hamburg raid one is lost.

During the raids on the Channel ports 7 planes are lost, 5 Blenheims and two Wellingtons. Both of the latter are machines from 149 Squad-ron. Joe Bull's plane is one of those which fails to return. Crippled by flak, it comes down into the sea.

Sgt Nugent Joseph Bull is one of those Australians listed on the Battle of Britain Roll of Honour at Westminster Abbey.

*

Daylight brings fair weather over the English Channel. The *Luftwaffe* remains quiet during the morning and in the early afternoon.

*

At Amesbury Abbey Kenneth Slessor interviews men who have been involved in the London raids. They tell how they helped in salvage and rescue work. Slessor can see that they have been shaken by what they have witnessed and their stories of casualties among women and chil-dren are horrifying.

Later Major St John, the deputy assistant adjutant general (DAAG), informs Slessor that 150 Australian Army reinforcements, plus a number of Australian sailors for service in the Royal Navy, disem-barked the previous day.

*

Park and Dowding are ready for the Germans. At 5.00 p.m. when the raid begins to materialize, 9 squadrons from 11 Group are in position while units from 10 and 12 Groups cover the factories and north Thames airfields. The *Luftwaffe* bombers are met early as they approach Kent and Sussex and most formations are broken up long before they can reach London. For the Germans it comes as a surprise because they had detected, so they thought, a weakening in the British defences during their first heavy raid on the 7th. Only a few bombs fall on the city.

*

Hurricanes of 111 Squadron being refuelled for another sortie (Imperial War Museum photograph CH 64).

[An order issued by the **Luftwaffe** command (**OKL**) dated 9 September outlines the systematic bombing of the British capital:

*The maintaining of the attack against London is intended to take place by day through **Luftflotte 2** with strong fighter and destroyer units; by night **Luftflotte 3** will carry out attacks with the object of destroying harbour areas, the supply and power sources of the city. The city is divided into two target areas, the eastern part of London is target area A with its widely stretched out harbour installations, target area B is the west of London which contains the power supplies and provision installations of the city. Along with this major attack on London the destruction raids will be carried on as much as possible against many sectors of the armament industry and harbour areas in England in their previous scope.[12]*]

In line with these orders, 195 of Sperrle's bombers raid London overnight for eight-and-a-half hours. By morning 370 more civilians are dead and 1 400 are injured. Three more railway stations are temporarily put out of action.

RAF Bomber Command divides its effort between 5 targets in Germany and the invasion barges in the Channel ports. Of the 76 bombers sent out, two fail to return.

TUESDAY, 10 SEPTEMBER

Dull weather covers most of Northern Europe and so German air activity is restricted to small nuisance raids.

At Sumburgh in the Shetland Islands, Clarrie Bennett of 248 Squadron in Blenheim WR-G has to abort a reconnaissance mission over the Sogne Fjord in Norway because the weather deteriorates further.

From St Eval three Blenheims of 236 Squadron take off to act as escorts for the *S.S. Scillonian*. Leading the formation is Dick Power. Over Penzance they rendezvous with the vessel and escort her to the Scillies.

*

For London at night there is no respite. Most of Sperrle's 148 bombers unload on the capital but Merseyside and south Wales are also raided.

Again most of RAF Bomber Command's effort is directed at the invasion barges in the Channel coast ports but a small force of Whitleys attacks Berlin. Two Hampdens of 50 Squadron are assigned to bomb the barges in Ostend Harbour. Both are piloted by Australians, Bob Reed in Hampden L4097 and Dereck French in P4408.

WEDNESDAY, 11 SEPTEMBER

Dereck French lands Hampden P4408 at Lindholme at 1.23 a.m.

Bob Reed and his crew will never return. They will never be heard of again. Reed's Hampden is one of two lost by Bomber Command during a mission to bomb the Potsdamer Station in Berlin. Two Whitleys are also lost. However, for the first time, the Germans have to admit that considerable damage has been caused in Berlin.

F/Lt Robert James Reed is one of the Australians listed on the Battle of Britain Roll of Honour at Westminster Abbey.

The British capital has suffered overnight too with hits registered on Thames-side factories and warehouses. Other bombs fall on the central London area where Buckingham Palace is damaged.

*

With daylight the weather is dull and cloudy so that in the morning *Luftwaffe* air activity is restricted to reconnaissance sorties over southern England. In the afternoon both *Luftflotte 2* and *Luftflotte 3* send out heavy co-ordinated attacks but this time the RAF is better prepared.

As the running battle approaches London, the long-range Messerschmitt Bf 110 *Zerstörers* pull away to the south and circle over the Croydon area in order to cover the bombers' retreat. Such is the fury of the fight that the short-range Messerschmitt Bf 109s, which had been briefed to cover the bombers over the target, are already low on fuel and are obliged to break off the action early. In London the city,

A 1944 sketch of John Hewson, who flew with 616 Squadron during the battle of Britain (photograph courtesy of John Hewson).

the docks and the suburbs of Islington and Paddington all receive hits but the German bombers, particularly a formation of Heinkel 111s from KG 26, are left to the mercy of many Hurricanes and Spitfires. At least 7 Heinkels are shot down and 10 damaged. The *Zerstörers* fail to cover because they are fighting for survival against a large force of Hurricanes.

Park is unable to draw assistance from Brand's 10 Group because at the same time two raids fly in over Portsmouth and Southampton. The bombers are heavily escorted by Bf 109s and Bf 110s which keep the British fighters at bay although the defenders are equally effective in ensuring that little damage is done.

Amid this widespread activity, a few bombs also fall on Biggin Hill, Kenley, Brooklands and Hornchurch.

*

John Cock reports back to 87 Squadron at Exeter after hospitalization. Through the day he makes three flights in Hurricane P3389. He has not been in the cockpit of an aircraft since being shot down on 11 August.

John Hewson leaves 616 Squadron to report to No. 7 ETS Peterborough as an instructor.

[John Hewson stayed at Peterborough for just under two months before being appointed to No. 31 SFTS Kingston, Canada. In February 1943 he left Canada and with promotion to temporary squadron leader was assigned to an army airfield construction group. This work remained his until late 1944 and he went with the army units as they moved from Algiers to Tunis and on into Italy from Salerno to Leghorn.

After returning to England, he was senior administrative officer to RAF Predannack in Cornwall until November 1945 when he took command of 567 Squadron at Manston. Hewson remained in command until April 1946, when he left the RAF.]

*

PDU Spitfires bring back alarming reports of the large number of German invasion barges assembling in the French Channel ports. Late in the afternoon Bomber Command and Coastal Command launch assaults by more than 100 aircraft on Dunkirk, Calais, Le Havre and Boulogne. Defending Bf 109s react violently and the British lose 15 planes but destroy about 100 barges.

One attack on Calais is carried out by a dozen lumbering Fairey Albacores of the Fleet Air Arm escorted by 6 Blenheims of 235 Squadron. Leading the Blenheims is Fred Flood in Blenheim L9396, QY-G. Over the target they run into Bf 109s and although the Blenheims put up a desperate defence they are hopelessly outmatched. In a running fight, one Blenheim goes down at 8.10 p.m. and just over 10 minutes later QY-G falls and disappears.

F/Lt Frederick William Flood is the 9th Australian deemed eligible for the Battle of Britain Clasp to be killed in action.

*

The *Luftwaffe* begins its usual night assault on London early, and 180 bombers attack the British capital while stray aircraft are active over Scotland, Bristol Channel, Lincolnshire and Norfolk.

THURSDAY, 12 SEPTEMBER

London has suffered again from the overnight bombing but since the 7th the city's anti-aircraft defences have doubled. Bombing accuracy suffers accordingly and many aircraft unload outside the city's central area.

*

The weather is unsettled and because of poor conditions the *Luftwaffe's* effort over the south and east coasts is greatly reduced.

At Warmwell a section of Spitfires from 152 Squadron, one of them flown by Ian Bayles, is scrambled. The fighters climb through the cloud using full throttle, are vectored towards a bandit and are told to 'Buster' (hurry). Shortly afterwards the ground controller hears a cry of 'Tally ho', indicating that the bandit has been sighted. Bayles recognizes a Junkers Ju 88 which is making good use of the cloud cover.

*

At Acklington John Crossman is only in the air for 15 minutes in Hurricane V6551 and when he lands he is told to report to 46 Squadron at Stapleford Tawney. He does not like leaving 32 Squadron but his posting means that he is going to 11 Group and the fighting.

Also moving southwards to Redhill, near London, is Charles Pritchard and 600 Squadron which will be better positioned to intercept incoming night bombers. Besides its standard equipment of Blenheim If night fighters, it now has a Douglas Havoc I for evaluation and a couple of fast and powerful, heavily-armed Bristol Beaufighters.

*

The *Luftwaffe's* night sorties are much reduced with the main bomber force heading for London, but single aircraft carry out raids over a wide area. A delay action bomb falls close to St Paul's Cathedral. It will take three days to remove it.

Near Warmwell Ian Bayles and his wife, Rowena, receive news that there is an unexploded bomb close to their home. However, they carry on as normal and retire for the night.

*

Weather conditions seriously curtail Bomber Command operations overnight so that only 40 Wellingtons are despatched to docks and railway yards in Germany and at Brussels.

FRIDAY, 13 SEPTEMBER

The weather is unsettled with bright intervals followed by showers, so German aerial activity is limited to reconnaissance sorties.

*

Upon arrival at Stapleford Tawney John Crossman is shocked by the primitive facilities but at the same time he is impressed by the friendliness of the pilots. The unit's commanding officer is S/Ldr J.R. MacLachlan and P/O 'Pat' Patullo is Crossman's section leader.

A detachment of Defiants from 141 Squadron (Noel Constantine) is sent from Turnhouse to Biggin Hill to reinforce the sector's night fighting strength. Left alone by the *Luftwaffe* since the attacks began on London, 'the Bump' is recovering because staff have been able to effect repairs.

*

The *London Gazette* announces the award of the DFC to two officers of 10 Squadron, RAAF, F/Lt J.A. Cohen and S/Ldr W.N. 'Hoot' Gibson.

*

Rumours of invasion are heightened by a report from No. 1 (Maidstone) Observer Group indicating that 10 large enemy transports, each towing two barges, are moving from Calais to Cap Gris Nez.

*

London is again the target for night raiders although there are smaller harassing attacks in several other areas. About 105 *Luftwaffe* bombers come over the capital.

RAF Bomber Command maintains pressure on the French invasion ports and 92 Hampdens, Blenheims, Whitleys and Wellingtons raid Boulogne, Calais and Antwerp. The British bombers discover that German defences have been strengthened with concentrations of searchlights and anti-aircraft guns. Two bombers, a Blenheim and a Hampden, are shot down while more than 70 landing barges are claimed destroyed.

SATURDAY, 14 SEPTEMBER

Showers and thunderstorms are widespread and the Straits of Dover, Thames Estuary and English Channel are shrouded in cloud. Sorties flown by the *Luftwaffe* are limited. Radar stations between Poling and Great Bromley are subjected to electronic interference by the Germans.

Just after 3.00 p.m. three small raids cross the coast on course for London via the corridors over Kent and the Thames. Several 11 Group squadrons are scrambled but about 20 Heinkel He 111s of KG 4 manage to get through to the capital. They bomb at random, causing 49 deaths around Wimbledon and Kensington. One of the British units up is No. 46 Squadron from Stapleford Tawney and the Hurricanes encounter a huge formation of Messerschmitt Bf 109s. The ensuing brief clash is John Crossman's first combat. One Messerschmitt is shot down while the Hurricanes manage to emerge unscathed.

Around 4.30 p.m. the Hurricanes of 73 Squadron's 'A' Flight are taken by surprise, by mistake, by a squadron of aggressive Spitfires, and tragically 5 are shot down.

At 5.15 p.m. a raid builds up over Cherbourg and heads towards Bournemouth but before crossing the coast it suddenly turns away. This feint is designed to oblige RAF Squadrons to scramble and patrol so that they will be back on the ground refuelling when, shortly afterwards, numerous small raids appear on radar. Electrical interference makes tracking extremely difficult and only a few are intercepted by British fighters.

Between 6.00 p.m. and 9.00 p.m. raids by individual and small groups of aircraft hit targets in south-eastern England and many strike at London. Among the defenders hurriedly scrambled are 73 Squadron's remaining Hurricanes with Charles McGaw in Blue Section. The Hurricanes do not sight the enemy.

The fragmented RAF effort is noted by *Luftwaffe* pilots. To the German commanders it seems that the RAF is showing signs of being worn down at last. It is a mistaken impression. The *Luftwaffe's* concentration on London, although causing heavy damage and carnage among the civil population, is actually having the reverse effect on Fighter Command. Park's airfields, while they are left alone, are being repaired so the Germans are making a fundamental error in not keeping the pressure on them. Biggin Hill has recovered to the extent that Desmond Sheen's unit, 72 Squadron, can come back from Croydon.

*

In the evening London is again the target but the *Luftwaffe's* effort is on a much reduced scale.

The fact that the overnight weather is fine and German action is relatively slight does not go unnoticed at Fighter Command headquarters. The situation had been similar a week ago and next day saw the first huge daylight attack on London. To many it seems obvious that something ominous is planned for tomorrow. Invasion?

*

Bomber Command cannot afford to rest and 157 aircraft are sent out to widespread targets. The largest single raid is made by 43 Wellingtons on Antwerp but the major effort is again directed against invasion barges in the French Channel ports.

No. 61 Squadron at Hemswell has two targets, barges in the docks at Calais and Dunkirk. Ray Earl and his crew in Hampden X2911 are ordered to attack Dunkirk. Visibility is excellent but as Earl comes in over the dock basins he meets blinding searchlights and concentrated anti-aircraft fire. Unable to positively identify his target because of the glare, he does not release his bombs and brings the Hampden about for another run. Around him most of the other bombers are obliged to do the same. After they bomb, fires break out in various locations but Earl and his crew find it impossible to judge the results of their attack.

The target for Dereck French of 50 Squadron is the railway marshalling yard at Mannheim which he reaches after a flight of three hours. The area is alive with flak and searchlights and, as he flies across the marshalling yards, about 24 barrage balloons are spotted nearby. His gunners fire at them as he continues his bombing run and one is seen to collapse. It is 10.44 p.m. when the aircraft's 4 bombs are dropped but because of searchlights, it is impossible to observe the results.

The Australian's return to Lindholme is eventful too. The auto-pilot becomes unserviceable and the Hampden has to fly through a snowstorm during which the starboard engine cuts out. In spite of this French lands safely at base at 1.59 a.m.

Bomber Command losses for the night are two Whitleys.

SUNDAY, 15 SEPTEMBER

At 4.00 a.m. the pilots of 152 Squadron are brought to 'Readiness'. They are told to bring their revolvers with them to dispersal. A signal has been received:

'Invasion Imminent.'

By 5.30 almost all of them, including Ian Bayles and 'Dutchy' Holland, are present and the atmosphere in the hut is tense with expectation. As the time drags on tension builds ... until at last somebody cracks a joke and there is a sudden release of laughter.

They wait for hours until, with daylight, the fears of an invasion evaporate. At 7.00 a.m. 'B' Flight is released for a quick breakfast.

*

[AVM Dowding's redeployment of rested airmen back into 11 Group is bolstering the defences with refreshed experienced pilots. During 8–14 September, because of the enemy's preoccupation with bombing London, Park's Group has had a chance to repair airfields and sector stations.]

*

Dawn brings fine weather with early scattered mists and cloud patches which will build up during the day. Strong enemy action seems probable and all three southern Groups, Nos 10, 11 and 12, order standing patrols along the coastline between Harwich and Land's End. For over two hours these patrols are vectored to intercept elusive German reconnaissance planes without conclusive results. Ian Bayles logs his first patrol for the day between Portsmouth and Southampton but does not encounter the enemy.

A similar patrol is carried out by a section of Hurricanes of 87 Squadron from Exeter. John Cock is flying his new Hurricane, V7207. Over Torquay a Heinkel He 111 is spotted high above. Cock and his companions climb but lose sight of their adversary when he disappears into the haze.

*

At 10.00 a.m. AVM Park and his staff officers, including Thomas Lang, settle down to their morning conference at 11 Group head-quarters, Uxbridge. The meeting is interrupted by an unexpected visitor, Prime Minister Winston Churchill. Park rings the duty controller in the underground operations room who replies that there is nothing happening at present but that something could be building.

Lang and the others exchange glances. Does the Prime Minister know or sense something?

Lang and his companions disperse to their various duties while Churchill and his wife are taken to the bomb-proof operations room some 50 feet (15 m) below ground.

'I don't know whether anything will happen today', says Park. 'At present all is quiet.'[13]

Fifteen minutes pass, then a raid of over 40 planes is plotted building up over Dieppe. Light bulbs along the bottom of the display panel begin glowing as various squadrons are brought to 'Stand By' . . .

By 11.00 a.m. radar shows huge formations building over Calais and Boulogne. The German bomber force consists of over 100 Dornier Do 17s which have taken off from Antwerp, flown westward to meet up with its massive fighter escort behind Pas de Calais and then set off across the English Channel.

At 11.03 a.m. 92 and 72 Squadrons, the latter down to 7 Spitfires, are scrambled from Biggin Hill to meet the enemy between Canterbury and Dungeness. They hit the incoming Germans at about 11.35 a.m. Operating in pairs, 11 Group squadrons become fully committed while 10 Group sends one squadron and 12 Group launches its Duxford wing of two Spitfire squadrons and three Hurricane squadrons, all led by S/Ldr Douglas 'Tinlegs' Bader.

*

As they advance on London the Germans run into more British fighters. By noon the capital is in sight but the Dorniers and Messerschmitts are beginning to break up under the concussion of constant attack. Suddenly, over the capital, no fewer than 9 squadrons of defenders engage simultaneously. The tidy bomber formations are irrevocably smashed and their bombing is scattered and ineffective.

Six Hurricanes of 73 Squadron's 'B' Flight meet the Germans west of Canterbury. Charles McGaw is in Blue Section and the battle is already in full swing with German planes scattered everywhere. Two Messerschmitt Bf 109s cross in front of him in an echelon port formation. McGaw lines up for a beam attack, presses the firing button and immediately one enemy fighter begins to burn and plummet down.

The unit from 10 Group is 609 Squadron up from Warmwell whose Spitfires engage 30 Do 17s surrounded by many Bf 109s over east London. John Curchin is Green 3. As he waits for a target he notices one Dornier break away from its formation and immediately fires at it. The crippled Dornier glides down with Curchin's Spitfire circling above it.

John Crossman becomes involved in his first heavy dogfight as 46 Squadron meets 20 Dorniers south-east of London. There is a layer of protecting Bf 109s further up. Crossman sees two 109s detach themselves from the escorts to come down behind the Hurricanes. The order to break is given at the right instant and the Australian turns inwards, evading the Messerschmitts and heading after the bombers. Coming from behind, he sits on the tail of a Dornier and sends out 8 showers of bullets. The machine-guns seem to have no effect at first, but when he is almost out of ammunition, smoke pours from the bomber's port engine and it begins to lose height.

At Uxbridge, from his controller's position, Thomas Lang watches the plotters pushing their discs backwards and forwards with the changing situation. Churchill's presence has almost been forgotten in the pressure of the situation and the ritual of organization. Now the lights on the board show that every squadron is engaged. Park sends a request to Dowding for three more squadrons from 12 Group to be put at his disposal should another major attack develop while his own units are returning to their bases to refuel and rearm.

Churchill is aware of the gravity of the situation and asks of Park, 'What other reserves have we?' 'There are none,' Park answers quietly.[14]

*

With the Germans retreating the British fighters break off and return to their respective airfields.

While the Hurricanes and Spitfires are refuelled and rearmed as swiftly as possible, sandwiches and mugs of tea are brought out to pilots. At Stapleford Tawney it is time for excited congratulations while the men are still eating. John Crossman's section leader and friend, 'Pat' Patullo, has also shot down a Dornier while Crossman is credited with his first 'probable' kill. Even so, time is critical. Should a new raid suddenly appear they would be caught on the ground.

*

The operations room at RAF Uxbridge from which battles were monitored and directed (Imperial War Museum photograph CH 7698).

There is a respite before new concentrations of German aircraft are picked up by radar at 1.00 p.m. The build-up over France continues for over an hour as the bombers, Dorniers and Heinkels from KG 2, KG 53 and KG 76, manoeuvre into three large waves. They come in towards London just after 2.00 p.m.

Given ample warning by radar 11 Group has its 23 squadrons of fighters in the air reinforced by 3 from 10 Group and Douglas Bader's Duxford wing from 12 Group. The Germans are shocked by the ferocity of their reception as 170 Hurricanes and Spitfires engage them over Kent. Although the escorting Messerschmitt Bf 109s from JG 26 and JG 54 manage to keep many of the British fighters at bay the intervention of the Duxford wing over east London completely shatters *Luftwaffe* hopes of making a concentrated attack. Moments later, 6 more 11 Group squadrons, plus two from 10 Group, meet the German bombers head-on, totally splintering what remains of the once tidy formations. Bombs are unloaded without accuracy and the remnants of the Heinkel and Dornier force retreat.

*

Along with the others John Crossman is involved in a hectic chase. He singles out a Dornier but, as he is closing in, it suddenly dives away heading for nearby cloud and disappears.

Near Rye the Spitfires of 'B' Flight, 609 Squadron, fall upon two fleeing Do 17s, launching devastating attacks as the Germans desperately seek safety. John Curchin follows his section in and fires two short bursts at a Dornier which is forced to land.

*

Taking advantage of the fact that most British fighters must be concentrated in the London area, 27 Heinkel He 111s of 3/KG 55 are detected by radar approaching 10 Group's western flank around 3.00 p.m. Twelve Spitfires from 152 Squadron at Warmwell are scrambled. The bombers seem to be heading towards Southampton so 'A' Flight, containing Ian Bayles, is vectored in that direction but, as insurance, 'B' Flight, containing Ken ('Dutchy') Holland, is sent to cover Portland.

At the last moment the German bombers wheel towards the naval installation at Portland. Holland can see that they are flying in vics of three stepped up in an irregular line-astern and there is no fighter escort — the Messerschmitts are needed elsewhere. The bombers manage to carry out a pattern bombing of the naval base before heading out to sea with the Spitfires in close pursuit. One bomber begins to lag behind and draws the full attention of Green Section. Green 1 concentrates his fire on the German's starboard engine and then breaks away. Green 3, which is Ken Holland, attacks next with a five-second burst from astern and above. Thickening black smoke pours from the starboard engine and the Heinkel starts to lose height.

Blue Section concentrates on the other side of the German formation but without success. The chase continues 10 miles (16 km) out to sea before the Spitfires break away and return to Warmwell.

*

[British citizens listening to the BBC evening news hear of 185 German planes shot down.]

*

During the day Sgt Bill Crook rejoins No. 264 (Defiant) Squadron at Kirton-on-Lindsey.

*

After dark the *Luftwaffe* renews its pressure on London. For the Germans it is obviously safer to operate at night and 180 bombers fly in from Le Havre and the Dieppe-Cherbourg area.

Simultaneously, RAF Bomber Command sends 150 aircraft the other way on various widespread operations but with its major effort concentrated on the Channel ports.

MONDAY, 16 SEPTEMBER

The positioning of 600 Squadron at Redhill, in the path of the incoming bombers, pays dividends when Charles Pritchard takes off at 12.20 a.m. and climbs his Blenheim If up to an intersection of search-lights where an enemy aircraft is illuminated. Because the lights stay firmly locked on target he is able to stalk his victim and approach to within very short range. Identifying it as a Heinkel He 111, the Australian fires off two long bursts and shoots it down into the sea. His victim is actually a Ju 88.

At this time the squadron has 6 of the newly heavily-armed Beaufighters on its strength although two have been detached to have radar fitted. A radar-equipped Beaufighter from 25 Squadron also operates from Redhill but has no luck even though several contacts are made with hostile aircraft.

*

Daylight reveals most of the country covered by cloud and rain which prevents heavy attacks by the *Luftwaffe*.

Goering orders a conference of his *Luftflotten* and *Fliegerkorps* commanders and decides to revert to a policy of attacking RAF Fighter Command itself. He instructs that bomber formations are to be reduced in size and are to bomb targets in the London area with the absolute maximum fighter escort in order to shoot down as many intercepting RAF fighters as possible. He repeats his old prophecy that in this way the RAF will be completely annihilated in 4 or 5 days. Massed bomber formations are to be used only in perfect weather conditions and raids will be increased on aircraft production centres.

On the British side of the Channel Park is still a long way from being satisfied with the efficiency of his defences. He lists the main problem areas such as individual squadrons failing to rendezvous, lone squadrons being detailed to large raids, paired squadrons meeting up too far forward and too low, delays by group controllers in vectoring the paired squadrons onto raids, high-flying large formations of German fighters attracting the group while the bombers get through, and errors in sector reports upon pilot and aircraft effective strengths. In an effort to eliminate these faults he details Spitfire squadrons from Biggin Hill and Hornchurch to attack the enemy's top cover of Messerschmitt Bf 109s while Hurricanes take care of the bombers at medium height. If time allows they are to operate in groups of three squadrons each from Tangmere and Northolt.

*

Because of the absence of the *Luftwaffe* and the poor weather RAF sorties are low in number.

*

At night the Germans again direct heavy attacks on London. Approximately 170 aircraft drop over 200 tons (203 tonnes) of bombs. Smaller harassing raids are made on Merseyside and the Midlands, including Liverpool and Bristol.

TUESDAY, 17 SEPTEMBER

The weather is poor with squalls, showers, local thunder in the Channel and leaden skies over the estuary. Some brighter intervals appear during the afternoon.

Photographic interpretation of the material brought back by the Heston-based PDU Spitfires portrays a grim picture. In spite of RAF bombing the build-up of the German invasion barge fleet continues in the Channel ports and photos disclose that there are 600 barges at Antwerp, 266 at Calais, 230 at Boulogne, 220 at Dunkirk, 205 at Le Havre and 200 at Ostend.

The weather is not suitable for a large-scale German raid on London and, in accordance with Goering's new instructions, Kesselring's *Luftflotte 2* sends two waves of fighters over South Kent which cross the coast at Lympne, Deal and Dover between 3.00 p.m. and 4.00 p.m. When the composition of the raiding force is realized, RAF fighters avoid contact and relatively few clashes occur.

In accordance with AVM Park's instructions, 73 Squadron (Charles McGaw) patrols as a wing with 257 Squadron from Martlesham Heath and 17 Squadron from Debden but the enemy is not encountered.

At 1.50 p.m. Blue Section of 152 Squadron, consisting of three Spitfires patrolling over Portland Bill, is vectored after a Junkers Ju 88 flying north over Shepton Mallet. Blue leader is P/O Marrs, Blue 2 is Sgt Ken Holland and Blue 3 is F/O O'Brien. The German plane is a mile off when it is spotted and the Spitfires are well positioned to carry out a classic No. 1 attack. Holland follows Marrs, coming in from the starboard beam. In his turn, he fires off a two-second burst while closing in from 250–200 yards (230–180 m). At last alerted to its danger, the Ju 88 dives steeply for cloud cover at 6 000 feet (1 800 m) with the British fighters in close pursuit, attacking individually as the opportunity arises and trading shots with the German gunners. The German plane crash-lands near Warminster.

An inspection of Ken Holland's Spitfire reveals that it has been hit in three places by return fire.

*

In the evening, during a secret session, Prime Minister Churchill informs Parliament:

> . . . At any moment a major assault may be launched upon this island. I now say in secret that upwards of 1 700 self-propelled barges and more than 200 sea-going ships, some very large ships, are already gathered at many invasion ports in German occupation . . .[15]

*[What the British do not know is that Hitler has already, on this very day, postponed Operation **Seelöwe** until further notice because the RAF has obviously not yet been defeated and there is an adverse weather forecast for the coming week. At the same time he insists that a high state of preparedness be maintained.]*

Taking advantage of the full moon, the *Luftwaffe* returns in strength to raid London, flying in a stream via Dungeness and Selsey Bill while in the north a few planes attack Merseyside and Glasgow. As usual, night fighter sorties by the RAF prove ineffectual with the exception of a Defiant of 141 Squadron which shoots down a Ju 88.

WEDNESDAY, 18 SEPTEMBER

At 12.30 a.m. Hampden X2919 approaches Antwerp. There is no anti-aircraft fire, only a few searchlights which merely serve to betray the exact position of the target to the RAF. Five minutes later Dereck French flies his plane across the area, dropping his bombs in a long stick over the docks where barges have been reported. However, no explosions are seen.

In the morning the weather is much brighter but with squalls in some areas. PRU flights show that over 150 barges have been destroyed by Bomber Command overnight. The dock areas of Dunkirk and Antwerp have also suffered a great deal of damage. Two Hampdens have not returned.

*

The first sign of *Luftwaffe* activity appears on British radar around 9.00 a.m., building up over Calais. Two large formations of enemy aircraft cross into east Kent at 9.15 a.m. and to meet them 15 squadrons of Hurricanes and Spitfires are scrambled by the Uxbridge controllers. No. 73 Squadron, including Charles McGaw, is ordered up to patrol as part of a wing with 17 and 257 Squadrons. No. 46 Squadron, including John Crossman, is scrambled from Stapleford Tawney. Enemy fighters are seen in the distance but because there are no bombers, in accordance with Park's instructions, the Hurricanes make no attempt to engage.

Of the 15 defending squadrons only 6 clash with the enemy in a series of running dogfights. The rest, like 46 Squadron, turn away when it is realized that there are no bombers. The wing from Debden makes no contact and Charles McGaw is back on the ground at 10.35 a.m.

Around noon a small group of Ju 88s, escorted by 100 Messerschmitt Bf 109s, comes in over Kent. Some fan out over a wide area while at least 60 reach central London. A flight from 46 Squadron becomes heavily engaged and three Hurricanes are shot down. One pilot is killed. John Crossman's flight remains at 'Readiness' but is not involved.

In the early afternoon two groups of between 20 and 30 enemy aircraft fly up the Thames Estuary heading for London. Observers' Corps reports confirm that the forces include bombers so 11 Group orders 14 Squadrons up and assistance is requested from 12 Group. Douglas Bader's Duxford wing takes off at 4.20 p.m. and while it patrols over Hornchurch anti-aircraft fire betrays the presence of one of the bomber formations. Bader leads his Hurricanes down in a violent diving attack to break up the enemy formation which is severely mauled. The three squadrons from Debden are airborne between 4.15 p.m. and 5.50 p.m. but make no contact.

*

At Exeter a flight of Hurricanes from 87 Squadron (John Cock) is on its way to Bibury to carry out night time 'cat's eyes' patrols when it is recalled because of an impending 'flap'. The raid does not eventuate so in the afternoon Cock and his comrades set off again and this time reach their destination. On the move also is the detachment of 141 Squadron Defiants from Biggin Hill. Noel Constantine is on his way to Gatwick with the others.

German bombers are over London early in the evening and the first air raids occur at 7.30 p.m. They continue until 5.30 a.m., with the main targets being London and Liverpool but there is also scattered bombing over Kent, Surrey and Middlesex.

*

RAF Bomber Command despatches 174 aircraft, most of which are to raid the Channel ports while the remainder attack railway targets in Germany.

From Hemswell 8 Hampdens of 61 Squadron take off after 7.30 p.m. to raid Le Havre. Ray Earl and his crew encounter the usual searchlights and flak which are becoming more intense every night. Some ships can be seen in the harbour. Earl makes a successful bomb run which is followed by a huge explosion. Large fires also break out which act as a beacon for incoming bombers. Earl's return flight is uneventful until he reaches home. Enemy aircraft are in the vicinity so he has to circle before landing. When the runway is lit the Australian is the first one down but the lights have to be extinguished almost immediately because more German planes are detected.

THURSDAY, 19 SEPTEMBER

The bombing of the British capital lasts until 5.30 a.m. Piccadilly, Bond Street, Regent Street, Park Lane and many other famous roads in the centre of London are blocked. Police and the Civil Defence Corps labour to clear the rubble and to rescue people trapped under wreckage.

*

A lull in the fighting occurs because of rain which spreads across England from the west. Some German planes fly in singly, crossing the coast near Dungeness, and carry out individual attacks on Liverpool and around London. However a *Gruppe* of Junkers Ju 88s sent against London is met by paired Hurricane squadrons, Nos 249 and 302, which succeed in turning the Germans back, each unit claiming one bomber destroyed. No. 249 Squadron is stationed at North Weald and during the day Bill Millington, fully recovered from his injuries, is posted to this unit.

*

Around 4.00 p.m. Green Section of 152 Squadron, consisting of two Spitfires, is scrambled from Warmwell. The pilots are P/O Williams and 'Dutchy' Holland. Just after take-off it is realized that Williams' radio is not functioning so the Australian assumes the leader's position. Not long afterwards a bandit is sighted over the Channel and Holland signals Williams to go below the cloud base while he remains above it. The German plane, a Ju 88, disappears into the murk but moments later it reappears about two miles (3 km) in front.

The Australian closes in, making alternate quarter attacks from left and right. Aiming first at the gunners' positions and then at each engine, Holland opens fire. There seems to be a free cannon firing at his Spitfire from the port side of the cockpit but this stops after Holland's first burst. There are also machine-guns firing from each side of the cockpit as he sweeps in from each direction. Altogether he makes 6 attacks until he runs out of ammunition. The Ju 88 is badly battered and Holland watches as it dives into the sea.

*

Poor weather overnight hampers *Luftwaffe* operations but the Germans still manage to carry out minelaying operations in British coastal waters.

At Heston an enemy bomber drops a magnetic mine by parachute. All that remains of the main hangar is a flattened mass of twisted girders and scrap metal. Crushed under the debris are 5 precious PR Spitfires, together with Sidney Cotton's famous Lockheed 12A. Destroyed too, is a visiting Wellington bomber. Six other planes are damaged.

RAF Bomber Command sorties are also fewer.

FRIDAY, 20 SEPTEMBER

In the early morning 12 aircraft from 50 Squadron set out to bomb the German barge concentrations at Flushing. Out over the North Sea Richard Taylor runs into endless heavy rain and cloud. On making a landfall on the Dutch coast and finding no improvement in conditions, he and his crew turn back.

Equally frustrated, Dereck French is reluctant to go home with his bombs so he and his crew look for some other objective. After a search they find and bomb the aerodrome at Bergen Op Zoom.

*

The daylight hours are fair with bright periods although there are showers in some areas. German air activity is limited with a few early morning reconnaissance sorties. A build-up begins over Calais around 10.30 a.m. but this is actually a German fighter sweep which approaches in two waves, the first crossing the coast at 10.45 a.m. and the second around 11.05 a.m. Fighters from Biggin Hill and Hornchurch are scrambled and a dogfight develops over Maidstone. The Messerschmitt Bf 109s, not hampered by the need to protect bombers, shoot down 7 Spitfires for a loss of only two.

At night, although the moon is in the wane, it is still bright enough to help the *Luftwaffe's* bombing. As usual the enemy's main effort is directed towards London but, in general, the *Luftwaffe* seems less active. Operating from Gatwick, Noel Constantine in Defiant N1622 carries out a night patrol but is unable to find a target.

RAF Bomber Command again concentrates on the Channel ports but there are also some smaller raids on German railways, canals and French airfields. Several areas are mined. Over 170 aircraft are despatched and, among these, 61 Squadron is given the tasks of minelaying around St Nazaire and attacking shipping docks at Antwerp. Six planes are involved including Hampden P2090 flown by Ray Earl.

SATURDAY, 21 SEPTEMBER

The weather for the day is mainly fine and London, with a covering of haze, has a fairly quiet day. Daylight sorties by the *Luftwaffe* are limited to scattered raids by small groups and individual aircraft. Among these a Junkers Ju 88 makes a low level attack on the Hawker aircraft factory at Brooklands. Three bombs explode in open ground without damage.

At Middle Wallop the men of 609 Squadron, including John Curchin, run for cover when the airfield is raided without warning by a few stray bombers. Damage is negligible and no one is hurt.

Scrambled from Warmwell, a section of Spitfires from 152 Squadron led by Ian Bayles, manages to intercept a lone Ju 88 but, as so often happens, it proves too elusive and escapes into cloud.

Late in the afternoon the *Luftwaffe* mounts several fighter sweeps over east Kent and 5 raids cross the coast at Dover, Lympne and

Dungeness on their way in towards Kenley, Hornchurch, Biggin Hill and central London. Twenty 11 Group squadrons, one 10 Group squadron and the wing from Duxford are scrambled but only one unit actually engages. Biggin Hill's 92 Squadron has a brief nil-all clash.

No. 46 Squadron, with John Crossman flying his new Hurricane, joins up with 249 Squadron and this force, 24 aircraft strong, patrols over the Thames Estuary and Kent, venturing out over the Channel via Folkestone and returning above Dover. In the lead, 46 Squadron tends to fly too fast leaving the last sections of 249 struggling to keep up, a dangerous situation if the 109s are lurking around. They do not encounter the enemy.

After dark the Germans are relatively quiet and only moderate raids are carried out on such centres as London, Colchester, Nottingham, Liverpool and Werrington. As usual, the British night defences are woefully inadequate and, to bolster the overworked Blenheims and Defiants, several day fighter squadrons fly 'cat's eyes' patrols. Operating from Bibury John Cock takes off to patrol in Hurricane V7207 but he has to return 20 minutes later because of a 'dud contactor'.[16] Later, with the problem rectified, he is up again patrolling.

SUNDAY, 22 SEPTEMBER

[Last Sunday the battle of Britain had witnessed some of its heaviest fighting and it will become known as 'Battle of Britain Day'.]

Today is a complete contrast, the weather is dull and foggy in the morning and this breaks up into cloud with some rain during the afternoon. Few Luftwaffe aircraft venture out and the only plane intercepted by the British, a lone Junkers Ju 88, is shot down into the Channel.

AVM Wilfred Ashton McClaughry DSO, MC, DFC is appointed air officer commanding No. 9 Group, RAF Fighter Command, which was created in nucleus form at Barton Hall, Preston, Lancashire, a month before.

[Born on 26 November 1894 at Knightsbridge, South Australia, McClaughry had served with the 9th Australian Light Horse Regiment on Gallipoli and transferred in 1916 to the Royal Flying Corps. Between November 1917 and December 1918 he was commanding officer of No. 4 Squadron, Australian Flying Corps. In July 1917 he won the Military Cross for bombing attacks on stations and trains and this was followed in November 1918 by a DFC and a DSO in February 1919. After the first world war he accepted a permanent commission in the new Royal Air Force. In 1938 he was appointed to the Air Ministry as director of training. Now, in his new appointment as the first AOC of 9 Group, he is charged with the responsibility of building up its strength, creating stations and airfields and forming new squadrons as part of Fighter Command's programme of expansion. He will hold the position for the next two years.]

McClaughry will be made a Companion of the Order of the Bath in 1942 but he will be killed in an air accident on 4 January 1943.]

For the men of the Australian Infantry Brigade an order restricts weekend leave to within 25 miles (40 km) of headquarters but, in spite of this, there is a relaxing of 'Readiness'.

Throughout the day the RAF flies only 158 sorties, the smallest number since the beginning of the battle, but the peace is shattered at night as the *Luftwaffe* turns up in force over London. Four *Gruppen* of bombers, 123 aircraft in all, drop over 100 tons of high explosive and 50 tons of incendiaries on the capital. No German planes are brought down by the defences.

MONDAY, 23 SEPTEMBER

If the British night defences are ineffective, so are those of the Germans. Overnight 95 Blenheims, Hampdens and Wellingtons of RAF Bomber Command raid the Channel ports and 9 Whitleys bomb a factory near Dresden, all without loss. Over his target area, although the night is crystal clear, Ray Earl of 61 Squadron and his crew are not able to make out the barges themselves but the outlines of the docks are sufficiently clear to allow bombing with precision. Even the anti-aircraft fire and searchlights seem less effective than usual.

Dereck French's Hampden P4408 is one of four 50 Squadron aircraft which bomb the German barges at Antwerp. It is 4.10 a.m. when French makes his bomb-run and unloads 7 bombs across Inner Haven Wess and the harbour works. One bomb fails to release. The Australian drops the 'hung up' bomb over the aerodrome at Vlissinger.

For many airmen coming home proves to be the most hazardous part of the operation as German bombers are still active over England. Some mingle with the returning British planes in order to sneak through the defences and raid airfields in Lincolnshire.

*

With daylight the weather remains fine and around 9.00 a.m. radar detects a build-up of 200 aircraft over Calais. The raiders come over in several waves and spread out over Kent. However the Observers' Corps is quick to report that they all appear to be Messerschmitt Bf 109s.

Operating from North Weald, 249 Squadron is ordered up at about 10.30 a.m. Flying his first sortie with this unit is Bill Millington who has recovered from the injuries he received while a member of 79 Squadron. The squadron makes a rendezvous with Hurricanes of 46 Squadron from Stapleford Tawney. At the controls of one of these is John Crossman. Together they patrol but, like so many of the airborne units, fail to make contact with the enemy. Eighteen Bf 109s are spotted very high up but there is no chance of reaching them. The only other planes in the air appear to be British but it is still essential to remain on guard because the Germans use every opportunity to take the unwary by surprise.

This happens to a flight of Hurricanes from 73 Squadron, Charles McGaw's unit, which clashes violently with numerous Bf 109s in a battle which spreads over the Thames Estuary and east Kent. Four Hurricanes are shot down.

Later, back on the ground at Stapleford Tawney, John Crossman records in his logbook, 'Saw dogfight in the distance — but didn't join in.'[17]

Between 5.00 p.m. and 6.00 p.m. 5 more raids of Bf 109s come in over southern England, sweeping through South Foreland, Hythe and Dover. No. 11 Group scrambles 12 squadrons in 4 wings but the Germans prove too elusive. No. 73 Squadron is up again from Castle Camps as part of a wing and Charles McGaw, who had not been in the morning clash, is with them. There is no contact this time.

*

In a broadcast to the nation, H.M. King George VI declares the introduction of two new awards for bravery, the George Cross, which will rank next to the Victoria Cross, and the George Medal for wider distribution.[18]

*

As a reprisal for German night raids on London, the Air Staff agrees to launch a heavy attack on specified military targets in Berlin. To concentrate on just one German city is unique at this time of the war. Accordingly 129 Hampdens, Wellingtons and Whitleys set out for the German capital. The targets are railway yards, electrical power stations, three gas works and two factories making aero engines or aircraft parts. Over three to four hours, 112 bombers drop their loads although Berlin's many searchlights and a heavy mist make identification of the actual targets difficult.

American correspondent, William Shirer, is in Berlin and experiences the bombing. He afterwards records:

> The British really went to work on Berlin last night. They bombed heavily and with excellent aim for exactly four hours. They hit some important factories in the north of the city, one big gas works, and the railway yards north of Stettiner and Lehrter stations.[19]

However, while this is happening, 261 German bombers are again turning London into an inferno and causing widespread damage. Again the night defences are woefully inadequate.

TUESDAY, 24 SEPTEMBER

For the crews of the Blenheim IVs of 40 Squadron stationed at Wyton the target is Calais. Brian Best takes off at 3.40 a.m. Over the French port he and the others make their bomb runs at high altitude and he places his stick of bombs across the dockside. Fires stand out like beacons below and after each Blenheim makes its run explosions are observed in the target area.

*

There is early morning fog over northern France while the English Channel is cloudy.

At 8.30 a.m. a raid of over 200 aircraft, mostly bombers, crosses the coast heading towards London. No. 11 Group reacts strongly, meeting the German formations as they fly in. No. 249 Squadron (Bill Millington) is scrambled at 9.00 a.m. and patrols over the Thames Estuary. Elsewhere, the German formations are repulsed and fail to reach London.

After landing back at North Weald Bill Millington and the others remain on 'Readiness' and wait around at dispersal.

At 11.15 a.m. the squadron is scrambled again to patrol over London. Five formations of German aircraft have been detected setting out from Cap Gris Nez. Seventeen other British squadrons are airborne to intercept. Only two manage to engage the enemy formations which turn back.

*

F/Lt Bob Bungey of 145 Squadron watches closely as a Fairey Battle lands at Montrose. He walks over as it taxis in. Newly promoted, the Australian is to take over 'B' Flight and he is awaiting transport back to Dyce. Two men clamber down from the cockpit and Bungey recognizes P/O Paul Rabone, a New Zealander, who like him had transferred across from Bomber Command and joined 145 Squadron. The other man is P/O Jean 'Pyker' Offenberg, a Belgian. Bungey receives the news that 'B' Flight now contains three Belgians, a Czech and an Anglo-Argentine with the comment:

> Well that's fine. I'm a Digger. We shall be a fine bloody Russian salad and there won't be any chance of getting bored. You can call me Robert or Bob if you like . . .[20]

*

Between 3.30 and 4.00 p.m. a raid builds up over Cherbourg. The enemy's objective is the Supermarine factory at Woolston.

At Middle Wallop 609 Squadron is scrambled to intercept. Leading Green Section is John Curchin while Mick Miller is flying as Yellow 3. The Germans reach their target and drop a concentrated load of bombs. Five hits are scored on the factory itself but they do not cause serious damage. However, another strikes a works shelter, killing 98 employees and injuring 40 others.

The Spitfires intercept the raiders over Swanage and 'A' Flight, containing Miller, launches an attack on the bombers while John Curchin's flight circles above to guard against enemy fighters. Three single-engined aircraft are spotted overhead and shortly afterwards another passes below. Curchin turns Green Section after it and gives chase. He fires a short burst and the fighter turns, coming into line with Green 2 who also snaps off a burst. It then tries to outdistance them by heading out to sea towards France but Curchin, pushing his Spitfire to the limit, is able to close in. White smoke pours from his victim's engine and the fighter crashes into the sea. While he circles the spot Curchin is suddenly attacked by another German fighter and has to quickly break into a tight turn.

The bombers are identified as Do 17s. Miller, with Red 2, attacks one and leaves it heavily damaged. He watches the crippled machine fall into the sea.

*

The *London Gazette* announces the award of the DFC to F/Lt Gordon Olive of 65 Squadron.

*

After mess at Amesbury Abbey a radio announcement causes a hush. The Australian government has decided to make separate divisions of its forces abroad, with reinforcements to be sent from Australia. Animated conversation follows and many believe that troops already in England will be expanded into a 9th Division and will remain in the British Isles.

*

Rumours spread like wildfire overnight to the effect that German minesweepers have been active in the English Channel — the prelude to invasion?

WEDNESDAY, 25 SEPTEMBER

Because of rumours that German ships had been clearing the English Channel of mines the previous day, no one in 249 Squadron is surprised when 'Readiness' is called for 5.50 a.m. The pilots, including Bill Millington, assemble at North Weald's dispersal although many of them are the worse for wear after an hilarious evening spent at 'The Thatch', Epping. Overnight, the Germans have bombed Merseyside and, of course, London.

With dawn, the weather is fine in most areas but with cloud over the English Channel.

Around 9.00 a.m. 249 Squadron takes off to patrol in brilliant morning sunshine. They can see a convoy in the Estuary with three destroyers steaming into Sheerness.

Meanwhile, British radar has detected a large volume of enemy air activity over France. It had started as early as 8.20 a.m. so, as well as 249 Squadron, numerous other units have been ordered into the air. Although they seem busy the Germans send out only the usual lone reconnaissance sorties.

*

Away to the west out over the Atlantic, Ivan Podger and his crew of 10 Squadron, RAAF, are on convoy patrol in Sunderland P9603 (RB-H), together with a RAF Sunderland, when a Focke-Wulf Fw 200 Condor is spotted stalking the ships. Before the Australian machine can intercept, it drops a bomb which lands just behind a vessel below. Then it turns to port and heads towards the Sunderland at a slightly higher altitude. The two big planes close with their gunners firing for all they are worth. Firing continues until they are past each other and out of range.

After this clash the Condor makes for the convoy again with the Sunderland in pursuit. As it approaches the ships one of the escorting destroyers opens up with its anti-aircraft guns. Next it is attacked by the RAF Sunderland which chases it off to the south-east. The Condor has had enough and does not come back.

*

The aerial activity witnessed by British radar through the early morning has actually been the redistribution of several *Luftwaffe* bomber units along the French coast in preparation for making renewed day and night attacks on the west of England. At 11.00 a.m. large raids begin building up in front of 10 Group.

At Warmwell 152 Squadron starts taking off in pairs. Some are already airborne but Blue 1 and Blue 2 (Ken Holland) take off with Green Section only when enemy aircraft are already visible from the aerodrome. Following close behind comes Black Section led by Ian Bayles with P/O Marrs as his number 2. No. 601 Squadron is scrambled from Exeter at 11.20 a.m. and instructed to patrol over Portland Bill. Leading 'A' Flight's Red Section is Clive Mayers. Up from Middle Wallop 609 Squadron is also directed to Portland Bill but shortly afterwards is diverted to Swanage. Leading Green Section is John Curchin while Mick Miller is flying as Red 3.

While diversionary raids head towards Plymouth, Falmouth, Swanage and Southampton, 58 Heinkel He 111s, heavily escorted by Bf 109s, cross the coast of Dorset at 11.15 a.m. and an attack on Portsmouth is mounted by Junkers Ju 88s. The main force of Heinkel bombers has orders to attack the Bristol factory at Filton which not only builds the Blenheim bomber but also manufactures aero engines for such aircraft as the Blenheim, Beaufort, Hampden, Wellington, Lysander, Gladiator and the new Beaufighter. The Heinkels reach Filton before being intercepted and their bombing is concentrated and accurate. Eight newly-built Blenheims and Beauforts are destroyed and a dozen others are badly damaged while the factory's production stops for several weeks. Afterwards the raiders turn south for their homeward run but start running into aggressive British fighters.

Following the rest of 609 Squadron John Curchin leads Green Section in to attack the main formation of bombers. After a couple of passes he notices three Heinkels which have fallen behind the main formation and he makes these his targets. Two of the bombers commence diving towards cloud cover so the Australian follows, selects one and attacks it from above. Discharging a couple of two-second bursts as he closes in, Curchin sees the German machines melt into the clouds but he follows them. He sees one of the Heinkels falling but can only watch helplessly as it crashes onto a house in Bournemouth. Curchin then searches for the other Heinkel and locates it trying to escape back into the cloud. Hauling back on his control column, he hurtles up after it at full throttle and triggers off two more two-second bursts. The Heinkel looms in front of him and he has to reef his Spitfire away. As he does so the German plane's wheels come down and it glides down shakily to land in a field near Swanage.

Mick Miller of 609's Red Section sights three stragglers flying below the main formation and goes after them. He singles out the centre He 111 and, as he closes in, he sends out a stream of machine-gun bullets

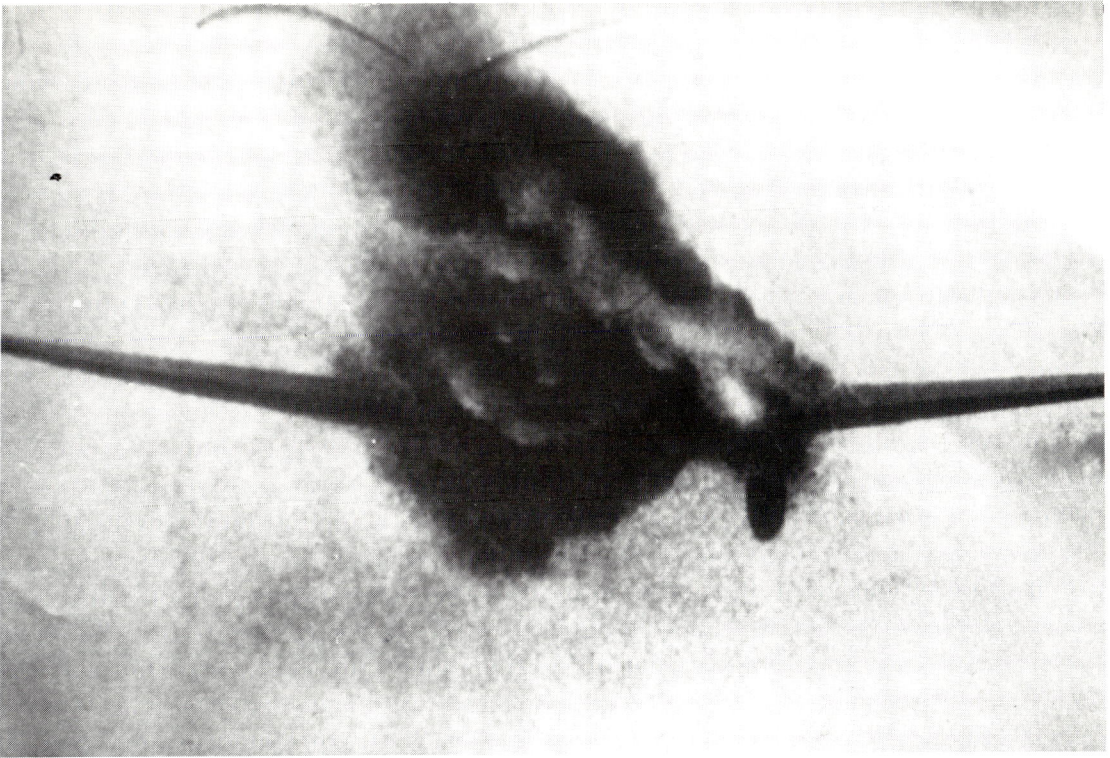

A Heinkel He 111 is destroyed (Imperial War Museum photograph).

until the hiss of compressed air reveals that he is out of ammunition . . . but it is enough. The Heinkel is in trouble and it crashes west of Bournemouth.

The various scattered sections of 152 Squadron have been unable to join up in the air for a combined assault on the enemy bombers and instead carry out a series of nibbling, stinging attacks in ones and twos, swarming around them like persistent flies. The enemy force is identified as a mixed formation of 60 Junkers Ju 88s, Heinkel He 111s and Dornier Do 17s. Accompanying the bombers is a circle of Messerschmitt Bf 110s flying above and behind, and above this formation is an echelon of Messerschmitt Bf 109s.

The 4 Spitfires of Blue and Green Sections intercept the bombers as they fly over Bath. Blue 1 who is leading, orders an attack on a vic of three Ju 88s. They sweep in and Blue 1 damages a Ju 88 before he is blinded by petrol from a punctured fuel tank which causes him to force-land. Now it is every man for himself and Blue 2, Ken Holland, closes in and attacks a Heinkel He 111. After several bursts it begins to trail smoke. Inside the Heinkel the fire spreads rapidly so its crew prepares to bail out. As they are about to jump, the German gunner notices that the attacking Spitfire has stopped firing and is coming closer, apparently for a better look. He stays at his gun until the last second and at point-blank range opens fire on the British machine which suddenly lurches and goes down. The crippled Heinkel plunges down too and only one man manages to bail out before it crashes. Nearby is the wreckage of Spitfire N3173.

Kenneth Holland, also known as Kenneth Holland Ripley, of 152 Squadron. He was killed in action on 25 September 1940 (photograph courtesy of Philip Markham and John Lindsay).

[When Holland's body was recovered from the wreckage it was found that he had been shot in the head. He was 20 years of age. He was cremated at Weymouth, Dorset, and his guardian had a memorial stone erected in the field at Woolverton, Somerset, where his Spitfire crashed. The stone has since been moved to the church in Woolverton.]

Sgt Kenneth Christopher Holland is the 10th Australian deemed eligible for the Battle of Britain Clasp to be killed.

Ian Bayles, Black 1, notices a Spitfire as it crashes but he is too far away to identify it as that belonging to Holland and he has his own hands full. Bayles and his wingman had been the last to leave the ground and they had caught up with the bombers south of Bristol. After climbing into position, they attack head-on from out of the sun. Bayles cannot see any obvious effect from his firing and as he hurtles through the Ju 88s he encounters heavy return fire. Breaking downwards, he then attacks another Ju 88 which is flying lower than the others. Coming in from astern, he opens fire until the distance narrows to 100 yards (90 m) and he has to break away. Again there does not seem to be any visible result of his attack but there is no time to loiter because covering crossfire from the other bombers is coming dangerously close. The Australian pulls his Spitfire up into a climb and once he has sufficient height he levels out waiting for another opportunity. Moments later he attacks three Ju 88s with familiar yellow spinners. Looking back at them as his Spitfire turns tightly, he is elated to find that one has gone down.

At the same time Bayles' attention is caught by a lone Heinkel He 111 which is trying to dive towards cloud cover but is being hampered by two Hurricanes and a Spitfire. He is in an ideal position and attacks it from above and astern. Closing in from 300 yards (275 m) he presses the firing button on his spade grip for 4 seconds. The Heinkel does not come out of its dive but before it crashes in a field two men manage to bail out.

Hurricanes from 601 Squadron circle over Weston-Super-Mare, having been unable to catch up with the enemy aircraft as they flew north north-west. They see them turn southwards around Gloucester. Seizing their opportunity, they fly east with the sun behind them and intercept a formation of 12 to 15 Messerschmitt Bf 110 escort fighters. They meet them head-on and Clive Mayers presses his firing button for about 5 seconds as one of the twin-engined fighters looms in front of him. Both of its engines belch smoke and it drops away and crashes as the Australian fires on another Messerschmitt to the right. Leaving this apparently undamaged, he dives into the path of another formation of 25 German aircraft. Everything happens so quickly that he is unable to identify with certainty the type of enemy planes coming at him and by reflex he is able to launch a quarter head-on attack on one enemy machine in the lower formation and then dive out.

*

Short Sunderland N9050 (RB-D) from 10 Squadron, RAAF, finishes its anti-submarine escort patrol around a convoy of ships in the North Atlantic in mid-afternoon. With the arrival of a relief Sunderland, Bill Garing is given his course to the base at Oban. After 30 minutes flying along this heading, a lifeboat with set sails is spotted in the water.

A Heinkel He 111 pursued by a Spitfire (photograph courtesy of Bundesarchiv-Militarchiv).

Garing alters course to investigate and descends to 500 feet (150 m). As they come close, the Australians can see that the boat is full of people and standing on a seat amidships is a boy in a scout's uniform. He is signalling in semaphore! Circling directly overhead, the crew of the Sunderland work out that he is spelling the words 'CITY of BENARES'. The realization brings elation for this ship had been sunk 8 days ago and hope of finding any more survivors had faded. There are 45 survivors on board including 6 children.

After supplies wrapped in Mae Wests are dropped to the lifeboat Garing leads an escort destroyer to it. Because of their shortage of fuel the Australians have to leave the scene.

News of the rescue spreads quickly and in Oban's Alexandra Hotel that night the crew of the Australian Sunderland receive free drinks.

[The survivors picked up by the destroyer are landed at Greenock, Scotland, next day.]

*

Air Vice-Marshal Keith Park, the officer commanding 11 Group (Imperial War Museum photograph CM 5631).

*[Animosity between AVM Keith Park and AVM Trafford Leigh-Mallory festers. Park believes that his tactic of sending his squadrons up individually or in pairs is the best to use against the Germans. It is a tactic born of necessity because of 11 Group's closeness to the enemy and the fact that, in spite of radar advanced warning, there is not really time to form up 3, 4 or 5 squadrons into wings to meet the raiders **en masse**. Leigh-Mallory, on the other hand, argues that the more fighters there are in the air to meet the Germans, the more of them will be brought down. In any case, from 12 Group's position in the Midlands he **does** have time to assemble a big wing to send southwards. By then, Park counters, the Germans will have already reached their targets, bombed and be flying home. In Leigh-Mallory's opinion it is better to decimate a German formation after it has bombed than only manage to bring down a few beforehand . . . and so the argument goes on . . .]*

*

At night the *Luftwaffe* raids London plus targets in north Wales and Lancashire. Around 11.00 p.m. a land mine is dropped on North Weald aerodrome, home of 249 Squadron, but it does not explode.

THURSDAY, 26 SEPTEMBER

Overnight RAF Bomber Command sends almost 120 aircraft to bomb the Channel ports, Kiel docks and other German targets. For 40 Squadron the target is Boulogne. Brian Best in Blenheim N3592 leaves Wyton at 3.40 a.m. Over Boulogne, he makes a high-level attack, dropping a stick of bombs. His crew, as they gaze down for results, see their bombs exploding across the target area.

*

Air Vice-Marshal Trafford Leigh-Mallory, the officer commanding 12 Group (Imperial War Museum photograph CH 11943).

Dawn brings fair weather but with cloud which builds up during the day. Bill Millington and the pilots of 249 Squadron at North Weald wake up to a morning of unexpected rest. Because of the unexploded mine dropped last night they are not even allowed to start an engine, let alone take off.

In mid-afternoon a raid of over 70 builds up over Brittany. By 4.30 p.m. the Germans are sweeping in over Southampton to attack the home of the Spitfire, the Supermarine aircraft factory at Woolston. Coming up the Solent, they turn and carry out a precision pattern bombing attack in a single run across the factory, dropping 70 tons (71 tonnes) of explosive. Three completed Spitfires are destroyed, more than 20 others are damaged and production of this vital fighter is halted. Fortunately for the British, a second factory has already been constructed at Birmingham and is just coming into production. By early October deliveries will be again back to normal. Thirty-seven people perish in the bombing of the factory itself and in the surrounding area 52 are killed.

Caught off balance, only 4 RAF fighter squadrons are scrambled and these only intercept the enemy after the bombing. One of these units is 609 Squadron from Middle Wallop.

The enemy force is identified as Dornier Do 17s and Heinkel He 111s with escorting Messerschmitt Bf 109s. Leading Green Section in 'B' Flight is John Curchin who follows Blue Section into the attack. He concentrates on the leader of the second formation of bombers and delivers three two-second bursts from the beam. Meanwhile other British fighters are beginning to join the fight and Curchin is startled by two single-engined machines which hurtle past, a Bf 109 chasing a fleeing Hurricane. He turns after the German plane but is not fast enough and the two fighters are out of sight before he can help. Turning his attention to the bombers, he finds two He 111s lagging behind their formation and he makes these his targets. As he fires the Heinkels split up. One makes for cloud cover, so Curchin goes after it and manages to fire another short burst before it disappears. Unfortunately for the German plane there are gaps in the cloud and each time the Heinkel reappears the Australian is there to send off a few more pot shots. Finally, with no more cloud left, the bomber has to emerge into clear sky. Closing swiftly, Curchin fires for three seconds and at long last the Heinkel loses height and crashes into the sea.

*

Three-quarters of an hour after John Curchin's dogfight, at the opposite end of the British Isles, Lockheed Hudson N7251 of 233 Squadron, Coastal Command, while on patrol over the North Sea, suddenly encounters an enemy aircraft. It is a Dornier Do 17, apparently on a similar patrol. Flying the Hudson is P/O Forbes with an Australian, P/O John McIntosh. The sudden meeting is over almost as soon as it occurs because before anyone can react both aircraft have passed each other. The Hudson continues with its patrol but, when it returns to Fifeshire, its undercarriage does not function and Forbes makes a forced landing, skidding along on the plane's belly.

*

During the night the Germans keep up their raids on London and Merseyside.

RAF Bomber Command despatches 77 aircraft to bomb the Channel ports, Dortmund and Kiel. In all of these operations only two aircraft are lost, a Blenheim and a Hampden. The briefing at Hemswell nominates two targets, the German battleship *Scharnhorst* at Kiel and the new aqueduct built for the Dortmund-Ems Canal. It is 8.29 p.m. when Hampden P2090, flown by Ray Earl and his crew, leaves the runway for the last time. This is the Hampden which does not return.

P/O Raymond Patrick Earl is one of the Australian airmen listed on the Battle of Britain Roll of Honour at Westminster Abbey.

FRIDAY, 27 SEPTEMBER

The weather promises to be fine with haze and some cloud over the Channel. At Uxbridge, at 8.00 a.m., the first signs of major German activity are indicated. Radar detects a number of fast-flying aircraft approaching the coastlines of Kent and Sussex on a 50 mile (80 km) front. Park's squadrons are quick to react, scrambling and joining up in the air to fly as wings of three or in pairs.

At 8.50 a.m. No. 46 Squadron is ordered to patrol North Weald. There is fog and visibility is limited to about 700 yards (640 m). The Hurricanes take off singly or in pairs and assemble over Stapleford Tawney, meeting with Hurricanes from 249 Squadron (Bill Millington) which are to lead.

At 9.00 a.m. No. 73 Squadron (Charles McGaw) is ordered to patrol Hornchurch-North Weald accompanied by 17 Squadron from Debden. No. 73 Squadron is to lead.

As the Germans cross between Dover and Brighton, they are identified by the Observers' Corps as Messerschmitt Bf 110 fighter-bombers escorted by many Messerschmitt Bf 109s. The German tactics are to draw up the British fighters in order to exhaust their fuel and ammunition so that a following raid by bombers will be able to reach London with a minimum of interference. The ruse seems to be succeeding as Park's fighters react strongly. South of Maidstone, the 24 Hurricanes of 249 and 46 Squadrons sight 20 Bf 110s milling around in a defensive circle. No. 249 leads into the attack and in the ensuing battle 8 Messerschmitts are claimed shot down in 20 minutes. One 249 Squadron Hurricane is damaged but its pilot manages to reach home safely. No. 46 Squadron claims 4 of the Messerschmitts.

Shortly after this 73 and 17 Squadrons encounter another *Staffel* of circling Bf 110s over the Weybridge/Kenley area. Charles McGaw observes that the German machines have dark green top surfaces and blue undersides. Besides circling, the Germans employ no other tactics. McGaw finds that the particular enemy plane he has selected to attack turns outwards from the circle as if to counter-attack but then it tries to rejoin the defensive ring. Seizing his chance, McGaw closes in and fires several bursts which smash the fighter's port engine. The 110 begins to lose height but in the same instant McGaw's Hurricane comes into heavy crossfire from the other Messerschmitts and he has to break away. In doing this the Scottish-born Australian loses sight of his adversary.

No. 73 Squadron claims three Bf 110s destroyed, 1 probable and 1 damaged (McGaw's) for 2 Hurricanes damaged.

While all this is happening, at St Eval, Dick Power in Blenheim ND-L leads off three aircraft to escort an Empire flying boat from Lundy Island to a point west of the Scillies. After a smooth flight with no incidents they return at 12.50 p.m.

At about the same time as Dick Power and his Blenheims take leave of the flying boat for their return flight, the *Luftwaffe's* next heavy raid crosses the Channel on course for London. It consists of 60 Junkers Ju 88s but the bombers have been late assembling over the French coast and have missed their fighter escort. Coming over Kent they are confronted by 120 Hurricanes and Spitfires which create havoc among their two neat formations. The Ju 88s jettison their bombs and send out frantic calls for help but before the relieving Messerschmitt Bf 109s and Bf 110s can arrive, a dozen of them are brought down.

No. 46 Squadron is ordered to patrol North Weald where it meets up with 249 Squadron. With No. 249 leading again the Hurricanes climb on course for Rochford where they spot a large dogfight in progress. Several Bf 109s cross in front but, as the RAF fighters prepare to attack, they are taken by surprise by another group of 109s coming from behind. In the battle which follows the pilots of 249 Squadron claim the destruction of three Messerschmitts while 46 Squadron accounts for another. One of 46 Squadron's Hurricanes force-lands at Rochester with a damaged engine.

The *Luftwaffe* has actually made a two-pronged attack. In the west, at the same time as the attack on London is in progress, 80 German aircraft invade 10 Group's air space to raid Bristol. AVM Brand deploys 5 squadrons to meet them. Among these are 152 and 609 Squadrons. The German formations are made up of 30 Heinkel He 111s, 19 bomb-carrying Messerschmitt Bf 110s and 27 Bf 110 escort fighters.

Mick Miller is leading Yellow Section and the whole of 609 Squadron because the radios of both flight commanders have failed. When they encounter the Germans, Miller realizes that the squadron is not in a position to intercept the bombers so he leads the Spitfires after the escort fighters which, at that moment, are circling over Warmwell.

The Spitfires attack the Messerschmitts head on. The leading British machine comes on relentlessly with its machine-guns winking ... it is coming too close ... impossible to avoid. With sickening impact the two planes collide and the Spitfire explodes, scattering wreckage in all directions. What remains of Miller's Spitfire (X4107) falls east of Doles Ash, and the wreckage of the Messerschmitt crashes nearby.

[According to British sources P/O Rogers Freeman Garland Miller is one of the Australians deemed eligible for the Battle of Britain Clasp and the 11th to be killed in action. He was designated 'Australian' when the list of battle of Britain pilots was first compiled. However this writer has been unable to discover any solid evidence to connect him with Australia. He was born at Weymouth, England, was educated in England, and his parents seem to have been English.[21] Rogers Freeman Garland Miller's name is not listed as Australian on the Roll of Honour at Westminster Abbey.]

No. 152 Squadron is 9 aircraft strong and Ian Bayles is flying as Yellow 2 in Spitfire X4025. The Germans are spotted proceeding south from Bristol. They are flying very fast and keeping no definite formation. Following Yellow 1, Bayles goes after a Messerschmitt Bf 110, presses his firing button for 6 seconds as he closes and the Messerschmitt drops back and down out of the formation. Bayles comes around for a second attack but a warning from Yellow 1 crackles in his earphones that yellow-nose Messerschmitt Bf 109s are closing in from the east. As the Australian breaks from his second attack, he sees Bf 109s approaching from behind so he dives down and away before they can come into range. Watching them carefully, he waits for a moment and then begins to climb up over the coast waiting for a chance to attack them. He counts 9 fighters and, hauling back on his controls, fires two snap shots and then turns quickly away. The 109s, apparently undamaged, fly out to sea.

Supermarine Spitfire Mk I, X4025, UM-K of 152 Squadron RAF. X4025 was delivered to 152 Squadron on 18 August 1940 and became the regular aircraft of Ian Bayles. It was the machine he was flying when he was almost shot down on 27 September. It is depicted in the mural on the walls of Aircraft Hall in the Australian War Memorial, Canberra, shown next to Hawker Hurricane L1963, LK-N, an aircraft flown in France by John Cock during the 'Phoney War'. X4025 went to an OTU in July 1941 and was involved in a flying accident next month. It was struck off charge on 18 August, exactly a year after it had been delivered to 152 Squadron.

Suddenly, there is a loud bang and a flash underneath the instrument panel. Has his engine blown up? No. Looking along his left wing Bayles can see that a hole has been blasted right through it. He has been bounced from behind. Instinctively, he throws his Spitfire into a quick half-roll and hurtles down in a vertical dive to get out of trouble. He is not sure of anything at this stage . . . whether his engine is going or not . . . It has all happened so quickly. His air speed indicator shows the same reading as before, when he had been climbing, so it is obviously no good. Close to the ground he manages to level out and throttle back. No one has followed him down so now he has time to test his controls. In spite of obvious damage the Spitfire responds as normal. There is a gaping hole in the port wing. His leg stings a little and there are small holes down the side of his cockpit, the result of shrapnel from the explosion.

Bayles makes his way back to Warmwell but he is not out of trouble yet. Although the wheels come down he has no flaps and no brakes. The tyre of his left wheel has been ripped to shreds. With his air speed indicator not working, the Australian has to judge his approach and it soon becomes obvious that he is coming in too fast. Fortunately for him, Warmwell is a grass aerodrome and the wheel of the wrecked tyre digs in and acts as a brake, swinging the Spitfire around until it comes to a halt.

Safely out of the cockpit, Bayles now becomes fully aware of the discomfort in his leg. During the explosion pieces of flying aluminium punched in from the side of his cockpit, have pierced his skin. Although there is nothing seriously wrong the injury is checked by the squadron's medical officer.

[Overnight, mechanics will remove the damaged wing and have it replaced with another, ready for operations next day.]

While the heavy fighting has been in progress John Crossman has been flying quietly in 46 Squadron's Magister on his way back from leave. He arrives at Stapleford Tawney and is greeted by exciting stories of the morning's air battles. As more enemy activity is expected, Crossman immediately joins the others waiting at 'Readiness'.

A scramble is ordered at 2.50 p.m. and, once airborne over Stapleford Tawney, 46 Squadron with only 11 aircraft, is instructed to patrol the Hornchurch line after making the usual rendezvous with 249 Squadron.

Just on 3.30 p.m. enemy aircraft are sighted over south London. There are 12 to 15 Junkers Ju 88s accompanied by the usual huge escort of Messerschmitt Bf 110s and Bf 109s. Quickly the Hurricanes manoeuvre to a favourable position and launch an attack which is made more difficult because the Ju 88s are going at full throttle. 'Pat' Patullo leads his section, consisting of John Crossman and Sgt Gooderham, down on 5 Ju 88s south of Chislehurst and orders each to single out a target. The pace is frantic and the bombers' machine-gunners put up a heavy crossfire. The Messerschmitts are coming down too. Crossman sees Patullo open fire on a Ju 88 and its engine blows up then Patullo breaks away.

Bill Millington of 249 Squadron is climbing to 1 000 feet (300 m) above the bombers. Once in position, he makes a steep diving quarter attack on the rearmost Ju 88. At this stage there are only 7 or 8 bombers left and these are being subjected to continuous attack from the swarming Hurricanes. Millington's target drops from the formation trailing smoke. Seizing his opportunity, the Australian attacks again and the Ju 88 explodes and crashes.

The Ju 88s split up and it seems that not one of them will escape. Joining up with another Hurricane, Millington attacks one of the remaining bombers which is beset by several other British fighters but is still managing to retain height. The Australian opens fire and the enemy plane loses height rapidly and crashes into the sea.

During the day 249 Squadron has had two pilots killed and one wounded but on the credit side it can claim 20 confirmed destroyed plus 8 probables.

*[Once again the German attempt to launch heavy daylight attacks on the British capital has failed and resulted in heavy casualties. The British claim to have destroyed 133 enemy planes (in fact 57 have been brought down) for a loss of 28. It is a rate of attrition which the Germans can no longer afford, not only in terms of aircraft lost, but also in terms of the loss of valuable aircrew, including some of the **Luftwaffe's** most experienced fliers.*

Meanwhile, in the Berlin Chancellery, representatives of Japan, Germany and Italy have signed a military alliance, the Tripartite Pact, which will recognize the right of the Germans and Italians to establish a 'new order' in Europe and of the Japanese to impose their 'new order' in Asia.

News of the Tripartite Pact between Germany, Italy and Japan reaches Britain at the same time as there is a meeting of the War Cabinet. Prime Minister Winston Churchill is quick to point out that the conditions of the Pact seem to be designed as a safeguard against possible intervention in the war by the United States of America.]

SATURDAY, 28 SEPTEMBER

With dawn the weather is fine with moderate winds and cloud over the English Channel, Straits of Dover and Thames Estuary.

*

Churchill sends a message of congratulations to Dowding:

> Pray congratulate Fighter Command on the results of yesterday. The scale and intensity of the fighting and heavy losses of the enemy . . . make 27th September rank with 15th September and 15th August, as the third great and victorious day of the Fighter Command during the course of the Battle of Britain.[22]

*

Australian-born New Zealander, P/O Douglas Whitney, reports for duty to 245 Squadron at Aldergrove in Northern Ireland. The squadron's duties include convoy patrols and the defence of Belfast.

*

At 8.45 a.m. Clarrie Bennett of 248 Squadron takes off from Sumburgh in Blenheim WR-G on yet another anti-invasion patrol. Mostly on such patrols there is nothing to see except for more and more water but at 9.40 a.m. the Australian and his crew find a Dornier Do 18 flying very low over the water north to north-west across their flight path. The Do 18 is a reconnaissance flying boat powered by two 880 hp Junkers Umbo 205D 6-cylinder, double-opposed liquid-cooled diesel engines. It is similar in shape to the PBY Catalina, it carries a crew of 4 and its armament consists of one 13 mm machine-gun in a bow position and one 20 mm cannon in a dorsal turret. This cannon is the real danger but against it Bennett's Blenheim is faster, carries a belly pack of 4 .303 machine-guns and two more .303 Brownings in its dorsal turret. However all of these have a shorter range than the cannon.

Bennett pushes the Blenheim into a dive, coming down fast from 1 500 feet (500 m). The German airmen are not taken by surprise. As the British machine opens fire from 400 yards (370 m) and closes in rapidly, they return fire immediately. Bennett can see his tracer hitting the Dornier's wings and smoke pours from the flying boat's engines but, because he is overshooting, the Australian has to break away to starboard. In the same instant the Blenheim is hit, with bullets entering its fuselage from the lower port side. Bennett is struck in the leg, his observer is hit in the shoulder and suddenly there is a strong smell of petrol. The Dornier seems to be slowing and it turns sharply to port still flying low over the water.

Bennett's wound is superficial but he is worried about the possibility of fire. The fuel tanks have obviously been hit and even if there is no fire they are a long way from home. The German flying boat is a long way off now, still low and hugging the waves. Faced with the prospect of coming down in the North Sea if he lingers too long, the Australian breaks away from the engagement and sets course for the Shetland Islands. Fortunately his observer's wound is not serious and his own leg has only been nicked.

Bennett does not make a claim for the Do 18 and he and his crew are unaware that the enemy flying boat has been obliged to come down on the sea. The German crew abandons the aircraft before it sinks.

*

At the same time as Charles Bennett is approaching to land, down at North Weald, 249 Squadron is scrambled to patrol over London and the Thames Estuary. As usual the Hurricanes rendezvous with those

Clarrie Bennett shows the rip in his trousers caused by a German bullet while fighting on 28 September (photograph courtesy of Len Bennett).

of 46 Squadron (John Crossman) and they are ordered up to 25 000 feet (7 600 m) where, in spite of many layers of warm clothing, the pilots find it uncomfortably cold. The Hurricanes do not perform well at such a height. They find a lot of aircraft in the air, many of them Messerschmitt Bf 109s flying back towards France. One 249 Squadron Hurricane pursues a Messerschmitt which flies tantalizingly close and manages to bring his victim down.

The three squadrons of the Debden wing (Charles McGaw of 73 Squadron is flying Hurricane V7501) are also up but fail to make contact with the enemy.

*

The deputy chief of the Air Staff, AVM Sholto Douglas, visits North Weald. Millington and the other pilots of 249 Squadron expect that he will congratulate them on their successes of the previous day but he just asks the usual polite questions and does not even mention the squadron's record score. They are noticeably disappointed.

[The Germans are changing tactics because of their heavy losses of the previous day. It is now abundantly clear that massed formations of bombers operating in daylight will suffer losses which are much too heavy so the decision has been taken to cut back on the number of bombers and to multiply the fighter escort.]

After midday several large groups of German aircraft, each consisting of about 30 bombers under heavy escort, appear between Deal and Dungeness. All 11 Group squadrons are scrambled and more are requested from 12 Group. The bombers turn back before reaching London but such is the aggressiveness of the Bf 109s that they heavily punish the British interceptors, especially the Hurricanes.

Nos 46 and 249 Squadrons are together again with 46 in the lead, much to the chagrin of the pilots in 249. The latter are critical of the pace which 46 Squadron sets. Control informs them that there are no enemy aircraft in their vicinity but on their way back from patrol two Bf 109s surprise them from behind. The German fighters fire a quick burst and break away into cloud cover below. Although 249 Squadron gives chase it is hopeless; they are left far behind. The Hurricanes of 46 Squadron have been too slow to react and take evasive action although they have witnessed the attack. One Hurricane is on fire. It falls engulfed in flames, but the pilot jumps clear.

Between 5.00 p.m. and nightfall several German aircraft carry out reconnaissance sorties. The attacks on London are resumed around 9.00 p.m. Blenheim and Defiant night fighters fly numerous night patrols but as usual, because of the inadequacy of the equipment, certainly not the efforts of the men, results are negligible.

SUNDAY, 29 SEPTEMBER

The early morning is fine but cloud builds up as the day goes on. In the north at Leuchars, the Lockheed Hudsons of 233 Squadron are prepared for operations. The first to take off at 6.19 a.m. is Hudson M7326 containing P/O Forbes and his Australian crewman John McIntosh, for convoy escort duty.

At 6.35 a.m. McIntosh's aircraft makes its rendezvous east of Montrose. There are 11 merchant vessels and two escort ships. Back and forth around the convoy they fly until 10.40 a.m. when it reaches May Island. There they turn back for Leuchars.

*

Two telegrams, one from Sir Archibald Sinclair, secretary of state for Air, and the other from the chief of Air Staff, Air Chief Marshal Sir Cyril Newall, arrive at North Weald congratulating 249 Squadron for its outstanding success on Friday.

For Bill Millington and the others the morning passes quietly and this relative calm is shared throughout Fighter Command. Aside from a few light harassing attacks on convoys and the odd reconnaissance sortie, the *Luftwaffe* remains inactive until mid-afternoon when several high-flying formations are detected by radar. No. 249 Squadron is scrambled at 4.00 p.m. to patrol with 46 Squadron (John Crossman) over the Thames Estuary and south London. By now the clouds have built up and the pilots cannot even see the ground. The wing formation becomes totally confused and the Hurricanes are hopelessly scattered, sitting ducks for any 109s which might be lurking about.

After landing back at North Weald, the pilots decide to invite 46 Squadron over from Stapleford Tawney after dinner so that their mutual problems can be discussed and solved before someone is shot to pieces.

*

During the day Kenneth Slessor and his wife Noela visit Southampton, searching for evidence of the bombing. There is very little in the business and shopping district but as they reach the wharves and industrial area the damage becomes much more obvious. Across the river they can see the Vickers factory. It has one end completely blown off and its roof is riddled with holes.

Many people are found outside the hospital reading the month's casualty list. As Slessor reads he is shocked to notice that it contains the names of scores of children between 5 and 9 years of age.

*

After dark the Germans renew their night blitz on London and Merseyside. There are, however, a number of other stray attacks and the Australian Army camp at Lipcombe Corner receives the enemy's attention at 10.00 p.m. Four high explosive bombs are dropped into the camp area but no one is injured and there is no damage.

MONDAY, 30 SEPTEMBER

The weather is generally fair with some clouds and light winds.

*

RAF Fighter Command prepares for a day of heavy activity. Around 9.00 a.m. after the usual early single reconnaissance sorties, the *Luftwaffe* raids begin. The first formation consists of approximately 30 bombers escorted by 100 Messerschmitt Bf 109s and the second group is estimated at over 60. Both forces cross the coast at Dungeness where they are met by RAF fighters up from the advanced aerodromes.

Around London No. 46 Squadron (John Crossman) is scrambled from Stapleford Tawney while at North Weald 249 Squadron (Bill Millington) is also ordered up. The two units meet as usual, patrol above the south of the capital and then out over the Thames Estuary. It is the first opportunity they have had to try out their new formations. One squadron flies in section vics in line astern while the other is above in two flights of 6 weaving, with the last aircraft of each 6 also weaving. On sighting enemy aircraft above, the first squadron is to go into a defensive 'snake' in close line astern and commence weaving too. Several yellow-nosed Bf 109s are spotted above but an opportunity to attack does not present itself. While keeping a sharp eye on the Messerschmitts, the Hurricanes continue to patrol for bombers but these do not come further than Maidstone where they turn away after a fierce dogfight with 8 squadrons of Hurricanes and 4 of Spitfires. Three Ju 88s and 4 Bf 109s are destroyed for the loss of three Hurricanes.

Back at Stapleford Tawney John Crossman pencils into his Log Book, 'Large formation Me 109s passed us but we did not attack — were looking for bombers'.[23] It is his last entry.

*

To reinforce 11 Group No. 609 Squadron is scrambled at 10.30 a.m. and sent to the London area. Thirty minutes later it receives a recall signal. At more or less the same time a mixed force of Messerschmitt Bf 110s and Bf 109s flies across from Cherbourg towards Weymouth Bay. The Middle Wallop controller informs the returning Spitfire squadron that there are 'a hundred bandits approaching Swanage at Angels 20'. The Spitfires climb for height and can soon make out the enemy in the distance. There seems to be at least 60. The squadron flies out over Weymouth Bay. 'A' and 'B' Flights split up to engage different enemy formations. Oblivious to the presence of British fighters, 6 Bf 109s fly across in front and are swiftly attacked.

To John Curchin it seems that there are two Spitfires for each Messerschmitt so he holds back, waiting above to ambush any other German fighters which might join the fight. After waiting several minutes he is startled by a 109 which suddenly dives past him. Quickly lining it up in his sights, he discharges a short burst but misses because it is diving too fast. The Australian turns to give chase but loses sight of his quarry. Then, suddenly, the sky is empty of aircraft.

Curchin patrols over Portland until he receives orders to land. As a result of the dogfight 609 Squadron claims three Bf 109s destroyed, one probable and one damaged, without loss.

*

After midday there are minor raids put up by the Germans over Kent but a couple of hours later a formation of 100 bombers escorted by about 200 fighters appears over the coast of Sussex en route for

London. The Hurricanes of 46 Squadron and 249 Squadron are up again and this time they find what seems to be hundreds of Bf 109s above them. The Germans are too high and well out of reach. A tense situation develops. As the Hurricanes continue to patrol looking for the bombers they are shadowed by the enemy fighters. One formation of Ju 88s manages to reach the outskirts of London and unload its bombs but damage is light. They are not detected by either 46 Squadron or 249 Squadron because the attention of the British pilots has become rivetted on the trailing Bf 109s in case they are jumped.

When a brief opportunity presents itself a few Bf 109s make a swift hit-and-run attack on 46 Squadron. Further back, at least one pilot of 249 Squadron, P/O George Barclay, sees a Hurricane falling in flames, plunging downwards towards the village of Forest Row . . .[24]

In the grounds of Tablehurst Farm, Forest Row, a man paints watercolour scenes of the tranquil English countryside. The peace is suddenly shattered when a burning Hurricane hurtles out of the sky and crashes directly in front of him, into the middle of the very scene he is painting! The pilot has not bailed out.

*

The painter was Edmund Wimperis, a cousin of H.A. Wimperis, former Director of Research at the Air Ministry, who had visited Australia before the war to advise the government on air defence. Edmund was able to discover that John Crossman was the pilot. He finished the painting, showing the burnt out Hurricane almost submerged into the seeming

As artist Edmund Wimperis was painting a watercolour of the English countryside near Forest Row, Sussex, a burning Hurricane crashed out of the sky into the very scene he was painting. He included the wreckage in his picture and recorded forever the last moments of John Crossman.

John Crossman, who flew with 32 and 46 Squadrons. He was killed in action on 30 September 1940 (photograph courtesy of Joan Bowden).

unchanged countryside, and sent it with two others, to John's parents and girlfriend in Newcastle, NSW.]

P/O John Dallas Crossman is the 11th of those Australian airmen deemed eligible to receive the Battle of Britain Clasp to be killed in action.

*

A large German raid crosses the Dorset coast just after 4.30 p.m. The Germans are after the Westland factory at Yeovil but 4 squadrons of British fighters bar their way. One unit is 152 Squadron. Ian Bayles, who is flying as Red 3, can see an estimated 70 Heinkel He 111s escorted by about 40 Messerschmitt Bf 110s and Bf 109s. The Heinkels are flying in vics of three in one large vic with the Messerschmitts weaving astern and above. The Spitfires are in a good position west of Portland with the sun directly behind them. They are slightly above the enemy fighters on which they launch an attack, the whole squadron charging in as one, trying to break up the German formations. A huge dogfight begins.

Bayles spots three Bf 110s and attacks them from the forward quarter but he is seen and they turn into him head-on. Neither side is able to score hits and they roar past each other unscathed. The Australian then climbs, finding as he does so a Heinkel which has dropped out of formation. Seizing his chance he closes in and opens fire. The Heinkel takes hits but is able to disappear into surrounding cloud cover before it can be seriously damaged. Bayles realizes that he has little chance of finding his target again so he climbs once more to a position where he can make another attack on the bomber formation.

While Bayles is engaged in this fight, to the west at Exeter, 8 Hurricanes of 87 Squadron have been taking off in pairs between 4.20 p.m. and 4.25 p.m. John Cock in Hurricane V7207 is paired with F/Lt Ian Gleed DFC and they climb rapidly, heading for Portland. Meanwhile the German bombers have been unable to identify their target through the scattered cloud. They bomb blind but are several miles away from Yeovil. As they turn for home they have to run the gauntlet of 4 more British squadrons racing to intercept them. The running battle which develops is not all one-sided for the German escort fighters stage an aggressive defence.

The Hurricanes from Exeter meet the Germans inland of Portland. John Cock and Ian Gleed find a large group of bombers escorted by a few Bf 109s and 110s. Cock prepares to attack from out of the sun but suddenly he is attacked from behind by a Bf 109. The Messerschmitt overshoots and in an instant the Australian pounces, firing as he closes in. Black smoke immediately pours out of the German fighter and it dives into a layer of cloud.

Determined to finish it off, Cock hurtles down into the cloud but when he breaks through it is not the Messerschmitt that he finds. Looming in front is a lone Junkers Ju 88. Cock is coming in swiftly on its beam and just has time to fire for two seconds before breaking away to avoid a collision. He throws the Hurricane into a tight turn, comes around onto the bomber's tail and sets it on fire.

After landing back at Exeter the pilots of 87 Squadron lodge claims for two destroyed, a Ju 88 and a Bf 110, plus three probables, two Ju 88s and a Bf 109.

*

As night falls RAF Bomber Command sends 104 bombers to a wide variety of targets, including one force of Wellingtons and Whitleys headed for Berlin to bomb the German Air Ministry building. It is an ambitious idea because the techniques of attacking with such precision at night have not yet been developed and, for a loss of 5 aircraft, only 6 bombs actually fall on the German capital. Blenheims and Hampdens are allocated closer targets including minelaying in the river Elbe. No. 40 Squadron is to bomb the dock areas of Ostend and Boulogne. Brian Best and his crew in Blenheim N3592 go to Boulogne where he drops a stick of bombs across Bassin Loubet. Bomb bursts are observed followed by vivid flashes and then two fires.

Overnight the *Luftwaffe* makes heavy raids on London, East Anglia, Bristol and Liverpool. Of 175 bombers which head for the British capital, not many are inclined to risk the heavy flak batteries around the centre of the city.

*

[September has seen a complete change in the battle of Britain. Whereas at the end of August, Dowding had reached the grim conclusion that Fighter Command was not winning, in the last 30 days the crisis has passed particularly after the great aerial victory of the 15th. The **Luftwaffe** *has not achieved anything like local air superiority, the necessary prerequisite for invasion, and now German bombers cannot hope to fly with any degree of safety over southern England during daylight. Growing numbers of RAF fighters patrol British airspace.]*

Of those 'Australian' airmen deemed eligible for the Battle of Britain Clasp, 5 have been killed during September:

7 September	F/Lt Pat Hughes	234 Squadron
7 September	F/Lt Dick Reynell	43 Squadron
11 September	F/Lt Fred Flood	235 Squadron
25 September	Sgt Ken Holland	152 Squadron
30 September	P/O John Crossman	46 Squadron

Of those not considered eligible for the Clasp but included as 'Australian' on the Battle of Britain Roll of Honour at Westminster Abbey, three have been killed in September:

26 September	P/O Ray Earl	61 Squadron
10 September	P/O Bob Reed	50 Squadron
8 September	Sgt Joe Bull	149 Squadron

Five Australians are still recovering from injuries:

P/O John 'Tiger' Pain of 32 Squadron, wounded 18 August
G/C Ron Lees, formerly 72 Squadron, wounded 2 September
Sgt Desmond Fopp of 17 Squadron, wounded 3 September
P/O Richard Hillary of 603 Squadron, wounded 3 September
F/Lt Desmond Sheen of 72 Squadron, wounded 5 September.

OCTOBER, 1940

TUESDAY 1

Records indicate that the Australian personnel listed below are on strength in RAF Fighter Command Squadrons at 9.00 a.m. on 1 October 1940:

SQUADRON	[AIRCRAFT]	AIRMAN	BASE	
32	[Hurricane]	P/O J.F. Pain	Acklington	[13 Group]
		(In hospital recovering from wounds received 18-8-40)		
65	[Spitfire]	F/Lt C.G.C. Olive DFC	Turnhouse	[13 Group]
72	[Spitfire]	F/Lt D.F.B. Sheen DFC	Biggin Hill	[11 Group]
		(Recovering from wounds received 5-9-40)		
73	[Hurricane]	P/O C.A. McGaw	Castle Camps	[11 Group]
87	[Hurricane]	F/O J.R. Cock	Exeter	[10 Group]
141	[Defiant]	F/O A.N. Constantine	Gatwick	[11 Group]
145	[Hurricane]	F/Lt R.W. Bungey	Dyce	[13 Group]
152	[Spitfire]	F/O I.N. Bayles	Warmwell	[10 Group]
249	[Hurricane]	P/O W. Millington DFC	North Weald	[11 Group]
264	[Defiant]	Sgt V.W.J. Crook	Kirton-in-Lindsey	[12 Group]
600	[Blenheim]	F/Lt C.A. Pritchard	Redhill	[11 Group]
601	[Hurricane]	AF/Lt H.C. Mayers DFC	Exeter	[10 Group]
609	[Spitfire]	P/O J. Curchin	Middle Wallop	[10 Group]

In addition three Coastal Command Squadrons are, or have been, attached to Fighter Command or operate under its control:

236	[Blenheim]	F/Lt R.M. Power	Middle Wallop	
		F/O W.S. Moore		
248	[Blenheim]	P/O C.C. Bennett	Sunburgh	
		P/O A.L. Hamilton		
		P/O J.D. Peterkin		

The telegram informing John Crossman's family of his death; many other Australian families received similar news (photograph courtesy of Joan Bowden).

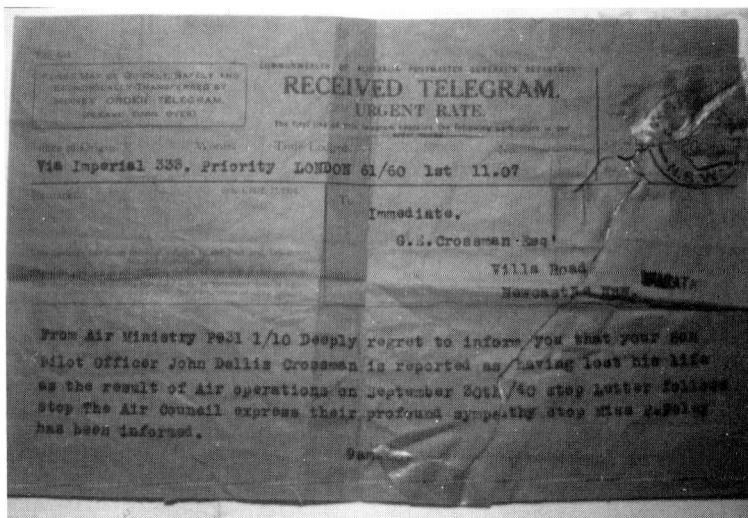

The Air Ministry sends a telegram to John Crossman's family in Australia:[1]

*

Clive Mayers of 601 Squadron has his award of the DFC gazetted, as does Bill Millington, of 249 Squadron.

Millington's squadron has an uneventful day. The Hurricanes fly two patrols over Kent. High above they can see large formations of Messerschmitt Bf 109s but there is no chance to engage them in combat.

Likewise Charles McGaw and 73 Squadron scramble at 2.00 p.m. and rendezvous with 257 Squadron for a similar patrol but they, too, do not make contact with the enemy.

*[German tactics on this day pose serious problems for Fighter Command, forcing the defending Hurricanes and Spitfires to fly many fruitless sorties. They are obliged to do this because, mixed in with the enemy's fighter formations, are groups of bomb-carrying Bf 109s. A third of the German fighter force is in the process of converting its aircraft so that the Bf 109s can carry a 250 kg bomb and the Bf 110s can carry a total load of 700 kg. While it is far from popular with the Messerschmitt pilots, the problems thus created for the RAF are difficult to solve. It is the presence of these fighter bombers which makes it essential for every **Luftwaffe** raid to be intercepted. No longer can formations which are apparently all fighters be allowed to roam unmolested. Unfortunately the Hurricanes are unable to climb high enough fast enough to intercept effectively and at high altitude they are no match for the Messerschmitts. The Spitfires, too, unless they are scrambled early enough, are having difficulty reaching the high-flying enemy planes which, once across the coast and behind the radar wall, cannot be accurately plotted by the Observers' Corps because of cloud and their extreme height.]*

*

Clarence Bennett of 248 Squadron. He is presumed to have died on 1 October 1940 after failing to return from a mission (photograph courtesy of Len Bennett).

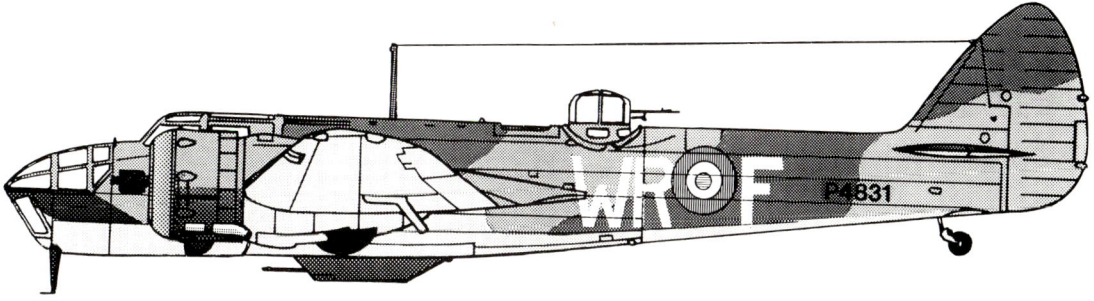

Bristol Blenheim Mk IVF, P4831, WR-F of 248 Squadron RAF. 'Short nose' Blenheim Mk IFs began to be replaced by 'Long nose' Blenheim Mk IVFs in 248 Squadron as early as February 1940, these also using the ventral pack of four 0.303 in. (0.77 cm) Browning machine-guns. P4831 was often used by Lewis Hamilton during August/September 1940 and also by Clarrie Bennett during August. Bennett was flying Blenheim R3626, WR-J, when he was posted missing on 1 October.

At 1.20 p.m. Blenheim WR-J of 248 Squadron takes off from Sumburgh to fly a photographic reconnaissance sortie of the Norwegian coast. Its crew consists of Charles Bennett with Sgt Clark and Sgt Brash, both non-commissioned officers who were with the Australian during his attack on the Dornier Do 18 on 28 September. The Blenheim flies out over the North Sea and disappears into the distance. It will never be seen again . . .

P/O Clarence Charles Bennett is the 12th of those Australians deemed eligible for the Battle of Britain Clasp who will not return.

[*Clarrie Bennett was listed as 'Missing in Action' but it was not until 18 December 1941 that a Notification of Death was issued stating that Pilot Officer Clarence Charles Bennett, Royal Air Force, '. . . was reported missing and is presumed, for official purposes, to have lost his life on the 1st day of October 1940, as the result of air operations.'[2]*]

*

German bombers, relieved from the pressure of daylight operations, now concentrate their effort on night attacks. The first raiders begin coming in over the Isle of Wight, Beachy Head and Dungeness shortly before 8.00 p.m., all on course for London.

WEDNESDAY, 2 OCTOBER

It is a clear morning and the German air force sends large numbers of high-flying fighters and fighter-bombers to attack London and Biggin Hill. The first raids are detected around 8.30 a.m. and south London begins to experience attacks half an hour later. They continue throughout the morning. Because of their poor high-altitude performance No. 11 Group's Hurricanes are ineffective in defence.

Flying from North Weald, 249 Squadron (Bill Millington) has a fairly active morning with two patrols high over the south of London. Some Bf 109s are seen but they are out of reach high above.

The large number of patrols which Fighter Command is obliged to make is leading to maintenance problems and most of 249 Squadron's Hurricanes are developing oil leaks because of wear and tear. Because of this fault, after half an hour of flying, an opaque film spreads over the aircraft's windscreen considerably reducing visibility.

During the afternoon Dowding visits North Weald and, in a talk to the pilots and men, he tells them of the new Hurricane Mk II with a more powerful Rolls Royce Merlin XX engine and an armament of 4 20 mm cannons. Perhaps some of these will provide an answer for the high-flying Messerschmitts which are making life so difficult. At the moment, out of all of 11 Group, only half a dozen Spitfire squadrons are capable of reaching the Germans before they drop their bombs.

After midday the German fighter-bombers are active again although on a much more limited scale owing to the thickening cloud. Some manage to get through to central London.

*

Over south-western England there is little activity. No. 601 Squadron at Exeter flies no operational sorties at all.

Meanwhile 87 Squadron, which is also stationed at Exeter, swaps flights at Bibury. John Cock leads 'B' Flight to Bibury where it will remain for about a week to carry out 'cat's eyes' patrols. 'A' Flight returns to Exeter.

*

With the days becoming shorter and the nights longer, RAF Bomber Command sends out 81 aircraft to targets in Germany and the Channel ports. For 6 Blenheims of 40 Squadron the target is Antwerp and they begin taking off just after 7.00 p.m. Brian Best leaves Wyton in Blenheim N3592. Cloudy conditions make visibility difficult but Best drops his stick of bombs across the target area. Neither he nor his crew are able to observe the results. Of the 6 planes despatched, one fails to find the target and brings its bombs home and only one, which goes in at low level, sees bombs landing on the quay.

The *Luftwaffe* starts early too and between 7.15 p.m. and 6.15 a.m. about 180 bombers conduct heavy and widespread raids over England, although the majority concentrate on London. Of 33 British night fighters in the air, not one manages to intercept.

THURSDAY, 3 OCTOBER

There is a rude awakening for North Weald Sector station when, at 5.00 a.m., there are sudden loud explosions as bombs are dropped near the officers' mess. Rain, drizzle and low cloud preclude any widespread aerial activity by either side.

*

Sidney Cotton's patience has reached an end. Over three months have passed and still no orders for a new assignment have arrived from the RAF Pool Depot at Uxbridge. To establish his Photographic Development Unit he has been given the rank of acting wing commander but, to his chagrin, he has been given no work and has therefore been unable to make any further contribution to the defence of England. During this time of forced inactivity he has tried to find a method of successfully combating the *Luftwaffe* night bombers. He has con-

A reunion in 1942 of Air Chief Marshal Sir Hugh Dowding and men who had fought in the battle of Britain. Desmond Sheen is second from the left and Richard Hillary is fifth from the right (Public Archives of Canada photograph PA 139034).

cluded that the best immediate solution would be to fit a radar-equipped aircraft with a powerful searchlight so that, once it has found its intended target, it can illuminate the German plane for a visual attack by an attending fighter. It is obvious to the Queenslander that something has to be done, and done swiftly, because the night raids are becoming more intense.

Determined to pursue his ideas to the limit, Cotton realizes that he will not be able to do so while remaining a member of the RAF because of its bureaucracy so he obtains his release from the service. Now he is free to approach other parties who may be interested. He visits Lord Beaverbrook who passes him on to his chief production director, Trevor Westbrook. After listening to Cotton Westbrook agrees that at least the idea should be tried. The Night Interception Committee had rejected a similar proposal in July but if anyone can make such an idea work he believes that Cotton is that man.

*

At Leuchars in Scotland the weather is not as bad, being hazy. Three Hudsons from 233 Squadron fly on an offensive patrol to the coast of Norway. Australian members of the squadron, Bill Weaber and John McIntosh, are engaged in the usual solitary reconnaissance patrols over the North Sea.

*

At Lindholme Dereck French is posted from 50 Squadron to 106 Squadron at Finningley.

[*Dereck French was a cadet at Point Cook in 1937 and in January 1938 sailed to England. For a courageous attack on the German cruiser* **Königsberg** *near Bergen on 9 April 1940 he was awarded a DFC. Flying operations practically non-stop, French remained with 50 Squadron until this day when he transferred to 106 Squadron. Thereafter he served with 207 and 87 Squadrons before joining 455 Squadron, RAAF, the first Australian medium bomber squadron, on 30 June 1941 while it was being formed at Swinderby, Lincolnshire. The aircraft, Hampdens, were slow in coming, only arriving in ones and twos, and it was on 29 August that French began the unit's operational life when he flew the only plane available, Hampden AE 296 (UB-F), to bomb Frankfurt-on-Main. This sortie went without incident. However, during a later mission to the same target, French's aircraft was hit by flak but he continued to carry out a glide bombing attack and return home safely. French's promotion to temporary squadron leader was recorded in the* **London Gazette** *in December 1941 and he remained with 455 Squadron as commander of 'A' Flight until March 1942. His work earned him a Bar to his DFC. He next flew Wellingtons with 108 Squadron stationed at Kabrit in Egypt. In November he was posted to the far east. Early in 1943 he commanded No. 215 (Wellington) Squadron at Jessore, India, for missions over Burma. In June 1943 he left the RAF and transferred to the RAAF.*]

*

Richard Hillary, who is in The Royal Masonic Hospital in London under the care of the gifted New Zealand plastic surgeon, Archibald McIndoe, has his promotion to flying officer recorded in the *London Gazette*.

[*The next two years for Richard Hillary were filled with numerous operations involving new and experimental techniques of skin-grafting surgery and slow recovery. The terribly maimed RAF casualties of 1940 brought to McIndoe completely new problems and his work was pioneering and experimental — each man was, in effect, a 'guinea pig'. Such was the spirit kindled in these men by the brilliant New Zealander that they formed their own exclusive club, The Guinea Pig Club, which is still in existence today.*

While still recovering, Hillary's promotion to flight lieutenant was recorded in the **London Gazette** *on 3 October 1941.*

Surgical skill and Dick Hillary's own fortitude eventually enabled him to leave hospital and he was sent by the Ministry of Information to give lectures in the USA. Upon his arrival there he was claimed by the British Air Communiqué Committee and given an office job. It was here that he wrote his book, a work detailing his own thoughts and experiences in 1940, which he called **The Last Enemy**. *The title was taken from Corinthians XV, 36: 'The last enemy that shall be destroyed is death.'*[3]

The book was released in June 1942 and was immediately popular.

Back in England, as his health improved, Dick Hillary began to pester the authorities to allow him to go back into operations. By November 1942 he was passed fit for active service and began training to fly night fighters at Chatterhall in Berwickshire.

On the night of 8 January 1943 he and his navigator, F/Sgt Kenneth

Fison, took off just after midnight. They were told over the radio to circle around a flashing beacon. The duty officer on the ground watched their Blenheim circling slowly and as it did so its port wing tilted towards the beacon. The Blenheim swung around and down in wide sweeps until it crashed into the ground where it burst into flames. Dick Hillary and Ken Fison were both killed.

So died Richard Hope Hillary.]

FRIDAY, 4 OCTOBER

The bleak weather continues with mist, rain and extremely poor visibility all over the British Isles. Bill Moore of 236 Squadron in R3878 leads a section of three Blenheims off on a fighter patrol. They take off from St Eval at 7.30 a.m. but conditions soon force them to abort the mission and they are all back on the ground by 8 a.m.

*

John Crossman, 22 years of age, formerly of 46 Squadron, is buried at Chalfont St Giles Churchyard, Buckinghamshire.

*

[AVM Park issues his Instructions to Controllers No. 24 and in it he refers to measures to be taken to combat the high-flying Germans. With the prevailing cloudy skies and inaccurate heights given by radar, the group controller's most difficult problem has been to establish the height of incoming raiders. Tip-and-run raids coming across Kent by Bf 110s carrying bombs, or small formations of long-range bombers escorted by fighters, give such short notice that the group controller has been sometimes compelled to detail even single fighter squadrons, that happen to be in the air, to intercept. Because of this and the delay in the receipt of both radar and Observers' Corps reports at Group control, plus longer time recently taken by squadrons to take off, paired squadrons have been meeting enemy formations above them before they can get to their ordered height.]

*

The poor weather of the daylight hours continues into the night with fog and intermittent rain. Even so the *Luftwaffe* maintains its pressure on London by sending over 100 bombers while others raid Liverpool. Conditions render the night fighter defences totally impotent.

SATURDAY, 5 OCTOBER

Weather conditions continue to be poor with showers in most areas. The Germans launch a series of fighter-bomber raids over south-eastern England and some venture as far inland as London. From the point of view of the German fighter-bomber pilots, their new duty is more than unpopular because they consider themselves to be at a serious disadvantage when confronted by Spitfires and even Hurricanes. When a dogfight is imminent they jettison their bombs at random, ready for the forthcoming battle. During the intervals of brighter weather the people of London and Kent witness the spectacle of twisting vapour trails high in the air as the Messerschmitts, Spitfires and Hurricanes duel overhead. Throughout the day there are 5 distinct attacks.

'B' Flight of 73 Squadron is given the task of convoy escort. Charles McGaw in Hurricane V7501 takes off from Castle Camps at the head of Green Section at 11.40 a.m. The 6 Hurricanes form an umbrella over the convoy as it leaves the Thames estuary and sets course northward hugging the coastline. They continue to escort until they are relieved by another flight shortly before 1.00 p.m.

No. 249 Squadron flies its first patrol around 10.30 a.m. The Hurricanes fly over Kent together with 46 Squadron which takes the lead. There is a brief clash with two Bf 109s which try to surprize a section of Hurricanes but they are spotted in time, diving from a layer of cloud. Both sides escape unscathed.

There is a second patrol after lunch, again at 20 000 feet (6 100 m) over Kent.

*

At Leuchars 8 Hudsons from 233 Squadron are involved in patrols throughout the day. In the morning one flies up and down the Scottish coast while three go on an offensive patrol along the coast of Norway. In the early afternoon 4 aircraft set out on routine solitary patrols over the North Sea. One is Hudson QX-S containing John McIntosh.

By 6.40 p.m. all of the Hudsons except for QX-S are back at Leuchars. McIntosh's patrol has been extended so it is known that he will be late but at the same time the weather is deteriorating rapidly. By the arrival of darkness the weather is atrocious and the Australian's plane has not returned. Time is running out. The men on the ground can only look out into the darkness and listen, hoping for some sign of the missing aircraft. Then much later, the telephone rings . . . Hudson QX-S has crashed near Berwick but there is no trace of its crew. Possibly, when they were unable to find Leuchars in the rain and darkness, they had bailed out . . . Perhaps into the sea.

SUNDAY, 6 OCTOBER

The foul weather persists overnight and into Sunday. In the early morning radar detects a large raid building up near the Straits of Dover but, because of continuous rain and low cloud, it disperses. The *Luftwaffe's* major operations are cancelled but a few minor attacks are launched.

At Leuchars there has been no news of McIntosh and his crew and it is assumed that they must have bailed out over the sea. In spite of conditions an aircraft is sent out to search but to no avail. The men are never found.

P/O John McIntosh is one of the Australian airmen whose names appear on the Battle of Britain Roll of Honour at Westminster Abbey.

*

The pilots of 609 Squadron are relaxing in the mess at Middle Wallop when, at 12.30 p.m., the loud speakers announce that an enemy aircraft is approaching the airfield. Because of the thick weather there is no chance of scrambling a pair of Spitfires to intercept so they just ignore the warning and order another round of drinks. Moments later there is a sharp, piercing whistle. There are two big flashes just outside the window followed by two massive explosions which rock the building.

When it is safe they rush outside to find two bomb craters in the field outside the mess and 6 others within the airfield's perimeter.

At Biggin Hill a solitary bomber makes a low-flying attack and destroys three barracks blocks, damages one aircraft and causes minor damage to the airfield's surface. The offending German aircraft collides with a balloon and cable but they are not enough to bring it down.

For Thomas Lang and the personnel at 11 Group headquarters, Uxbridge, an extremely dangerous situation develops when 4 parachute mines, one of them a delayed-action type, are dropped in the vicinity.

[Thomas Lang remained a senior group controller at No. 11 Group headquarters, Uxbridge, and a staunch supporter of Keith Park, until May 1941, and afterwards served under Leigh-Mallory. Thus he was uniquely placed to witness the tactical methods of both commanders and was highly critical of the results of a simulated raid carried out by the latter to demonstrate the effectiveness of his 'Big Wing' theory early in 1941. Lang was mentioned in dispatches in September 1941 and awarded the AFC a year later. He remained in the RAF after the war and retired in November 1955. He died in January 1970.]

*

Overnight high winds and low cloud give London its first quiet evening since 7 September. Only a few brave, or foolhardy, German bombers venture over the capital.

MONDAY, 7 OCTOBER

The weather is much improved with good visibility and varying degrees of cloud.

Throughout the morning the *Luftwaffe* sends waves of Messerschmitt Bf 109 fighters and fighter-bombers over Kent in a practically continuous stream. No. 11 Group has difficulty combating these tactics and many squadrons fly fruitless patrols.

After lunch 249 Squadron carries out another uneventful patrol but later, during the afternoon's second mission, there is a clash with the enemy. While flying north of Ashford at 21 000 feet (6 400 m) Bill Millington and the others see 6 or 8 Bf 109s circling in a *mêlée* with Spitfires. Much higher up there are about 20 more 109s in a loose formation, apparently heading for France. The Hurricanes break into sections and join the fight. Millington starts after a 109 which dives steeply with a Spitfire in hot pursuit but then he breaks away and climbs to a position with the sun at his back. Almost immediately he spots a Bf 109 which is on the tail of a Spitfire and dives after it. The German fighter breaks away and turns steeply in front of him. Millington fires a short burst and the Messerschmitt turns over and dives away with smoke pouring from its engine.

Millington is about to follow when he notices two other aircraft preparing to attack him. He breaks off violently and in the same instant realizes that his would-be attackers are Spitfires. He dives away carrying with him the distinct feeling that his is not the only Hurricane which has been wrongly attacked by Spitfires.

*

The largest single raid of the day is an attack on the Westland Aircraft factory at Yeovil. At 10 Group headquarters AVM Brand scrambles his squadrons to meet the threat. The Spitfires of 609 Squadron take off from Middle Wallop and climb steadily in a south-westerly direction trying to get as much height as possible before reaching the coast. The pilots are impressed by the clarity of the air and from 15 000 feet (4 600 m) they can see Plymouth and far beyond into Cornwall.

Three squadrons, Nos 152, 238 and 601, engage the Germans near Portland. No. 152 Squadron is at 20 000 feet (6 100 m) and to one side of the bombers. Ian Bayles looks down at 25 Junkers Ju 88s flying in a loose formation with a guard of about 50 Messerschmitt Bf 110s coming in behind and above them. The Spitfires are in pairs. They dive after the bombers and through the formation, trying to split it up. Two sections of Hurricanes from 601 Squadron, one of them led by Clive Mayers, sweep into the fight.

The Germans drop 80 high explosive and 6 oil bombs on the Westland complex. In material terms the damage is light but one bomb makes a direct hit on an air raid shelter, causing more than 100 casualties.

The running battle continues but the timely arrival of about 30 Bf 109s saves the battered Ju 88s and Bf 110s from suffering really heavy casualties. Ian Bayles blazes away at a Ju 88 but without any obvious effect. It just refuses to fall. His wingman is more successful and shoots down one of the bombers.

At least 9 of the raiders, two Ju 88s and 7 Bf 110s, are shot down but it is not a wholly one-sided contest. Two Spitfires are lost by 152 Squadron and one pilot is severely burned. No. 238 Squadron loses a Hurricane and 601 Squadron has one aircraft badly damaged. The latter is Hurricane R4218 flown by Clive Mayers. Mayers manages to crash-land near Axminster but he is shaken up and slightly injured. No. 609 Squadron loses two Spitfires shot down and two others damaged.

During a conference at Australian Force headquarters, Amesbury Abbey, General Wynter informs the officers that the proposed move-

The radar-equipped Beaufighter Mk 1s which came into service towards the end of the battle of Britain. The aircraft shown is clad in post-1940 markings (Imperial War Museum photograph CH 6723).

ment of the Australian troops to their winter quarters at Colchester will take place on 14, 15 and 16 October.

*

Between 5.00 p.m. and 9.00 p.m. numerous scattered raids are detected by radar. The main German targets are London and Merseyside but other attacks are scattered from Harwich to Newcastle and the Firth of Forth.

Although the use at night of day fighters such as Hurricanes and Spitfires continues to illustrate the inadequacy of the British defences after dark, new equipment is starting to filter through into the squadrons. Charles Pritchard of 600 Squadron flies a night patrol too, his first in one of the new generation of night fighters. His aircraft is Bristol Beaufighter R2056. Although roughly the same length and wingspan as a Blenheim, the Beaufighter is a stronger, heavier and more powerful machine. On either side is a 1 590 hp Bristol Hercules XI radial engine and both of these project ahead of the aircraft's very short nose. Its firepower is enormous; four 20 mm cannons in the lower portion of the fuselage nose with 240 rounds each and six .303 inch machine-guns, two in the port wing and 6 in the starboard, each with 1 000 rounds.

While taking off Pritchard finds that he has to correct the Beaufighter's tendency to swing off line and as it climbs away there is some further instability caused by the small surface area of its dorsal tail fin. In general, however, the new machine handles well. Pritchard is on patrol for one hour and 50 minutes.

The Beaufighter will eventually prove to be the answer to Britain's night fighting problems but there are not yet enough of them. Also, airborne radar is still suffering from teething problems and requires a skilled operator to interpret the electronic blips on its display screen.

TUESDAY, 8 OCTOBER

It is a windy day with clouds over south-eastern England but no rain. The *Luftwaffe* sends over its usual early morning reconnaissance sorties and at 8.00 a.m. two formations of about 50 and 100 approach the coast of Kent. From North Weald 249 Squadron is one of the units scrambled but the take-off turns into a shambles. Bill Millington is faster into the air than his squadron commander and everyone starts to formate on him. As soon as he realizes what is happening the Australian tries to 'buzz off'. At the same time one of the other section leaders has radio failure. It is some time before any semblance of order is restored so that the squadron can go on its patrol. If the Messerschmitts had been around they would have had a lot of easy targets.

Shortly afterwards 249 Squadron is on patrol over London. High above, formations of German planes can be seen making heavy vapour trails over the south-east and the capital but there is nothing the squadron can do about them. When the Hurricanes finally land back at North Weald, the pilots are informed that London has been bombed through the clouds by Bf 109s.

At 10.30 a.m. another group of 30 bomb-carrying Bf 109s makes a follow-up attack on London and the *Luftwaffe* continues this pressure by sending more formations across, at 60-minute intervals, for the next few hours. No. 249 Squadron is scrambled, along with other units, twice in the morning but each time the enemy is too high and too far away.

*

At 9.55 a.m. in the far north Gordon Olive of 65 Squadron leads three Spitfires from Turnhouse to Drem. There they fly in co-operation exercises with the Westland Whirlwinds of 263 Squadron, the RAF's first twin-engined, single-seat fighters.

On close inspection, the Whirlwind looks streamlined and fast with a very thin fuselage containing four 20 mm Hispano cannon in the nose, giving it a dense concentration of fire, enough to bring down any bomber. The view from the all-round-vision cockpit canopy seems excellent and the pilots of 263 Squadron claim that its handling characteristics are delightful. Unfortunately, however, the plane's 885 hp Rolls Royce Peregrine engines are suffering from numerous teething problems.

[It was late November before Gordon Olive and 65 Squadron came south again, this time to Tangmere. On 9 December he shot down a Bf 110 for what turned out to be his sixth and final victory although he claimed a probable Ju 88 on 15 February 1941. In March he was promoted acting squadron leader and took up fighter controller duties at Tangmere for the next three months. On 20 June 1941 he was appointed to command 456 Squadron, Australia's first night fighter unit. The squadron became operational in August and its first victory came on the night of 10–11 January 1942 when a Dornier Do 217 was shot down in flames. Olive carried out 17 sorties with 456 Squadron before ill-health cut short his tour of duty. On 3 June 1943 he joined the RAAF, relinquishing the rank

of acting wing commander which he had attained on 29 December 1942.

On 20 October 1943 he left England for Australia. In February 1944 he went to RAAF Command where he received the rank of acting wing commander on 1 April.

Altogether, W/Cdr Gordon Olive DFC completed 4 tours of operational flying involving 219 sorties, many of them during the hectic days of the battle of Britain. He was discharged from the RAAF on 7 March 1946.

In civilian life Olive returned to Brisbane and joined Rheem Australia in an executive position. He retired in 1972 and died towards the end of 1987.]

*

As darkness falls the winds become gusty. Even so, RAF Bomber Command sends more than 100 Whitleys, Hampdens, Wellingtons and Blenheims to numerous targets in France and Germany. The largest concentrated effort is made by 38 Blenheims on the Channel ports. The aircraft of 40 Squadron are allocated two targets. Three Blenheims are to attack Flushing and three others are to bomb Boulogne. Brian Best, in aircraft N3592 (BL-C), makes a shallow diving attack on the docks at Boulogne but because of the weather he and his crew are unable to see direct results.

The *Luftwaffe* is busy too and over 100 raiders converge on London to carry out a continuous bombardment until 4.00 a.m.

WEDNESDAY, 9 OCTOBER

The weather remains windy and gusty with rain and clouds over northern France and the Straits of Dover. High-flying Messerschmitts are active again, concentrating their efforts on the fighter airfields in Kent and on London.

*

At North Weald 257 Squadron (Hurricanes) arrives to take the place of 25 Squadron (Blenheim night fighters). This unit is to combine and form a wing with 249 Squadron and 46 Squadron from Stapleford Tawney.

Bill Millington and 249 Squadron are scrambled just before tea and climb up over Maidstone. The Messerschmitts are nowhere to be found.

[AVM Park has been far from satisfied with the RAF's lack of success in combating the high-flying Germans. In a directive dated the previous day he has ordered that, when a Spitfire squadron is on readiness patrol on the Maidstone line, its function will be to cover the area of Biggin Hill-Maidstone-Gravesend, while other RAF squadrons are gaining height, to protect them from the German fighters. This squadron is not to be ordered to intercept a raid during the early stages of the engagement, but the sector controller must keep the squadron commander informed as to the height

and direction of the approaching raids. The object of ordering the squadron to patrol at 15 000 feet while waiting on the patrol line for raids to come inland is to conserve oxygen and to keep the pilots at a comfortable height. Pilots must watch this carefully so that they have ample oxygen in hand when the Spitfires are ordered to 30 000 feet as soon as enemy raids are about to cross the English coast.[4]

Meanwhile, arriving in squadrons now is the improved Spitfire Mk II with a Rolls Royce Merlin XII engine, rated at 1 175 hp for take-off and 1 150 hp at 14 500 feet (4 400 m), driving a Rotol three-blade Jablo constant-speed propeller. Unfortunately its use will not become widespread until December.]

*

John Cock of 87 Squadron leads the Hurricanes of 'B' Flight back to Exeter after their stint of night operations at Bibury.

Overnight German bombers stream in and attack a wide variety of targets but they concentrate on London.

THURSDAY, 10 OCTOBER

Dawn reveals haze in the Thames Estuary and over East Anglia and the weather is showery. The German effort continues to consist of high-flying fighter-bombers coming over southern England in a steady stream — a tactic which continues to be difficult to counter. For the British pilots, especially those of the Hurricanes which cannot reach the upper altitudes, the situation is particularly dangerous. The enemy is always above and therefore retains the advantage in a fight.

At 12.40 p.m. the Hurricanes of 145 Squadron begin landing at Tangmere. They have flown south from Dyce. Most of the pilots begin to find quarters and look around their new home but Bob Bungey does not bother. He tells the others to relax because they will have plenty of time to explore later and they are certain to be scrambled shortly.

The Australian's words are prophetic for an order comes to take off before the hour is up. They leap into action and within minutes are strapped into their aircraft and airborne, climbing quickly in 4 sections of three aircraft each. Following instructions issued by control, they fly along the coast as far as Beachy Head and then turn south and head back. Shortly afterwards the controller orders them to 'pancake', i.e. return home and land.

During a patrol over Portland John Cock and 'B' Flight encounter a large group of escorted Messerschmitt Bf 110s and the Australian leads his section after three Bf 109s. He opens fire on one of the fighters and its engine suddenly belches out thick black smoke. Before Cock can observe any further results the 109 escapes into thick cloud.

At about 3.00 p.m. 249 Squadron scrambles and climbs to 24 000 feet (7 300 m) with 46 Squadron.

When 249 Squadron lands at North Weald one Hurricane is missing. It is learned afterwards that it has crashed, smashing into two cottages and killing three people. An investigation suggests that the pilot's oxygen supply had failed and that he had lost consciousness.

Spitfire Mk IIs were introduced towards the end of the battle of Britain. It was hoped that they would be effective against the high-flying Messerschmitt Bf 109Es (AWM SUK 15204).

FRIDAY, 11 OCTOBER

The overnight pattern of *Luftwaffe* attacks is the same as the previous night with a concentration of effort on London and on airfields in Kent.

In the early hours, mists blanket the Straits of Dover and Thames Estuary but these clear for a mainly fair day. Bob Bungey leads his section on 145 Squadron's first dawn patrol out over the Isle of Wight. They return to Tangmere for breakfast.

Throughout the day the Germans send out 4 waves of fighter sweeps over Kent and Sussex and two over Weymouth. Almost all of them come at heights over 30 000 feet (9 100 m).

Just before 9.00 a.m. all of 145 Squadron is scrambled. Following the controller's instructions the Hurricanes struggle up to reach 30 000 feet (9 100 m). Bungey and the others almost freeze because of the aircraft's lack of heating and the controls become difficult to use. Ice forms on their windscreens making it necessary for the squadron to lose some altitude.

During the rest of the day 145 Squadron is involved in 4 more scrambles, each of them without contacting the enemy. Likewise, at North Weald, 249 Squadron is scrambled for a similar number of patrols, all without result.

*

In the night the German raids are widespread with the main attacks centring on London, Liverpool, Manchester and as far north as Newcastle-on-Tyne.

SATURDAY, 12 OCTOBER

With daylight the weather over much of the British Isles consists of mist and fog which only clears gradually.

In spite of the fog the Germans carry on with their high level penetrations. The Hurricanes of 249 Squadron take off from Middle Wallop around 9.00 a.m. and patrol over Kent and south London. Their controller warns them of Messerschmitt Bf 109s in the area which are, for once, at a lower level than the British fighters. After an hour of searching over Kent and Dover without finding their quarry the pilots conclude that their controller is imagining things. Guarding 249 Squadron's tail are Hurricanes from 257 Squadron but in spite of their presence they do not see several Bf 109s which suddenly launch a swift hit-and-run attack on both units. It costs 257 Squadron two Hurricanes shot down and one pilot slightly wounded while 249 loses one Hurricane.

No. 145 Squadron suffers a similar fate. At about 10.30 a.m. its Hurricanes are on patrol over Cranbrook, well above the fog and mist, when the controller reports bandits 20 miles (32 km) from their position. The squadron banks eastward into the sun. Bob Bungey is heading 'B' Flight.

A number of Messerschmitts have crept up from behind and the Hurricanes scatter. There follows 10 minutes of twisting, turning, dodging and firing in utter confusion until at last the Germans are gone. The squadron leader calls for his aircraft to reform over Selsey Bill. In ones and twos they arrive at the rendezvous until all who can make it are there. Two Hurricanes are missing but one pilot is known to have bailed out.

The squadron is more fortunate during a second clash later in the day. They are bounced again by the Messerschmitts but this time the Germans are spotted. One Bf 109 is shot down and a second is damaged. Lower down, two other pilots surprize an unsuspecting Arado 196 and shoot it down into the sea.

*

[During the day, in Germany, General Wilhelm Keitel issues a circular to the German forces on behalf of Adolf Hitler:

The Führer has decided that from now until the spring, preparations for Seelöwe shall be continued solely for the purpose of maintaining political military pressure on England. Should the invasion be reconsidered in the spring or early summer of 1941, orders for a renewal of operational readiness will be issued later. In the meantime military conditions for a later invasion are to be improved.[5]

The notice, in effect, concedes that the British have won this round. There will be no invasion of England in 1940.]

*

At night the *Luftwaffe* again raids London but it is a fairly light attack.

SUNDAY, 13 OCTOBER

The perpetual fog which has covered most of southern England for the past two days now spreads across to France, Belgium and Holland, cutting back the number of sorties flown by the *Luftwaffe*. Nevertheless, there are several small-scale raids by bomb-carrying Messerschmitt Bf 109s beginning with a convoy attack off the east coast and continuing with three separate missions to London. The third formation of 25 Bf 109s reaches London around 4.00 p.m.

Earlier the Hurricanes of 17 Squadron on patrol over Chatham had been fired upon by defending anti-aircraft batteries. One had been shot down. The pilot had bailed out but was injured. Meanwhile 17 Squadron's Australian member, Desmond Fopp, is still in hospital recovering from burns.

[Fopp's stay in hospital lasted for three months, one month of which he was totally blind. When he was fully recovered he was posted back to 17 Squadron in 1941. On 3 November he was granted an emergency commission as a pilot officer and posted to 132 Squadron to fly Spitfires. Six months later, as a flight lieutenant, he was put in charge of 'A' Flight and stayed with this unit until the end of 1943. He was mentioned in dispatches on 1 January 1943. Other postings after 132 Squadron included flight tactics liaison officer to the USAF, an instructors' course on Oxfords and then instructor at an Advanced Flying Unit at Wrexham. During this time he was awarded an Air Force Cross for managing to bring an aircraft back safely after a mid-air collision.[6]

When the war ended he was posted to RAF College, Cranwell, as a flight commander of the first post-war Cranwell cadet entry and he remained there until 1949. He then went to an Elementary Flying School near High Wycombe for 9 months, prior to leaving the RAF and joining Airworks Ltd. For a year he trained naval pilots to fly Mosquito aircraft and then in March 1951 he rejoined the RAF.

On 12 March 1975 S/Ldr Desmond Fopp AFC retired from the RAF after 34 years of distinguished service. At the time of writing he was living in Salisbury, Wiltshire.]

At North Weald 249 Squadron's Hurricanes are scrambled on three occasions. The first is in the morning when a section is ordered up to intercept a bandit coming up the Thames Estuary. In spite of good visibility in the air they are unable to find it. The second and third scrambles are almost complete failures.

*

Desmond Sheen DFC, completely recovered from the injuries he received on 5 September, rejoins 72 Squadron at Biggin Hill. It is his third return since the beginning of the war and his second this year. The squadron's complement of experienced pilots has been reduced to 7 and Sheen's return is most welcome. This squadron has been in the forefront of the fighting for 6 weeks.

[On 30 October, 72 Squadron went to Mutlask in Norfolk and then Acklington. While at Acklington, Desmond Sheen was promoted to acting squadron leader and from April 1941 he took over command. Around this time he shot down a Ju 88 at night.

Early in July 1941, 72 Squadron returned to Biggin Hill and took part in offensive sweeps over the continent. Sheen led the squadron, and sometimes the wing, on fighter sweeps, bomber escort missions and anti-shipping sorties. On 17 August he damaged a Bf 109 and on the 29th, he damaged another. Sheen was leading the Biggin Hill wing near Abbeville on 2 October when he claimed a 'probable'. The Bar to his DFC was announced in the **London Gazette** on the 21st.

Desmond Sheen left 72 Squadron in November 1941, having flown 260 operational hours, officially destroyed 6 enemy aircraft, probably destroyed 2 and damaged at least 5. Between March 1944 and January 1945 he commanded 148 Wing of the British Liberation Army in France and Belgium. After this he held a staff appointment at Middle East Headquarters, Cairo, until demobilization in January 1947.

Sheen returned to Australia where he stayed for the next two-and-a-half years before returning to England and rejoining the RAF for a long and distinguished career. At the time of writing Gp/Capt. Desmond Sheen DFC and Bar, was retired and living in Surrey, England.]

*

The afternoon becomes cloudy and the cloud thickens as night falls. Shortly afterwards the sirens wail as London settles down for its usual night raids. The Germans send over about 100 bombers and, although the moon is bright, the 22 night fighters scrambled to intercept them are without success.

Bomber Command sends 125 aircraft to attack the Ruhr, Kiel, Wilhelmshaven and the Channel ports but because of deteriorating weather conditions only 41 of these are able to bomb their primary targets. One Wellington fails to return.

MONDAY, 14 OCTOBER

In the morning the cliffs on either side of the English Channel are shrouded by fog and drizzle. Rain spreads to the south-east and conditions are cloudy over the North Sea. The Germans only send out very small raids over the south-east of England and the Midlands.

Australian troops begin their move from Salisbury Plain to Colchester.

While they are on the move the *Luftwaffe* makes a series of heavy night attacks on London. During the early part of the evening the East

End is badly hit and as the night goes on damage spreads to the other side of the city.

[Many historians regard this night as marking the real beginning of the 'Blitz'.]

The accuracy of the bombing is aided by a full moon and 591 civilians are killed and 2 300 are injured. Coventry is also severely hit.

British night fighters — Blenheims, Defiants and 'cat's eyes' Hurricanes — fly over 50 sorties but they are ineffective as usual. Noel Constantine of 141 Squadron and his gunner, Sgt Coxon, are airborne in their Defiant between 7.40 p.m. and 8.05 p.m. without success.

TUESDAY, 15 OCTOBER

Barrage balloons over London (Imperial War Museum photograph HC 3725).

Taking advantage of brighter weather, beginning around 9.00 a.m., the Germans send several waves of Messerschmitt Bf 109 fighter-bombers towards London. Thirty of them reach the centre of the city and drop a number of 250 kg bombs, one of which hits Waterloo Station. The damage is such that all rail services are brought to a halt. There is also widespread damage among factories on the south bank. This is only

the beginning. Another 50 Messerschmitts, the first of many follow-up raids throughout the day, arrive an hour later. Other Bf 109s come in and spread out over Kent and southern England.

The Hurricanes of 145 Squadron fly in zig-zags over the sea south of the Isle of Wight for half an hour until Tangmere control notifies them that there are bandits approaching. Bob Bungey is leading 'B' Flight. Although they are on the alert, they are taken by surprize as the Messerschmitts dive on them from out of the sun before anyone can spot them. The Hurricanes scatter as tracer bullets whip through their formation. The 109s dive through like meteors with Hurricanes trying to follow in pursuit. The squadron commander manages to shoot one down at long range. It is all over in a matter of seconds.

No. 609 Squadron (John Curchin) is scrambled from Warmwell to intercept a raid of fighters and fighter-bombers near Southampton. The Spitfires arrive in the area at 10 000 feet (3 000 m) but discover that they are in a hopeless position well below the Messerschmitts. Not only that, they are plainly visible to the enemy because they are out-lined against a layer of white cloud. They are trapped and can only wait for the Germans to come down as they continue to climb. With their attention on the German planes above, the Spitfire pilots fail to notice more 109s coming down from behind until it is almost too late.

The Spitfires break away in all directions, turning sharply away and diving hard for cloud cover. In ones and twos they return to Warmwell.

No. 249 Squadron flies as a pair with 257 Squadron over Folkestone where they too run foul of the Bf 109s. Again the Hurricanes are ambushed and most dive away to escape. One 257 Squadron Hurri-cane is shot up and lands at Hawkinge.

At North Weald in the evening the pilots of 249, 257 and 46 Squadrons hold a meeting and decide on a change of tactics. The German method of flying in fours is to be tried and, if the wing is attacked, these sections will break further into pairs for fighting.

*[From Berlin Reichsmarschall Hermann Goering issues a directive to the **Luftwaffe** specifying the principal objectives of the **Blitzkrieg** against England.[7] In essence, they are:*

1. *London*
2. *Factories*
3. *Industrial zones such as Birmingham and Coventry*
4. *Airfields of English fighter squadrons.]*

Goering's bombers use the full moon to launch heavy attacks on London and these again cause widespread damage to the city. In the Greater London area 512 people are killed, around 1 000 seriously injured and between 10 000 and 11 000 lose their homes and lodgings.

RAF Bomber Command sends out 134 aircraft to attack the Chan-nel ports, oil storage depots and several other targets in Germany.

John Pain of 32 Squadron (photograph courtesy of Doug Peterkin).

WEDNESDAY, 16 OCTOBER

To Bill Millington and the airmen at North Weald German planes seem to be overhead all night. The bright moonlight apparently shows up the aerodrome, making it a good landmark and target. Bombs drop all around the area.

Birmingham is bombed but, with daylight, fog inhibits further *Luftwaffe* operations.

*

John Pain, who is recovering from the injuries he received on 18 August, is promoted to pilot officer.

[John Pain's injuries were serious enough to keep him in hospital for two months and he did not rejoin his squadron until 31 October. On 26 November 1940 he transferred to 249 Squadron at North Weald but was only with this unit for a few weeks and left for No. 70 OTU on 18 December. After this he was posted to 261 Squadron in Malta where he scored numerous successes. In May 1941 261 Squadron was disbanded and Pain was posted to Takoradi Headquarters Air Defence Unit. By March 1942 he was flying on operations with 73 Squadron at Gambut. With this squadron, on 3 July, near El Alamein, Pain had his most successful day of combat when he destroyed a Bf 109, probably destroyed a Ju 87 Stuka and damaged a second.

Pain was posted to 123 Squadron early in 1943. Then, after various administrative appointments, he returned to England and at the end of March 1944 resigned his commission. Back in Australia after the war, he lived in Brisbane and afterwards in Sydney. He died in September 1980.]

*

The weather deteriorates to mist and rain in the evening so that even London is exposed to only light overnight attacks.

Bomber Command's effort is widespread but on a much-reduced scale. Returning British bombers have difficulty finding their own bases and, besides three aircraft which fail to return, 10 Hampdens and 4 Wellingtons crash because of fog.

THURSDAY, 17 OCTOBER

Some German bombers operate in the darkness, mist and drizzle and, so too, must the British night fighters. Visibility is poor so take-off and landing conditions are extremely hazardous. Flying from Gatwick Noel Constantine patrols in his Defiant with his chances of meeting a German plane far more remote than usual.

*

Flying conditions are better out over the Atlantic and Sunderland P9600 of 10 Squadron, RAAF, is returning to Oban from an all-night patrol. The sea is still dark but one of the gunners spots a red light on the water several miles away. Ivan Podger, who is the flying boat's captain, circles the area waiting for daylight and, as visibility improves, the Australians can see a lifeboat. They are about 150 miles (140 m) from the nearest land. The lifeboat contains 21 survivors from the S.S. *Stangrant* which had been sunk 4 days earlier. Podger decides to land on the sea and after half an hour, despite a heavy swell, the transfer of survivors to the Sunderland is completed.

The Sunderland crews of 10 Squadron, RAAF, operating from Mount Batten, have been ordered since the 10th to co-operate with Royal Navy submarines in blockading U-boat bases which are being prepared by the Germans in the Bay of Biscay ports. The east-bound U-boats spotted by the aircraft are not to be attacked but their position, speed and course are to be reported so that the RN submarines can intercept. Permission has been given, however, to attack west-bound U-boats because they would have already passed through the screen.

Charles Pearce DFC and S/Ldr Owen Dibbs in Sunderland N9050 are presented with identification problems later in the day when, just to the west of the restricted area, they sight a submarine. To prevent the possibility of a mistake, Pearce flies low and challenges using the Aldis lamp. The submarine replies by firing a rocket which emits blue stars.

Suddenly a machine-gun opens fire from the conning tower. It is a U-boat. As Pearce manoeuvres the Sunderland around for an attack the submarine crash-dives and disappears. The Australians drop 4 anti-submarine bombs and, after the explosions, Pearce circles to observe results. A moment later a green patch bubbles to the surface but there is nothing else.

*

For the pilots of Fighter Command Messerschmitt Month continues and at 11 Group Park issues more instructions to his controllers on tactics to combat the menace. In general his plan is to have one or two Spitfire squadrons to engage enemy fighters from above, around the middle of Kent, in order to cover other Spitfire and Hurricane squadrons which are climbing to operational height on patrol lines south and east of London. He details the tactics to be adopted by each unit with special mention of the use of one or two reconnaissance aircraft to be kept on patrol near the coast of Kent. Once enemy formations are plotted over the French coast or the Straits of Dover these 'spotter' planes are to be despatched to the area to locate the enemy raids and then report their strength, height and direction.

In the morning at Margate, Stanmore and Broadstairs, almost 100 German fighter-bombers carry out heavy attacks. They return and maintain continuous raids with small and medium size formations which use cloud cover to evade British interceptions.

In accordance with Park's instructions Hurricane squadrons from Debden are ordered to patrol in pairs over mid-Kent to form a screen of fighters east and south-east of London. Charles McGaw in Hurricane P3207 is airborne at 1.20 p.m. with the rest of 73 Squadron to rendezvous with 17 Squadron and patrol over Hornchurch. He is up again at 3.25 p.m. but the patrol over Debden is uneventful.

Boulton Paul Defiant Mk I, N1795, TW-W of 141 Squadron RAF. Powered by the same engine as a Hurricane and Spitfire, the two-seat Defiant was heavier, slower and less manoeuvrable than its single seat contemporaries and at a serious disadvantage in fighter vs fighter combat. N1795 was delivered to 141 Squadron after the disastrous 'Slaughter of the Innocents' on 19 July 1940, after which the squadron was rebuilt and switched to night fighting. It was one of the machines flown by Noel Constantine. The aircraft was later wrecked when its pilot misjudged his take off and struck the road embankment at Gravesend.

Meanwhile Bill Millington and 249 Squadron have also been scrambled. As soon as they are in the air they hear their controller ordering 46 Squadron, with which they are supposed to rendezvous, to chase a plot of 17 enemy bombers. Both squadrons respond but there is no sign of the enemy planes.

*

The *Luftwaffe* begins the evening with several raids over Kent and Kenley airfield is hit, damaging 4 Hurricanes of 501 Squadron. Later Liverpool and Birmingham, as well as London, share in the bombing.

FRIDAY, 18 OCTOBER

Fog covering the Straits of Dover and the Thames Estuary reduces visibility so badly that air operations over England are very few during the morning. After lunch the Germans carry out a number of high-flying fighter-bomber sorties.

At Warmwell only Ian Bayles and Sgt Edmund Eric Sheppherd are kept at 'Readiness'. In spite of the miserable weather they are scrambled to intercept an intruder but there is no sign of an enemy aircraft.

Messages from control inform them that the weather is deteriorating and an order is received recalling Sgt Sheppherd. Bayles continues with the patrol as the other Spitfire breaks away and disappears. Shortly afterwards Bayles, too, is ordered to return but it is with some trepidation that he begins to lose height. As he descends the cloud becomes progressively thicker and he has no idea where he is. Then the greyness at last brightens below and he is through . . . the cloud base is now as low as 150 feet (45 m).

Bayles searches for a landmark and at last he finds a railway line and follows it until he recognizes his surroundings. Shortly afterwards he lands back at Warmwell only to discover that Sheppherd has not returned. News is received later that the sergeant's Spitfire has crashed near Dorchester and that this cheerful young man from the Isle of Wight has been killed.

[Ian Bayles remained in 152 Squadron until 18 August 1941 when he was posted to Training Command. In August 1942, after a short gunnery course, he received an urgent posting to 224 Group in India. On 5

Ian Bayles of 152 Squadron (photograph courtesy of Ian Bayles).

February 1943 S/Ldr Ian Bayles took command of 135 Squadron which operated along the Arakan coast and flew Hurricane Mk IIs. He was given command of 273 Squadron stationed at Cox's Bazaar on 16 December 1944. The unit flew Spitfire VIIIs.

On 14 April 1945 Bayles left the squadron to become W/Cdr Flying, 902 Wing. He continued on operations, flying P-47 Thunderbolts, until leaving India early in July. The **London Gazette** *of 2 October 1945 announced the award of his DFC.*

Back in England, after the war, reunited with Rowena, Ian left the RAF in July 1946 and they came to Australia. He invested in a property at Tabilk in northern Victoria.]

In the far north, at 1.13 p.m., Lewis Hamilton of 248 Squadron takes off from Sumburgh in Blenheim WR-V. His mission is to carry out a reconnaissance of the Norwegian coast. At Sando Island Hamilton bombs a lookout, scoring several hits and causing dense smoke to pour from a shattered building. Continuing along the coast he finds and records two merchant vessels in the fjords.

*

London is again the *Luftwaffe's* overnight target but, because the weather does not improve, only a limited number of aircraft venture out.

SATURDAY, 19 OCTOBER

Again fog throughout the morning brings operations to a standstill. In mid-afternoon the weather clears. At 3.00 p.m. 'B' Flight of 73 Squadron from Castle Camps has a convoy patrol. As they gain height over Cambridge and prepare to fly out over the Thames Estuary Charles McGaw's aircraft, Hurricane V7501, gives trouble and he returns to base. Meanwhile 249 Squadron's 'B' Flight (Bill Millington) patrols over the convoy off Harwich.

Fully recovered from the previous day's nightmarish experience, Ian Bayles of 152 Squadron is up again to intercept another lone bandit plotted on radar. The weather is much better but there is still plenty of cloud. This time the Spitfires manage to find their quarry and identify it as a Heinkel He 111. They even manage to close in but that is all because the German has spotted them and evades them completely.

*

[Sidney Cotton has been working with W/Cdr William Helmore concerning his idea of airborne night interception using a radar and searchlight-carrying aircraft to illuminate the enemy bomber while an accompanying fighter shoots it down. Helmore and Cotton have named their project 'Aerial Target Illumination' and the former has discussed it with Sir John Salmond, a retired Marshal of the RAF who is working under Lord Beaverbrook at the Ministry of Aircraft Production and the Chairman of the Night Defence Committee. On the previous day Helmore and Salmond had broached the subject with Beaverbrook who had

promised that, provided that Dowding was in favour, he would provide facilities for trials.

Dowding himself has been giving the problems faced by the British night defences serious consideration. Among other measures he has pressed for the urgent introduction of the new Beaufighter but so far only 30 have reached the squadrons and although they, unlike the poor lumbering Blenheims, are fast enough to catch the German bombers, the airborne radar installations are still suffering from teething problems.

Another aircraft undergoing trials with 600 Squadron is a Douglas DB-7 Boston and it is this type of plane that Sidney Cotton has requested to be fully equipped with the latest airborne radar and a searchlight for his scheme to combat the German bombers.]

On this day Dowding writes a letter to Lord Beaverbrook about the idea.

[To put the idea into effect No. 1422 Flight (Air Target Illumination Unit) was formed at Heston. This was expanded into 10 flights between May and December 1941 and each was attached to a fighter squadron. Eventually, in September 1942 these became 10 separate 'Turbinlite' squadrons, Nos 530–539, each equipped with a flight of Turbinlite aircraft and a flight of Hurricanes. Although numerous contacts were made, by January 1943 only one German plane could be claimed destroyed plus one probably destroyed and two damaged. The idea had not lived up to its promise and by now the advances in Aircraft Interception (AI) had rendered this cumbersome technique outmoded. All 10 squadrons were disbanded.

*Sidney Cotton was awarded the OBE. He died in England in 1969. His biography is recorded in **Aviator Extraordinary** by Ralph Barker.]*

*

At Tangmere Bob Bungey is due for 48 hours leave and together with one of his Belgian pilots, Jean Offenberg, he sets out for the Olde Ship Inn at Boshham, a popular haunt of the pilots from Tangmere.

[For 145 Squadron October continued to be a month of numerous patrols and brief skirmishes with its Hurricanes ill-matched against Bf 109s at high altitude where most encounters took place. On 7 November the squadron was bounced by a large number of Bf 109s west of Plymouth and 5 Hurricanes were shot down. Bob Bungey managed to bail out into the sea off the Isle of Wight. His knee was injured but this did not prevent him from flying again on the 9th when he and Jean Offenberg surprised a Ju 88 and damaged it. Bungey and Offenberg were paired again on 11 December when they met a He 111. They shot it up until their ammunition ran out. It was later confirmed destroyed. February 1941 saw the squadron re-equipped with Spitfire Mk IIs and the following month cross-Channel sweeps began. Bungey and his section destroyed a Ju 88 over the Channel on 10 March. The Australian's knee injury continued to plague him and on 30 March he went into hospital for an operation.

On 10 June 1941 Bungey was appointed commanding officer of 452 Squadron, RAAF, the first Australian unit to be formed under the Empire Training Scheme. By early July it was judged ready for offensive operations.

It transferred south to Kenley in 11 Group on the 21st and became continually involved in 'Circus' and 'Ramrod' operations. During this period it became one of Fighter Command's most successful units. Bungey had a team of excellent men under his command, including the Irish flight commander, 'Paddy' Finucane, who was well on his way to becoming one of the RAF's leading fighter aces, Keith 'Bluey' Truscott, who became a leading RAAF ace, and Ray 'Throttle' Thorold-Smith, another ace in the making. Then there was Keith Chisholm who shot down 5 planes before being shot down himself and captured . . . to name but a few. In these large 'Circus' operations 452 Squadron, headed by Bungey and his team, frequently led the Kenley wing until October when weather conditions curtailed activities. The **London Gazette** *announced the award of Bungey's DFC on 7 October.*

At the end of January 1942 Bob Bungey handed over leadership of 452 Squadron to 'Bluey' Truscott and, with promotion to acting wing commander, took up a posting to RAF Station, Shorham. Just prior to this he married Sibyl Ellen Johnson of Berkshire. Later he was posted to RAF, Hawkinge. W/Cdr Bungey relinquished his commission in the RAF upon receiving an appointment to the RAAF Reserve on 25 January 1943. He and his wife returned to Australia. He was on leave in Adelaide, pending an appointment to take command of a wing in the north, when they both died in tragic circumstances.]

*

The Germans carry out scattered attacks at night with London, the Midlands, Liverpool and Bristol receiving most attention.

SUNDAY, 20 OCTOBER

There is fog again over the south in the morning which thins out as the day goes on. At various times the Germans send out 5 waves of high-flying Messerschmitt Bf 109 fighters and fighter-bombers. Fighter Command flies 475 sorties and there are several sharp clashes but for the most part the RAF fighter pilots are involved in long patrols and fruitless flights. Charles McGaw and 73 Squadron are scrambled at 12.50 p.m. to patrol over their base but soon they land again after a flight without incident. Later in the afternoon, with the weather clearing, McGaw and the others are up again for a patrol with 17 Squadron over Hornchurch. Likewise, 249 Squadron patrols south of Maidstone without meeting the enemy.

In the north at Sumburgh 248 Squadron has a disastrous day. One Blenheim on patrol over the Norwegian coast in the morning is shot down by Messerschmitt Bf 109s. Because of the chance that the crew may have succeeded in ditching, other Blenheims are sent out to conduct a search but one of these fails to return.

Two new Australian pilots report for duty to 50 Squadron at Lindholme. They are P/Os Philip Moore and Hugh Macrossan, both of whom were members of the last contingent of Australian airmen to join the RAF under the short-service commission scheme.

*

Overnight the Germans send 300 bombers to London and they inflict serious damage on the city's railway system. Other German bombers raid industrial centres in the Midlands and at Coventry the Armstrong-Siddeley and Singer Motor factories are hit.

The RAF force directed against Berlin is one-tenth the size and consists of 30 Hampdens but altogether 140 British bombers are active over the continent. Two targets are given to 40 Squadron at Wyton. Six Blenheims are to bomb Rotterdam while the remainder are ordered to attack Forest de Guines. Brian Best in Blenheim N3592 (BL-C) takes off at 6.05 p.m. Over the target he makes a high level-run, drops his stick of bombs in the forest area and watches them burst. He is back home by 9.25 p.m.

*[Brian Best was awarded a DFC recorded in the **London Gazette** of 12 November 1940. He attained the rank of temporary squadron leader late in June 1944, but is listed as 'Missing (flying battle), presumed dead,' later that year.]*

MONDAY, 21 OCTOBER

Poor weather spreads over the British Isles and conditions over the continent are only marginally better. However the *Luftwaffe* despatches single raiders and small formations of fighter-bombers and bombers whenever possible. The number of sorties flown by Fighter Command is only half of those flown the previous day but they still represent hours of fruitless, tiring effort for the pilots. Nevertheless a memorable success is scored by two Spitfires of 609 Squadron flown by F/Lt Frank Howell DFC and P/O Sidney Hill when they intercept a stray Junkers Ju 88 strafing Old Sarum airfield. They shoot it down at 1.47 p.m. to score the unit's 100th victory, making it the first Spitfire squadron to achieve this figure. At Middle Wallop in the evening there is a huge celebration party.

Clive Mayers DFC, fully recovered from the injuries he received while crash-landing his Hurricane on 7 October, is back with 601 Squadron at Exeter. He takes part in a patrol at 12.30 p.m. and three hours later test-flies a new aircraft, Hurricane V7539.

*

In the morning at Colchester, winter quarters for the Australian troops, Kenneth Slessor visits the new headquarters. He is seeking General Wynter's approval for release of his story of the troop movement from Salisbury but he finds that the general has just left on leave. He is referred instead to Brigadier L.J. Morshead.

[Born in Ballarat, Victoria, on 18 September 1889, Leslie James Morshead was educated at Mount Pleasant and the Victorian Teachers' College and enlisted in 1914. He commanded a company on Gallipoli. After being invalided back to Australia, he became commanding officer of the 33rd Battalion which served in France in 1917–18, and during demobilization he acted as assistant adjutant-general, AIF. During the

second world war he commanded the 18th Brigade in England and the middle east and, with promotion to major-general commanded the 9th Australian Division at Tobruk and El Alamein. He became general officer commanding, AIF, Middle East, before returning to Australia to command the New Guinea Force. His appointment to GOC, I Australia Corps, in 1944 led to his commanding the Allied forces which captured Tarakan and Balipapan the following year. After the war he returned to civilian life and became general manager of the Orient Line and held the chairmanship of the NSW Savings Bank. Sir Leslie James Morshead died in September 1959.

Henry Wynter was born at Burnett River, Queensland, on 5 June 1886, and was regarded as one of the clearest thinkers in the Australian army of his time. He served in the 1st AIF and was assistant adjutant-general in 1917-18. In the mid-1920s he analysed the deficiencies of the Singapore base theory and warned that the fortress was vulnerable from the landward side. He further warned that if war occurred in the Pacific area it would happen at a time when Britain would be unable to send a force sufficient to defeat a first-class power because of commitments in Europe. His appointment to command the Australian Force in the UK came on 18 June 1940, the day after the troops began to disembark. On 29 September he was appointed GOC of the 9th Division and in mid-November movement of the Australians to the middle east began. Lieut-Gen. Henry Douglas Wynter CB, CMG, DSO died on 7 February 1945, while in charge of Land Headquarters, Australia, a position he had held since 1942.]

*

In spite of continuing rain and fog the Germans hammer the British capital again overnight. Other targets are Coventry, Birmingham, Liverpool and Wolverhampton.

TUESDAY, 22 OCTOBER

It is another poor day for flying with widespread fog over southern England which disperses gradually into scattered rain. The *Luftwaffe* sends over a few small fighter-bomber attacks but otherwise the morning is very quiet.

*

The *London Gazette* announces a number of awards to RAF pilots and among these the DFC is awarded posthumously to Pat Hughes. Another DFC goes to Ron Lees.

[On 9 January 1941 Lees was posted to command RAF Station, Coltishall, Norfolk, a position he retained until September 1942. During this time he remained active with regard to flying and took part in numerous operations. He was mentioned in dispatches on 24 September 1941 and on 26 December received a Bar to his DFC.

Lees was posted to the middle east and command of No. 234 Wing, one of the three major RAF wings to provide cover for **Operation Torch**, the invasion of Tunisia. In March 1943 he was appointed senior air staff officer (SASO) at Headquarters 242 Group, North-West African Air Force. Two months later, on 26 May, he was appointed to the head-quarters of the Tactical Air Force. The **London Gazette** of 2 June 1943 announced that he had been made a CBE and a month later he was promoted temporary group captain.

On 26 August he was appointed aide-de-camp (ADC) to H.M. King George VI and in October 1944 was attached to the staff of the Mediterranean Allied Tactical Air Force with the new rank of acting air commodore. He was awarded a mention in dispatches three times in 1945.

With the war over servicemen wishing to stay in the RAF and the other armed forces had to be prepared to lose some seniority and in December 1945 Ron Lees relinquished his rank of acting air commodore. In October 1946 he was re-appointed wing commander.

In 1946 he was appointed CB and he received a Legion of Merit, Degree of Commander, conferred by the president of the USA.

In 1947–50 Lees was stationed at the Staff Central Fighter Establishment and Headquarters Fighter Command. In 1951 he became commanding officer, Metropolitan Sector, Headquarters, RAF, and by then he had risen once more to the rank of acting air commodore.

He remained ADC to the king and when George VI died he was ADC to H.M. Queen Elizabeth II in 1952–53. There followed numerous high ranking appointments.

On 3 February 1966, with 35 years of distinguished service, Air Marshal Sir Ronald Beresford Lees KCB, CBE, DFC & Bar retired from the RAF and returned to Australia to become a grazier near Albury, NSW. Afterwards he moved to Adelaide, South Australia.]

Among all these awards to RAF officers there is one for a member of the RAAF. Bill Garing picks up 10 Squadron's fourth DFC.

*

With the arrival of darkness, the poor weather continues, curtailing operations by RAF Bomber Command.

WEDNESDAY, 23 OCTOBER

The weather on this day is described as 'foul' with fog, low cloud and drizzle all over southern England making it one of the quietest days of the battle of Britain.

From St Eval Dick Power and his wingman escort a Douglas DC-2 out into the Atlantic.

At Castle Camps 73 Squadron does not go up at all especially after new orders are received for it to change over to night fighter duties as soon as possible. The order is not popular but it shows how frustrated Fighter Command has become with the nocturnal German raids. The commanding officer gives each pilot the opportunity of applying for a posting to another unit if they want to stay on day fighters. Six pilots do so and among these Charles McGaw is posted to 66 Squadron at Biggin Hill. Meanwhile the CO also requests that 73 Squadron be taken off operations for 10 days, so that a training programme can be instituted for each remaining pilot to build up 25 hours of night flying experience before being called for 'cat's eyes' patrols.

Across at North Weald where, likewise, there are no operations, Bill Millington introduces a new pet to 249 Squadron. It is a white duck he calls 'Wilfred'.

At night, with fog and low cloud keeping most British night fighters on the ground, the Germans come over in force to attack London. Victoria Docks, London Bridge and St Pancras Station are all hit by bombs. In the north an aircraft from Stavanger in Norway, flies across the North Sea and attacks Glasgow.

A report comes in to Sumburgh in the Shetland Islands that an enemy aircraft is shadowing Royal Navy destroyers operating in the North Sea. Lewis Hamilton takes off in Blenheim P4825 to try and shoot it down or drive it off but in the darkness, with no radar, it is a hopeless task.

THURSDAY, 24 OCTOBER

Overnight RAF Bomber Command sends 79 aircraft to attack several targets. Brian Best of 40 Squadron takes off into low cloud and drizzle at 2.35 a.m. His is one of two Blenheims which have been ordered to bomb Krefeldt but neither is able to find the target.

*

Daylight brings an overcast sky with haze hanging over the English Channel. This clears gradually and besides a few reconnaissance flights the *Luftwaffe* is quiet in the morning. Things liven up in the afternoon when the Germans launch a few fighter sweeps over the south-east and East Anglia.

From Leuchars in Scotland Bill Weaber takes off at 1.32 p.m. in Hudson N7257 (QX-H) on a patrol over the North Sea. He and his crew spot a Heinkel He 115 floatplane, a type used by the Germans for torpedo bombing, minelaying and reconnaissance. Weaber positions his Hudson with the sun at its back and attacks using his front guns. His firing seems to have little effect on the German plane.

At 3.30 p.m. another He 115 is found. Weaber readies for a similar attack but this time the German spots him and meets him head-on. Both aircraft blaze away, Weaber using his two forward-firing 0.30 inch (7.62 mm) machine-guns in the nose while the Heinkel uses its single, flexible, forward-firing 7.9 mm MG 15 machine-gun. Weaber then dives to allow his rear gunner, Sgt Knowles, to open fire but as he does so he hears the rattle of bullets striking the Hudson's fuselage. Knowles is killed instantly. Weaber turns homeward.

Apart from the occasional German reconnaissance plane the sky over south-west England has become almost peaceful. RAF fighter squadrons are kept busy with routine patrols and training new pilots.

Winston Churchill, the British prime minister, talking to Australian airmen later in the war (AWM 2815).

Sharing Exeter with 601 is 87 Squadron and one of its formation practices ends with tragedy. John Cock is leading a formation of 4 Hurricanes on patrol at 3 000 feet (900 m) when the engine of his aircraft suddenly cuts out. He quickly pushes the nose down to avoid striking his wingmen and these, reacting swiftly, swing away but the fourth Hurricane in the box of the formation has no chance to evade. Its propeller smashes into Cock's tail tearing it to shreds. The Australian's plane drops like a stone. After plummetting almost to the ground it suddenly pulls up and climbs steeply. Cock is barely able to retain control. For him now there is a nightmarish trip back to base during which he wrestles with the controls to keep the limping plane in the air. Exeter finally looms into view but Cock finds it impossible to use either his flaps or his wheels. Fortunately he manages a smooth belly-landing just off the runway. He scrambles out quickly in case of fire. When the others return he learns that his No. 4 pilot has been killed while trying to bail out.

*

The cloudy day gives way to a clear night. RAF Bomber Command sends over 100 aircraft to numerous targets in Germany and France. There is a particularly successful raid on Hamburg. At the same time about 50 German bombers are active over London while 70 others attack widespread targets in England with a concentrated effort on Birmingham.

FRIDAY, 25 OCTOBER

The skies are grey and overcast all day but visibility stays reasonably good and the *Luftwaffe* carries out fighter and fighter-bomber raids over Kent and south London.

Just after noon Bill Millington and 249 Squadron are caught up in a fierce dogfight with Bf 109s north of Hastings. The Australian is flying as the rearguard and amid the confusion he discovers that he is ideally placed up-sun of an unsuspecting Messerschmitt. He approaches from behind, closing in to a range of about 50 yards (45 m) before opening fire. His bullets tear large pieces off the German fighter which reacts quickly and dives down through the clouds leaving a column of black smoke in its wake. During the battle 249 Squadron loses two Hurricanes.

At Exeter 601 Squadron has 4 operational take-offs but the day's flying mostly consists of formation practice. Although many RAF squadrons have come to realize the flexibility and superiority of the *Luftwaffe's* method of flying in fours and in pairs and have adopted similar formations themselves, as a whole the RAF is slow to change and the majority continue to fly in the old style.

*

Pending the result of the inquiry into the previous day's mid-air collision John Cock is grounded. The investigation will reveal that the abrupt loss of power was caused by the Hurricane's gravity fuel tank suddenly running dry. A representative from Hawker Aircraft Ltd remarks that, considering the damage to the tail, it is a miracle that Cock was able to bring the plane back at all.

Cock's DFC is announced in the *London Gazette*.

John Cock of 87 Squadron; in 1983 he watched as his Hurricane V2233 was recovered from Portland Harbour (photographs courtesy of Simon Parry).

[Towards the end of the year John Cock attended an instructors' course and from February 1941, carried out the duties of instructor at various Flying Training Schools until 15 July 1942 when he was posted as a flight commander to 453 Squadron, RAAF, at Drem (although he remained a member of the RAF). On 30 August he left to train as a pilot gunnery instructor and for a short period, late in October, he was with the 93rd Fighter Squadron USAF, instructing on gunnery and tactics. At the end of November he left England to come to Australia via the USA, where he lectured for a short time.

He was attached to the Spitfire Wing in Darwin as a supernumerary. Then, after a short spell at Mildura Gunnery School, he transferred, lecturing again to Australian airmen at Kiriwina, Merauke and Horn Islands.

Cock's promotion to temporary squadron leader was announced on 1 January 1944 and in April he returned to England. In September 1944 he was flying Hawker Tempest Vs in France with 3 Squadron, specializing in train busting and armed reconnaissance. After completing his final tour he returned to England on 31 December.

John Cock had flown a total of 510 hours 5 minutes on operations against the enemy and by his own reckoning destroyed 10¼ aircraft and probably destroyed 5. After the war he remained in the RAF until February 1948. He moved to Queensland in the early 1970s where he built a supermarket in Tewantin. He retired in 1983.

He died on 29 August 1988.]

*

During the night a new element is added to the bomber force raiding England in the form of 20 Breda BR.20 bombers of the Italian *Reggia Aeronautica*. They are there both as a gesture of support for the Germans and in retaliation for RAF bombing attacks on targets in northern Italy.

[Across the Atlantic the second draft of 40 Australian pilot trainees arrives in Canada under the Empire Training Scheme.]

Richard Power of 236 Squadron (Imperial War Museum photograph CH 5964).

SATURDAY, 26 OCTOBER

In spite of the large number of German bombers over southern and eastern England the British night fighters again fail to achieve any success.

Dick Power in Blenheim ND-O leaves St Eval at 6.15 a.m. for a night/morning patrol between Trevose Head and Newquay. The sky gradually lightens to reveal a cloudy grey day.

In the north the weather is far worse with heavy clouds and local showers. Lewis Hamilton of 248 Squadron takes off from Sumburgh in Blenheim P4825 (WR-D) for another anti-invasion patrol. These long flights out over the North Sea and around the eastern and southern coasts of the British Isles, although essential, are routine and monotonous.

The *Luftwaffe* engages in a series of high-altitude fighter sweeps which keep the southern groups of Fighter Command on alert for most of the day. Several raiders penetrate to London and convoys in the Thames Estuary are bombed.

As Hamilton is landing, at the other end of England, Dick Power is taking off again from St Eval for his second sortie of the day. He is leading an escort of three Blenheims over a packet steamer as it makes its way to Penzance. After the vessel has reached safety Power and the others stay on to escort an accompanying destroyer to Lizard.

[Power remained with 236 Squadron until July 1941 when he was posted to No. 3 OTU at Chivenor with a promotion to squadron leader. On 22 August 1943, after a period of instructing, he was posted to 248 Squadron which was involved in anti-shipping sorties, flying Beaufighters and later Mosquito Mk VIs. Then with his third operational tour complete, Dick Power left 248 Squadron on 12 March 1944.

He reported to the Air Ministry and was appointed to the Directorate of Accident Prevention as air accidents officer. He was later given a new position in the Directorate General of Organization in 1945–46. His promotion to acting wing commander was noted in the **London Gazette** of 18 June 1945.

Alan (W.A.S.) Butement, the man responsible for Britain's Chain Home Low radar chain (photograph courtesy of Alan Butement).

In August 1946 he was released from the RAF and returned home to Australia. His last day of service is recorded as 7 February 1947. He and his family lived in Melbourne until 1960 when they moved to Adelaide.]

*

Alan Butement is no longer involved in the development of his radio proximity fuse for anti-aircraft shells because the results of his research have been handed over to the Americans. However he continues to be involved in many research projects as the war progresses.

[The fuse evolved by the Americans proved highly successful and, because of their massive production facilities, all of those used during the war were manufactured in the USA. Used in conjunction with highly developed centrimetric radar, the fuse gave to the anti-aircraft guns of both the British and Americans a deadly precision not imagined at the beginning of the war.

Butement's next most successful project was his Wireless Set No. 10, the first narrow beam speech radio communication system using multi-channel interlaced pulse modulation. It was first used operationally in June 1944.

During the war Butement received promotion to principal scientific officer of the Ministry of Supply at its Headquarters in London and when it ended he was promoted further to senior principal scientific officer. He was also awarded the OBE.

Late in 1946, he was appointed to a special unit under Lieut-General John Evetts for the planning of a rocket range in Australia. He came into the team as deputy chief scientific adviser and returned to Australia early in 1947. Shortly afterwards the chief scientific adviser left and Butement took over. A few months later he became chief superintendent of the organization which became known as the Long Range Weapons Establishment comprised of the rocket range at Woomera, South Australia, and the base establishment at Salisbury, England, together with air support. In 1949 he was appointed chief scientist of the Department of Supply in Australia and given executive charge of Australian Defence Scientific Research and Development. In this role he had to merge the functions of Woomera and Salisbury with the Munitions Supply Laboratory and the Aeronautical Division of the CSIRO to weld them into an integrated Defence Science Service for Australia. He was now responsible for the general oversight of the whole scientific programme for the Service and in charge of some 650 scientists with all supporting staff.

Work developed under his auspices during this time included the 'Wombat' radar system which would allow an aircraft primarily on coastal defence duties to determine its position at any time in any conditions of visibility and the Infra Red Image Converter to give a picture on a screen of an area of terrain below.

A number of other works were initiated by Butement himself. Among these were a semi-solid mono-propellant rocket motor using a new system of propulsion, the **'Malkarra'** short-range command control guided anti-tank missile, and the deadly anti-submarine missile **'Ikara'** which was accepted by the Royal Navy and went into service in 1967.

Butement was appointed CBE in 1959 and next year he submitted a record of his scientific work (subject to security restrictions of the time) to Adelaide University for the degree of Doctor of Science which was duly *granted.[8] He continued as chief scientist for the Department of Supply in executive charge of Australian Defence Scientific Research and Development until 1967 when he left to become research director of Plessey Pacific Pty Ltd, a position he retained until 1981.*

After a career of remarkable achievement Alan Butement retired to Melbourne where he died on 25 January 1990.]

*

At night the *Luftwaffe* raids London, the Midlands, Liverpool and Manchester. British night fighters are up in strength only to fly back and forth in frustration after the invisible enemy.

Meanwhile, over Germany and France, it is the RAF bombers which fly in the safety of darkness. Eighty-four are despatched after various targets, the largest raid being by 17 Hampdens on a power station in Berlin.

SUNDAY, 27 OCTOBER

The *Luftwaffe* begins its work early although the weather is cloudy. Some formations of fighter-bombers are large, consisting of up to 50 aircraft, and these begin attacking convoys in the Estuary and penetrating to London as early as 7.45 a.m. By 9.00 a.m. several London suburbs have been bombed and damage has been inflicted on the dock area.

Along with many other units in the south and east of England, 145 Squadron is scrambled early from Tangmere so many of its pilots miss their usual religious services. Bob Bungey leads Blue Section. The Hurricanes climb, straining their way up to 32 000 feet (9 800 m) where the air is so cold that the pilots are almost frozen in their cockpits. They find a dozen Bf 109s below. It is a pleasure to be above the Messerschmitts for once and they dive onto the German planes. Seconds later Bungey sees the 109s scattering in all directions and one of them spins down. Most of the German planes seem to zoom upwards, climbing at full throttle. Bungey and the other pilots find that they are losing ground. Their Hurricanes have no hope of keeping up with the Messerschmitts at such a high level.

Reforming, 145 Squadron climbs back to 30 000 feet (9 100 m) and continues its patrol until fuel runs low. In the distance a dogfight is in progress where the Bf 109s have run into patrolling Spitfires. On the flight back to Tangmere two Hurricanes have to force-land because of lack of fuel.

Over Yarmouth a section of Spitfires from 72 Squadron intercepts and chases off a stray Messerschmitt Bf 110 around 2.30 p.m. Many patrols are sent up through the afternoon in the hope of catching others. Desmond Sheen leads a section up twice but has no luck.

*

Dull, cloudy conditions persist, making interception difficult for the defending RAF. At 4.30 p.m. the *Luftwaffe* launches simultaneous raids on Southampton, London and Martlesham Heath.

John Curchin of 609 Squadron. He did not return from a mission on 4 June 1941 and is presumed to have died on that date (Public Records Office, London, photograph).

Charles McGaw has been quick in his conversion from Hurricanes to Spitfires with 66 Squadron at Gravesend in Kent. At 4.35 p.m. he flies his first operational sortie with his new unit. The 6 Spitfires find themselves climbing through eight-tenths cloud. They patrol for over an hour without meeting the enemy.

No. 145 Squadron from Tangmere is up again over the Isle of Wight. Bungey is again leading Blue Section. The Hurricanes have not been on patrol for more than 5 minutes when a formation of Bf 109s suddenly pounces on them from out of the sun. Control has not warned them of the enemy's presence and they are taken completely by surprize. Three Hurricanes are shot down and one pilot is killed.

The squadron has had a bad day with 5 aircraft lost and one pilot dead.

*

Air Ministry Bulletin No. 2098 announces that John Curchin has been awarded the DFC.[9]

*[Curchin's DFC was announced in the **London Gazette** on 1 November and his squadron moved to Warmwell on the 29th. In February 1941 the first Spitfire Mk IIs began to arrive and, equipped with these, 609 Squadron transferred to Biggin Hill on the 24th to take part in 'Circus' operations over the continent. In May the squadron started to re-equip with Spitfire Vs. On 8 May Curchin shot a Bf 109 down into the sea and shared in destroying a second to bring his score of confirmed kills to 9.*

During the afternoon of 4 June the squadron was bounced by Messerschmitt Bf 109s and emerged from the clash claiming two 109s destroyed and one damaged, but one Spitfire was missing. An aircraft, at first thought to be a Messerschmitt, was seen to splash down into the water but it was realized later that it had been a Spitfire:

> *. . . Then it suddenly dawns on us, the almost unbelievable: the missing pilot is Johnie — Johnie Curchin.[10]*

The Australian ace was presumed killed in action.]

*

During the night the *Luftwaffe* carries out its usual attacks on London, Liverpool and Bristol. German bombers are also active over the south-east, aggressively bombing and machine-gunning many airfields.

MONDAY, 28 OCTOBER

Autumn mist persists through the morning, covering German airfields in northern France and restricting *Luftwaffe* activities to a few nuisance raids by individual aircraft.

In a daring attack a lone Dornier Do 17 raids North Weald. It dives through the cloud, unloads hurriedly and then slips back up into the murk.

Just before this the Hurricanes of 249 Squadron had taken off and they are now on patrol above the clouds. Bill Millington is Blue 1 and is acting as weaver. They are over Hawkinge when control reports a bandit about 10 miles (16 km) north-east of their position. It is the same Do 17 running for home and Bill Millington is the first to spot it as it breaks cloud. Millington starts after it, reporting its location to the squadron commander as he goes. At the same time two anti-aircraft shells burst close to the German machine and these help the squadron leader find it. He sends three more Hurricanes to follow the Australian who is now diving on the Dornier from above and behind. He closes in to about 200 yards (180 m) before firing. The Hurricane's tracer bullets are clearly visible penetrating the Do 17's fuselage and Millington breaks away after silencing the German rear gunner. Smoke streams from the damaged bomber as it vanishes into the clouds.

The Australian next joins forces with another Hurricane (Yellow 1) and, following instructions from the controller, the pair orbit over Dungeness. Little time passes before they sight a Junkers Ju 88 which breaks cover nearby for a few seconds. Millington and his companion wait for the bomber to come into the clear and ambush it from above, Yellow 1 coming in from behind while Millington carries out a quarter attack from above, allowing full deflection. He fires a long burst, using up all of his ammunition and the Ju 88's starboard engine begins to burn. Even though his guns are empty the Australian continues with mock attacks from above to keep the German rear gunner busy while Yellow 1 opens fire. The gunner stops shooting and there is a small explosion in the bomber's rear fuselage. It leaves a trail of white smoke behind as it continues south-eastwards. Even though neither has any more ammunition, both Hurricanes follow until it is necessary for them to break off. It seems that the bomber may escape. However the Ju 88 runs into yet another 249 Squadron Hurricane (Yellow 3) which delivers the *coup de grâce* and sends it crashing down into the sea.

While Bill Millington and his companions are shooting down the Ju 88, out over the North Sea Lewis Hamilton and his crew in Blenheim T2078 (WR-Q) are on another anti-invasion patrol. The likelihood of invasion now seems quite remote, even to the British, because of the weather and tidal conditions and because the *Luftwaffe* has been unable to establish the air superiority needed.

[In January 1941 No. 248 Squadron at last moved south to Dyce. The next move came in June 1941 to Bircham Newton where it began to re-equip with Beaufighters. Just before this Lewis Hamilton left the squadron with a posting to Rhodesia as an instructor but Doug Peterkin remained. At this stage both held the rank of flying officer.

In mid-1944 Hamilton returned to England. He flew Mosquitos with 464 Squadron, an Australian unit attached to the RAF. At this time the squadron was operating from Thorney Island in support of the 2nd Tactical Air Force on the continent. Specializing in night bombing, he served with this unit until 26 April 1945. At the end of the war he decided not to leave the RAF and on 19 June 1947 was granted an extended service commission and later a permanent commission. W/Cdr A.L. Hamilton retired from the RAF in April 1961 after almost 22 years of service and returned to Australia to eventually settle in Canberra. In a

Lewis Hamilton of 248 Squadron, with his gunner (photograph courtesy of John Hamilton).

*tragic accident on 1 October 1977 he drowned while fishing off the NSW
south coast.*

*Doug Peterkin left 248 Squadron after having taken part as a gunner
in 66 operations, including 12 with 612 Squadron (Whitleys) from Dyce
on Atlantic patrol to Iceland. On 2 March 1942 he was promoted to flight
lieutenant and resumed flying training at Cambridge where he at last
qualified as a pilot. Early in 1944 he was posted to 141 Squadron. This
unit was a member of 100 Group, Bomber Command, although it
actually flew de Havilland Mosquito Mk II night fighters on bomber
support missions. On the night of 4–5 July he and his navigator/radar
operator shot down an Me 410 but next night their luck ran out. The
Mosquito was shot down by flak over France. Peterkin managed to bail
out but his companion was killed.*

*Peterkin was captured by the Germans that night but managed to
escape 4 or 5 days later and establish contact with the French Underground. He made a deal with the French that in return for looking after
him he would instruct them in the use of various weapons which were
being supplied to the Resistance by the RAF. When Pas de Calais was
liberated he returned to England. After the war, early in 1946, he
resigned his commission with the rank of squadron leader and on 29 May
he returned to civilian life.*

*Doug Peterkin retired in 1978 and, at the time of writing, was living in
Perth, Western Australia.]*

With the improved afternoon weather the Germans despatch 8 *Gruppen* of Messerschmitt Bf 109s over the Thames Estuary and Kent. The
first, a raid of 50, crosses the coast at Folkestone and heads for London.
It is followed by 4 waves of aircraft totalling about 100.

The Spitfires of 66 Squadron are scrambled from Gravesend on an
interception patrol. Returning down through the clouds, Charles
McGaw in Spitfire P7440, becomes separated from the others and he is
the last to make it back to Gravesend.

*[McGaw stayed with 66 Squadron until 8 December when he was posted
to No. 7 CFS Cranwell. There followed several periods of instructing and
training. His promotion to flight lieutenant was gazetted in April
1942.*

*He applied for another tour of operations but by now there was a
greater demand for bomber pilots so he trained to fly twin-engined aircraft. In July 1943 he went to the Mediterranean to take up a posting in
No. 18 Squadron which was equipped with Douglas Bostons. In August
the unit moved to Sicily to begin interdiction bombing of enemy communications in Italy and the Balkans.*

*On 1 October 1943 Charles McGaw and his crew, along with 7 other
Boston crews, were given the task of bombing a bridge in Italy. They took
off from Gerbini near Mount Etna but encountered violent electrical
storms on the way to the target. Six out of the 8 planes turned back. On his
way home in the darkness the engines of McGaw's Boston cut out and he
had to ditch into the sea near Messina. As the bomber struck the waves it
overturned violently and broke up. Only one man was rescued. The body
of Charles McGaw was never found.*

McGaw never saw his son who was born on 29 February 1944. After the war, in 1946, Margaret McGaw sailed to Australia and visited Charles' parents so they at least met their grandson.[11]

While Charles McGaw is on patrol high over Kent Bill Weaber of 233 Squadron is patrolling in Hudson N7269 over the North Sea. Several mines are spotted floating in the water at about 3.30 p.m. Weaber brings the Hudson down low and tries to sink them using gunfire but is unsuccessful.

*

Although he is the official correspondent for the Australian army, Kenneth Slessor has been contacted by Australia House with the suggestion that he should write something on the RAAF and RAN volunteers at present serving in Britain.

At Australia House, London, Slessor meets Air Cdr Frank McNamara VC who is to make arrangements for the RAAF in England story.

[AVM Frank Hubert McNamara VC, CBE, BA, RAAF was RAAF liaison officer in London 1938–41. He won the Victoria Cross in the first world war while a member of No. 1 Squadron, Australian Flying Corps. In spite of the fact that he was severely wounded in the thigh, that Turkish cavalry was closing in and that his aircraft was being subjected to heavy firing, he landed in the desert and rescued a downed pilot. When his own plane crashed he took off in the other aircraft and flew 70 miles (112 km) back to base where he collapsed from loss of blood.

Invalided to Australia, he was given a hero's welcome. He resigned from the AFC shortly afterwards but, not content with civilian life, rejoined in September 1918 and was reappointed to his former rank and seniority. When the RAAF was formed he passed into the new service and eventually rose to the rank of air vice marshal. He died in England on 2 November 1961 at the age of 67.]

The *Luftwaffe's* overnight effort is widely dispersed and many towns throughout England experience alerts and light bombing. London's all-clear sirens wail at 7.00 a.m.

TUESDAY, 29 OCTOBER

The morning mist gradually gives way to haze over northern France and the Straits of Dover, very suitable conditions for fighter-bomber attacks and the Germans seize the chance. First there are the usual early morning reconnaissance sorties by single aircraft but around 11.00 a.m. the first raid of 30-plus is plotted approaching the coast near Deal. These raiders are successfully intercepted but a few manage to break through to London and drop their bombs.

At 10.30 a.m. 12 Group is asked by AVM Park's headquarters to launch the Duxford wing against German aircraft breaking through 11 Group's area. It leaves the ground at 10.47 a.m. but takes 20 minutes to form up in the air and so does not leave Duxford until 11.07 a.m. As a result it is too late and fails to intercept the enemy formation. Around noon, as the wing is landing, the Germans begin sending over more raids and because of this timing 12 Group is again unable to be of help.

The next raid of Messerschmitt Bf 109 fighters and fighter-bombers, numbering 100-plus, is intercepted by 5 squadrons of Spitfires and 4 of Hurricanes from 11 Group. The British fighters are well positioned and inflict heavy losses on the German formations. At least 8 109s are shot down in under 10 minutes while the remainder are forced to jettison their bombs and turn back, racing for the Channel at full throttle.

At about the same time two raids of 50 and 12 aircraft from *Luftflotte 3* attack Portsmouth. In the west at Exeter, Clive Mayers and his wingman are scrambled at 1.00 p.m. but after 20 minutes of orbiting they are ordered to land — the enemy has not come their way.

While Portsmouth is bombed 15 Breda BR. 20 bombers and 73 Fiat CR.42 biplane fighters raid Ramsgate in the first large-scale daylight attack by the *Reggia Aeronautica* on a target in Britain. The Italians are not intercepted and escape unscathed.

At 4.30 p.m. the Hurricanes of 249 and 257 Squadrons are ordered to scramble from North Weald but as they taxi out, a *Staffel* of Messerschmitt Bf 109s suddenly appears over the airfield. Each Messerschmitt is carrying three 100 kg bombs for this special dive-bombing mission.

Realizing their peril, the Hurricanes rush to take off. Bill Millington is Blue 1 and, as soon as he sees the bombs coming down, he takes off behind Red Section. Only one aircraft from 249 Squadron is damaged as it takes off but 257 Squadron bears the brunt of the attack. As its Hurricanes hurtle forward the end of the runway in front of them seems to explode. One plane is caught up in the blast, toppled onto its back and thrown down. It bursts into flames and its pilot is burned to death. A second Hurricane is badly damaged but its pilot manages to coax it up to 1 500 feet (450 m) so he can bail out.

The Messerschmitts, after their hit-and-run attack, make off due west and Red Section gives chase as they skim low across the countryside. Millington is behind them and he opens his throttle to maximum speed. Several of the Bf 109s, probably believing that they are in the clear, begin to climb and so give the Australian a chance to catch up. There are 6 German planes and by the time they reach 3 000 feet (900 m) they are nearing the coast. Millington believes his quarry to be 4 Bf 109s in the lead with two He 113s *(sic)* weaving slightly behind. On the right, one Messerschmitt lags behind the others so Millington works his way behind it until he is 100 yards (90 m) back in line astern. He fires and instantly the 109 reacts by diving for the haze over the sea. The Australian follows and when the opportunity presents itself he fires a long, continuous burst. Pieces are torn off the German fighter and it disappears vertically into the haze leaving a trail of thick smoke. Millington judges that it will fall into the sea. He flies back to North Weald where 27 bombs have been dropped on the aerodrome, killing 19 people and injuring 42 others.

As 11 Group has 17 squadrons committed, 12 Group's Duxford wing is again instructed to patrol Maidstone/Sheerness. When Hornchurch Control tries to direct it to intercept two raids heading for Essex, it is unable to break into the wing's continuous radio conversations with Duxford. After it becomes obvious that the Germans can no longer be cut off, 12 Group is asked to order the wing to intercept other raiders. Instead, because the weather is reportedly closing in at Duxford, it is recalled. To cap this fiasco off, as the wing is landing, aerodromes in East Anglia, 12 Group's own area, come under attack.

[Group Captain G.M. Lawson, 'Strath' Evill's chief assistant at Fighter Command Headquarters, Bentley Priory, called attention to the total ineffectiveness of the 'Big Wing' on this day. In the morning the wing had taken too long to assemble over Duxford and in the afternoon it had proved all but impossible to control by either group headquarters when flying over the south. Finally, it was out of action when its own area was raided. These incidents demonstrated the correctness of the tactics adopted by Park.

'Strath' Evill was born of English parents in Broken Hill, NSW, on 8 October 1892. The family returned to England in October 1897. He continued on as SASO after Dowding's retirement and in 1942, with the rank of temporary air marshal, was appointed head of the RAF delegation to Washington. Next year he returned to England and served as the chief of air staff and additional member of the Air Council of the Air Ministry from March 1943, a position he held until his retirement. For his service he received numerous awards.

Air Chief Marshal Sir Douglas Strathern Evill GBE, KCB, CB, DSC, AFC retired from the RAF with effect from 15 January 1947. However in December 1949 he was appointed honorary air commodore of No. 3617 (County of Hampshire) Fighter Control Unit, a position he held until 1960.]

*

At 6.15 p.m. Noel Constantine and his gunner, Sgt Coxon, take off from Gatwick for a night patrol in Defiant N1566. The Germans begin a series of heavy attacks on London and the Midlands and, as has happened so often before, they pass by the British night fighters unchallenged in the darkness. Like the others the Australian and his gunner are unable to find the enemy.

[On 16 April 1941 Constantine and Coxon flew their last sortie together in Defiant N1798, the Australian's last operation before leaving 141 Squadron. Constantine's promotion to flight lieutenant was gazetted on 3 September 1941 and shortly after this he left England for India and the Burma theatre of operations. In April 1942 he was promoted acting squadron leader and given command of 273 Squadron at China Bay. He remained in command until June 1943, at which time he moved to Baigachi to take over 136 Squadron which was also equipped with Hurricanes. At the time he took over it moved back to India for 6 months to re-equip and rest. The new planes were Spitfires VCs and operations using these began in December 1943, when the squadron started to fly fighter defence patrols and escort missions over Burma. Over 4 months, 136 Squadron built up an impressive tally of victories of which Constantine accounted for at least 6. In April 1944 he was promoted acting wing

commander and placed in charge of Air Fighter Tactics Air Command for the rest of the war.[12]

He remained in the RAF until 9 December 1946 when he was discharged. He returned to Australia but continued to fly in Asia. On 29 July 1947 he was reported killed in an air crash while flying medical supplies to the Javanese. Another unconfirmed story has it that, while flying a civil-registered Anson, he was shot down over Indonesia.[13]]

The Defiants of 264 Squadron (Bill Crook) which have moved from Kirton-in-Lindsey to Rochford are equally frustrated by the darkness.

[Bill Crook left the squadron on 20 March when he was posted to No. 3 Group Training Flight at Stradishall. From there he left for the middle east where he reported to 37 Squadron at Shallufa, Egypt. This unit operated Vickers Wellington ICs and at this time was engaged in night bombing raids on enemy ports and bases in Libya. In May it took part in suppressing the Iraqi uprising but its main work was concentrated upon Libya and the Desert.

During this time Crook flew as a gunner with a regular crew. Their usual aircraft was Wellington N2917 although they did fly others. On the night of 6–7 June 1941, 5 aircraft from 37 Squadron were detailed to attack enemy stores and vehicles in Benghazi and it was from this raid that Wellington N2917 failed to return. After bombing the port's docks, heavy flak was encountered and the Wellington crashed into the sea. Bill Crook and the others, although shaken up, were able to take to the dinghy. After two days of exposure a seaplane picked them up.

Upon completing his second operational tour early in September Bill Crook returned to the UK. After a period of instructing and training during which he was promoted flight sergeant and received a mention in dispatches in 1942, he joined 160 Squadron in Palestine. No. 160 Squadron's main duties consisted of bombing enemy bases and ports in Libya and Crete. On 7 November, after a raid on Crete, the Liberators flew back to a new base at Shandur in Egypt. From here they struck at targets over a vast area ranging from Tunisia to Italy, Tripoli and Benghazi but now the number of bombers on strength began to slowly decline as the Liberators left for India; those that remained were merged into 178 Squadron in January 1943.

Operations continued at a hectic pace and on 4 March Bill Crook's new squadron moved to Libya to attack targets in North Africa, Italy and the Balkans and to carry out supply-dropping flights to partisans as far afield as Poland and northern Italy. Crook's promotion to warrant officer came through in April and his stay with 178 Squadron ended two months later when his third tour of operations finished.

He returned to England and shortly afterwards sailed for New Zealand. In April 1944 he was in No. 1 Squadron, RNZAF, but he had applied to transfer to the RAAF and the following month he left New Zealand bound for Australia. His official discharge from the RNZAF took effect from 9 June. During his service he had logged a total of 750 hours flying and, of these, 520 were on operations. Bill Crook served with the RAAF in Melbourne and was discharged in February 1945 for medical reasons. He died in the 1950's under tragic circumstances.[14]]

*

Bill Crook, an air gunner with 264 Squadron (photograph courtesy of Kenneth Wynn).

No. 609 Squadron has its official 'Century Celebration Dinner', marking it as the first Spitfire Squadron to destroy 100 enemy aircraft. The squadron has been 'in the line' since May and has achieved one of the best kill/loss ratios, having lost only 8 pilots since July and won 7 DFCs, including one for its current Australian member, John Curchin.

*

Bomber Command sends out 98 aircraft to bomb numerous targets. The biggest raid, consisting of 30 Hampdens and Wellingtons, is ordered to attack Berlin. Because of poor weather only four aircraft bomb the capital.

WEDNESDAY, 30 OCTOBER

At the beginning of the battle RAF fighters flew in sections of three aircraft and flights of six. By the end of October many squadrons were adopting the more flexible German formations and using sections of two and flights of four (Imperial War Museum photograph).

The poor weather which has developed overnight continues through the day with low cloud and continuous drizzle everywhere. At Exeter Clive Mayers is up in Hurricane P3831 for 35 minutes to test the weather.

A few German reconnaissance planes venture into the air and at 9.05 a.m. 4 Spitfires from 66 Squadron take off from Gravesend for an interception patrol. Charles McGaw is in Spitfire P7433. The patrol follows the controller's directions back and forth but their quarry is too elusive.

The first serious radar plots start showing around 11.30 a.m. By noon 80 German aircraft are flying up the Thames Estuary and these are followed 15 minutes later by two waves of 50 and 60-plus, coming in via Dymchurch. To meet them Fighter Command has 10 squadrons of Hurricanes and Spitfires in the air and 6 of these units make contact. No. 249 Squadron is one of them. Around 1.00 p.m. Bill Millington in Hurricane V7536 finds himself caught up in a series of sporadic actions with Messerschmitt Bf 109s over the Channel. His aircraft is last seen chasing a German fighter out over the sea.

Back at North Weald two Hurricanes are missing and one has been damaged by a cannon shell. News comes that one of the missing Hurricanes has force-landed at Blackford Farm. The second aircraft, Hurricane V7536, will never return.

P/O William Henry Millington DFC is the 13th of those Australians deemed eligible for the Battle of Britain Clasp to be killed in action.

*

H.M. King George VI inspects the Australian troops at Colchester. At 4.00 p.m. he leaves Colchester to continue his inspection of other soldiers in the Australian contingent.

*

At the same time as the king is leaving Hurricane V7301 of 253 Squadron is crash-landing at Southfleet after a clash with Bf 109s. Its pilot is Sgt Peter Moore of Melbourne who had joined the squadron at Kenley earlier in the month. Moore is slightly injured.

[Peter John Moore was commissioned as a pilot officer on 8 November 1941 and served with 616 Squadron. He was killed in action on 3 June 1942 and buried in Etaples Military Cemetery, France.]

*

With the coming of darkness the first German bombers are picked up on radar heading, as usual, for London. The weather, however, continues to deteriorate so that most of them turn back and by midnight the radar screens are clear.

RAF Bomber Command sends out only 28 Blenheims and Wellingtons to Antwerp, Flushing, Duisburg and Emden. All of the aircraft return safely.

THURSDAY, 31 OCTOBER

In spite of the poor weather a few German raiders are plotted by radar as they fly around Yorkshire in the morning. Charles Pritchard of 600 Squadron takes off on a patrol at 5.15 a.m. in Blenheim BQ-G. After searching in vain for an hour-and-a-half, he lands back at Catterick.

[Pritchard's promotion to acting squadron leader was recorded in the **London Gazette** *of 14 December 1940, two days after he took command*

of the squadron. A week later 600 Squadron ceased to be operational and devoted its energy to training on Beaufighters.

By May it was based at Colerne, Wiltshire, and was gaining more successes against enemy night bombers. On the night of 16–17 May there was a serious mishap. In Beaufighter X7544, Charles Pritchard's AI operator, Sgt Gledhill, located a bandit south of Gloucester and they followed it to Coventry. Searchlights failed to illuminate the German plane but frequently lit up the Beaufighter. This alerted the enemy pilot to the fact that he was being followed and he took violent evasive action by twisting, turning and climbing. Gledhill managed to keep him on radar and eventually Pritchard obtained visual contact after a long chase. While Pritchard was manoeuvring to attack searchlights again illuminated the British fighter. It was only 100 yards (90 m) from the enemy, a Ju 88, and the German gunners had a perfect silhouette. They opened fire and blew in the starboard side of the Beaufighter's cockpit, setting alight the petrol feed and causing flames to envelop the Australian. The two men managed to bail out but they were both injured, Pritchard with serious burns to the face and Gledhill with a bullet wound in the leg.[15]

Charles Pritchard's promotion to acting wing commander was gazetted on 3 September 1941 and it was then that he left the squadron. On 24 June the **London Gazette** had announced his award of the DFC.

After this, information on Charles Pritchard's activities becomes fragmented but he is known to have been in command of RAF, High Ercall, in mid-1943 and he also received an Air Efficiency Award that year. W/Cdr C.A. Pritchard DFC left the RAF in 1945 and during the 1960s was living in Port Elizabeth, South Africa. He is now believed to be deceased.]

*

Clive Mayers later served with 601 Squadron in north Africa; he is shown here sitting in the doorway shortly before he was declared missing, presumed dead, on 20 July 1942 (Imperial War Museum photograph CH 2923).

Daylight shows low cloud and drizzle over the English Channel, haze in the Thames Estuary and similar conditions blanketing the Straits of Dover. The *Luftwaffe* sends over a few scattered raiders. It is the quietest day for 4 months.

Over at Exeter Clive Mayers takes off at 8.45 a.m. for a weather test. Satisfied that conditions are clear enough he radios back for his flight to join him to practise formation flying.

Because of deteriorating weather this is the only flying carried out by 601 Squadron during the day.

[Clive Mayers' promotion to acting squadron leader was gazetted on 1 November 1941 and two weeks later he became an acting wing commander. By then he had transferred to the middle east where he had taken over command of 94 Squadron in August and shared in the destruction of a Ju 88 with two other pilots on 11 September. On Christmas Day 1941, Nos 94 and 260 Squadrons carried out a strafing attack on a German column travelling along the Antelat-Agedabia Road. A member of Mayers' Squadron, Sgt McKay, was shot down by ground fire. What happened next is recorded in the citation for Mayers' Bar to the DFC:

One day in December 1941, during a machine-gun attack against an enemy column, Wing Commander Mayers observed a member of his formation shot down by anti-aircraft fire. When the attack was concluded, he skilfully landed near the crashed aircraft and, although enemy vehicles were approaching, coolly waited for his comrade to reach him. Putting him in the seat, Wing Commander Mayers clambered in on top of him and took off as the enemy neared the aircraft. He finally flew safely to base. This officer has always shown great courage and leadership. He has destroyed at least 11 enemy aircraft.[16]

On 26 April 1942 Mayers was appointed wing leader of the newly-formed 239 Wing established at Gambit. This placed him in charge of three squadrons, Nos 112, 250 and 3 Squadrons, RAAF. During May **Luftwaffe** *Junkers Ju 52 transport aircraft were flying numerous sorties between Crete and North Africa with reinforcements and on the 12th a special mission was planned to ambush one of these formations. The mixed force of Beaufighters and Kittyhawks was led by Mayers with F/Lt J.L. Waddy in charge of the top cover. Along with an escorting Bf 110, 9 Ju 52s were shot down and two others crash-landed along a beach. Mayers claimed two Junkers and another damaged.*

On 17 June Mayers led 239 Wing in a strafing attack on Gazala. They shot up 15 Bf 109s on the ground and other German aircraft which tried to become airborne were swiftly shot down, one by Mayers. He led another successful wing attack on 8 July on enemy airfields.

Because of his work as a wing leader Mayers was recommended for a DSO but before this could be awarded the Australian failed to return from a heavy raid on Fuka Daba on 20 July. He was probably the victim of ground fire but he could have been shot down by 4 Bf 109s scrambled to intercept the raid. His downed Kittyhawk was found by British aircraft but he had vanished. It seems likely that he survived the landing and was captured. He is said to have been killed when the Ju 52 which was transporting him to a POW camp in Italy was intercepted and shot down

Robert Bungey of 145 Squadron. He later commanded 452 Squadron, RAAF, Australia's first fighter squadron in the UK (AWM 10823).

The battle of Britain chapel in Westminster Abbey; the Roll of Honour records the names of 24 Australians (Ministry of Defence, UK).

by Spitfires. If so, it was an ironic ending for a pilot who had led many similar sorties.

*Just 9 days after he failed to return, Clive Mayers' DSO was recorded in the **London Gazette**.]*

*

At 10.20 a.m. a flight of three Lockheed Hudsons of 233 Squadron leaves Leuchars for an offensive patrol off the coast of Norway. At the controls of Hudson T9372 (QX-R) is Bill Weaber. After flying across the North Sea they reach Norway north of Lister and spot a merchant vessel heavily laden with timber. It is accompanied by a smaller ship and a flakship.

The Hudsons concentrate on the largest ship. Weaber makes a run in at 500 feet (150 m) and drops four 250 lb (114 kg) bombs, all of which narrowly miss. The explosions cascade water over the vessel's decks. Bombs from the second Hudson also miss, landing in the water 50 yards (45 m) in front. The third Hudson scores with its second bomb run and there is an explosion amidships which sends up clouds of white smoke.

All this time the flakship has been firing an intense barrage and Weaber's Hudson is last seen flying into it. Shortly afterwards a sheet of flame erupts on a beach 10 miles (16 km) north of Lister.

Meanwhile a Messerschmitt Bf 109, apparently responding to a call for help, appears and attacks one of the two retreating Hudsons from below. There is a furious exchange of fire and machine-gun bullets perforate the bomber in several places before it manages to escape. Fortunately none of the damage is serious. With German fighters about, it is obviously too dangerous to go back and look for the missing Hudson so they set course for home. Bill Weaber's aircraft does not return.

P/O William Owen Weaber is among the Australians whose names are listed on the Battle of Britain Roll of Honour at Westminster Abbey.

*

John Pain returns to 32 Squadron which is now based at Acklington. He is fully recovered from the wounds he received on 18 August.

*

The *Luftwaffe's* activity at night is much reduced owing to the continuing rain and drizzle.

*

On the stroke of midnight on this day the battle of Britain is considered to have ended.

ENDNOTES

INTRODUCTION

1. Herington, John, *Australia in the war of 1939–1945 (Air)* Vol. III, *Air war against Germany and Italy, 1939–1943* (Australian War Memorial, 1962), p.35
2. Werner Kreipe served with KG 2 from December 1939 to June 1940, after which he was appointed chief operations officer of the Third Air Fleet. He considered the battle to have started on 28 May 1940, the day the *Luftwaffe* first met the RAF head-on over Dunkirk. Cajus Bekker, author of *The Luftwaffe war diaries*, noted that on 30 June, only a week after the end of the French campaign, Goering issued his 'General Directions for the operations of the *Luftwaffe* against England'. Others have put forward 2 July when the *Luftwaffe* received its first specific operational instructions for the campaign against England or the next day when regular attacks on shipping began and eighty-seven Junkers 87 Stukas escorted by Messerschmitt Bf 109s attacked naval installations at Portland. Most German battle of Britain pilots are in agreement on this.
3. Many questioned such rigid parameters. For example Air Cdr Alan Deere DSO, OBE, DFC and Bar, DFC (US), the famous New Zealand air ace, suggested the beginning of July. Noted air historian Chaz Bowyer, author of *Fighter Command 1936–68*, wrote that between 1–9 July Fighter Command pilots shot down at least 56 German aircraft for the loss of 28 planes with 23 pilots either killed or wounded. These men were therefore declared ineligible to receive the Battle of Britain Clasp. Bowyer nominates 4 June, when the Dunkirk evacuation was officially over, or 1 July, when the Germans occupied Guernsey, as equally valid dates for the commencement of the battle.
4. The fighting tapered off throughout November and December but there were sporadic and sometimes fierce battles such as: 7 November when 145 Squadron lost 5 Hurricanes in an encounter with 50 Bf 109s, 11 November, when the *Reggia Aeronautica* launched its first and only heavy daylight attack and was cut to pieces by the RAF, the night of 14–15 November when Coventry was razed, and the night of 29–30 December when a fire raid on London was considered to have caused the most disastrous blaze since the Great Fire of 1666.
5. Herington, John, op. cit., p.37.

PRELUDE TO THE BATTLE

1. Hughes, W., Letter of P.C. Hughes, 6 Sept. 1940.
2. Bowden, J., RAF pilot's flying log book of J.D. Crossman, 30 Sept. 1939.
3. Bf 109 and Bf 110. These fighters were referred to during the war years as the 'Me 109' and 'Me 110' but at the time of their design the manufacturing company was *Bayerische Flugzeugwerke* and the prefix 'Bf' was used in official German handbooks and documents. The design team was headed by Professor Willy Messerschmitt who

joined the company in 1927 and eventually took over when it was reconstituted as the *Messerschmitt A.G.*

4. Wood, D. & Dempster, D., *The narrow margin* (Arrow, London, 1969), p.97.

5. Refer to Appendix 6.

6. He 113 — actually the He 100D. It was generally believed that this fighter had entered service with the *Luftwaffe* when in fact only 12 were produced and none were accepted for service. In a successful bid to fool Allied Intelligence, they were painted with different insignia several times for propaganda photographs, thus creating the impression that the type was in widespread use. In the heat of battle, on numerous occasions, Bf 109s were mistakenly identified as 'He 113s' and entered as such in RAF combat reports and official records.

7. Churchill, W.S., *The second world war* Vol. 3 (Cassell, 1964), p.201.

JULY 1940

1. Kreipe, W., in Richardson, W. & Freidin, S., *The fatal decisions* (Harborough, 1956), p.14.

2. Coward, Air Cdr J., Correspondence to author, 17 Aug 1983.

3. Butement, W.A.S., *Record of scientific work* (Butement, 1960), pp.48–49.

4. Power, R.M., Correspondence to author, 6 Sept. 1983.

5. Trevor-Roper, H.R., *Hitler's war directives 1939–45* (Pan, 1964), pp.74–79.

6. Churchill, W., op. cit., p.231.

7. Operations record book, 65 Squadron, 20 July 1940 (Public Record Office, London).

8. Mason, F.K., *Battle over Britain* (McWhirter, 1969), p.185.

9. Wood, D. & Dempster, D., op. cit., p.142.

10. Olive, G., Taped interview, 16 May 1985.

AUGUST 1940

1. ORB, 236 Squadron, 1 Aug. 1940 (PRO).

2. Trevor-Roper, H.R. (ed.), *Hitler's war directives 1939–1945* (Pan, 1966), p.79.

3. *London Gazette*, 6 Aug. 1940.

4. Ibid., 6 Aug. 1940.

5. Olive, G., Taped interview, 4 Sept. 1985.

6. ORB, 248 Squadron, 9 Aug. 1940 (PRO).

7. Cock, J., Taped interview, 12 May 1985.

8. Parkinson, R., *Blood, toil, tears and sweat* (Hart-Davis MacGibbon, London, 1973), pp.93–94.

9. Mason, F.K., op. cit., p.285.

10. Parker, V., Record of interview, 29 Aug. 1945, via C. Burgess.

11. Reid, P.R., *The latter days of Colditz* (Coronet, London, 1965), p.97

12. James, R.R. (ed.), *Winston S. Churchill, his complete speeches 1897–1963* Vol. 11, *1935–1942* (Chelsea House, New York, 1978), p.6266.

13. Parkinson, R., op. cit., p.102.

14. Hillary, R., *The last enemy* (Pan, London, 1956), p.106.

SEPTEMBER 1940

1. Long, G., 'AIF in the United Kingdom' in *Australia in the war of 1939–45 (Army)* Vol. I, *To Benghazi* (Australian War Memorial, 1961), p.308. Originally these newly formed battalions were numbered 2/28th, 2/29th and 2/30th, but because these numbers were already allotted to units to be formed in Australia, they were changed temporarily to 70th, 71st and 72nd respectively. Later, in October, they were renumbered permanently to 2/31st, 2/32nd and 2/33rd.
2. Shirer, W.L., *Berlin Diary 1934–1941* (Sphere, London, 1970), p.388.
3. Combat report, F/Lt P.C. Hughes, 41 Sqn, 5 Sept. 1940 (PRO).
4. Willis, J., *Churchill's few* (Michael Joseph, London, 1985), pp.128 & 135.
5. Parkinson, R., op. cit., p.108.
6. Orange, V., *Sir Keith Park* (Methuen, London, 1984), p.105.
7. Mason, F.K., op. cit., p.355.
8. Combat report, P/O J. Zurakowski, 235 Sqn, 7 Sept. 1940 (PRO).
9. As already noted Pat Hughes became the most successful Australian pilot of the battle of Britain before his death on 7 September 1940. His combat record included 15 confirmed shot down, 1 probable, 3 shared and 1 unconfirmed shared. Refer Appendix 8.
10. Semmler, C., *The war diaries of Kenneth Slessor* (University of Queensland Press, 1985), p.108.
11. Shirer, W.L., op. cit., p.392.
12. Wood, D. & Dempster, D., op. cit., p.222.
13. Churchill, W.S., op. cit., p.14.
14. Ibid., p.16.
15. Smith, C.B., *Evidence in camera* (Penguin, 1961), p.74.
16. Cock, J., Log book, 21 Sept. 1940.
17. Crossman, J.D., Log book, 24 Sept. 1940.
18. Mason, F.K., op. cit., p.406.
19. Shirer, W.L. op. cit., p.406.
20. Houart, V., *Lonely warrior* (Corgi, 1957), the journal of Jean Offenberg, p.68.
21. British Ministry of Defence, Correspondence to author, various dates.
22. Wood, D. & Dempster, D., op. cit., p.240.
23. Crossman, J.D., op. cit., 30 Sept. 1940.
24. Barclay, G., *Angels 22* (Arrow, London, 1977), p.72.

OCTOBER 1940

1. Bowden, J., Letters of J.D. Crossman, 1 Oct. 1940.
2. Air Ministry, Notification of death, 18 Dec. 1941, via Len Bennett.
3. Hillary, R.H., op. cit. Quoted at the beginning of the book.
4. Wood, D. & Dempster D., op. cit., p.255.
5. Ibid., p.258.
6. AWM 65, S/Ldr D. Fopp AFC.
7. Salmaggi, C. & Pallavismi, A., *2194 days of war* (Windward, 1979), p.80.
8. Butement, W.A.S., op. cit., p.56.
9. AWM 65, F/Lt J. Curchin DFC.

10. ORB, 609 Squadron, 4 June 1941 (PRO).
11. McGaw, M., Correspondence to author, 26 Feb. 1983.
12. Air Ministry and Central Office of Information, *Wings of the Phoenix* (His Majesty's Stationery Office), p.46.
13. Olive, G., Taped interview, 16 May 1985.
14. Wynn, K.G., *A clasp for 'The Few'* (Kenneth G. Wynn, Auckland, 1981), p.99.
15. ORB, 600 Squadron, 16–17 May 1941 (PRO).
16. AWM 65, W/Cdr H.C. Mayers DSO, DFC & Bar.

APPENDIX 1

AIR MINISTRY ORDERS
RE THE BATTLE OF BRITAIN CLASP

A.M.O. A.544/1946
Section 12

CLASP TO THE 1939–45 STAR

Issues of silver-gilt rose emblems denoting a clasp to the 1939–45 Star may be made to flying personnel who flew in fighter aircraft engaged in the Battle of Britain between 10th July, 1940, and 31st October 1940. Issues are to be confined to those who operated with the undermentioned squadrons:-

Nos. 1, 17, 19, 23, 25, 29, 32, 41, 43, 46, 54, 66, 72, 73, 74, 79, 85, 87, 92, 141, 145, 151, 152, 213, 219, 222, 229, 234, 235, 236, 238, 242, 248, 249, 253, 257, 264, 266, 302, 303, 310, 312, 401 (R.C.A.F. Squadron), 501, 504, 600, 601, 602, 603, 604, 605, 607, 609, 610, 611, 615 and 616. Service with the fighter interception unit will also qualify.

The following details must be inserted in line 2 of the claim form for claimants for this emblem:-
(a) Squadron and Station
(b) Dates of qualifying service
(c) Date of one sortie during (b) above

C.Os are not to admit claims for this highly-prized emblem which are open to any possible doubt. The clasp is not available for personnel who flew in aircraft other than fighters, notwithstanding that they may have been engaged with the enemy during the qualifying period.
A.M.O. N.850.- BATTLE OF BRITAIN
(A.344696/60/S.7 — 9th November, 1960)

1. The 20th anniversary of the Battle of Britain has prompted the publication of the following list of operational units that took part in the battle between 10th July, 1940 and 31st October, 1940:-
Squadron Nos. 1, 3, 17, 19, 23, 25, 29, 32, 41, 43, 46, 54, 56, 64, 65, 66, 72, 73, 74, 79, 85, 87, 92, 111, 141, 145, 151, 152, 213, 219, 222, 229, 232, 234, 235, 236, 238, 242, 245, 247, 248, 249, 253, 257, 263, 264, 266, 302, 303, 310, 312, 401 (No. 1 R.C.A.F. Squadron), 501, 504, 600, 601, 602, 603, 604, 605, 607, 609, 610, 611, 615 and 616.
Flight Nos. 421 and 422.
Fighter Interception Unit.

2. Aircrew who flew at least one operational sortie in fighter aircraft
    of these units during the period shown in paragraph 1, above, may
    submit a claim for a silver-gilt rose emblem denoting a Clasp to the
    1939–45 Star. The Clasp will not be issued to aircrew who did not
    fly in fighters even though they may have been engaged with the
    enemy in the air during the qualifying period.

*

*[It should be noted that both AMOs emphasized that only operational
sorties counted for this Clasp and only the personnel of defending fighter
squadrons qualified. However three of those listed, Nos 235, 236 and 248
Squadrons, were Coastal Command units which were attached temporarily, for varying lengths of time, to Fighter Command. Later were added
Nos 804 and 808 Squadrons of the Fleet Air Arm.]*

APPENDIX 2

Most historical works written in the United Kingdom seem to be unanimous in their assessment that only 21 Australians took part in the battle and that, of these, 14 were killed. The names of these men are to be found in such excellent publications as *The narrow margin* by Derek Wood and Derek Dempster, Winston G. Ramsey's *Battle of Britain — then and now* Mk II-Mk IV and Francis K. Mason's *Battle over Britain* although the latter, by conceding that F/Lt H.C. Mayers DFC was an Australian, raised his number to 22. That outstanding storyteller, Len Deighton, in his book *Fighter — the true story of the battle of Britain*, apparently using Mason as a source of information, stated that of 22 Australians, 14 were killed. The epic film *Battle of Britain* did not include a list of names but stated that there were 21 Australians involved. This was because the screenplay relied heavily on *The narrow margin* for information. While I was researching this book the historian of the Battle of Britain Fighter Association of Great Britain, G/Cpt Tom Gleave CBE, furnished me with a list of names of 21 Australians.

At first inspection all this evidence was convincing in its uniformity. Even so, there seemed to be room for doubt, especially as sources in Australia put the number at 29. Closer investigation revealed that all of these authorities had based their lists upon the remarkable work of one man, F/Lt John Holloway MBE.

In 1955 F/Lt John Holloway had been a serving officer in the RAF stationed at Kenley during the making of the film *Reach for the sky* based on Paul Brickhill's biography of G/Cpt Douglas 'Tin Legs' Bader CBE, DSO, DFC. There, he was in a position to collect many autographs of battle of Britain airmen in his own copy of the book and from then on it became his obsession to continue collecting these autographs. Holloway retired from the RAF in 1958 and began work in earnest to obtain autographs of all battle of Britain pilots and aircrew. It did not stop there. As time went on his aims widened — he would compile a 'diary' for every airman.

The worthiness of his project was recognized by official organizations such as the Air Historical Branch and Airmen Records Establishment of the Ministry of Defence and the staff of these co-operated fully as he searched through records and documents pertaining to the battle of Britain period, i.e. 00.01 hours on 10 July 1940 to 23.59 hours on 31 October 1940. This meant searching through the records of some 67 squadrons and subsidiary units until he had the names of 2 946 qualifiers for the Battle of Britain Clasp. By 1961 he had completed the first list of 'The Few' which was made available to Wood and Dempster for their book, *The narrow margin*. In appreciation of his work, members of the Battle of Britain Fighter Association presented him with a model of a silver, mounted Spitfire. John Holloway's outstanding work took 14 years to complete and since then he has presented plaques and diaries to the Imperial War Museum in London and the Smithsonian Institute in Washington (honouring 7 American pilots who flew in the RAF). In 1982 he visited Australia to honour his 21 'Australians' by presenting a plaque and diaries to the Australian War Memorial.

Holloway's dedication can only be described as incredible and, for the most part, highly accurate. Over the years others conducting research have made only minor modifications to his work.

In 1983 I wrote to John Holloway informing him of my research and I received a detailed reply dated 9 June 1983. His list of names of 21 Australian pilots, plus 8 others he declared to be 'British', appears below.

AUSTRALIAN BATTLE OF BRITAIN PILOTS AND AIRCREW

RANK 1940	INITIALS	NAME	PILOT OR AIRCREW	DECORATIONS	SQNS FLOWN WITH DURING THE BATTLE OF BRITAIN	DATE KILLED OR DECEASED
P/O	C.C.	Bennett	Pilot		248*	1/10/40
"	R.W.	Bungey	"	DFC	145	Deceased
F/O	J.R.	Cock	"	DFC	87	
P/O	F.W.	Cale	"		266*	15/8/40
"	A.N.	Constantine	"		141	29/7/47
"	J.D.	Crossman	"		46*	30/9/40
F/Lt	F.W.	Flood	"		235*	11/9/40
F/O	R.L.	Glyde	"	DFC	87*	13/8/40
P/O	A.L.	Hamilton	"		248	Deceased
Sgt	K.C.	Holland	"		152*	25/9/40
F/Lt	P.C.	Hughes	"	DFC	234*	7/9/40
"	J.C.	Kennedy	"		238*	13/7/40
P/O	B.M.	McDonough	"		236*	1/8/40
"	R.F.G.	Miller	"		609*	27/9/40
"	W.H.	Millington	"	DFC	79–249*	30/10/40
F/Lt	C.G.C.	Olive	"	DFC	65	Deceased#
"	R.M.	Power	"		236	
"	R.C.	Reynell	"		43*	7/9/40
"	D.F.B.	Sheen	"	DFC	72	
"	S.C.	Walch	"		238*	11/8/40
"	L.C.	Withall	"		152*	12/8/40

ALL BRITISH

R.B. Lees

J.F. Pain (later Brooker-Pain)

V. Parker

C.A. McGaw

H.G. Hardman

I.N. Bayles

R.H. Hillary

J.D. Curchin

* Indicates killed during the battle of Britain.

Gordon Olive died in 1987 after this letter was received.

John Holloway died a few years ago and the task of looking after the 'official' list of airmen qualified to belong to the Battle of Britain Fighter Association now rests with the organization's historian.

APPENDIX 3

AUSTRALIANS ON THE BATTLE OF BRITAIN ROLL OF HONOUR AT WESTMINSTER ABBEY

On the 7th anniversary of the officially declared first day of the battle of Britain, 10 July 1947, H.M. King George VI unveiled the Battle of Britain Memorial in Westminster Abbey. The Roll of Honour, on parchment bound in blue leather, originally resting on a wrought-iron lectern north of the Royal Air Force Chapel, was the gift of Bruce S. Ingram, designed and executed by William F. Matthews and illustrated by Miss Daisy Alcock. It contained the names of 1 497 (later updated to 1 503) pilots and aircrew killed or mortally wounded during the battle numbering:

449 in Fighter Command
732 in Bomber Command
268 in Coastal Command
  14 in other RAF Commands
  34 in the Fleet Air Arm

In a letter to *Flight* magazine of 17 April 1947 Mr E.H. Keeling, the honorary secretary of the Battle of Britain Memorial wrote:

> ... Those killed in other than Fighter Command are included in the Roll because their attacks on enemy shipping, invasion barges and bases of various kinds, were an essential contribution to the winning of the Battle which is deemed to have begun on July 10 and ended on October 31, 1940.

There can be no doubt that, although men of Fighter Command were the 'front rank' of the defence, in an overall consideration of the battle of Britain the part played by the others, as stated by Mr Keeling, has to be included. The roll includes the names of:

1 300 men from the United Kingdom and her colonies
47 Canadians
47 New Zealanders
24 Australians
17 South Africans
35 Poles
20 Czechoslovakians
6 Belgians
1 American

The Australians listed in the roll of honour are:

42104	P/O Cale, Francis Walter	266	Sqn
43283	P/O Crossman, John Dallas	46	"
39983	F/O Glyde DFC, Richard Lindsay	87	"
754503	Sgt Holland, Kenneth Christopher	152	"
39461	AF/Lt Hughes DFC, Paterson Clarence	234	"
40052	AF/Lt Kennedy, John Conelly	238	"
42720	P/O Millington DFC, William Henry	249	"
32091	F/Lt Reynell, Richard Carew	43	"
40063	AF/Lt Walch, Stuart Crosby	238	"
39361	AF/Lt Withall, Latham Carr	152	"
42097	P/O Bennett, Clarence Charles	248	"
37582	AF/Lt Flood, Fredrick William	235	"
741151	Sgt Gannon, Benjamin Peter	206	"
41399	P/O Gilbert, John Allan	206	"
41417	P/O Horan, James Henry	233	"
42137	P/O McDonough, Bryan Martin	236	"
83709	P/O Weaber, William Owen	233	"
43289	P/O McIntosh, John	233	"
41770	P/O Earl, Raymond Patrick	61	"
40059	F/Lt Reed, Robert James	50	"
41471	P/O Robson DFC, Angus	144	"
40060	F/O Ross DFC, Ellis Henry	83	"
904181	Sgt Bull, Nugent Joseph	149	"
77944	P/O Leach, Phillip Allen	38	"

This information was obtained from Ministry of Defence, correspondence reference no. D/DPS1(R.A.F.)/44/7. 25 January 1985.

APPENDIX 4

AUSTRALIAN AIRMEN IN
THE BATTLE OF BRITAIN
ACCORDING TO AUSTRALIAN SOURCES

As already noted the *Official history of Australia in the war of 1939–45* stated that some 30 Australians fought in Fighter Command during the battle of Britain. In researching this figure, the following data were obtained:

1. A letter obtained from the Department of Defence via Australian Archives, listing the Australian personnel eligible for the prized Battle of Britain Clasp for the 1939–45 Star, which had been prepared before 1960 and showed 25 names.
2. A letter which showed that the above was later modified in accordance with Air Ministry Orders (AMO) N.850 which allowed the inclusion of squadrons and flights temporarily attached to RAF Fighter Command 10 July-31 October 1940, and added 4 more names to the list, making the total 29.
3. Another list obtained from the Australian War Memorial included the same 29 names but with additional information such as dates of birth and enlistment where known, address and fate.

Shown below are the relevant portions of 2:

VICTORIA BARRACKS
27 Jun 1957
Medals
Overseas Headquarters,
R.A.A.F.
Australia House,
Strand,
London W.C.2.

BATTLE OF BRITAIN CLASP TO THE 1939–45 STAR
(Your 1228/1/2/P3 (77A) 0990 — 18th March 1957)

1. A list of Australians known to have taken part in the Battle of Britain is as follows:-

*P-O	C.C. Bennett KIA 1/10/40
Plt. Off.	Francis Walter Cale KIA 15/8/40
Plt. Off.	John Dallas Crossman
*F-Lt	F.W. Flood KIA 11/9/40
Flg. Off.	Richard L. Glyde, D.F.C.
*P-O	A.L. Hamilton
Sgt.	Kenneth C. Holland KIA
A/Flt. Lt.	Patterson Clarence Hughes, D.F.C. KIA 7/9/40
A/Flt. Lt.	John C. Kennedy — KIA 13/7/40

Plt. Off.	William H. Millington, D.F.C. KIA 30/10/40
Flt. Lt.	Richard Carew Reynell KIA 7/9/40
A/Flt. Lt.	Stuart C. Walch KIA 11/8/40
A/Flt. Lt.	Latham Carr Withall KIA 12/8/40
Plt. Off.	Bryan M. McDonough
A/Wg.Cdr.	L.S. Constantine (A.N.?) (later KIA)
T/Gp. Capt.	R.B. Lees (later AVM: CB.CBE.DFC)
Flt. Lt.	J.F. Pain
*F-Lt	R.M. Power
Flt. Lt.	U. Parker [obviously V. Parker]
Flt. Lt.	C.A. McGaw
Sqn. Ldr.	H.G. Hardman
Sqn. Ldr.	I.N. Bayliss [obviously Bayles]
Flt. Lt.	R.N. Hillary
Plt. Off.	J.D. Carchin, D.F.C. [obviously Curchin]
Flg. Off.	J.R. Loch, D.F.C. [obviously Cock]
Flt. Lt.	R.W. Bungey, D.F.C. (later died)
Flt. Lt.	C.G.C. Olive, D.F.C.
Flt. Lt.	D.F. Sheen, D.F.C.
Flg. Off.	H.C. Mayers, D.S.O., D.F.C. (later KIA)

* These are additional names added to original list.

2.   Of those listed only Sg.Cdr. C.G.C. Olive (277457) and Sqn. Ldr.

R.W. Bungey, D.F.C. (257414) (deceased) are known to have been members of the Royal Australian Air Force. The remainder, therefore, would be Australians who enlisted in the Royal Air Force and whose records of service and personal files would be held by the Royal Air Force . . .

3.   As records of campaign awards are held under the names and numbers of ex-members rather than types of awards it is possible that the foregoing information is not exhaustive. However, it is the best that can be obtained from all possible sources in practice.

(W.R. King)
Squadron Leader
For Air Member for Personnel

APPENDIX 5

AUSTRALIAN CADETS TRAINED FOR THE ROYAL AIR FORCE

At the Imperial Conference of 1923 the UK proposed offering four-year short-service commissions in the RAF to RAAF officers. By this method it was reasoned, a reserve of trained aircrew would be built up which could be used to reinforce RAF squadrons in an emergency and Australia would benefit when the men returned after four years' operational training at British expense. The scheme was accepted by the Australian Government and began in 1927 when the first Point Cook graduates took up their commissions.

EMBARKED FOR UK	NAME	REMARKS
27/11/26	TOWNSEND, F.	RAAF Reserve
"	MURRAY, L.C.L.	Rel. comm. on completion of service 7/8/39
"	COLMAN, C.H.A.	Remained in UK
"	KOCH, A.A.	RAAF Reserve
"	SELK, G.	Resigned 23/11/29
"	IRVING, E.H.	Remained in UK
"	FOREMAN, J.G.	Resigned RAF
18/12/27	CAMERON, I.M.	Killed 28/9/39
"	CLARKE, C.R.	Reserve
"	KLEIN, G.E.	Returned UK
"	LINDELL, J.H.	Reserve
"	McKENNA, J.F.	Remained in UK
"	SAVILLE, D.T.	Discharged 30/4/36
3/4/29	FRITH, R.R.	Discharged 3/4/29
"	GRIFFIN, R.V.	Killed
"	JORDAN, R.C.	PC (Discharged officers)
"	SAMPSON, G.E.	PC (N196/36)
"	TULLOCK, G.K.	PC (Discharged officers)
"	WELLS, J.M.	Ret. to Australia MU
2/7/30	BATES, E.C.	RAAF (Permanent)
"	COLEMAN, G.S.	RAAF (CAF)
"	HARRISON, R.W.	MU
"	SPENCER, C.E.	MU
"	WOODHOUSE, H.O.	MU RAF Reserve 12/8/34
27/1/31	CAMERON, D.A.	Died 10/5/40
"	WEBB, A.C.D.	Killed 25/10/38
"	MATHESON, A.W.S.	PC (N196/36)
31/1/31	LEES, R.B.	PC (N196/36) DFC
"	KAYSER, E.A.	Discharged RAF
3/2/31	PROUD, J.C.	MU
9/1/31	RANKIN, W.E.	RAF Reserve (183/2/287)

EMBARKED FOR UK	NAME	REMARKS
30/6/31	BENNETT, D.C.T.	Rel. comm. 7/8/39
"	DREW, A.C.	Killed
"	LITTLEJOHN, N.B.	Joined RAF
"	PAGET, J.R.	RAAF Reserve
"	SMITH, C.H.	SSC Extended (Eng. Cse)
27/11/31	BOWMAN, A.McD.	PC (N196/36) DFC
1/12/31	GLEN, J.G.	PC (N196/36)
3/12/31	GRACE, A.D.	PC (N196/36)
18/11/31	DRAPER, A.J.	Died
27/11/31	RAE, R.A.R.	PC (N196/36)
5/7/32	GIBSON, D.A.	SSC Extended to Sept. 1937 PC? MID
"	JUDGE, J.W.B.	PC (N196/36)
"	BOSS-WALKER, H.F.	RAAF Reserve
2/7/32	STRANGEMAN, G.E.	Died 24/2/37
11/7/32	STEWART, A.G.F.	Medm Svc. to 1941 MID
7/1/33	HOBLER, J.	
"	PALMER, E.J.	
10/1/33	LEE, H.G.	DFC AFC
"	OLIVER, W.W.E.	RAF Reserve 2/8/38
30/6/33	MULHOLLAND, N.G.	DFC
"	SALMON, E.J.	SSC (Attd Eng. Cse)
4/7/33	HURLEY, H.B.	
10/7/33	MILLS, A.C.	RAF Reserve 8/6/38
"	GLASHEEN, V.W.	RAF Reserve 8/6/38
"	SPENCER, L.V.	MU
2/12/33	CHAPMAN, F.B.	RAAF
28/6/34	BANDIDT, A.F.	
"	BLOOMFIELD, H.D.	
"	McKAY, K.J.	
9/7/34	McGUIRE, J.W.	
5/1/35	CARR, W.E.	RAF Reserve
"	GROOM, A.D.	
"	HOSKINGS, H.V.C.	
12/7/35	LINDEMAN, G.M.	
16/7/35	DUPONT, R.E.	
"	WELLAND, R.D.	
"	WOOD, V.C.	
10/1/36	FLOOD, W.	KIA 11/9/40
10/1/36	SHEEHAN, G.H.	Seriously injured 7/5/40
"	WHITELY, E.A.	
"	WRIGHT, N.W.	
14/1/36	NEWMAN, H.D.	
"	PASCO-WEBB, J.B.	Killed 13/4/37
16/1/36	RAY, V.	
20/1/36	HORNE, G.E.	
11/1/36	DAISH, H.C.	
"	SISLEY, A.F.M.	

EMBARKED FOR UK	NAME	REMARKS
14/7/36	HARVEY, T.F.M.	MU
"	PITFIELD, A.L.	Reported missing 12/6/40
16/7/36	WATSON, R.A.M.	Killed 11/1/37
20/7/36	EDWARDS, H.I.	
"	WILLIAMS, W.C.	
20/12/36	MARSHALL, D.	
5/1/37	KAUFMAN, K.W.	DFC
"	MACE, C.R.	Killed 31/3/40
"	POWER, R.	
"	ALLSOP, J.W.	Killed
"	BROUGH, J.F.T.	DFC
7/1/37	FOWLER, H.N.	
"	GILBERT, C.L.	Injured in air operations 21/10/40
"	GOOD, D.C.F.	Seriously wounded in air operations 5/6/40
"	PAINE, J.	
"	BOEHM, D.C.	
9/1/37	CAMPBELL, D.	
"	HUGHES, P.C.	KIA 7/9/40
"	HULLOCK, C.L.	
"	KELAHER, C.R.	
"	ROBINSON, A.E.	Exchange duty in Australia
"	ROGERS, K.R.	Killed 14/5/40
"	SHEEN, D.F.B.	
"	WIGHT, W.B.	
"	YATE, E.W.	Killed in crash 1/8/39
"	JOHNSTON, L.L.	MID
"	OLIVE, C.G.C.	
11/1/37	GREY-SMITH, G.E.	Missing 12/5/40 POW
"	KINANE, W.	Killed in crash ?/8/39
12/1/37	COSGROVE, R.J.	Missing
17/7/37	DILWORTH, J.F.	Exchange duty in Australia
"	EDWARDS, W.H.	Missing 12/5/40 DFC
"	FARRINGTON, A.L.	
"	FRY, C.H.	
"	GIBBES, A.R.	Missing 2/9/41 DFC
"	HUBBARD, A.L.G.	DFC
"	HUNTER, D.H.	Returned to Australia
"	KENNEDY, J.C.	Killed 13/7/40
17/7/37	LEIGHTON, J.W.E.	
"	LEWIS, O.J.F.	Missing 18/12/39
"	McGHIE, A.F.	
"	McKINLAY, J.F.	
"	MESSERVY, N.H.E.	
"	MULLIGAN, A.R.	Missing 12/8/40 DFC
"	ROSS, E.H.	Killed 12/8/40 DFC
20/7/37	AMBROSE, B.S.	
"	BLOM, W.M.	Killed 27/7/40 DFC
"	GRAHAM, G.F.	
"	SADLER, J.F.B.	
"	WALCH, S.C.	Killed

EMBARKED FOR UK	NAME	REMARKS
22/7/37	BUNGEY, R.W.	
"	CLISBY, L.R.	Missing 14/5/40 DFC
"	SKINNER, W.B.	
"	WALSH, K.H.	
26/7/37	REED, R.J.	
31/12/37	BOYLAN, T.H.	DFC
"	CREMIN, D.E.	DFC
"	OAKLEY, A.E.	Missing 12/5/40
"	YOUNG, A.M.	
4/1/38	FRENCH, D.J.	DFC
"	TAYLER, G.R.	DFC
6/1/38	GIBSON, H.K.	
10/1/38	ROWAN, P.J.	Missing 10/5/40
16/7/38	EDWARDS, M.A.	
"	CURTIS, A.G.	Missing 11/8/40
"	PETTIGREW, J.F.	
19/7/38	STRAHAN, P.E.	
"	McCRACKEN, W.G.	Believed killed 6/8/40
"	EVANS, M.D.	
21/7/38	SIEBERT, J.A.	DFC
25/7/38	TAYLOR, H.H.	Missing 19/5/40

The scheme, offering four-year short-service commissions in the RAF to RAAF officers, was officially suspended in Australia in July 1938 but short-service commissions in the RAF continued to be advertized in the Australian Press and intakes continued until mid-1939. Those accepted at these later dates, although they were selected by a board of RAAF officers in each state, did not have the benefit of initial flying training at Point Cook and some, such as John Crossman, had not had any flying training at all.

EMBARKED FOR UK	NAME	REMARKS
9/3/39	BAILEY, R.E.	
"	BENNETT, C.C.	Missing 1/10/40
"	CALE, F.W.	
"	CONWAY, J.P.	
"	HAMILTON, A.L.	
"	HANNAH, K.T.	
9/3/39	HORAN, G.E.J.	
"	HYDE, J.R.	
"	MacPHERSON, R.I.C.	
"	McDONOUGH, B.M.	
"	ROBINSON, G.M.	
"	ROYLE, P.G.	
"	WRIGHT, R.J.	
"	MATHERS, B.M.	

EMBARKED FOR UK	NAME	REMARKS
12/8/39	ASH, R.	
"	BURRASTON, J.	
"	CHAPMAN, C.	
"	COOPER, J.	
"	CORNISH, G.	
"	CROSSMAN, J.D.	
"	DALE, J.	
"	GUILDERTHORP, T.	
"	HERON, J.	
"	HOLLAND, A.	
"	HUGHES, K.	
"	KERR, R.	
"	MacROSSAN, H.M.	
"	MacMEIKAN, D.	
"	McINTOSH, J.	
"	MOORE, M.	
"	PAIN, J.	
"	PETERKIN, J.D.	
"	PREECE, M.S.	
"	SLATTER, J.	
"	TINDALE, A.	
"	WOOD, W.	

APPENDIX 6

AUSTRALIANS SERVING IN RAF FIGHTER COMMAND 1939–40

This list is based on a document, obtained via Australian Archives, which is believed to have been compiled c.1944. It has been modified by the inclusion of the names of others discovered through recent research. These men are indicated * below, otherwise the data remain unchanged except for the omission of serial numbers.

RANK	NAME	SERVICE	HOME	REMARKS
TS/Ldr	BALDIE, S.W.	1 Sqn 8/9/39 (AASF) 43 Sqn 6/11/39 111 Sqn 21/11/39–14/6/40	New Guinea (Wau)	Killed flying accident 21/9/43
AS/Ldr	BAYLES, I.N.	152 Sqn 20/4/40 249 Sqn 29/5/40 152 Sqn 7/6/40–18/8/41	Melbourne Vic.	
AG/Cpt	BAYNE, D.W.	257 Sqn 17/5/40–21/7/40	Sydney NSW	
P/O	BENNETT, C.C.	248 Sqn 6/11/39–30/9/40	Mallala SA	DP 1/10/40
SW/Cdr	BUNGEY, R.W.	79 Sqn 18/9/40 145 Sqn 19/9/40–31/3/41	Glenelg SA	DFC 7/10/41
P/O	CALE, F.W.	266 Sqn 6/11/39–15/8/40	Perth WA	KIA 15/8/40
F/O	CAMERSON, D.Q.	266 Sqn 2/9/39–9/5/40	Croydon Vic.	DP 10/5/40
TS/Ldr	COCK, J.R.	87 Sqn 9/9/39–10/8/40 87 Sqn 3/12/40–6/12/40	Renmark SA	DFC 25/10/40
AW/Cdr	CONSTANTINE, A.N.	141 Sqn 4/12/39	Moama NSW	
F/Lt	CRIMP, G.S.	234 Sqn 6/11/39–12/4/40	Claremont WA	
W/O	CROOK, V.W.J.*	264 Sqn May/40–26/7/40 264 Sqn 15/9/40–20/3/41	Orange NSW	
P/O	CROSSMAN, J.D.	32 Sqn 14/7/40–2/8/40 46 Sqn 12/9/40–29/9/40	Mackay Qld	KIA 30/9/40
AF/Lt	CURCHIN, J.	609 Sqn 8/5/40–3/6/41	Hawthorn Vic.	DFC 1/11/40 DP 4/6/41
AF/Lt	FOPP, D.*	17 Sqn 24/5/40–3/9/40 17 Sqn Mid 1941–3/11/41	Adelaide SA	AFC 29/9/44
S/Ldr	FOWLER, H.N.	3 Sqn 22/4/39 615 Sqn 3/10/39	Adelaide SA	MC 14/12/43 Killed flying accident 26/3/44
F/O	GLYDE, R.L.	87 Sqn 9/9/39–13/11/39 87 Sqn 27/11/39–12/8/40	Perth WA	DFC 4/6/40 DP 13/8/40
S/Ldr(?)	GRAEME-EVENS, F.R.	26 Sqn 9/9/39–7/10/39 26 Sqn 8/10/39–2/8/40	Launceston Tas.	
F/Lt	HAMILTON, A.L.	248 Sqn 6/11/39–26/6/41	Adelaide SA	
S/Ldr	HARDMAN, H.G.	111 Sqn 17/9/38–9/3/39 111 Sqn 6/7/40–8/9/40 111 Sqn 6/11/40–6/1/41	Arncliffe NSW	

RANK	NAME	SERVICE	HOME	REMARKS
S/Ldr	HEWSON, J.M.*	616 Sqn 19/8/40–11/9/40		DFC 6/8/40
F/Lt	HILLARY, R.H.	603 Sqn 6/7/40–2/9/40	Sydney NSW	Killed flying accident 8/1/43
Sgt	HOLLAND, K.C.*	152 Sqn ?/?/40–25/9/40	Sydney NSW	KIA 25/9/40
W/Cdr	HOLMWOOD, R.A.*	64 Sqn 10/11/40–17/12/40 615 Sqn 18/12/40–26/2/41	Vic.	KIA 26/2/41
F/Lt	HUGHES, P.C.	64 Sqn 22/5/37 234 Sqn 8/11/39–7/9/40 247 Sqn 1/8/40	Haberfield NSW	KIA 7/9/40 DFC 22/10/40
AF/Lt	KENNEDY, J.C.	65 Sqn 19/3/37–21/1/40 65 Sqn 29/1/40–31/5/40 238 Sqn 1/6/40–13/7/40	Hurlstone Park NSW	KIA 13/7/40
TG/Cpt	LANG, T.F.U.	FCHQ 8/7/40–10/5/41	Melbourne Vic.	
TG/Cpt	LEES, R.B.	CO 72 Sqn 28/12/38–22/7/40	Broken Hill NSW	DFC 22/10/40
AVM	McCLAUGHRY, W.A.*	AOC 9 Group FC 22/9/40–42	Adelaide SA	CB, DSO, MC, DFC Killed aircraft accident 4/1/43
P/O	McDONOUGH, B.M.	236 Sqn 6/11/39–1/8/40	Melbourne Vic.	DP 1/8/40
F/Lt	McGAW, C.A.	73 Sqn 11/5/40–23/10/40 73 Sqn 24/10/40–8/12/40	Qld	
AW/Cdr	MAYERS, H.C.	601 Sqn 3/8/40–20/5/41	Sydney NSW	DFC 1/10/40 Missing DP 20/7/42
P/O	MILLINGTON, W.H.	79 Sqn 17/6/40–18/9/40 249 Sqn 19/9/40–30/10/40	Edwardstown SA	DFC 1/10/40 DP 30/10/40
AW/Cdr	OLIVE, C.G.C.	65 Sqn 22/5/39–28/5/40 65 Sqn 1/6/40–11/6/41	Brisbane Qld	Missing 28/5/40 DFC 24/9/40
F/Lt	PARKER, V.	234 Sqn 10/4/40–15/8/40	Townsville Qld	Missing 15/8/40 POW 16/8/40
F/Lt	PAIN, J.F.	32 Sqn 29/7/40–26/11/40 249 Sqn 27/11/40–18/12/40	Brisbane Qld	
F/Lt	PETERKIN, J.D.*	248 Sqn 5/3/40–42	Perth WA	Missing 5/7/44
TS/Ldr	PETTIGREW, J.F.	74 Sqn 17/12/38 151 Sqn 28/4/39–14/9/39 151 Sqn 14/4/40–6/6/40	Haberfield NSW	Missing 6/6/40 Killed aircraft accident
AW/Cdr	PRITCHARD,* C.A.	600 Sqn?/4/36–3/9/41	Manildra NSW	DFC 24/6/41
F/Lt	REYNELL, R.C.	43 Sqn 26/8/40–7/9/40	Reynella SA	KIA 7/9/40
AW/Cdr	ROBINSON, G.M.	53 Sqn 13/4/40–27/5/40 219 Sqn 12/12/40 23 Sqn 23/12/40-16/11/41	Perth WA	DFC 22/2/44
F/O	RUSSELL, I.B.N.	609 Sqn 25/11/39–12/5/40 245 Sqn 13/5/40–31/5/40	Melbourne Vic.	DP 1/6/40 DFC 14/6/40
G/Cpt	SAMPSON, G.E.*	CO 74 Sqn ?/4/38–?/3/40	Brisbane Qld	OBE 24/9/41

RANK	NAME	SERVICE	HOME	REMARKS
P/O	SCOTT, E.W.S.	616 Sqn 19/9/39		KIA 4/6/40
TW/Cdr	SHEEN, D.F.B.	72 Sqn 16/8/39–19/4/40	Sydney NSW	DFC 7/5/40
		212 Sqn 20/4/40–28/7/40		Bar 21/10/40
		72 Sqn 29/7/40–27/2/41		
		CO 72 Sqn 28/2/41		
AS/Ldr	SKELTON, G.F.A.	264 Sqn 1/2/40–12/5/40	Mosman NSW	
P/O	STEVENSON J.W.B.	266 Sqn 6/11/39–2/6/40	Melbourne Vic.	DP 2/6/40
P/O	TRALINTON, J.J.	79 Sqn 17/12/38–15/2/40	Cobargo NSW	DP 16/2/40
AF/Lt	WALCH, S.C.	238 Sqn 15/5/40–11/8/40	Hobart Tas.	DP 11/8/40
P/O	WRIGHT, R.J.	245 Sqn 6/11/39–22/11/39	Spotswood Vic.	
P/O	WILKIE, J.L.	266 Sqn 6/11/39–5/4/40	Perth WA	DP 2/6/40
		263 Sqn 4/5/40–2/6/40		
AF/Lt	WITHALL, L.C.	152 Sqn 3/10/40–12/8/40	Toodyay WA	DP 12/8/40
P/O	WICKHAM, S.McD.	615 Sqn 20/10/39–17/12/39	Sydney NSW	Killed flying accident 18/12/39
AS/Ldr	WOOD, V.T.L.	610 Sqn 1/3/40–4/6/40	Geelong Vic.	

APPENDIX 7

CLAIMS AND LOSSES JULY — OCTOBER 1940

Like so many aspects of the battle of Britain the losses and victory claims of the combatants have always been subject to controversy. A typical example is provided by the various figures cited for the *Luftwaffe* losses of 15 September. Claims made by the British at the time were as follows:

175 — *Daily Express*
183 — Reported to Churchill on the evening of the 15th
185 — *Official history of the second world war*

These were amended after the war in the light of evidence from the other side:

50 — *German high command diary*
56–60 — Post-war RAF claims
61 — Latest research (Ramsey, *Battle of Britain then and now* Mk III, p.707)

The figures quoted in this appendix for the *Luftwaffe* and RAF Fighter Command are those which have gained general acceptance in the light of up-to-date research. Figures in brackets indicate stated RAF claims and losses made in 1940. Australian claims are based on information found in Combat Reports, ORBs, Log Books etc.

DATE	LUFTWAFFE	RAF	AUSTRALIAN CLAIMS			AUSTRALIAN CASUALTIES
			Confirmed	Probable	Damaged	
1 July	10	1	—	—	—	
2	3	—	—	—	—	
3	4	—	—	—	1	
4	3	1	—	—	—	
5	2	1	—	—	—	
6	3	—	—	—	—	
7	5	6	—	—	—	
8	7	4	1	—	—	
9	11	6	1	—	—	
10	11	3	—	—	—	
11	17	6	2 1 shared	1	1	
12	9	5	2 shared	—	—	
13	6	6	1 shared	—	1	J. Kennedy KIA
14	3	1	—	—	—	
15	5	2	—	—	—	
16	4	1	—	—	—	
17	4	1	—	—	—	
18	6	5	—	—	—	

| DATE | LUFTWAFFE | RAF | AUSTRALIAN CLAIMS | | | AUSTRALIAN CASUALTIES |
			Confirmed	Probable	Damaged	
19 July	5	10	—	—	—	
20	12	9	1	1	—	
21	12	2	1	1	—	
22	4	2	—	—	—	
23	5	2	—	—	—	
24	15	5	—	—	—	
25	19	9	—	—	—	
26	5	1	2	—	—	
27	5	2	—	—	1	
28	11	6	1 shared	—	—	
29	11	6	—	—	—	
30	9	1	—	—	—	
31	7	7	—	—	—	
1 Aug.	13 [2]	4 [1]	—	—	—	B. McDonough KIA
2	7	3	—	—	—	
3	6	—	—	—	—	
4	2	1	—	—	—	
5	8 [4]	2 [1]	—	—	—	
6	6 [1]	6	—	—	—	
7	3	4	—	—	—	
8	24 [60]	21 [16]	1	2	—	
9	6 [1]	3	—	—	—	
10	1	—	—	—	—	
11	38 [60]	28 [26]	1	2	—	S. Walch KIA J. Cock wounded
12	32 [62]	18 [13]	—	1	—	L. Withall KIA
13	39 [78]	15 [13]	4	4	2	R. Glyde KIA
14	20 [31]	9 [7]	—	1	—	
15	76 [180]	35 [34]	6 1 shared	1	—	F. Cale KIA V. Parker POW
16	44 [75]	24 [22]	5	6	—	
17	5 [1]	2	—	—	—	
18	67 [153]	33 [22]	2	—	1	J. Pain wounded
19	11 [6]	5 [3]	—	—	—	
20	8 [7]	2 [2]	—	—	—	
21	14 [13]	4 [1]	1	—	—	
22	4 [10]	4 [5]	—	—	—	
23	8 [4]	1	—	—	—	
24	41 [50]	20 [19]	—	1	—	
25	23 [55]	18 [18]	1	—	—	
26	42 [47]	29 [15]	3	—	—	
27	11 [5]	7	—	—	—	
28	32 [28]	15 [14]	—	—	—	
29	24 [11]	10 [9]	1	1	—	
30	40 [63]	25 [25]	1	1	1	
31	39 [94]	41 [37]	4	—	1	W. Millington wounded

DATE	LUFTWAFFE	RAF	AUSTRALIAN CLAIMS			AUSTRALIAN CASUALTIES
			Confirmed	Probable	Damaged	
1 Sept.	16 [29]	13 [15]	—	—	—	
2	37 [65]	14 [20]	3	1	1	R. Lees wounded
3	20 [25]	15 [15]	1	1	—	D. Fopp wounded
						R. Hillary wounded
4	28 [64]	17 [17]	4	1	—	
				1 shared		
5	27 [39]	20 [20]	2	—	—	D. Sheen wounded
6	33 [46]	20 [19]	1	2	—	
7	41 [103]	25 [22]	2	1	—	R. Reynell KIA
						P. Hughes KIA
8	16 [11]	5 [3]	—	—	—	
9	30 [52]	17 [13]	—	—	—	
10	13 [2]	3	—	—	—	
11	29 [93]	29 [24]	—	—	—	F. Flood KIA
12	7 [3]	1	—	—	—	
13	7 [2]	3	—	—	—	
14	13 [18]	13 [9]	—	—	—	
15	61 [185]	31 [25]	1	1	—	
			3 shared			
16	10 [7]	1	1	—	—	
17	8 [12]	6 [3]	1 shared	—	—	
18	20 [48]	12 [12]	—	—	—	
19	10 [5]	—	1	—	—	
20	8 [6]	8 [7]	—	—	—	
21	11 [2]	1	—	—	—	
22	6 [1]	1	—	—	—	
23	17 [12]	11 [11]	—	—	—	
24	11 [9]	6 [4]	1	—	1	
25	16 [26]	6 [4]	5	—	—	K. Holland KIA
			2 shared			
26	9 [34]	8 [8]	1	—	—	
27	57 [133]	28 [34]	2	—	2	R. Miller* KIA
			1 shared			
28	12 [6]	17 [7]	1	—	—	
29	9 [10]	6 [4]	—	—	—	
30	47 [49]	21 [22]	1	—	3	J. Crossman KIA

* Considerable doubt exists as to whether or not R.F.G. Miller was an Australian.
Refer to biographical outline War Diary, 27 September 1940.

| DATE | LUFTWAFFE | RAF | AUSTRALIAN CLAIMS | | | AUSTRALIAN CASUALTIES |
			Confirmed	Probable	Damaged	
1 Oct.	9 [5]	7 [3]	—	—	—	C. Bennett missing
2	18 [12]	2 [1]	—	—	—	
3	9 [1]	1	—	—	—	
4	15 [3]	1 [1]	—	—	—	
5	14 [23]	7 [9]	—	—	—	
6	9 [2]	2	—	—	—	
7	19 [28]	17 [16]	—	1	—	C. Mayers injured
8	17 [8]	8 [2]	—	—	—	
9	9 [4]	3 [1]	—	—	—	
10	12 [5]	8 [5]	—	1	—	
11	10 [9]	9 [9]	—	—	—	
12	13 [12]	11 [10]	—	—	—	
13	6 [2]	4 [2]	—	—	—	
14	4	1	—	—	—	
15	16 [18]	15 [15]	—	—	—	
16	15 [6]	3	—	—	—	
17	16 [4]	5 [3]	—	—	—	
18	14	6	—	—	—	
19	6 [2]	1	—	—	—	
20	11 [8]	5 [3]	—	—	—	
21	7 [4]	2	—	—	—	
22	12 [3]	6 [6]	—	—	—	
23	4	1	—	—	—	
24	12 [3]	3	—	—	—	
25	24 [17]	14 [10]	—	1	—	
26	10 [6]	8 [2]	—	—	—	
27	16 [13]	14 [8]	—	—	—	
28	14 [6]	—	1 shared	—	1	
29	28 [33]	12 [7]	—	1	—	
30	8 [9]	9 [5]	—	—	—	W. Millington missing
31	2	—	—	—	—	

APPENDIX 8

PAT HUGHES'S COMBAT RECORD

Flight Lieutenant Pat Hughes was the highest-scoring Australian ace to serve in the battle of Britain. There is, however, some ambiguity over his actual tally of victories. At the time of his death in action on 7 September 1940 he had been credited with shooting down fourteen enemy aircraft. The circumstances of his death and the irreconcilable differences in eye-witness accounts of it preclude a definitive conclusion as to whether he gained a last victory in his final combat. If he had collided with the Dornier Do17 then it became his fifteenth victim. If he had in fact been shot down, and the bomber was downed by another British fighter, then his tally remained unchanged. In the latter case he would have become the third highest-scoring battle of Britain ace. The figure of fourteen individual and three shared kills is, however, widely accepted, making him the sixth ranking ace.

VICTORIES (Total)	NAME	SQN	COMMENTS
17 (28)	Sgt J. Frantisek DFM, Croix de Guerre	303	(Czech) Top-scoring Allied pilot. Killed in crash 8/10/40
16 +1 shared (26)	P/O E.S. Lock DFC & Bar	41	Top-scoring British pilot. KIA 3/7/41
15 +1 shared (15)	F/O B.J.G. Carbury DFC	603	Top-scoring New Zealand pilot. Shot down 6/8/41
15 +1 shared (28)	Sgt J.H. Lacey DFM	501	British
15	P/O R.F.T. Doe DSO, DFC	238 234	British
14 +3 shared (or 15+3 shared?)	F/Lt P.C. Hughes DFC	234	Top-scoring Australian pilot. KIA 7/9/40

The ranks and decorations shown are those held during the battle of Britain.

APPENDIX 9

AUSTRALIA'S FEW

And who, after considering all of the requirements set down in the Introduction, the details in the War Diary and the data outlined in the preceding Appendices, were Australia's Few?

1	P/O I.N. Bayles	152 Squadron		(Spitfire)
2	S/Ldr D.W. Bayne	257	"	(Hurricane)
3	P/O C.C. Bennett (KIA)	248	"	(Blenheim)
4	F/Lt R.W. Bungey	145	"	(Hurricane)
5	P/O F.W. Cale (KIA)	266	"	(Spitfire)
6	P/O J.R. Cock DFC	87	"	(Hurricane)
7	F/O A.N. Constantine	141	"	(Defiant)
8	Sgt V.W.J. Crook	264	"	(Defiant)
9	P/O J.D. Crossman (KIA)	32 & 46	"	(Hurricane)
10	P/O J. Curchin DFC	609	"	(Hurricane)
11	F/Lt F.W. Flood (KIA)	235	"	(Blenheim)
12	Sgt D. Fopp	17	"	(Hurricane)
13	F/O R.L. Glyde DFC (KIA)	87	"	(Hurricane)
14	P/O A.L. Hamilton	248	"	(Blenheim)
15	F/O H.G. Hardman	111	"	(Hurricane)
16	F/Lt J.M. Hewson DFC	616	"	(Spitfire)
17	P/O R.H. Hillary	603	"	(Spitfire)
18	Sgt K.C. Holland (KIA)	152	"	(Spitfire)
19	F/Lt P.C. Hughes DFC (KIA)	234	"	(Spitfire)
		247	"	(Gladiator)
20	F/Lt J.C. Kennedy (KIA)	238	"	(Hurricane)
21	W/Cdr R.B. Lees DFC	72	"	(Spitfire)
22	P/O B.M. McDonough (KIA)	236	"	(Blenheim)
23	P/O C.A. McGaw	73	"	(Hurricane)
		66	"	(Spitfire)
24	F/Lt H.C. Mayers DFC	601	"	(Hurricane)
25	P/O W.H. Millington DFC (KIA)	79	"	(Hurricane)
		249	"	(Hurricane)
26	Sgt P.J. Moore	253	"	(Hurricane)
27	F/O W.S. Moore	236	"	(Blenheim)
28	F/Lt C.G.C. Olive DFC	65	"	(Spitfire)
29	P/O J.F. Pain	32	"	(Hurricane)
30	P/O V. Parker (POW)	234	"	(Spitfire)
31	F/O J.D. Peterkin	248	"	(Blenheim)
32	F/Lt R.M. Power	236	"	(Blenheim)
33	F/Lt C.A. Pritchard	600	"	(Blenheim)
		600	"	(Beaufighter)
34	F/Lt R.C. Reynell (KIA)	43	"	(Hurricane)
35	F/Lt D.F.B. Sheen DFC	72	"	(Spitfire)
36	F/Lt S.C. Walch (KIA)	238	"	(Hurricane)
37	F/Lt L.C. Withall (KIA)	152	"	(Spitfire)

Total: 37   KIA: 13   POW: 1

SELECT BIBLIOGRAPHY

Air Ministry, *The battle of Britain — an air ministry account of the great days from August 8 to October 31, 1940* (Ministry of Information, London, 1941).

Air Ministry and the Central Office of Information, *Wings of the phoenix* (His Majesty's Stationery Office, London, 1949).

Allen, W/Cdr H.R., *Battle for Britain* (Corgi, London, 1973).

Allen, W/Cdr H.R., *Who won the battle of Britain?* (Panther, St Albans, 1976).

Australian Military Forces, *Soldiering on : the Australian army at home and overseas* (Australian War Memorial, Canberra, 1942).

Bader, Douglas, *Fight for the sky* (Fontana, Glasgow, 1975).

Baff, F/Lt K.C., *Maritime is number ten* (Baff, Netley, South Australia, 1983).

Baker, E.C.R., *The fighter aces of the R.A.F.* (New English Library, London, 1974).

Barclay, George & Wynn, Humphrey (eds), *Angels 22* (Arrow, London, 1977).

Barker, Ralph, *Aviator extraordinary* (Chatto & Windus, London, 1969).

Bartlett, Norman (ed.), *Pictorial history of Australia at war, 1939–45*, Vols I & II (Australian War Memorial, Canberra, 1957).

Beedle, J., *43 Squadron* (Beaumont, London, 1966).

Bekker, Cajus, *The Luftwaffe war diaries* (Corgi, London, 1969).

Bishop, Edward, *The battle of Britain* (Transworld Publishers, London, 1961).

Bishop, Edward, *Their finest hour — the story of the battle of Britain 1940* (Macdonald, London, 1968).

Bolitho, Hector, *Combat report* (Batsford, London, 1943).

Bowyer, Chaz, *Fighter Command 1936–68* (Sphere, London, 1981).

Bowyer, Chaz, *Bristol Blenheim* (Ian Allan, London, 1984).

Braham, W/Cdr J.R.D. 'Bob', *Scramble!* (Pan, London, 1961).

Brickhill, Paul, *Reach for the sky* (Collins, London, 1954).

Bryant, Arthur, *The turn of the tide 1939–1943* (Fontana, London, 1965).

Burns, Michael, *Spitfire! Spitfire!* (Blandford Press, Poole, 1986).

Burt, Kendal & Leasor, James, *The one that got away* (Granada, London, 1956)

Butement, W.A.S., *Record of scientific work undertaken by W.A.S. Butement CBE*, submitted to Adelaide University for the degree of Doctor of Science. (Privately published by W.A.S. Butement, Adelaide, 1960).

Caidin, Martin, *Me 109* (Macdonald, London, 1969).

Champ, Jack & Burgess, Colin, *The diggers of Colditz* (George Allen & Unwin, Sydney, 1985).

Churchill, Winston, *The second world war*, Vols 1, 2, 3 & 4 (Cassell, London, 1964).

Collier, Basil, *The battle of Britain* (Fontana, London, 1969).

Collier, Richard, *Eagle day* (Pan, London, 1968).

Collier, Richard, *1940 — The world in flames* (Penguin, Harmondsworth, 1980).

Cooksley, Peter G., *1940 — The story of No. 11 Group, Fighter Command* (Robert Hale, London, 1983).

Crook, David, *Spitfire pilot* (Faber & Faber, London, 1942).

Deere, Gp Capt. Alan W., *Nine lives* (Hodder, London, 1969).

Deighton, Len, *Fighter — the true story of the battle of Britain* (Triad/Panther, St Albans, 1979).

Deighton, Len, *Battle of Britain* (Coward, McCann & Geoghegan, London, 1980).

Dezarrois, Andres (ed.), *The Mouchette diaries 1940–1943* (Panther, London, 1957).

Dickson, Lovat, *Richard Hillary* (Macmillan, London, 1951).

Fleming, Peter, *Operation sea lion* (Pan, London, 1975).

Flight magazine, October 1940, 'Dick Reynell', p. 373.

Forrester, Larry, *Fly for your life* (Collins, London, 1960).

Franks, Norman, *Fighter leader* (William Kimber, London, 1978).

Franks, Norman, *The air battle of Dunkirk* (William Kimber, London, 1983).

Galland, Adolf, *The first and the last* (Methuen, London, 1955).

Gallico, Paul, *The Hurricane story* (Michael Joseph, London, 1959).

Gelb, Norman, *Scramble — a narrative history of the battle of Britain* (Pan, London, 1986).

Gibson, Guy, *Enemy coast ahead* (Pan, London, 1955).

Gleed, Ian, *Arise to conquer* (Gollancz, London, 1942).

Golding, James & Moyes, Philip, *RAF Bomber Command and its aircraft 1936–1940* (Ian Allan, Shepperton, 1973).

Green, William, *Famous fighters of the second world war* (Macdonald, London, 1957).

Green, William, *Famous bombers of the second world war*, First & Second Series (Macdonald, London, 1960).

Gunston, Bill, *Night fighters* (Patrick Stephens, Cambridge, 1976).

Halley, James J., *The squadrons of the Royal Air Force* (Air-Britain, Tunbridge, 1980).

Herington, John, *Australia in the war of 1939–1945 (Air)* Vol. III, *Air war against Germany and Italy, 1939–1943* (Australian War Memorial, Canberra, 1962).

Hillary, Richard, *The last enemy* (Macmillan, London, 1942).

Houart, Victor (ed.), *Lonely warrior* (Hamlyn, Feltham, 1978).

Irving, David, *The rise and fall of the Luftwaffe* (Futura, London, 1976).

James, R.R. (ed.), *Winston S. Churchill, his complete speeches 1897–1963* Vol.II *1935–1942* (Chelsea House, New York, 1978).

Johnen, Wilhelm, *Duel under the stars* (William Kimber, London, 1957).

Johnson, Frank (ed.), *R.A.A.F. over Europe* (Eyre & Spottiswoode, London, 1946).

Johnson, AVM J.E., *Full circle* (Pan, London, 1968).

Jones, W/Cdr Ira 'Taffy', *Tiger squadron* (W.H. Allen, London, 1955).

Jullian, Marcel, *The battle of Britain* (Johnathan Cape, London, 1967).

Kent, Gp Capt. J.A., *One of the few* (William Kimber, London, 1971).

Kreipe, Werner, 'The battle of Britain' in Richardson, William & Freidin, Seymour (eds), *The fatal decisions* (Harborough, London, 1959).

Lanchbery, Edward, *Against the sun* (Pan, London, 1957)

Legge, J.S. (ed.), *Who's who in Australia*, XIXth edition, 1968 (Herald and Weekly Times, Melbourne, 1968). (Plus later editions).

Long, Gavin, 'The A.I.F. in the United Kingdom' in *Australia in the war of 1939-1945 (Army)* Vol.I, *To Benghazi* (Australian War Memorial, Canberra, 1961).

Lucas, Laddie, *Flying colours* (Granada, London, 1983).

McCarthy, John, *Australia and the imperial defence 1918-1939* (University of Queensland Press, St Lucia, 1976).

McClelland, James, *Where Australians fought and died* (McClelland, Silverdale, 1980).

McKee, Alexander, *Strike from the sky* (New English Library, London, 1977).

Mason, Francis K., *Battle over Britain* (McWhirter, London, 1969).

Middlebrook, Martin & Everitt, Chris, *The Bomber Command war diaries* (Viking, New York, 1985).

Middleton, Drew, *The sky suspended* (Pan, London, 1963).

Morgan, E.B. & Shacklady, E., *Spitfire, the history* (Key, Stamford, 1987).

Mosley, Leonard, *Battle of Britain* (Pan, London, 1969).

Mosley, Leonard, *The Reich Marshal* (Pan, London, 1977).

Moulson, Tom, *The flying sword (601 Squadron)* (Macdonald, London, 1964).

Murray, Williamson, *Strategy for defeat: the Luftwaffe 1933-1945* (Quintet, London, 1986).

Orange, Vincent, *Sir Keith Park* (Methuen, London, 1984).

Orde, Capt. Cuthbert, *Pilots of Fighter Command* (Harrap, London, 1942).

Parkinson, Roger, *Blood, toil, tears, and sweat* (Hart Davis Mac-Gibbon, London, 1973).

Parry, Simon, 'The Reunion', p. 32, *Flypast* magazine, December 1983.

Pawle, Gerald, *Secret weapons of World War II* (Ballantine, New York, 1967).

Price, Alfred, *Luftwaffe* (Macdonald, London, 1973).

Price, Alfred, *Battle of Britain: the hardest day* (Macdonald and Jane's, London, 1979).

Quill, Jeffrey, *Spitfire — a test pilot's story* (John Murray, London, 1983).

Ramsey, Winston, G. (ed.), *The battle of Britain then and now, after the battle* (London, 1980). (Plus versions Mk II, Mk III & Mk IV).

Ramsey, Winston G. (ed.), *The Blitz then and now*, Vol.1, *After the Battle* (London, 1987).

Rawlings, John D.R., *Fighter squadrons of the R.A.F. and their aircraft* (Macdonald and Jane's, London, 1976).

Rawlings, John D.R., *Coastal support and special squadrons and their aircraft* (Jane's, London, 1982).

Rawnsley, C.W. & Wright, Robert, *Night fighter* (Corgi, London, 1959).

Reynolds, Quentin, *A London diary* (Angus & Robertson, London, 1941).

Ricketts, P/O V.A., 248 Squadron line book (Unpublished, 1941, via John Hamilton).

Robinson, Anthony, *R.A.F. fighter squadrons in the battle of Britain* (Arms & Armour Press, London, 1987).

Saunders, Hilary St George, Hillary, Richard & Bekker Cajus, *The battle of Britain* (Tandem, London, 1969).

Semmler, Clement (ed.), *The war diaries of Kenneth Slessor* (University of Queensland Press, St Lucia, 1985).

Semmler, Clement (ed.), *The war despatches of Kenneth Slessor* (University of Queensland Press, St Lucia, 1987).

Shaw, M., *Twice vertical (1 Squadron)* (Macdonald, London, 1971).

Shirer, William L., *Berlin diary 1934–1941* (Sphere, London, 1970).

Shores, Christopher & Ring, Hans, *Fighters over the desert* (Spearman, London, 1969).

Shores, Christopher & Williams, Clive, *Aces high* (Spearman, London, 1966).

Smith, Constance Babington, *Evidence in camera* (Chatto & Windus, London, 1957).

Stokes, Doug, *Paddy Finucane: fighter ace* (William Kimber, London, 1983).

Taylor, John W.R., Taylor, Michael J.H. & Mondey, David, *The Guinness book of air facts and feats* (Guinness, Enfield, 1977).

Terraine, John, *The right of the line* (Hodder & Stoughton, London, 1985).

Thompson, Laurence, *1940: year of legend, year of history* (Collins, London, 1966).

Townsend, Peter, *Duel of eagles* (Corgi, London, 1970).

Trevor-Roper, H.R. (ed.), *Hitler's war directives 1939–1945* (Pan, London, 1973).

Vader, John, *Spitfire* (Macdonald, London, 1970).

Wallace, Graham, *R.A.F. Biggin Hill* (Four Square, London, 1958).

Williams, Peter & Harrison, Ted, *McIndoe's army* (Sphere, London, 1981).

Willis, John *Churchill's few* (Michael Joseph, London, 1985).

Wood, Derek, *Target England* (Jane's London, 1980).

Wood, Derek, & Dempster, Derek, *The narrow margin* (Hutchinson, London, 1961).

Wright, Robert, *Dowding and the battle of Britain* (Corgi, London, 1970).

Wynn, Kenneth G., *A clasp for 'The Few'* (Kenneth G. Wynn, Auckland, 1981).

Ziegler, Frank, *Under the white rose (609 Squadron)* (Macdonald, London, 1971).

INDEX